Stabilization, Debt, and Reform

For my mother

Stabilization, Debt, and Reform

Policy analysis for developing countries

Rudiger Dornbusch
Massachusetts Institute of Technology

 Prentice Hall, Englewood Cliffs, NJ 07632

First published 1993 in the United States by
Prentice-Hall Inc.
A Simon and Schuster Company
Englewood Cliffs, New Jersey 07632

© Rudiger Dornbusch 1993

Typeset in 10/12 pt Times
by Vision Typesetting, Manchester

Printed and bound in Great Britain
by T J Press, Padstow, Cornwall

Library of Congress Cataloging-in-Publication Data

Dornbusch, Rudiger.
    Stabilization, debt, and reform : policy analysis for developing
countries / Rudiger Dornbusch.
        p. cm.
    Includes bibliographical references and index.
    ISBN 0-13-097395-5
        1. Developing countries—Economic policy. 2. Debts, External—
Developing countries. 3. Economic stabilization—Developing
countries. I. Title.
HC59.7.D668 1993
338.9′009172′4—dc20
                                                          93–9102
                                                            CIP

10 9 8 7 6 5 4 3 2

Prentice-Hall International (UK) Limited, London
Prentice-Hall of Australia Pty. Limited, Sydney
Prentice-Hall Canada Inc., Toronto
Prentice-Hall Hispanoamericana, S.A., Mexico
Prentice-Hall of India Private Limited, New Delhi
Prentice-Hall of Japan, Inc., Tokyo
Simon & Schuster Asia Pte. Ltd., Singapore
Editora Prentice-Hall do Brasil, Ltda, Rio de Janeiro

Contents

Acknowledgments

Some of the material in this book was previously published and because of this some repetition of material does occur. Permission to reprint was kindly granted by the copyright holders as follows:

"Lessons from Experiences with High Inflation," *World Bank Economic Review*, 1992.

"Policies to Move from Stabilization to Growth," *Proceedings of the World Bank Annual Conference on Development Economics* 1990.

"The New Classical Macroeconomics and Stabilization Policy," *American Economic Review*, 1990.

"Credibility and Stabilization," *Quarterly Journal of Economics*, 1991.

"The Case for Trade Liberalization in Developing Countries," *Journal of Economic Perspectives*, 1992.

"Priorities of Economic Reform in Eastern Europe and the Soviet Union," Center for Economic Policy Research (CEPR) *Occasional Paper*, 1991.

"Monetary Problems of Post-Communism: Lessons from the End of the Austro-Hungarian Empire," *Weltwirtschaftliches Archiv*, 1992.

"Our LDC Debts," in M. Feldstein, ed., *The United States in the World Economy*, University of Chicago Press, 1988.

"Debt Problems and the World Macroeconomy," in J. Sachs, ed., *Developing Country Debt and Economic Performance: Vol. 1; The International Financial System*, University of Chicago Press, 1989.

"Reducing Transfers from Debtor Countries," in R. Dornbusch, J. Makin and D. Zlowe, eds, *Alternative Solutions to Developing Country Debt Problems*, American Enterprise Institute, 1989.

"Macroeconomic Populism" (with S. Edwards), *Journal of Development Economics*, 1990.

"Brazilian Debt Crises: Past and Present," (with E. Cardoso), in B. Eichengreen and P. Lindert (eds), *The International Debt Crisis in Historical Perspective*. MIT Press, 1989.

"Mexico: Stabilization, Debt, and Growth," *Economic Policy*, 1988.

"Debt and macroeconomic instability in Argentina" (with J. C. de Pablo), in J. Sachs, ed., *Developing Country Debt and the World Economy*, University of Chicago Press, 1989.

Introduction

This collection of policy essays, written in the years 1988–92, addresses issues arising in developing and transition economies. The central focus is always a macroeconomic perspective, but the specific problem areas vary: inflation and stabilization, debt problems, exchange rate strategies, growth and modernization, or troubles of economies trapped in between the command economy and the market.

Part of the task of policy economics is precisely to highlight the common features of problems and thus make it possible to discern lessons from the very broad laboratory across history and across countries. Every experience has some unique features, but the basic belief underlying these essays is the view that there is an interesting precedent for every episode.

Here is a broad overview of the themes touched on in this book.

Inflation and stabilization

Milton Friedman argues that inflation is always and everywhere a monetary phenomenon. That is barely true in some cases and very true in others. The art is to know which is which. In the United States monetarism makes a comeback typically *after* a major inflation episode; monetarists come out of the corner after inflation has happened, because then a monetary expansion can clearly be documented and held responsible. There is always some lag in the link between inflation and money that will oblige. But when there is no inflation even though money has grown rapidly, monetarists stay in hiding. In the United States experience, monetarism does not do a lot for us, no more at least than the prediction that it is colder in winter than in summer.

But money comes into its own when we discuss high inflation experiences—say 10, 20 or more percent per month. These used to be episodes of history, in the aftermath of great social upheavals or wars, but they have become more common again both in Latin America and now in the former Soviet economies. In these episodes there is a close link between financing the budget and the growth of money. The link runs in two directions: rapid inflation wipes out the real value of tax revenues and thus leads to increased deficits and faster money growth. The other direction is the traditional one—money burning holes in people's pockets and thus becoming the source of inflation.

An inflation story is not complete without a role for the exchange rate. A balance of payments crisis, with a resulting collapse of the currency, is often the starting point for a dramatic escalation of inflation. The ability to hold the currency, by contrast, is seen as a way of avoiding accelerating inflation. In the monetarist rendition, the role of exchange rates in the inflation story is ordinarily omitted. Yet the discussion as to what is the cause of inflation goes back at least to the 1920s in the debate between the "quantity theory school"—it's all money— and the "balance of payments school"—it's the currency collapse.

Stabilizing a major inflation involves a two-pronged attack: on the one hand, the budget must be brought under control. That is a *sine qua non*. Without budget control, any stabilization is very temporary and will ultimately fail. In Germany in 1923, in the midst of hyperinflation, a moment of full price stability was achieved by pegging the currency. But the episode lasted only a few months and then the full blow-up followed. Budget balance is a necessary condition for stabilization.

But attention to the budget is not enough. Any inflation process has inertia, except possibly at the most extreme rates. There is always someone just about to raise his prices or wages, just one more adjustment while everybody else holds still. The presence of inflation inertia requires incomes policy as part of the complete stabilization package. Incomes policy means some program for wages, prices, and the exchange rate so as to establish *de facto* price stability.

Here we encounter a controversy: is it really true that both are needed, is it not enough to have just one? The orthodox approach highlights fiscal discipline and is more than weary of incomes policy. Incomes policy, adherents of orthodoxy will argue, covers up—for a while—the symptoms and thus makes it seem that deep surgery is not required. They argue that you cannot make omelettes without breaking some eggs. Adherents of heterodoxy focus on inertia and therefore will argue that incomes policy is *the* central instrument and that fiscal discipline ought to come sometime, possibly later, when the political conditions have become more propicious.

The debate is the same on every occasion. There are plenty of examples now of heterodoxy gone wrong. And there are examples of failed orthodoxy. Incomes policy is just as necessary as fiscal discipline. There are genuine coordination problems which need solving, and recessions are economically and politically just about the worst way of going about working off inflation inertia.

The exchange rate plays a very special role in stabilization. At the outset, fixing the rate immediately creates at least one spot of stability in the economy. But if inflation is not wiped out altogether, very soon the fixed exchange rate risks becoming overvalued. Once overvaluation is under way, increased interest rates will be necessary to defend the currency and then, sooner or later, a currency crisis will topple the stabilization program. The responsible solution is to sacrifice the quest for zero inflation, if in fact one has been unable to achieve that target, and start crawling very soon. That means accepting *some* inflation, but the strategy avoids a crisis sometime along the way.

What role does credibility play in all this? In the wake of Tom Sargent's work, credibility is one of the magic words in the trade: programs are said to fail because there was no credibility, and they are said to succeed because of credibility. Of course, that is circular reasoning and does not give credibility any testable content; it just sounds good.

Credibility is best measured by the substance of an adjustment program: given the size of a real depreciation or of a budget cut, how likely is it that this is enough to avoid a crisis or speculative attack? Viewed in this way, credibility is just a summary term for adjustment effort and it plays no independent role. Adjustment is all important, it is the *sine qua non*. Credibility means nothing by itself—you can't put it on a sandwich and it does not pay interest.

International confidence plays a key role in any stabilization effort. With confidence in world markets, fostered by the fact or strong prospect of adjustment efforts, capital inflows will support the currency and help stop inflation from day one. By contrast, with strained confidence abroad, high interest rates are necessary to maintain the exchange rate and they worsen the output effects of stabilization, worsen public finance, and thus impair the prospects for reform.

The trouble with international investors is that they can afford to wait while the economy cannot. If they do take a wait-and-see attitude, that very fact makes a stabilization less likely to succeed. There is little that can be done, except overkill in adjustment and stabilization loans. If reserves are plentiful, foreign investors need not be concerned about the prospects of adjustment. The ample reserves offer assurance that until further notice they can get out through the same door as they came in. Note that stabilization loans have an interesting twist: the larger they are, the less they will be used.

Modernization and prosperity

In the 1980s, in the aftermath of the debt crisis, opening up and modernization became the key message to Latin America. For over 60 years the region had followed inward-looking strategies, pervasive regulation and the model of a highly interventionist state. Whatever benefits there might have been from that strategy of development at the outset, in the midst of the Great Depression, by the 1980s there were none. Moreover, it was clear that the only way growth would return was by a radically different model with a much smaller role for government and a far bigger role for the market, less intervention and more rules. That setting, not by accident, combines well with free and open societies and thus was a good counterpoint to the authoritarian regimes of the past.

Chile took the lead in opening up, with the economics moving far ahead of the politics. Mexico followed, then Argentina, and by now more or less everybody has joined in, although the tail looks rather like the Boston Marathon.

In the meantime the research controversy continues on the question whether openness is, in fact, a critical ingredient for growth. But even though that question is unresolved, the episodic evidence is all too strong to dissuade any close observer from believing in openness. In highly protected markets, scale of operation is small, competition is absent, and rent seeking is pervasive. Resources thus are poorly used and the incentives for innovation are minimal. By contrast, in open economies the manifold channels for beneficial foreign influences on a country's economy are at work, ranging from technology and foreign investment to competition and the stability of rules. Open economies beget free societies; take that for granted until further notice.

But the enthusiasm for open economies must not blind us to the complications of getting there. Trade reform is politically difficult, and even on the economic front there are questions: should a country liberalize unilaterally or rather seek a regional agreement?; should unilateral liberalization be complete or should it stop at a uniform 20 percent tariff? And what is the exchange rate policy that goes with a liberalization process? There are no theorems here, but all the evidence suggests that a hefty real depreciation is an essential complement to a substantial liberalization. The reason is this: import liberalization produces what it promises, and fast—plenty of imports. The beneficial effects of liberalization on the export sector, by contrast, are much slower to come about. As a result, without a real depreciation and without open-ended financing from abroad, a payments problem is likely to emerge as a by-product of an overly radical trade liberalization.

Modernization also has to do with the attitude toward foreign investment in all forms. In the statist-nationalist model of the postwar period, foreign investment did not have a good name. Multinationals were branded exploitative, opportunistic, if not downright hostile. Today the opposite attitude prevails in many places: access to foreign capital is an essential piece of stabilization. Access to foreign saving is essential for modernization of plant and technology, and infrastructure.

The question then arises how to make a country attractive to foreign investors: stability of rules comes high on the list. But equally important are a country's prospects in world trade. Being part of a regional arrangement—say Spain in the European Community or Mexico in the North American Free Trade Agreement—is all important because it guarantees market access.

What kind of money should a country try and attract? One view is that money is fungible—little does it matter whether foreigners go to the stock market or set up new manufacturing activities. That is too simplistic a view: a country should stay far away from hot money and court direct investment above all. The social benefits of direct investment—technology, management skills, guaranteed market access, sharing of fixed costs with foreign firms—all make up important sources of growth. Debt finance and equity do very little beyond the sheer fact of financing trade deficits. The more a country lacks dynamism of its own, the more policy should bend toward courting direct foreign investment.

The state

Discussion of modernization cannot be complete without touching on the role of the state, especially in relation to social programs. One view is that poverty is there because the state, all powerful and interfering, simply stands in the way of progress. That view is common among extreme conservatives and those in despair with state intervention, most eloquently expressed by Hernan de Soto in his powerful statement *The Other Path*. There is also the other view: the state can, should and indeed must help bring about a better life for people at the bottom, not at the expense of the rest but rather for the common benefit. Poverty and unjustifiably bad income distribution are the chief economic problems of Latin America; there are solutions, and to bring them into play is within the economic responsibility of a modern democratic state.

From the broad perspective of economic progress and from a narrower one of containing and eliminating poverty, the good state must obey four criteria: a good ideology; a strong administrative capacity; targeted instruments; and determined leadership. We comment on two of these.

An economic ideology or, less threatening, an economic philosophy serves two purposes. First, it is a means to mobilize society around a set of key ideas and shape a consensus which then becomes the body of guiding principles by which society functions. Second, the economic ideology helps to judge measures and actions to ensure that they form a coherent program rather than a group of unrelated and often contradictory measures.

Where to find a good economic ideology? Not in President Bush's Washington or in the populism of García or the authoritarian rule of Fujimori in Peru, nor of course in Cuba. A good model is the German "social market economy". In this model, the presumption is the market as the central organizing principle, competition and all. But there is an overriding realization, too, that the market by itself does not yield the right outcomes in three areas. First, a market economy need not be automatically and of itself competition. On the contrary, left to themselves firms would tend to restrict competition. Thus government intervention is necessary to ensure competition.

Second, the market does not deliver a socially acceptable distribution of income. Hence government intervention is appropriate to even out the distribution produced by the market. A comprehensive, effective and progressive tax system is one of the means to do so. Education, health and stability are another set. Equality of opportunity and, to some extent, in results, is not only an ethical precept; increasingly it becomes apparent that excessive inequality fosters social strife. If there is in fact such a link then productivity and performance itself require some social cohesion as is fostered by moderation of inequalities. In the past the emphasis was uniquely placed on the motivating force of visible, stark inequality—top pay for star performers. Today there is a counter-current to recognize the social costs of inequality when it marginalizes certain groups and thus creates its own kind of costs. Third, there are obvious areas where externalities warrant and indeed call for public intervention. But the presumption is that intervention needs a specific, good excuse.

Underdevelopment is typically used as an apology and explanation for a lack of administrative capacity; sloth and corruption are accepted if not condoned as part of an underdevelopment culture. It is clear that low levels of per-capita income need not go hand in hand with poor administrative capacity. The counter-examples exist and the major changes under way in Mexico or Argentina demonstrate the contrary.

Two principles in particular help foster administrative capacity. One is decentralization and the other is accountability. Decentralization shifts power and responsibility from an all-powerful center closer to the users or targets of public policy. The closer the administration is to the user or target, the more easily it can become conscious of the specific requirements and opportunities and the less able it is to absolve itself of direct scrutiny and responsibility. Such a decentralization not only promotes effectiveness, but also represents a major step in the direction of a more effective democratic control of the public sector. It eliminates the overriding power of Buenos Aires or Mexico City in favor of the states or provinces and even the local communities.

Accountability is the other side of the coin. Those who exercise control and power must also be held accountable for their management of affairs. Accountability replaces the absence of a price system; without it there is patronage, waste and corruption. With accountability the public exercises direct, vocal control.

An effective administrative capacity cannot be built up in a year or two; it does require years and even a decade. Mexico's new tax administration is a concrete example, as is that of Argentina. The surprise, though, is that already within a very brief period dramatic results are possible. It used to be said that collecting taxes in Latin America was counter-cultural. Mexico and Argentina disprove the point; in fact, people not only do pay, they even think that it is by and large reasonable.

Other than education and health, macroeconomic stability is central to fighting poverty. Without it, and in particular in the aftermath of populist programs, dramatic cuts in real wages and in employment throw large parts of society into poverty. Peru under García is an example, and there are all too many to point to. Of course, tax collection is a first step toward macroeconomic stability and a stable real exchange rate is the second key ingredient. Without the former inflation is bound to emerge and ultimately financial instability; without the latter capital flight will provoke exchange crises and collapsing real wages.

When things are basically in place, as for example in Switzerland, there is no need for great political leadership; in fact, it would be downright worrying. But among developing countries in Latin America, Africa or the former Soviet bloc none can expect to emerge from the distress of the 1980s by simply plodding ahead, trying to do better today than they did yesterday. The changes that need to be made are large, often not easy and not popular. Political leadership of unusual quality is required to carry forward a progressive program. The leaders will ultimately be judged unsuccessful unless their campaign of economic modernization goes far beyond financial stability to a direct focus on poverty as the most urgent and pressing problem of Latin America. Economists know that poverty is a problem for which solutions do exist. Effective solutions cannot deliver instant relief, they do require time. Poverty can be abolished if a country chooses to do so.

Debt problems

The developing country debt problem is off the front page and has a hard time keeping its place even in the financial pages. The defaulted-restructured debts are actively traded on the rumors of the day. What belongs in the obituary of these 1970s debts?

Debt problems occur in history with great regularity, and every time they do, the lenders are almost as surprised as the debtors. In the 1800s debt problems were routine, and again in the interwar period. Access to credit was barely restored by the time the next round of trouble got underway. There is certainly something to the view that either a developing country gets too much capital from abroad or too little, but rarely the middle ground. Taussig (1928) remarked on this fact:

> The loans from creditor countries ... begin with a modest amount, then increase and proceed crescendo. They are likely to be made in exceptionally large amounts toward the culminating stage of a period of activity and speculative upswing, and during that stage become larger from month to month so long as the upswing continues. With the advent of crisis, they are at once drawn down sharply, even cease entirely.

Taussig might have added that debt crises come as a great surprise; from seeming ease of debt service on one day, the next day the country has no visible means of support. The sharp contrast is created by the fact that debt principal and interest are rolled quietly and automatically, until one day the seamless web tears for some reason. The very moment the slightest suspicion of solvency and even liquidity emerges, *all* lending freezes and creditors try to make off with whatever they can lay their hands on. That is the moment of crisis.

Nobody needs to feel very sorry for the lenders; they are paid to know better. But for the sake of curiosity, what is it they forgot about? Debt problems are transfer problems. They occur when in the budget, in the foreign balance, or in politics the resources for continued service are lacking. Accordingly transfer problems can come about in a number of ways and any one is enough to bring about cessation of debt service.

The first way a global debt crisis might emerge is the occurrence of a sharp tightening of capital markets in advanced countries. This forces lenders to ration credit, and if only a handful of banks fail to support their major debtors the debtor will go under in no time. It is in the nature of rolling principal plus interest that every year more credit is required. But in a global tightening less is available and that makes tight credit markets a fertile breeding ground for debt crises.

The second possibility is a major deterioration in the export revenues (or import costs) of debtors. This is the classical commodity collapse both in the 1930s and again in the 1980s. Of course, commodity collapses may well be the counterpart of a credit squeeze and to that extent they come hand-in-hand. When a country's export earnings collapse while debt service rises (more so, the shorter the debt), it is hard to avoid being on the ropes.

The third possibility is domestic mismanagement. This is typically the counterpart of money that has been coming too easily and with no questions asked. That money will typically have financed all too free spending and a grossly overvalued currency.

The fourth possibility is contagion. Countries which are perfectly healthy or at least reasonably healthy are tossed in the same pot as the defaulting ones; by sheer geographic proximity, they come to suffer the same poor rating as neighboring delinquent debtor countries. Colombia is a case in point—conservatively managed, never failing to pay interest, and yet falling into credit rationing just because of its location in Latin America—seen one, seen them all.

Once a debt crisis occurs, what does the script say next? In the past, developing country bonds quickly fell to a discount, reflecting the disillusion of lenders. For a decade or so debts would be serviced at most partially, if at all, and then a workout would come about because the country could afford to make a settlement and creditors did not want to hold on any longer to discounted bonds. Typically creditors would forgive part of the principal, debtors would pay part of the arrears. Mexico, for example, settled for 20 cents on the dollar.

In the 1980s the process was far more complicated because banks were the lenders and behind the banks stood the guaranteeing governments and their multilateral institutions. Forced lending was one side of the coin, early if not premature resumption of debt service was the other. In many countries the result was extreme inflation, extreme poverty, and political instability. Brazil, Peru and Argentina are still in the throes of the 1980s debt problem. Of course, it is not only the debt that is behind their poor performance but also an overriding measure of incompetent or unsuccessful government. But the basic point is this: there is a direct link that runs from a payments crisis to an extreme inflation, and the debt problems were the source of just such payments crises.

For much of Latin America the debt crisis, in the sense of credit rationing in capital markets, is already over. The debts still trade at a discount—barely 30 cents on the dollar in Brazil, 60 cents in Mexico—but access to the world capital market is already restored. New debts are cheerfully signed on even though the creditors of the old debts just took a haircut. In fact, we are seen to have moved already into stage two of the Taussig process—capital is becoming all too available as judged by currency overvaluation and the large trade deficits of the borrowing countries.

Problems of transition economies

With the fall of communism, a new challenge has come for economic analysis and for policy: how to move formerly communist economies to the market? The problem is far more formidable than anyone would have thought five years ago. The complications are due to a number of factors.

First and foremost, the fall of communism has opened up a political vacuum. There is lots of democracy, but no center of gravity in the process. As a result, everything difficult becomes basically very difficult if not impossible. "Politically impossible" includes, in particular, balancing the budget, liberalizing prices, shifting to a market-oriented trade and foreign exchange regime, and privatizing.

As a result of the opposition to full, radical change, the economy is caught in between the market and command. The latter no longer functions and the former is not allowed to function yet. In that no man's land economic results are bound to be very unsatisfactory. Production collapses, distribution breaks down, and nothing works except the printing press.

The second complication is the very poor state of the region. Five years ago, estimates of standards of living placed East Germany or Russia well above 60 percent of standards in West Germany or the United States. These estimates have now been revised radically: productivity is abysmally low, quality is low, and, except for raw materials, the prospects are commensurately poor.

The third problem has to do with the resurgence of nationalism. In the break-up of any empire, nationalism is quick to emerge. If repression was the rule then harmony can hardly be expected in the aftermath. The breakup of Comecon obeys the rule and so does the break-up of the Soviet state. Rivalries among ethnic groups and rivalries across the new republican borders bring with them important complications for trade and payments. If budgets are already a problem in themselves, the proliferation of independent, uncontrolled money issue is certain to make things worse.

Transition economics is rapidly becoming a new discipline. The essays in this volume take a different view. Here it is argued that many of the problems of transition are not unlike those encountered in other developing countries or in historical precedents such as the break-up of the Austro-Hungarian empire. The analogies are valuable because they give us a framework of analysis and tell us where to look for solutions.

Policy economics has a solid analytical basis and lots of practical case work to flesh out the lessons. The experience of developing countries, notably in Latin America, is relevant and useful for transition economies. The best evidence in support of the contention is this: from the very outset of transition, students of macroeconomic instability in Latin America predicted extreme inflation in Russia. For many other observers the future looked far less clear-cut and the prediction of chaos seemed far-fetched.

Reference

Taussig, F. (1928) *International Trade*. New York: Macmillan.

Part I

Inflation and stabilization

1

Lessons from experiences with high inflation

In early 1991 Argentina, Brazil, Peru, Poland, and Yugoslavia were in the midst of extreme instability or at best in the early stages of stabilization. Another group of countries, including the Soviet Union, Romania, and Bulgaria, was on the verge of slipping into high or even extreme inflation. A third group had already run the course and stabilized, as did Bolivia and Israel, or had avoided the extreme experience and opted for stabilization early and decidedly, as Mexico did.

The evidence from some 20 experiences with high inflation establishes that the similarities between the experiences of various countries become sharper and clearer and the differences less significant as the inflation rate rises. The particular mechanism by which monetary expansion occurs may differ—say, deficits of state enterprises rather than of a particular ministry—but the general pattern that runs from deficits to an expansion of money and credit is broadly the same, as is the dynamics of inflation. Of course the experience in the post-communist economies is special in that it starts from repressed inflation, but even that is not very different from experiences in Argentina or Brazil, where cycles of price controls and hyperinflation are now common (Cardoso 1991; Dornbusch, Sturzenegger, and Wolf 1990). The experience of Poland and Yugoslavia, and the extraordinary problems already apparent in the Soviet Union, Bulgaria, and Romania, suggest that discussion of high inflation is timely (Commander and Coricelli 1992; Coricelli and Rocha 1990).

1.1   Lessons from history

Should hyperinflation make policymakers opt for zero inflation at any price? Or is there room in between, with cost-benefit analysis and with the lessons from a rich inflation experience across time and space? Three questions are of special interest in the context of inflationary instability and stabilization. First, how does

Table 1.1 The Soviet budget deficit, 1985–90

	1985	1986	1987	1988	1989	1990[a]
Percentage of GNP						
Revenues	47.3	45.8	43.6	41.7	41.0	42.8
Spending	49.7	52.0	52.0	51.0	49.5	50.6
Budget deficit	2.4	6.2	8.4	9.2	8.5	7.9
Percentage per year						
Retail inflation	—	2.0	1.3	0.6	2.0	4.8
Money incomes	—	3.6	3.9	9.2	13.1	14.5

—Not available.
[a] Plan and estimates.
Source: IMF, World Bank, OECD, and EBRD (1990).

a country fall into hyperinflation? Second, what is necessary to stop high inflation and return to normal growth? And, third, will Eastern Europe and the Soviet Union soon resemble Latin America, with some success stories, a few countries on the verge of high or extreme inflation, and some countries experiencing hyperinflation?

The statistics are, of course, open to question, but the size of the Soviet Union's budget deficits in the past few years indicates the problem ahead (Table 1.1). The data show persistent and increasing deficits. Inflation is still negligible in official markets, but the stage is set for a dramatic inflation unless both the overhang and the deficit are addressed at the outset of any attempt to restructure the economy.

The answers to these questions can to a large extent be discerned from historical experiences of high inflation (Bruno *et al.* 1988; Yeager 1981; Dornbusch and Fischer 1986; Dornbusch, Sturzenegger, and Wolf 1990; Dornbusch and Wolf 1990). Some of the lessons from the past are described below.

1.1.1 *The similarity of inflationary experiences across countries*

It is a mistake to believe that the problems of a particular country are unique. But it is common that policymakers in Brazil, Peru, or the Soviet Union cannot accept that the experience of their country is not unique in the essential facts of inflation. Yet their situation is not substantially different from that of the 20 other countries where policymakers also thought that their unique situation set ordinary economics aside (Dornbusch and Edwards 1991).

1.1.2 *The danger of complacency*

Hyperinflation is not around the corner whenever there is a budget deficit. But inflation can easily become a habit—and from there an unstable process. Complacency comes at a disastrous price: society falls apart as the middle class disappears and society is divided between those who know how to get ahead with inflation and those that fall behind (see Guttman and Meehan 1976 and Fergusson 1975 for dramatic descriptions of the German experience). Pauperization of the middle class rapidly corrodes social institutions. Public administration, the tax system, and all social relations become undermined by corruption and fraud. The middle class revolts against the state, and the poor revolt against property.

1.1.3 *Participatory democracy and instability*

Political change toward a more participatory democracy has not been the traditional vehicle for stability. Political change may carry with it the expectation of an improvement in opportunities and living standards. An inflationary response to raised expectations occurred in Europe in the 1920s, in the Soviet Union in 1919–21, during the Allende period in Chile, and with the growth of Solidarity in Poland.

Destructive inflation may accomplish many things that had been considered politically impossible. The destruction that takes place calls for particularly stern measures to rebuild confidence and stability. Because democratic institutions do not facilitate hard choices, democratic countries have almost invariably implemented special procedures to adopt and implement the hard measures necessary for stabilization. The arrangements differ from national unity governments (Israel in 1985) to restricted special powers for the executive (Poincaré in France in 1926) or special parliamentary committees charged to interact expeditiously with the executive (Germany in 1923). In the end the politically impossible gets done because the destruction brought about by uncontrolled inflation is so devastating that it forces cooperation.

1.1.4 *Fiscal austerity*

Stabilization does not imply that zero inflation must be achieved at any cost. Some policies incorporate a moderate rate of inflation because there is a steeply rising cost of disinflation. Policies that do not set a limit on inflation or policies that merely repress it for a while do not encourage confidence and stability. Policymakers need to have a good grasp of the role of control of the budget and incomes policy in stabilization. Without fiscal austerity stabilization cannot last; without incomes policy it cannot start.

1.1.5 *Structural reform and external support*

A separate set of issues concerns the transition from stabilization to growth. What kind of policies at home and abroad can help to decrease the risk of protracted stagnation? Structural reform and external support play a role in reassuring potential investors and thus moving the economy to growth (Dornbusch 1991).

1.2 Varieties of inflationary experience

Table 1.2 shows inflation rates for several European countries in the range from moderate to acute and extreme inflation. Table 1.3 shows average annual inflation rates in industrial and developing countries. High inflation is a problem in the developing countries of Europe and Latin America; it is not endemic to Africa, Asia, or industrial countries.

Extreme inflation (hyperinflation) is rare. The generally accepted operational definition of hyperinflation proposed by Cagan (1956) sets the benchmark at an inflation rate of 50 percent a month (12,875 percent at an annual rate):

> The term hyperinflation must be properly defined. I define hyperinflation as beginning in the month the rise in process exceeds 50 percent and as ending in the month before the monthly rise in prices drops below that amount and stays below for at least a year. The definition does not rule out a rise in prices at a rate below

Table 1.2 Recent European experience with high inflation, 1986–90 (percentage per year)

Year	Hungary	Turkey	Poland	Yugoslavia	Soviet Union
1986	5.2	34.6	17.7	89.8	2.0
1987	8.7	38.8	25.2	120.8	1.3
1988	15.6	75.4	60.0	194.1	0.6
1989	16.9	69.6	251.1	1,239.9	2.0
1990	28.3	60.3	585.8	583.1	4.8

Source: IMF, *International Financial Statistics* (various issues): and IMF, World Bank, OECD, and EBRD (1990).

Table 1.3 Inflation around the world, 1970–89 (percentage per year)

Year	Industrial countries	Developing countries				
		Africa	Asia	Europe	Middle East	Latin America and the Caribbean
1970	5.6	5.4	6.5	—	3.0	12.4
1979	9.2	15.4	7.5	20.9	10.2	50.2
1988–89	4.7	23.3	11.8	126.0	17.0	208.0

— Not available.
Source: IMF, *International Financial Statistics* (various issues).

Table 1.4 Recent experiences with high inflation, 1981–89 (percentage per year, December to December)

Year	Argentina	Bolivia	Brazil	Mexico	Peru	Israel
1981	105	29	106	28	75	117
1982	165	133	98	59	64	120
1983	344	269	142	102	111	146
1984	627	1,281	197	66	110	374
1985	672	11,748	227	58	163	305
1986	91	276	145	86	78	48
1987	132	15	230	132	86	20
1988	343	16	682	114	10,205	16
1989	3,079	15	1,287	20	3,390	20
1990	2,314	17	2,938	27	7,482	16

Source: IMF, *International Financial Statistics* (various issues).

50 percent per month for the intervening months, and many of these months have rates below that figure.

Until recently there were few cases of hyperinflation in modern history. But now, with fresh cases emerging in Latin America and possibly in Eastern Europe, the phenomenon is more pervasive.

The distinction between hyperinflation and cases of lower and yet extreme inflation is somewhat arbitrary. Whether the inflation rate is really 50 percent a month or only 20 does not make too much difference because in either case inflation will be the dominant factor in the economy and will overshadow most other issues. Countries experiencing inflation rates of 10 or 15 percent a month for any length of time are moving toward hyperinflation. Table 1.4 shows the movement into high inflation in Argentina, Bolivia, Brazil, Mexico, Peru, and Israel in the 1980s. Unlike the inflation experiences associated with war dislocation or civil war, high inflation in these six countries is rooted in domestic mismanagement and, to some extent, in external shocks. In each case the transition to extreme high inflation started off with quite moderate rates, then suddenly gathered speed and became extreme. Only Mexico cut the process short and stabilized before all the mechanisms of instability could gather force.

Stabilization cannot afford to be weak. "Soft measures do not create hard currencies" the German authorities said in 1948 when a drastic monetary reform had to be administered (Dornbusch and Wolf 1990). The lack of thorough reform in Argentina, Brazil, and Peru shows up in the continuation for more than five years of off-and-on-again extreme inflation, which of course is accompanied by a dramatic decline in economic activity and the standard of living.

1.3   The sources and dynamics of high inflation

This section discusses the interaction of financing requirements and the financial structure by assuming full wage-price flexibility. It focuses on the role of contracts in the inflation process and the dynamics of the interaction among deficit finance, institutional innovation in financial markets, dollarization, and shortening contracts. Explosive inflation arises from the disintegration or melting of several institutions. A framework of the main determinants of inflation highlights the roles of budget finance, tax and financial institutions, and contracts in creating high inflation. The following analysis not only identifies the determinants of inflation but also explains the mechanics of the very sharp acceleration that has been witnessed on several occasions.

1.3.1 *Deficit finance*

There is considerable controversy in high-inflation countries about the exact, or even the approximate, size of budget deficits. Reliable public data, covering an extended period of time in a comparable fashion, are simply unavailable. Various series differ in their coverage of the public sector, in the distinction between budget and cash bases, and in the inclusion of certain expenditure items, especially with respect to the quasi-fiscal deficit of the central bank.

Both the adjustment of velocity and the presence of alternative means of financing the deficit (foreign borrowing, use of reserves, and domestic debt finance) help explain the lack of a tight link between inflation and the deficit. Controversies arise about the reason for the budget deficits, their endogeneity as a result of inflation, and their amplification of financial adaptation. That the actual outburst of inflation is often triggered by a foreign exchange crisis does not alter the fact that high inflation is a fiscal phenomenon.

The most common view asserts that high inflation is the result of budget deficits. If the government spends more than it receives in tax collection, the remainder is financed by creating money. That means more money—too much money—chasing too few goods with the predictable outcome of inflation. This view needs considerable refinement to be entirely correct. Three directions of correction are essential. First, there is some room for noninflationary deficit finance. Second, deficits can be financed by debt. Third, there is a channel of causation that runs from inflation to deficits, as well as the other way around.

A model of these important qualifications is given by equation (1.1). The deficit can be financed with high-powered money, with domestic debt, or with foreign debt:

$$gY = \dot{M}/P + \dot{B}/P + \dot{B}^* e/P \tag{1.1}$$

where g is the deficit ratio, Y is real gross domestic product (GDP), M is the domestic base money, B and B^* are domestic and foreign debt, e is the exchange rate (domestic currency over dollars), and P is the price level. (A dot over a variable denotes the rate of change.) It is clear that deficits can be financed by borrowing from abroad or at home, thus entirely avoiding an increase in the money stock, at least for the time being. Focusing on the situation in which the entire deficit is financed by money will show how much inflation can be generated by such a system.

Inflationary finance

Financing deficits by money creation means that any money that is not demanded at the current level of prices must be forced on the public by inflation. In a growing economy some extra real money balances are demanded in order to finance the growing level of transactions. But, beyond that, the demand for nominal money expands only to the extent that inflation erodes the purchasing power of existing real balances. To restore their real balances (at least partially), the public has to add to nominal money holdings. Thus inflationary finance automatically creates a demand for the money issue that finances the deficit.

Keynes (1923, p. 37), in his splendid description of the inflation tax, noted the scope for inflationary finance even in a country with the poorest economic and political conditions:

> A government can live for a long time, even the German government or the Russian government, by printing paper money. That is to say, it can by this means secure the command over real resources, resources just as real as those obtained by taxation. The method is condemned, but its efficacy, up to a point, must be admitted. . . . so long as the public use money at all, the government can continue to raise resources by inflation . . . a government can get resources by a continuous practice of inflation, even when this is foreseen by the public generally, unless the sums they seek to raise in this way are very grossly excessive. . . . What is raised by printing notes is just as much taken from the public as is a beer duty or an income tax. What a government spends the public pays for. There is no such thing as an uncovered deficit.

But, as Keynes has noted, significant inflation reduces the amount of money people choose to hold, because they will substitute toward assets that are more inflation-proof. Thus, just as high taxation erodes the tax base, high inflation leads to a reduction in real balances and hence to an increase in the rate of inflation necessary to finance a given deficit. Moreover, there may be a maximum amount of resources the government can extract.

The long-run relation between the money-financed budget deficit and the rate of inflation is shown in equation (1.2) (for a derivation, see Dornbusch 1985):

$$\pi = (\alpha g - y)/(1 - \beta g), \qquad 1 > \beta g \tag{1.2}$$

where π and y are the rate of inflation and the growth rate of real GDP. The term α represents the noninflationary level of velocity, and β is the responsiveness of velocity to the rate of inflation. This equation shows that because the deficit is financed by money creation, there is inflation. But it also shows that the inflationary impact of a given deficit can differ widely, depending on the financial structure and the growth rate of output.

There are three key points of this relation. First, the inflation rate is lower the higher the growth rate of output is. When output grows strongly, so does the demand for real money. Accordingly there is room for some extra money to be issued without introducing the risk of inflation. Second, inflation is higher the larger the budget deficit is. Moreover, this relation is nonlinear. As the government tries to finance a larger deficit, the required rate of inflation increases steeply. Depending on the particular form of the money demand equation, there may even be a maximum deficit that can be financed by money. Going beyond that range implies hyperinflation. Third, the inflation rate depends on the velocity parameters in equation (1.2). The higher is the level of noninflationary velocity (that is, because of dollarization) the higher the rate of inflation associated with any given deficit. A high degree of responsiveness of velocity to inflation also implies a larger rate of inflation.

The increase in inflation brought about by a one percentage point increase in the deficit is higher, the higher are inflation and the budget deficit from which one starts. Inflationary finance thus exerts a very powerful impact on inflation if it is used in large doses or in an environment where a high level of velocity, and strong responsiveness of velocity to inflation, leave little scope for an inflation tax. Likewise, dollarization or a drop in growth bring about large increases in the inflation rate, the more so the higher the initial extent of deficit finance.

The Olivera–Tanzi effect

One of the striking effects of inflation is the erosion of the real value of taxation. If there is any delay between accrual and payment of taxes, the inflation in the interim will mean that the real value of what is paid is lower the higher the rate of inflation. With moderate inflation it makes no difference that 1987 taxes are paid in 1988. But when inflation is high, this effect wreaks havoc with the real value of tax collection. Keynes, commenting on the impact of inflation on the budget noted this point, as did Bresciani-Turroni (1937). Tanzi (1978) and others have recognized this effect in the specific context of Latin American inflation. The empirical importance of this effect is large whenever inflation is high and tax collection lags are long and when there is no provision for tax indexation.

External shocks and inflation

Suppose, as is the case in Argentina, that the public sector has a large external debt and an external debt shock occurs. Specifically, assume that before the disturbance any existing external debt was rolled over with interest fully capitalized through automatic "new money" and that there is no domestic debt. Let d^* be the flow of external debt service (measured as a percent of gross national product [GNP]), and thus g is the total deficit ratio that is financed by money creation. Thus,

$$g = \sigma(\pi) + d^* \tag{1.3}$$

From equation (1.3) reduced access to automatic capitalization of interest payments implies that external debt service leads to increased deficit finance by money creation. The country has to earn the resources for external finance or else finance the purchase of foreign exchange by creating money. First, the government will issue more money to finance the purchase of foreign exchange for interest payments (assuming, of course, that there are no expenditure cuts or tax increases). Second, there will typically be a real depreciation in order to improve the external balance.

The increase in inflation resulting from an external financing disruption is larger, the larger is the debt service shock and the real depreciation, but it also depends on the responsiveness of velocity to inflation and on the degree to which increased inflation erodes real tax collection. Each of these factors will increase the inflationary impact of the debt shock significantly.

The "balance of payments school" would argue that external balance problems and the resulting depreciation of the exchange rate are the primary causes of the deficit. By contrast, the "quantity theory school" would point to budget deficits and their financing by money creation as the reason for inflation. Passive money is the essential ingredient in reconciling the quantity school and the balance of payments doctrine. Not surprisingly suspension of reparation payments in Germany and of debt service in Bolivia in 1985 were essential steps in the stabilization of inflation. In Argentina, involuntary external debt service after 1982 became an important source of inflation in exactly the manner the balance of payments school emphasizes. Deteriorating terms of trade further aggravated the external debt shock by forcing real depreciation and hence an increase in the real value (in terms of GDP or the tax base) of the existing external debt service.

Endogenous financial innovation and liberalization

The interest that traditional depository institutions can pay is typically controlled. There may be an outright limitation on interest rates, or else institutions may be required to hold reserves or government debt at controlled rates. These restrictions make institutions unable to compete in financial markets where nominal interest rates more nearly reflect the ongoing inflation. New, unregulated financial institutions that offer depositors higher interest rates spring up and thus draw customers away from traditional depository institutions. There is a fall in the ratio of conventional money to GDP. The government loses part of its inflation tax base, and hence equilibrium inflation increases. The government may aggravate matters when it responds to the increasing inflation by raising reserve requirements or forcing traditional banks to hold government debt.

Governments often promote this process, most obviously under the guise of financial liberalization. Since inflation is a tax on money (or commercial bank non-interest-bearing reserves), financial liberalization means that the public can avoid the tax on money. Financial liberalization may take the form of interest-bearing deposits or formal dollarization, each of which reduces the demand for high-powered money; velocity rises and so does the inflation rate associated with the financing of a given deficit by money creation. Thus, from an inflation point of view, financial repression, no liberalization, is appropriate. Financial liberalization requires that extra tax revenue be available to avoid the inflationary impact of a reduction in the captive inflation tax base. Governments that condone dollarization likewise promote inflation. Dollarization is captured in equation (1.2) by both the coefficients α and β. The shift from the domestic monetary base into dollars reduces the base for the inflation tax and hence must increase inflation.

One is tempted to explain inflation experiences in some countries by dollarization and new financial intermediaries. Thus countries with stronger dollarization have higher inflation. A government that experiences some inflation and makes dollarization easier will experience even more inflation. However, dollarization is also a response to inflation.

The financial adaptation to inflation intensifies the inflationary process. In response to inflation there is a flight from money into interest-bearing financial assets, to the extent that they exist at all, or into dollars. But there is also an institutional adaptation: financial institutions spring up that offer protection against inflation. The better the protection they offer, the more substantial the flight from money or the larger the increase in velocity.

Timing

Inflation controls and managed exchange rates can slow down the build-up of inflation. The loss of resources, or forced saving, is an alternative mode of financing. However, deficits do imply money creation and inflation. Moreover, the longer the delay the more dramatic the inflationary explosion. This is especially the case when a managed exchange rate and reserve losses have financed the deficit in a relatively noninflationary manner. When these mechanisms are no longer possible, there will be a sudden shift toward the inflation tax at the same time that a real depreciation is required.

1.3.2   *The role of contracts in the inflation process*

As inflation accelerates, contracts shorten, and that shortening of contracts is itself a factor that causes inflation to accelerate. Institutional wage-setting mechanisms often rely on a fixed contract length, with wage adjustments occurring at specified intervals. The adjustments are based on the cumulated increase in prices since the last adjustment. For example, earners might receive full compensation for past actual price increases at regular intervals, say yearly. Now suppose there is a shift to six-month intervals. There are two interesting questions. The first concerns the dynamics of shifting to shorter contracts. What is the threshold for inflationary erosion of wages that causes the shift, and what makes it economywide rather than just for a particular firm? The other interesting question is what happens when the frequency of adjustment increases yet further. This point has been developed especially by Pazos (1972). It is of interest here because contract deterioration is one of the important characteristics of an accelerating inflation and because exchange depreciation often plays an important role in setting off the process.

If nominal wages are adjusted only periodically, the real wage follows a sawtooth pattern. On each adjustment date the nominal wage is increased by the cumulated inflation since the preceding adjustment. Until the next adjustment date the real wage declines as the ongoing inflation erodes the purchasing power of the constant nominal payments. By the end of the adjustment interval the real wage has declined below its period average. The higher the rate of inflation, moreover, the lower the average real wage, given the interval of adjustment.

In a system of full, but lagged, indexation, the real wage can be cut only by moving to a higher rate of inflation. Thus, once-and-for-all depreciation of the currency immediately raises the rate of inflation and erodes existing contracts. But wage indexation ensures that inflation must be pushed to an even higher rate so that there is always some group of wage earners whose wages are still lagging behind the increasing rates of price increases. The same principle applies to the removal of subsidies undertaken to correct the budget. Measures undertaken to correct competitiveness or the budget can be effective only if they achieve a cut in the real wage, but because of full indexation that cut can take place only if inflation is allowed to run at a higher rate. This mechanism often sets the stage for inflation explosions.

Consider a country that requires adjustments in the budget and external competitiveness. Suppose that the government lacks the political force to suspend full indexation, so that the removal of subsidies or a real exchange depreciation will speed up the inflation rate. Workers in the middle of their contracts, for example, will find that their real wages fall below what they consider a minimum standard of living. They cannot borrow, even in perfect capital markets. Hence they will call for a shorter interval between wage adjustments in order to recover the real wage losses imposed by inflation. They will ask for an advance of what they think is due. If the economy does, in fact, shift from, say, six-month to three-month indexation intervals, the inflation rate will simply double (Simonsen 1986). But once the contract structure has moved to a three-month scheme, it is unlikely that the indexation structure will return spontaneously to a longer interval, even if shocks are favorable. And there is nothing to make the three-month interval more stable than the six-month interval that was just abandoned. New shocks will shift the economy to even more frequent adjustments and hence to correspondingly higher rates of inflation. At this stage the exchange rate becomes critical.

The dramatic escalation of inflation, seemingly out of proportion to the disturbances, arises from the endogeneity of the adjustment interval. This is due not so much to the direct impact on inflation of corrective exchange rate or price policies. It occurs because increases in inflation, which may be minor but highly visible (such as a 10 percent devaluation over and above a purchasing power parity rule or a removal of bread subsidies), lead to an increase in the frequency of wage adjustments, which brings on a much higher inflation rate. The endogeneity of adjustment intervals is the mechanism that connects small inflation disturbances with a shift from 50 to 100 percent inflation or beyond to hyperinflation. As long as full indexation remains, even seemingly small corrections are a dramatic threat to the stability of the inflation rate and hence may not be worth undertaking. Incomes policy designed to avoid inflationary explosion must avoid accelerating the frequency of adjustments.

1.3.3 *Dynamics*

The actual dynamics of the economy emerges from the interaction of the inflationary aspects of deficit finance and the contracting process. A stable equilibrium may not actually exist. When inflation rises significantly and permanently, institutions adapt. In doing so, they help to increase inflation. Under conditions of extreme inflation, institutions break down. There is a near-abandonment of domestic money, which means the government must continue to increase inflation to get any seigniorage. Contracts are set for a shorter duration and are more likely to be dollar-based.

In the analysis of inflationary experiences, it is common to assume adaptive inflationary expectations (Cagan 1956). There appears to be a significant sluggishness in the initial phases of high inflation as well as a subsequent acceleration, which suggests exactly such an expectations mechanism. Adaptive inflationary expectations are often the key model device to slowing the impact of money on inflation. An alternative and perhaps more accurate model focuses much more on the dynamics of deterioration in contracts, both in the goods and labor markets and on the inflationary adaptation of financial institutions. Institutional dynamics seems to offer a more suitable framework for studying high inflation.

As economic institutions break down and time intervals for contracts and adaptation to inflation become shorter, the inflation process becomes explosive. The economic time horizon shrinks along with contracts and maturities of financial assets until, when the economy converges to a spot market with dollar pricing, the budget or external balance deficit leads to hyperinflation. Hyperinflation is inevitable because the inflation tax, with sufficient financial adaptation, can be almost totally evaded, and hence the budget deficit cannot be financed. The Olivera–Tanzi effect, the shortening of contracts, and financial adaptation all react in a perverse way (from the perspective of stabilization) in that they widen the deficit and accelerate explosively the inflation process.

1.4 Stabilization

The preceding discussion helps to explain why stabilization is difficult and often takes more than one attempt to succeed. In the process of high inflation all institutions break down. When stabilization is undertaken, there is neither immediate, spontaneous resumption of longer adjustment periods for wages and prices nor an instant increase of real money demand to noninflationary levels. As a result more sizable adjustments in the budget are required, and more dramatic measures are necessary to create the confidence that stabilization will, in fact, last. Because the fiscal measures have to be particularly large they are also particularly difficult and hence often cannot be sustained. When they fail, inflation returns instantly at exceptionally high levels because institutional inertia has not recovered.

Incomes policy—freezing exchange rates, wages, and prices—can be an effective supplement to the inevitable budget cut. It makes up for institutional inertia and, to that extent, gives a government a better chance to start stabilization. But as is clear from the experiences of Argentina, Brazil, and Peru, failure to correct the budget implies that high inflation will soon return. The decline in the ratio of M1 to GDP is not typically fully reversed in the initial stabilization. As a result financing even a moderate deficit is much more inflationary than it was before the experience of extremely high inflation. This hysteresis effect of high inflation (similarly apparent in contracts, pricing, and tax collection) sharply reduces the chances of stopping inflation with anything short of a dramatic budget cut.

The task of stabilizing inflation involves stopping inflation quickly and avoiding the resurgence of inflationary pressures. To end inflation by incomes policy is relatively easy, but to keep it down requires fiscal support. The chief mistake in stabilization policy is to rely too much on incomes policy—fixed exchange rates and wage and price freezes—and too little on fiscal austerity. Such programs quickly lead to repressed inflation and overvaluation, in which tight monetary policy is introduced to sustain the imbalances. Ultimately that does not work, and another inflationary explosion offers the starting point for yet another stabilization. Argentina offers a clear example of this process with its successive failed stabilization programs in the past five years.

1.4.1 *Budget balancing*

Budget deficits are the ultimate source of inflation. When external financing or the domestic capital market cannot finance deficits, then the deficits must be adjusted. Two questions immediately emerge. The first is how large a deficit is consistent with stability; the second is how to cut deficits down to the required size.

Argentina, Brazil, and Peru failed to adjust fiscal deficits in the aftermath of their 1985 heterodox stabilization. Wage-price controls and fixed exchange rates quickly stopped inflation and raised the political popularity of the president. The resulting possibility for fiscal stabilization was, however, not used. Instead the deficits persisted and were financed by creating money. As a result, inflation continued.

Quasi-fiscal deficits

The starting point for budget balancing is the need for a transparent accounting of the consolidated government. Because the issue is control of monetary emission, it is essential that the central bank's "quasi-fiscal" deficit be part of the accounting. An accounting framework is needed for the consolidated government sector, including not only the central government and the central bank, but also state enterprises and local government. Extreme inflation invariably reflects deficits financed by writing checks on the central bank, whether it be by provincial authorities, as in China; by state enterprises, as in Yugoslavia; or by a government bank, as in Brazil. The deficits may have as a counterpart purchases of foreign exchange, payments of wages, deficits of the railroads, external debt service, election spending by a governor, or simply corruption. In any case a deficit leads to money creation.

Quasi-fiscal deficits arise from loans by the central bank at subsidized rates, losses on foreign exchange operations in the form of guarantees, forward contracts, or simply purchases at a high rate (under multiple exchange rates) and sales at a low one. In Peru in 1986–87, for example, exchange losses accounted for 2.3 percent of GDP. But central bank losses also arise from credit operations. Subsidized credit is no different from any other subsidy; in fact credit subsidies have long ceased being investment subsidies and have become simply a production subsidy that finances wages when prices are not allowed to reflect costs.

Revenues

The second point on the reform agenda is to achieve a productive tax system. The reform must raise revenue on a substantially larger scale and far more efficiently. Increasing the yield of the tax system is dictated by the need to eliminate deficits. Inflation stabilization makes an immediate contribution because the inflationary erosion of revenues ceases. But that is only a small part, perhaps as much as 2 percent of GNP in revenues. The major effort must be in reconstructing the tax system, including stopping the corruption and evasion that now undermine the collection of taxes as well as introducing and demonstrating mechanisms to increase compliance. The complacent acceptance of pervasive tax evasion is the most regressive aspect of the Latin American tax system, and it must be carefully watched as Eastern Europe moves to taxation as the chief source of government revenue.

The revenue effort must concentrate both on collecting taxes and on eliminating subsidies in public sector enterprises. Many countries now have pervasive systems to manage public sector prices, both to control inflation and to try to prevent a decline in real wages. The implied revenue losses are extraordinarily large and cannot be justified by any of the objectives. For example, in Peru controlled telephone rates have reduced the real price of the service to one-tenth the 1985 level. It is difficult to argue that telephone rates have an important effect either on inflation or on welfare of the poor, but they do contribute to deficits.

Governments should therefore totally eliminate all subsidies. The resulting revenue gains must be applied to eliminate inflation, which in itself raises the welfare of the poor since inflation is a highly regressive tax. Part of the revenues should also be used for targeted food and employment programs for the poorest groups.

Beyond cutting all subsidies and raising revenue under the existing structure, governments should use the crisis to institute a more efficient tax system. The system should produce more revenue with fewer distortions, which means eliminating the pervasive exemptions from direct taxes and raising the rates to higher levels. A comprehensive value added tax of 15 percent, with a 5 percent surcharge for luxuries, might be the starting point for discussion.

Government spending

For many observers the right direction for adjustment is to cut government spending, not to raise taxes. Inefficiency in government is pervasive, and public sector employment in many countries is unjustifiably high. But there is no presumption that the fiscal problem can be solved correctly by massive firing of public sector employees and privatization. There is a need to restructure public sector spending, from consumption to investment and productive services. But as for the level of spending, it certainly is not excessive. More of the spending absolutely and relatively should fall on infrastructure, health, and social services for the poorer groups. The current composition of spending is not only unproductive but probably also regressive.

Most of infrastructure investment could be done by the private sector. That is certainly the case, for example, for telephone services, but also for public transport and even the road system. Mexico is now exploring such options with very substantial success. But the fact remains that infrastructure spending should not be the priority in balancing the budget, certainly not at the expense of health and education.

1.4.2 *Incomes policy*

Fiscal austerity is the essential aspect of stabilization, but incomes policy is an important, desirable component. Incomes policy is designed to bring about a rapid, coordinated end to inflation. In a hyperinflation, incomes policy amounts to fixing the exchange rate. Because price setting is geared to the movements of the dollar, the move to a fixed exchange rate is enough to break the inflation and the expectation of inflation.

But when annual inflation is only 100 or 200 percent, incomes policy is both more essential and more complicated. Without incomes policy, ending inflation by demand management alone would create an extraordinary depression. The current inflation will be a weighted average of cost increases that are equal to past inflation, which enters costs by explicit or implicit indexation, and the current rate of exchange depreciation, $\dot{e}$, plus a cyclical component, which is denoted by "GAP":

$$\pi = \tau\pi_{-1} + (1 - \tau)\dot{e} + \Psi\,\text{GAP} \tag{1.4}$$

Because of the inertia represented by the cost increases resulting from explicit or implicit indexation, current inflation cannot get away from past inflation unless the government breaks the process by incomes policy. Incomes policy means fixing the exchange rate and stopping wage inflation. The government will have to intervene in loan contracts to reduce real interest burdens that otherwise would result from the unanticipated decline in inflation, and intervention will be required in wage contracts. Because these contracts have periodic adjustments for inflationary erosion, a sudden ending of inflation requires intervention. Some wage contracts have to be rolled back, and others need to be adjusted upward.

Exchange rate policy

Exchange rate policy assumes a strategic role in stabilization, as does pricing in the public sector. The starting point of a program is invariably a fixed exchange rate. But if inflation does not end completely, sooner or later adjustments in the exchange rate and public sector prices are needed. The decision to abandon the fixed rate is a difficult one because it signals the government's acceptance of inflation as something inevitable. As a result there is a temptation to postpone exchange rate adjustment until a significant overvaluation has developed.

Overvaluation in turn creates an expectation of a devaluation, and very high real interest rates become necessary to stop speculation. High real interest rates in turn increase domestic debt service and worsen the budget. Ultimately the exchange rate adjustment does have to come, but often the overvaluation has gone so far that an outright exchange crisis and collapse are the end of the abortive attempt to practice a fixed exchange rate. The pragmatic answer is to move after two or three months to a crawling peg, depreciating the exchange rate at a pace that maintains external competitiveness. The risk of an overvaluation maintains short economic horizons and stands in the way of recovery. The right time for a crawling peg is very early because the government should try to preserve maximum competitiveness. Holding on to an exchange rate too long may yield an extra month of low inflation, but it also sacrifices competitiveness and therefore prejudices the return of growth.

Indexation

A major stabilization decision regards indexation. The common view is that indexation is responsible for the inflation and that accordingly it should be abolished. Moreover, governments should declare a zero inflation target rather than create mechanisms that make it easier to live with inflation. However, it is not necessarily true that without indexation there is inflation stability because inflationary shocks, such as public sector price increases and depreciation, are not fully absorbed into lower real wages. Without explicit indexation the government becomes the judge of what wage increases to grant. The wage becomes politicized, which means invariably larger rather than smaller wage increases, and wage increases come sooner rather than later. In fact in economies in which a government seeks to avoid explicit indexation, as in Brazil after 1985, inflation soon becomes more unstable and susceptible to a far more rapid escalation than had ever been experienced under indexation.

Indexation is a mechanism that creates inertia and also preserves inertia. Reintroducing half-yearly indexation may therefore be a key step in establishing the expectation of low inflation. Once the wage is locked away, a very rapid resumption of inflation will not be expected. As a result horizons can lengthen far more effectively than under threshold provisions or in the absence of any kind of formal indexation.

Monetary policy

Monetary policy does not play an independent role in stabilization; it is dictated by the budget and the exchange rate policy. Following stabilization real interest rates are too high. One could argue that to resume growth the economy needs reliquification. There is very limited room for reliquification, but that is best done by monetizing reserve inflows rather than by deficit finance or domestic credit creation.

The alternative is an overly firm commitment to a zero inflation target. The policymaker might be tempted to make monetary policy (and the exchange rate) do what fiscal policy has not achieved. The risk is a long period of extraordinarily high real interest rates and possibly an exchange overvaluation. They might stop inflation, but they also will destroy the real economy. The best and only lasting way to bring about low real interest rates and to achieve moderate inflation is by a balanced budget (including state enterprises, except where they are financed in the capital market) and a very competitive real exchange rate.

1.5 Concluding remarks: Priorities

Without financial stability, economic reconstruction and growth will simply not occur. If inflation is high and variable, then it will be the most important issue. It will take up policymakers' precious time. It will tempt them into superficial remedies, which help in the short run but set back economic activity because they create uncertainty. It will also lead the private sector to focus on protection against inflation and government's arbitrary interventions. The first priority then must be to reduce inflation. A balanced budget that lasts is required to achieve financial stability.

In economies in which price control has been the rule, the recognition of the problem of inflation may be the most serious issue. There has been no experience with inflation, and most attention focuses on the popular revolt against removing some subsidies. But beyond the initial correction of subsidies there is the broader issue of the risk of a serious inflation. Serious inflation can emerge either because there is an initial monetary overhang or because the subsidy correction does not go far enough. Deficits remain, and money creation starts to interact with corrective inflation. (The Soviet Union is an obvious case in point.)

In countries with major fiscal problems it is not politically impossible to make the necessary adjustments; it is politically difficult, but the adjustments will ultimately be made. The only question is how large the loss in the standard of living has to be before it is done and how much time and political capital will be lost (Blanchard *et al.* 1991; Fischer and Gelb 1990; Dornbusch 1990).

References

The word "processed" describes informally reproduced works that may not be commonly available through library systems.

Blanchard, Oliver, Rudiger Dornbusch, Richard Layard, and Lawrence Summers (1991) *Reform in Eastern Europe.* Cambridge, MA: MIT Press.

Bresciani-Turroni, C. (1937) *The Economics of Inflation.* London: Allen & Unwin.

Bruno, Michael, Guido Di Tella, Rudiger Dornbusch, and Stanley Fischer, eds (1988) *Stopping High Inflation.* Cambridge, MA: MIT Press.

Cagan, Phillip (1956) "The Monetary Dynamics of Hyperinflation." In Milton Friedman, ed., *Studies in the Quantity Theory of Money.* Chicago: University of Chicago Press.

Cardoso, Eliana (1991) "From Inertia to Megainflation: Brazil's Macroeconomic Policies in the 1980s." In Michael Bruno and Stanley Fischer, eds, *Lessons of Economic Stabilization and Its Aftermath.* Cambridge, MA: MIT Press.

Commander, Simon, and Fabrizio Coricelli (1992) "Price-Wage Dynamics and Inflation in Socialist Economies: Empirical Models for Hungary and Poland." *The World Bank Economic Review,* 6(1).

Coricelli, Fabrizio and Roberto Rocha (1990) "Stabilization Programs in Eastern Europe: A Comparative Analysis of the Polish and Yugoslav Programs of 1990." World Bank, Washington, DC. Processed.

Dornbusch, Rudiger (1985) "Stopping Hyperinflation: Lessons from the German Experience in the 1920s." In Rudiger Dornbusch, Stanley Fischer, and John Bossons, eds, *Macroeconomics and Finance: Essays in Honor of Franco Modigliani.* Cambridge, MA: MIT Press.

Dornbusch, Rudiger (1990) "Priorities of Economic Reform in Eastern Europe and the Soviet Union." Massachusetts Institute of Technology, Department of Economics, Cambridge, MA. Processed. (See also Chapter 7, this volume.)

Dornbusch, Rudiger (1991) "Policies to Move from Stabilization to Growth." *Proceedings of the World Bank Annual Conference on Development Economics 1990.* Washington, DC: World Bank. (See also Chapter 2, this volume.)

Dornbusch, Rudiger and Sebastian Edwards (1990) "The Macroeconomics of Populism in Latin America." *Trimestre Economico* 57 (January–March): 121–62.

Dornbusch, Rudiger and Sebastian Edwards (1991) *The Macroeconomics of Populism in*

Latin America. Chicago: University of Chicago Press.

Dornbusch, Rudiger, and Stanley Fischer (1986) "Stopping Hyperinflations: Past and Present." *Weltwirtschaftliches Archiv* 122 (1, April): 1–14.

Dornbusch, Rudiger, Frederico Sturzenegger, and Holger Wolf (1990) "Extreme Inflation: Dynamics and Stabilization." *Brookings Papers on Economic Activity* 2: 1–64.

Dornbusch, Rudiger, and Holger Wolf (1990) "Monetary Overhang and Reforms in the 1940s." Massachusetts Institute of Technology, Department of Economics, Cambridge, MA. Processed.

Fergusson, A. (1975) *When Money Dies.* London: William Kimber.

Fischer, Stanley, and Alan Gelb (1990) "Issues in Socialist Economy Reform." Massachusetts Institute of Technology, Department of Economics, Cambridge, MA. Processed.

Guttman, William, and P. Meehan (1976) *The Great Inflation.* London: Gordon and Cremonesi.

International Monetary Fund. Various issues. *International Financial Statistics.* Washington, DC.

International Monetary Fund, World Bank, Organization for Economic Co-operation and Development, and European Bank for Reconstruction and Development (1990) *The Economy of the Soviet Union.* Washington, DC.

Keynes, John M. (1923) *A Tract on Monetary Reform.* Reprinted by the Royal Economic Society, London, 1971.

Pazos, Felipe (1972) *Chronic Inflation in Latin America.* New York: Praeger.

Simonsen, Mario (1986) "Indexation: Current Theory and the Brazilian Experience." In Rudiger Dornbusch and Mario Simonsen, eds, *Inflation, Debt and Indexation.* Cambridge, MA: MIT Press.

Tanzi, Vito (1978) "Inflation, Real Tax Revenue, and the Case for Inflationary Finance: Theory with an Application to Argentina." *IMF Staff Papers* 25 (September): 417–51.

Yeager, Leland (1981) *Experiences with Stopping Inflation.* Washington, DC.: American Enterprise Institute.

2

Policies to move from stabilization to growth

Discussions of economic stabilization traditionally have assumed that fiscal austerity, competitive real exchange rates, sound financial markets, and deregulation provide the conditions for a resumption of growth. One must distinguish the necessary from the sufficient conditions, however. Adjustment is a necessary, but not necessarily a sufficient, condition for a resumption of growth, because asset holders may postpone repatriating flight capital, and investors may delay initiating projects. These factors raise an important problem of coordination that classical economics does not recognize. This paper starts with a statement of the problem, reviews essentials of stabilization, and then turns to the question of structural adjustment and the return to growth.

2.1   The problem

Figures 2.1 and 2.2 show two very different cases of economic performance. In Chile (Figure 2.1), after serious domestic and external disturbances, a long effort at restructuring has been paying off. In 1989, Chilean output reached the level of potential, and the scope of growth in the years ahead is substantial.[1]

Argentina (Figure 2.2) represents the opposite experience. Output per capita has been declining for almost a decade and is now at the level of the early 1960s. Macroeconomic instability, particularly hyperinflation, stands in the way of normality. But even if stabilization occurs, is there any assurance that growth will resume promptly? The examples of Bolivia and Mexico suggest that it may not.

Thus, even if stabilization occurs in Argentina, Brazil, or Peru (and ultimately it must), there is little assurance that the onset of austerity will not translate into protracted stagnation. The policy issue, then, centers on the following questions:

The author is grateful to Vittorio Corbo and John Williamson for helpful comments.

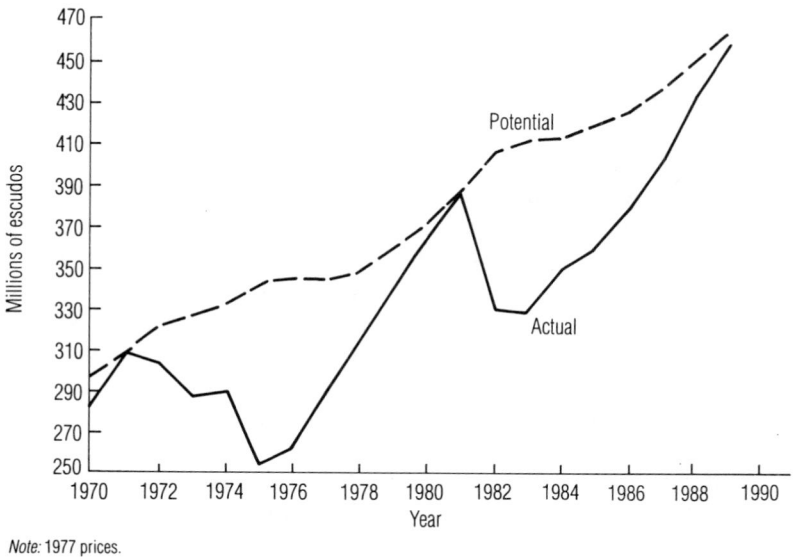

Figure 2.1 Actual and potential output, Chile, 1970–89.
(*Sources*: International Monetary Fund (IMF) data, and Marfan and Artiagoitia (1989).)

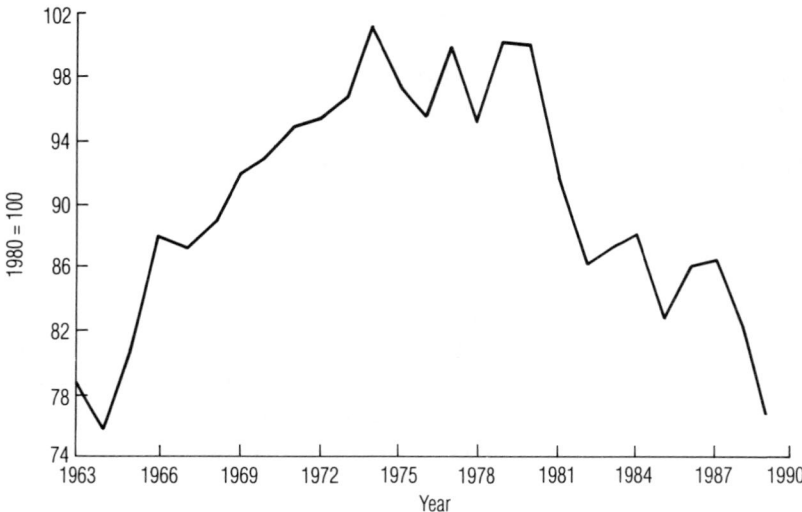

Figure 2.2 Index of per-capita output, Argentina, 1963–89.
(*Source*: IMF data.)

- What are the essential steps that assure stabilization?
- What are the key policy measures in the restoration of growth?
- What is the contribution of the external environment? Specifically, what role can debt relief and stabilization loans play in supporting a program?

The literature on these questions falls into two broad categories. The first is the optimistic approach, which, for example, represents the official view of the International Monetary Fund (IMF). The optimistic approach asserts that with the appropriate policies in place, stabilization will pay off rapidly in terms of growth. In support, the optimists can cite a few cases to suggest that vigorous reconstruction can give way to a period of strong growth—Brazil in 1964–67, Chile after 1983, and the Republic of Korea and Turkey at the beginning of the 1980s. The other trend in the literature, the skeptical approach, cites the experience of Mexico, Bolivia, or even Chile in arguing that there is no quick step from stabilization to growth and that the transition remains difficult to understand and even more difficult to accomplish. I discuss these two lines of argument after a review of prescriptions for stabilization.

2.2   Stabilization

The design of a stabilization effort comprises five elements:

- the post-stabilization inflation target;
- the extent and manner of fiscal stabilization;
- the appropriate monetary policy;
- the appropriate level of the exchange rate;
- the use of an incomes policy.

On each of these issues there is now a significant body of evidence, and therefore it is appropriate to draw some lessons.

2.2.1   Inflation targets

Two schools dominate thought on inflation targets. The intransigent school asserts that nothing short of zero inflation is a viable policy target. The most lenient school accepts, if necessary, moderate inflation of 20 or 30 percent.

The intransigents argue that only zero inflation is a stable target and that any concession on this leads to a cumulative departure. Fellner (1976) forcefully argued this view, drawing attention to the need for an explicit price target path because of the problem of "self-justifying lack of credibility" in the absence of such a commitment. This is a strong argument, and it should be the last word in an economy starting with zero inflation. But what of an economy that has fought its way down to 20 percent inflation, say, and whose policymakers now contemplate further disinflation? The policymakers face a cost–benefit issue if credibility in and of itself does not produce this further disinflation. If attaining further reduction in inflation takes protracted slack in the economy, then going all the way to zero inflation by spending an extra year or two with slack can be very costly. But it is equally clear that being too anxious to turn the corner by declaring victory over inflation too early keeps the inflationary virus fully alive and leaves the economy vulnerable to a resumption of high inflation.

On the issue of inflation targets, pragmatism must prevail. Central bankers should talk about zero inflation, but they also should compromise with reality. At the margin there are tradeoffs, and pursuing zero inflation at *any* cost is not only socially irresponsible but also bad economics.

2.2.2 *Fiscal policy*

Adjustment of the budget is the indispensable feature of a stabilization program. Protracted fiscal deficits that cannot be financed in the domestic capital market or abroad lead to high inflation and in time to megainflation or even hyperinflation. The evidence from Latin America and now from Eastern Europe in this regard is quite unambiguous. It is one thing to know what kind of deficit a stable country can run without getting into trouble; it is quite another to set the allowable deficit for a country that wants to restore stability.

Hysteresis effects in this context are more than a fad; they are a live issue because the preceding period of financial instability will have semipermanently deteriorated the scope for noninflationary deficit finance. Specifically, the demonetization that is always the consequence of high inflation—whether it be by dollarization, capital flight, or flight into fully liquid interest-bearing assets—reduces for a long time the scope for noninflationary deficit finance.

The size of the budget deficit that can be financed will depend on how far the financial instability has gone. If there has been hyperinflation, a budget surplus is required. If inflation reached only 50 percent, there is room for moderate deficits financed by money creation and debt finance. The size of the deficit also will depend on the inflation target. There is room for a moderate remonetization of the economy, but the scope is drastically limited. Beyond that, planned seigniorage revenues must be consistent with the inflation target. There is a close link between revenues and inflation, given by

$$\pi = \frac{(\alpha g - y)}{(1 - \beta g)} \tag{2.1}$$

where π is the rate of inflation, g is the budget deficit financed by money creation, y is the trend growth of output, and α and β are parameters of the velocity equation.[2] The higher the noninflationary level of velocity and the higher the response of velocity to inflation, the more inflationary is deficit finance. Therefore, it is appropriate to look at inflation in two ways: one is how to reduce inflation from high levels by restrictive aggregate demand policies and by an incomes policy: the other is what fiscal policies to put in place to finance the budget consistent with the inflation target.

Fiscal adjustment should take place on several fronts. The first is the introduction of a productive tax structure. A productive tax structure involves four elements:

- a broad tax base, without exemptions and only a few taxes;
- a firm attitude toward tax compliance;
- moderate, preferably uniform rates of taxation;
- absence of significant subsidies of any form and establishment of efficient public utility rates.

Not included here is a tax amnesty, which is often favored as part of fiscal reconstruction. Uchitelle (1989) shows the very limited success of such a measure.

In Latin America, to take a specific region, tax systems are defective in every one of these dimensions. Large parts of Latin American economies—for example, agriculture in Mexico and Brazil—were exempted from taxation until recently. Tax evasion is pervasive, especially among the privileged. In Argentina, for example, compliance is a joke, and government after government condones one of the worst compliance records in the world. Argentina has just now approved a law that penalizes tax evasion, but the government is far from starting its implementation. There is much room for change. Still, improvements in fiscal administration in countries traditionally plagued by poor tax compliance—Italy, Mexico, and Spain, for example—offer grounds for hope.

During periods of financial instability, public sector pricing becomes a macroeconomic issue. When inflation is too high, public sector price increases are slowed down to reduce inflation. The resulting deficit creates financial problems that then are solved by emergency increases in public sector rates. This yo-yoing is extremely inefficient. Public sector prices should be set on the basis of microeconomic efficiency considerations. Any income distribution consequences should be resolved through the general tax structure. Public utility rates should be indexed on a regular basis even if that means there is more indexation and hence more vulnerability to inflation in the economy. Inflation must be stopped by a permanent balance in the budget, not by a temporary slowdown of public sector price increases.

The tax rate structure in Latin America remains highly distorted. It is characterized by a proliferation of taxes and punitive rates for the sectors least able to evade taxation and by an excessive emphasis on regressive selected sales and trade taxes rather than by comprehensive expenditure or income taxes. Subsidies remain pervasive in the prices of public enterprises, in the credit market, for particular regions, and in particular sectors. The combination of punitive taxation of sectors, regressive taxes, and widespread subsidies produces a totally unproductive tax structure, a high marginal cost of revenue, and hence an almost inevitable bias toward inflationary finance in response to shocks.

Reform of the tax system is essential both for economic and social reasons. Financial stability cannot come about without far larger revenues at a much lower marginal cost. Fiscal reform has to do with establishing a tax and expenditure structure and a tax base such that the marginal cost of extra revenue is lowered. That in turn implies that extra taxes, not money creation, can become a plausible response to adverse fiscal shocks.

Along with the efficiency of the tax system goes the issue of emergency taxation. Take again the case of Argentina, where crises are solved by imposing export taxes and raising public utility prices. Subsequently, as inflation picks up and competitiveness deteriorates, the export tax comes off, and the utility rates are allowed to fall behind inflation. Soon the next fiscal crisis occurs, and everything starts all over again. The instability of Argentina's tax pressure is apparent in Figure 2.3. This process destabilizes public finance, capital markets, and economic efficiency. Only a fiscal reform that provides revenue to finance the government on a steady basis can help overcome these problems.

On the expenditure side, a number of reforms typically are necessary:

- efficient administration of public utility rates;
- cuts in public sector employment;
- privatization and closing of public sector firms;
- restoration, maintenance, and investment expenditures on social and economic infrastructure.

Public sectors, like attics, need occasional cleaning out. Employment in the

Figure 2.3 National taxes as a percentage of gross domestic product, Argentina, 1970–87. (*Source*: World Bank data.)

public sector gets bloated because of patronage and poor accountability. Productivity can be raised sharply by reviewing labor requirements The immediate savings—although not always as large as they would be in Brazil, for example, where public firms pay wages far above the industry averages—generally are worthwhile in most developing economies. There is also ample room for privatization. Like fashions, ideological fads change, and one can benefit from the mood of the day to sell off steel mills, airlines, or telephone companies—none of which today are considered to occupy the commanding heights of capitalism.

Privatization is useful for three reasons. First, the public sector does not have the managerial capacity to administer a major share of gross national product (GNP) in a cost-effective fashion. Second, the public sector does not have the investment resources required to provide *all* public services well. Third, revenues are required to avoid deficit finance. Low prices received in the privatization are a serious problem, but these low prices reflect the precariousness of the economy, and they may well become even lower if failure to privatize and thus obtain fiscal resources causes financial stability to deteriorate even further.

The available resources therefore should be allocated to sectors in which private initiative is less willing or able to function. Telephone companies need not be in the public sector, but rural schools should be. Privatizing appropriately ensures that public resources are freed for important jobs and that private investment is focused on upgrading infrastructure and supply of services.

Privatization thus should not be an ideological issue. It not only helps to reduce the budget deficit but also is essential to finance investment. We noted above that the inefficiency on the tax side implies a very large marginal cost of resources and hence leads to shocks that translate readily into inflation. On the spending side, poor resource management cuts into both physical and social capital and reduces prospective growth and political stability.

Fiscal adjustment, both on the spending and tax sides, must achieve a better mix of equity and efficiency. The mix has deteriorated dramatically in many countries in Latin America in the past decade. Real payments to pensioners in Argentina, for example, have declined to only half those of wage earners. At the same time, too many people are on pensions because the system permits retirement at an absurdly low age. As a result, younger workers qualify for pensions and then work in the underground economy while older pensioners are put into distress. A more sensible system is to raise the age of eligibility for retirement and to use the savings to support more viable payments to older pensioners. The same type of problem emerges in the public sector—too many people, paid too poorly and too randomly.

The result of this misadjustment is poor performance. The state's poor performance as a supplier of services in turn "legitimizes" tax evasion as a form of revolt against the state. This vicious circle must be broken. The solution is not to abolish the state but rather to have it function better—more efficiently and more equitably.

2.2.3 *Tight money or tight budgets?*

The typical stabilization program for an economy emerging from high inflation involves freezing wages and prices and making little fiscal adjustment. For the first month or two this program is successful, partly because expectations of a freeze will have led to prior price hikes. Soon the freeze wears off, however, and the deferred rise in public sector prices, the lifting of export taxes, and real appreciation combine to erode the budget position. Then, in phase two, policymakers implement tight money. This gives an unsustainable program another few months of life, but of course it also increases public indebtedness sharply. Next, in phase three, the problems with the program become widely perceived, and debtors plead their distress due to high real interest rates. When tight money goes, the house of cards collapses; the exchange rate collapses, inflation surges, and real interest rates turn very negative. Soon, another stabilization is under construction, ready for the spring, tottering in the summer, and blown away by fall.

The important lesson to draw is this: tight money is not a substitute for a balanced budget. Real interest rates ultimately should be low (New York plus 3 percent), and the only way such a situation is sustainable is by basically sound fiscal and real exchange rate policies. We return to the financial market issue below. Here we simply note that tight monetary policy—realized real interest rates of 30 or 40 percent—is a signal of serious misalignment in the budget, the real exchange rate, or both. Realized real interest rates at such levels, in the presence of domestic debt, soon give rise to fiscal problems.

2.2.4 *Exchange rates*

At the outset of a stabilization program, quick success in disinflation is critical in gathering the political capital for further progress on more basic adjustments. Fixing the exchange rate can help achieve this objective, more so the higher the initial inflation, and hence the more the level of the dollar serves as an indicator for economywide pricing. In fact, a fixed rate is far more preferable than a floating rate. Under a floating rate the inevitably tight money position will drive up interest rates sharply and thus attract capital flows that will lead to sharp real appreciation. Real appreciation is undesirable because, ultimately, it has to be undone. This is not a negligible issue, because if disinflation succeeds, it will be very inconvenient to have a large devaluation just as the program gathers momentum. Political resistance to the devaluation in turn forces policymakers into a high interest rate policy to defend a basically overvalued exchange rate. There should be a premium on removing pending problems, not on creating new ones.

The key issue then is to select the initial level of the exchange rate so that even with moderate inflation for a few months, the real exchange rate is not overvalued from the start. Moreover, very soon, exchange rate policy should shift from a

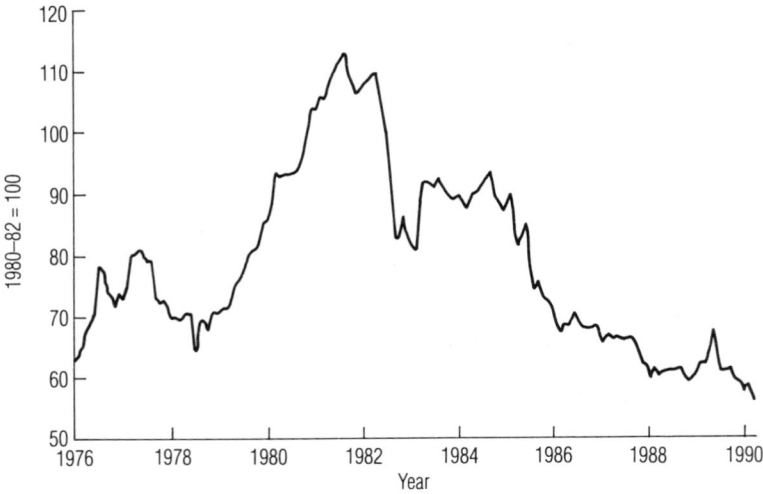

Figure 2.4 Index of the real exchange rate, Chile, 1976–90.
(*Source*: Morgan Guaranty Trust Company, unpublished data.)

fixed rate to a crawling peg to offset inflation differentials and maintain competitiveness. Once again, politically, it is extremely inconvenient to shift to a crawling peg (often seen as the source of inflation) just as inflation comes down. But if the decision is postponed too long, the real exchange rate becomes starkly overvalued, and the program ultimately fails.

Chile's experience illustrates these problems. Figure 2.4 shows Chile's real exchange rate. Following the coup in 1973 and a period of fiscal stabilization, the Chilean currency was placed on a *tablita* (schedule), and in 1978, when inflation was still above 20 percent, the currency was fixed to the dollar. As a result, the real exchange rate appreciated steadily and vastly. Inflation did come down over the next two years, but not fast enough to avoid a dramatic overvaluation. In 1981, net exports reached a deficit of 8.2 percent of gross domestic product (GDP) against an average of a surplus of 0.8 percent in the 1970s. For a while, the deficits were financed in the world capital market, but by 1982 confidence and credit had withered, and the policy collapsed.

Chile's exchange rate policy in the post-1983 stabilization was far more appropriate. Inflation targeting became more pragmatic, and the real exchange rate was pushed steadily into more competitive ranges. As a result, a steadily strengthening traded goods sector could support a sustained growth in the economy. The strength of the traded goods sector in turn translated into moderate real interest rates, thus facilitating management of the external debt and of the domestic budget.

Figure 2.5 and Table 2.1 show the case of Turkey. The initial exchange rate

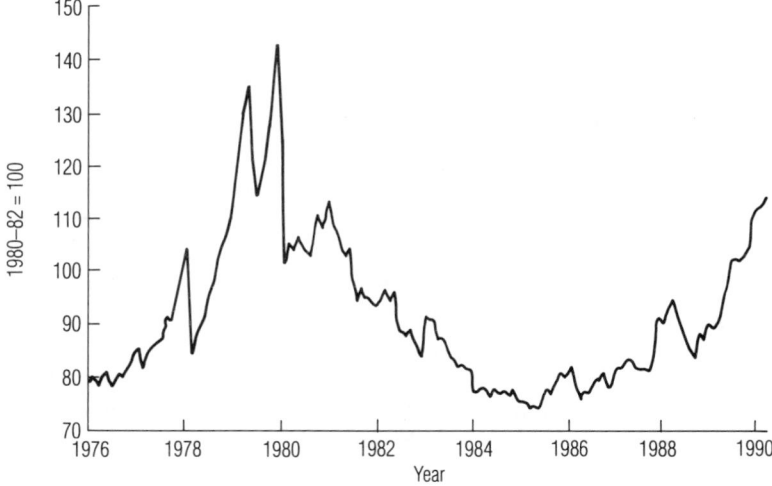

Figure 2.5 Index of the real exchange rate, Turkey, 1976–90.
(*Source*: Morgan Guaranty Trust Company, unpublished data.)

Table 2.1 Restructuring success, Turkey (average annual growth and shares in percent)

Measure of success	1973–79	1981–87	Share of GDP 1980	1987
GDP	5.1	5.6	100.0	100.0
Exports	−1.1	24.6	7.3	21.3
Imports	1.8	12.0	15.4	22.9
Manufacturing values added	4.9	8.4	22.4	26.0

Source: Organization for Economic Co-operation and Development data.

policy, following the 1980–81 problems, supported the strong restructuring and recovery of the economy shown in Table 2.1 (see Celasun and Rodrik 1989; Sareacoglu 1987; and Dervis and Petri 1987 on the Turkish stabilization).

In 1989–90 this sound exchange rate policy has given way to a dramatic real appreciation. This may well become a Chile-style problem, particularly because Turkey does not have preferential European Community (EC) access and because serious competition from Eastern Europe in the European market is a certainty. In fact, the slowdown in growth and the widening current account imbalances already indicate major problems.

When fiscal austerity reduces demand, full employment growth requires an offsetting mechanism for crowding-in. A competitive real exchange rate does provide such a mechanism. This may not be the case in the short run, as discussed below, but in the medium term it does work.

2.2.5   *Incomes policy*

The discussion of exchange rates has already introduced the topic of incomes policy. Here, we go a step further to raise two questions. First, is incomes policy an important ingredient in stabilization? Second, how should it evolve in the course of stabilization?

Without fiscal austerity stabilization cannot start. Without incomes policy it is unlikely to succeed. Incomes policy is necessary as a coordinating device when wage and price setting are not fully centralized. Because of built-in inflation expectations in contracts, adjustments have to be made. It is also important to intervene to stagger wage and price setting over time so that different contracts are spread across various points along the adjustment cycle.

In principle, all this could be accomplished by enough austerity and tightness of aggregate demand. But if substantial inertia prevails, via implicit or explicit indexation, incomes policy can help reduce the unemployment cost of indexation. To take the extreme example of an economy in which all wages and prices are both fully flexible and entirely forward looking—and thus capable of falling into line on the mere announcement of a credible program—is not realistic. Thus, incomes policy comes to play its role by shifting all wages and prices to a new regime.

But although temporary incomes policies, including wage-price controls, are useful, their perpetuation is certain to create deep problems. Ample examples exist. Policymakers thus should move quickly to a system of indexation of public sector prices, the exchange rate, and wages. The temptation to postpone the shift to a crawling peg exchange rate is often responsible for an ultimate overvaluation of the exchange rate. Wage indexation on a semiannual or annual basis will create a new inertia around a low inflation rate. Far from being a source of inflation, wage indexation protects the economy against rapid inflationary escalation provided that monetary and fiscal policies are sound. (It is understood that real exchange rate changes and changes in real public sector prices must be purged from the indexation formula.) If monetary and fiscal policies are not sound, nothing can protect against inflation.

Indexation has gotten a bad reputation in Latin America because it has been blamed for the instability of inflation. There is no merit to that argument, because it implicitly assumes that in the absence of indexation real wages would have adapted more easily to the shocks of the 1970s and 1980s. An argument to the contrary is that real wage resistance would have translated into faster and politically more troublesome wage adjustments in response to shocks.

Next we turn to a discussion of the supply side, which serves as a background for the review of structural adjustment.

2.3   The supply side

The starting point for discussion is an aggregate production function. The determinants of output are the available labor force, N, the capital stock, K, and the state of knowledge and institutions, captured by the parameter A.

$$Y = AF(K, N) \tag{2.2}$$

The basic approach to growth relies on a production function in the tradition of Solow–Dennison growth accounting (the distinction between GNP and GDP is omitted here):

$$y = a + (1 - \alpha)k + \alpha n \tag{2.3}$$

where lowercase letters a, k, and n represent growth rates, and α is the share of labor in income.

Estimates of the sources of growth have been collected by Chenery, Robinson, and Syrquin (1986) and are shown in Table 2.2. The data reflect the significant role of total factor productivity, the catchall for the poorly understood mechanics of economic growth.

The growth accounting approach can be expanded in a direction that highlights three aspects of factor inputs: the available supply in the economy; the efficiency with which a given supply is allocated; and the level of utilization of the given supply. For simplicity, let X refer to an index on the interval 0–1 for the degree of utilization. And let E be an index that measures the extent to which distortions in the allocation of resources impair the efficiency of factor utilization and hence their productivity, again on a range 0–1, with unity representing the undistorted economy. Moreover, let these efficiency and utilization indexes be common to both capital and labor.[3] Then the growth equation becomes

$$y = \theta + \alpha n + (1 - \alpha)k; \quad \theta = a + x + e \tag{2.4}$$

In this form we can separate out five sources of growth in income. In addition to technical progress and increasing capital intensity, we now identify as separate contributing factors both the efficiency of resource allocation and the level of utilization. Cyclical recovery, for example, would yield transitory extra growth over and above what factor accumulation gives, as would an improvement in the allocation of resources. The central point of this decomposition is to highlight that capital formation is only one avenue to growth. In view of the scarcity of saving available for capital formation, increased attention must focus on improving productivity.

Table 2.2 The sources of growth in developing countries (average growth rates in percent)

Source of growth	Chenery sample of 20 countries[a]	Korea, Rep. 1963–73	Korea, Rep. 1973–86
Value added	6.3	9.5	7.8
Total factor input	4.3	5.4	4.1
Capital	2.5	3.2	2.2
Labor	1.8	4.1	3.8
Total factor productivity	2.0	4.0	2.4

[a] Sample of twenty developing countries in various time periods.
Source: Chenery, Robinson, and Syrquin (1986, Table 2.2); and Song (1990, Table 5.5).

Moving a step further, we note that capital formation relies on domestic saving or a noninterest current account deficit. Rewriting the growth equation we have

$$y = \theta + \alpha n + r(s + \lambda) \tag{2.5}$$

where s is the national saving rate, λ is the noninterest current account deficit expressed as a fraction of GDP, and r is the marginal return on capital formation.[4]

Equation (2.5) highlights the role of domestic saving, s. Higher saving rates finance capital accumulation and growth. But the equation makes the important point that the immediate impact of saving on growth is minor. Assume that the return to capital is 10 percent. Raising the saving rate by 5 percentage points of GDP will then raise the growth rate of output by only 0.5 percentage points. Of course, the compound growth effects of an extra 0.5 percent growth are considerable, but only in the long run.

Recent literature on growth economics has struggled with the fact that empirically total factor productivity growth accounts for so much of growth and is so poorly explained (Romer 1989a; Helpman 1988). One important direction for further studies of sources of growth is in the scale of the market and related externalities (see Romer 1989b; Murphy, Shleifer, and Vishny 1989a; 1989b).

The growth accounting framework leads to a number of policy-oriented questions:

- Is there a link between economic policies and total factor productivity growth?
- Is there a link between policies and the national saving rate?
- What kind of policies will ensure the full utilization of resources?
- What kind of policies ensure that national saving is invested at home rather than abroad and that foreign saving will become available?

These questions are naturally familiar from the discussion of structural adjustment and stabilization. They center on the issue that a country must use the limited availability of resources most effectively; sound regulatory and trade policies are at issue here. They also deal with the need to mobilize effectively domestic saving and to create an environment in which it will be invested at home. That has to do with a stable, productive financial framework for economic development.

2.4   Structural adjustment

Two areas of structural reform are singled out here for special attention: deregulation, including trade reform; and reform of the financial sector. Both areas are focal points of adjustment efforts, and structural adjustment in both fields can play a central role in the long-run success of a stabilization effort.

2.4.1   *Deregulation and trade reform*

Growth accounting consistently shows that most of growth in per-capita income is not explained by capital accumulation but by growth in total factor productivity. It is appropriate, therefore, to ask whether a country can identify policies that would lead directly to a more efficient use of resources. Deregulation and trade reform can play that role.

The effect of an improved resource allocation, by trade liberalization or by deregulation, can be represented as a gain in productivity (see, for example, Easterly 1989). Suppose the production function for output is linearly homogeneous in capital, labor, and intermediate inputs, H:

$$Q = F(K, N, H) \tag{2.6}$$

The value-added function, Y, can then be written as

$$Y = \psi(p)\, G(K, N) \tag{2.7}$$

where p measures the real price of intermediate goods. A decline in the real price of intermediate goods because of competition or reduced costs of transborder shipments therefore operates in the way of technical progress by shifting out the aggregate production function.

Another way in which a more open competitive market or improved trade opportunities translate into productivity gains can be represented in a model that places importance on the variety of intermediate products available to firms. In the formulation of Romer (1989a), emphasis is placed on the size of the market in sustaining the profitable production of specialized intermediate goods. Because of the presence of fixed costs, the larger the market, the larger the range of specialization that can take place. Let the production function for final goods be

$$Y = N^{1-\alpha}\Sigma x^{\alpha} \tag{2.8}$$

where x denotes the quantity of each intermediate good.[5] Let there be M intermediates, and assume that it takes one unit of labor to produce a unit of the intermediate. The labor requirement for intermediates, N_{I}, then is $N_1 = Mx$, and that leaves $N_{\mathrm{F}} = N - N_{\mathrm{I}}$ of labor for final goods production. Therefore, we can rewrite the aggregate production function for final goods as

$$Y = (N - N_{\mathrm{I}})^{1-\alpha}N_{\mathrm{I}}^{\alpha}M^{\alpha} \tag{2.9}$$

The point of the Romer formulation is to highlight that, in addition to labor, input variety (proxied by M, the number of different inputs) is a determinant of the level of output. A larger and more open market increases the aggregate output not because of scale economies to labor but because it allows the production of a larger variety of specialized inputs.

But gains also result from the more traditional economies of scale that stem from declining average variable cost attributable to wider markets. Raising the scale of operation of individual firms is in this case the source of gain in productivity. Worldwide operation for firms with scale economies raises their productivity and frees resources as firms merge into more efficient units. De Melo and Robinson (1990) emphasize the correlation between growth rates and the growth of total factor productivity and interpret one of the channels as export-led growth, which provides the resource base for imports of capital goods. Pecuniary externalities become available in export-led development that accelerates growth over what the classical growth model allows. Opening of markets that are closed by licenses or by government monopolies or restrictions thus provides an important source of productivity growth.

In fact, aggressive deregulation may well be one way to achieve a Schumpeterian change (Schumpeter 1934, pp. 64–66): "Development in our sense is a distinct phenomenon. . . . it is spontaneous and discontinuous change in the channels of the flow, disturbance of equilibrium, which forever alters and displaces the equilibrium state previously existing. . . . Development in our sense then is defined by the carrying out of new combinations."

In Schumpeter's analysis, development originates in the following:

- the introduction of a new good;
- the introduction of a new method of production;
- the opening of a new market;
- the conquest of a new source of supply of raw materials or intermediate goods;
- the carrying out of the new organization of any industry.

Deregulation and trade reform may be effectively the instruments that take an economy out of the trap of slow growth toward an acceleration of growth that then develops its own dynamics and financing.

Even though the search for productivity growth is essential and obvious, caution is required when trade reform is at stake. The elimination of obstacles to trade—the movement away from a system of quotas and licenses that effectively closes the economy, as in Chile or Mexico—invariably spills over into a large increase in imports. The beneficial effects on exports are much slower to appear, because although inputs become more readily available and technology improves, exports do not rise immediately even if a real depreciation is undertaken. Without real depreciation, exports will scarcely help pay for the higher imports. If real depreciation is not possible, then liberalization should occur in two rounds. First, the country should move from quotas and licenses to a uniform high tariff of, say, 50 percent. Later, when the economy booms, and the external balance can support liberalization without the risk of an exchange crisis, tariffs can be taken down to 10 percent.

Such a policy does change radically the openness of the economy, because tariffs allow competition at the margin, whereas quotas and licenses prevent such competition. But at the same time, a two-round liberalization policy avoids the

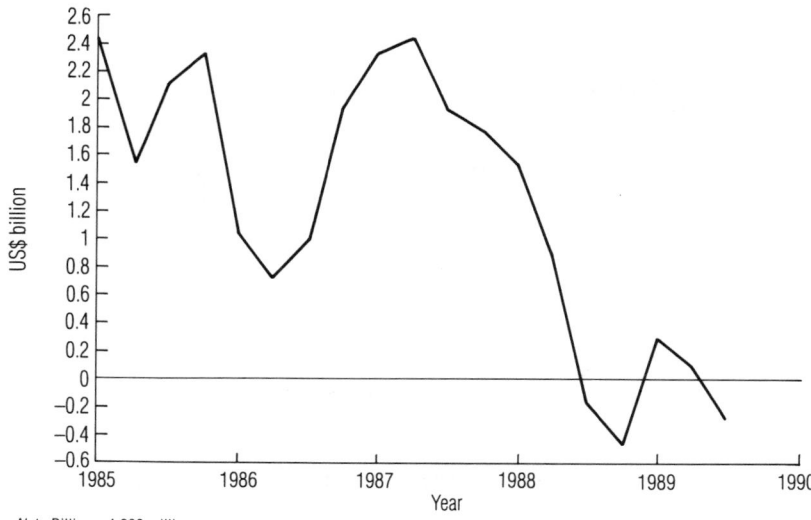

Note: Billion = 1.000 million.

Figure 2.6 Trade balance, Mexico, 1985–89.
(*Source*: Banco de México data.)

grave risk of an exchange crisis. When Chile liberalized imports almost fully in the late 1970s (and overvalued its currency), import levels exploded and could not be financed. The exchange rate collapsed, and another stabilization had to be undertaken. Similarly, Mexico, when the country moved from a closed economy almost immediately to a tariff of only 10–15 percent, import levels increased very sharply, the trade surplus disappeared (see Figure 2.6), and the exchange rate thus became overvalued. Incomes policy packages and a concern for inflation now make it impossible to devalue. As a result, very high real interest rates are being used to defend the premature liberalization. The policy is clearly unsustainable unless capital inflows, fostered by modernization and the free-trade agreement with the United States, provide the financing.

2.4.2 *Reform of the financial sector*

Fiscal mismanagement and the resulting financing of deficits by persistently large negative real returns on assets ultimately cannot fail to divert savings abroad and reduce investment. Once again, Argentina is an example. Figure 2.7 shows the cumulative real value of an investment in Argentina's financial market at the active and passive (lending and deposit) rates. Starting from 1983, the real value of an investment would have declined to only 5 percent by 1989. A country that runs a financial system with dramatic negative rates of return, on average, cannot expect to retain saving or investment. The variability of real rates adds to the loss because it forces everybody to become a speculator in a negative-sum game.

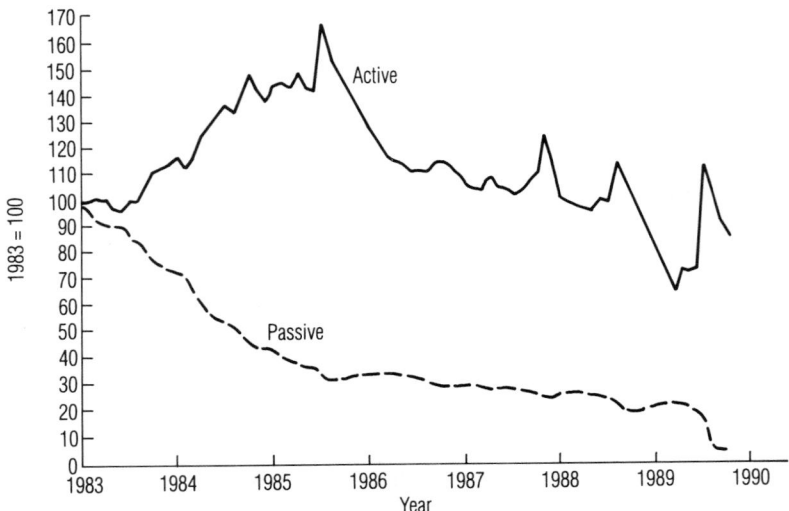

Note: Active rate is the lending rate; passive rate is the deposit rate.

Figure 2.7 Index of the real value of an investment, Argentina, 1983–89.
(*Source*: Data from Fundación de Investigaciones Económicas Latinoaméricas (Argentina).)

The policy package of international institutions rightly emphasizes the inevitable need for budget balancing and for competitive real exchange rates. But it also gives strong emphasis to the need for positive real interest rates and, more generally, to the need to abolish financial repression (see Polak 1989; World Bank 1989b; Gelb 1989; and Molho 1986). The evidence in support of this policy recommendation on positive real interest rates is less decisive than that in support of competitiveness and a balanced budget.

Two arguments ordinarily are presented for the positive real interest rate recommendation:

- Positive deposit rates mobilize saving. Specifically, with positive rates there are higher saving rates, and saving will be efficiently channeled by financial intermediaries rather than going into goods or dollars.
- Positive real active rates ensure a higher quality of investment and therefore higher growth rates of output.

The World Bank has expounded the view that positive real interest rates and financial liberalization can help promote growth. *World Development Report 1989* (World Bank 1989b) reports evidence of a positive relation between real growth and real interest rates. A study by Polak (1989) similarly concludes that real interest rates have a positive effect on growth. Table 2.3 presents their evidence.

Table 2.3 Effects of real interest rate on growth of real gross domestic product

Source	Constant	r	dum	R^2
World Bank (1989b)	−0.12	0.2	−0.02	0.45
	(−2.5)	(5.2)	(−3.4)	
Polak (1989)	5.21	0.21		0.32
	(15.3)	(4.5)		

Note: r = real interest rate on deposits; dum = dummy variable for 1974–85. The *t*-statistics are reported in parentheses.

In both cases averages of growth rates for a sample of thirty-three developing countries were used in a cross-section regression. The results for *World Development Report 1989* further allow for a shift dummy variable to separate the 1965–73 period from the 1974–85 period. Both studies support the view that a 5 percentage point increase in the real interest rate raises the real growth rate by an entire percentage point. If these results are at all representative, they of course have extraordinary implications for growth policy. The evidence in support of a linkage between real interest rate and growth is less strong, however, than the World Bank or Polak would lead us to believe. Gelb (1989), on whose research *World Development Report 1989* is based, is in fact far more circumspect than the report itself.

Persistently large negative real deposit rates misdirect saving. Similarly, random and priceless allocation of investment has negative consequences for the productivity of resources. Most of the evidence about the harmful consequences of misdirected capital market policy come from the outliers—countries that have vastly negative asset returns. Once these outliers are isolated, the evidence no longer supports the claim that positive real interest rates help growth.

Figure 2.8 and Table 2.4 support this view. The data shown here are the averages (1970–79 and 1980–86) of per-capita growth rates of real income and real deposit rates for fourteen Asian economies. Regression analysis using twenty-seven data observations (two subperiods, fourteen economies, less one observation not available for China in the 1970–79 period) yield no significant evidence of an effect of real interest rates.[6]

In the sample of Asian countries there is no correlation between saving rates and real interest rates, between investment rates and real interest rates, or between per-capita growth rates and real interest rates.

With so striking an absence of any real interest rate effects in this particular sample, we return to the World Bank data. Figures 2.9–2.12 show the data for the investment rate, the growth rate, and the real interest rate (the data are shown in the form 1 + growth rate or 1 + real interest rate). As in Figure 2.8, these data represent period averages. Even when real interest rates were averaged over the nine- and eleven-year periods, for several countries the rates were strongly negative.

In looking further at the evidence, we want to separate two issues. First, do

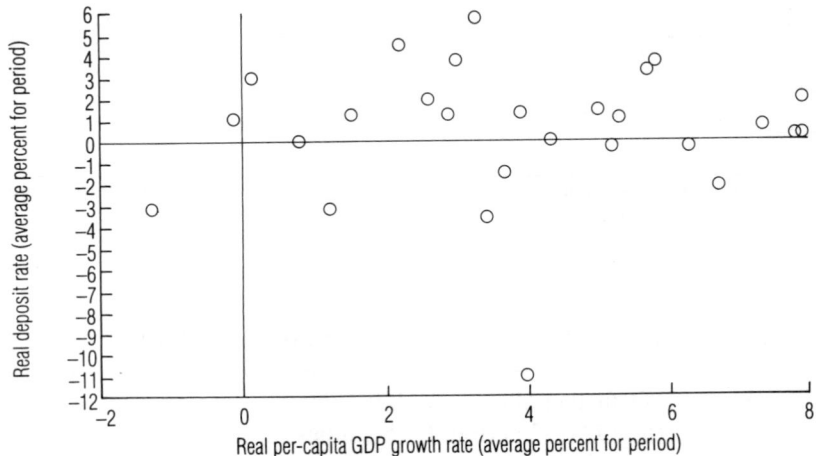

Note: Data are one observation in each period for each of the fourteen Asian economies listed in footnote 6, less one observation not available for China in the 1970–79 period.

Figure 2.8 Real deposit rates and growth, fourteen Asian economies, 1970–79 and 1980–86.
(*Source*: Okita and Faber (1989, Tables AII-2 and AII-7).)

Table 2.4 Real interest rates, saving, investment, and growth

Rate	constant	r	$\bar{R}^2$
S/Y	22.7	0.23	−0.033
	(12.4)	(−0.41)	
I/Y	25.4	0.21	−0.031
	(17.2)	(−0.47)	
$\Delta y - n$	3.9	0.05	−0.03
	(7.7)	(0.34)	

Note: S/Y is the saving rate, I/Y the investment rate, and $\Delta y - n$ the growth rate of per-capita income. The variable r denotes the real deposit rate. The t-statistics are reported in parentheses. *Source*: Okita and Faber (1989).

positive real interest rates have *all* the positive effects predicted above, or do they apply only to growth, to investment, or to saving? Second, are adverse effects caused by a regime of negative real rates or by isolated instances of *very* negative rates?

On the first question, the World Bank sample indeed confirms a positive effect of real deposit rates on investment and growth. But, interestingly, there is no significant effect on saving. A key part of the story is missing, and therefore one must ask whether this does not seriously limit any policy implications.

To test the second hypothesis—the impact of outliers—a dummy variable was used for countries that had more than three years of strongly negative real interest rates (of less than −10 percent). The results are shown in Table 2.5.

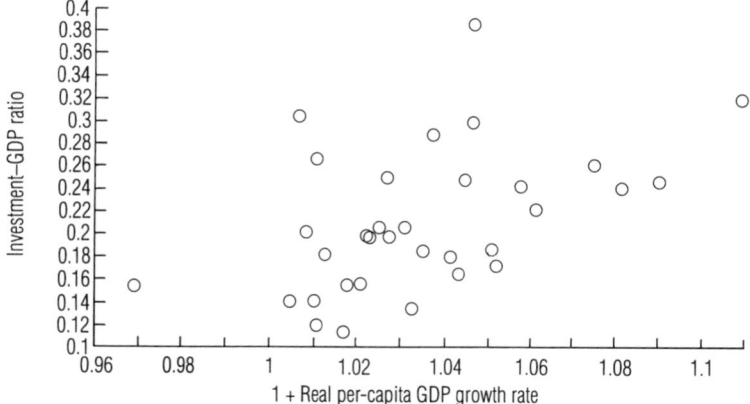

Note: Data are for Algeria, Argentina, Brazil, Chile, Ecuador, Ghana, India, Ivory Coast, Jamaica, Korea, Malawi, Malaysia, Mexico, Morocco, Nigeria, Pakistan, Peru, Philippines, Portugal, Senegal, Sierra Leone, Singapore, Sri Lanka, Taiwan, Tanzania, Thailand, Tunisia, Turkey, Uruguay, Venezuela, Yugoslavia, Zaire, and Zambia.

Figure 2.9 Investment-GDP ratio and growth, thirty-three economies, 1965–73. (*Source*: World Bank data.)

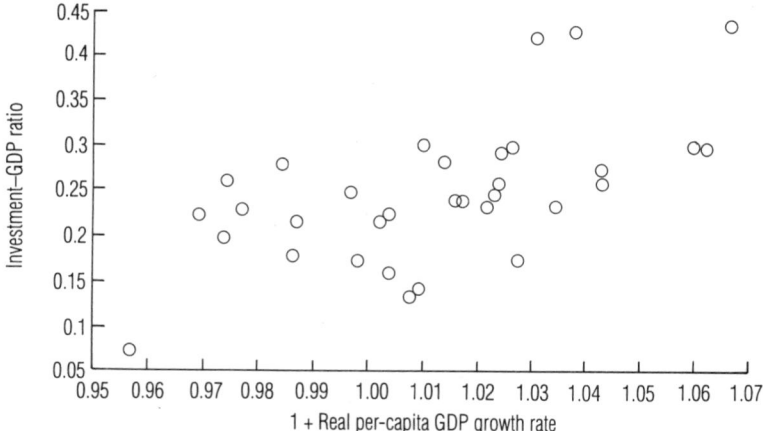

Note: Data are for the thirty-three economies listed in the note to Figure 2.9.

Figure 2.10 Investment-GDP ratio and growth, thirty-three economies, 1974–84. (*Source*: World Bank data.)

Note that the effect of positive real interest rates on growth continues, although the dummy for large negative real interest rates is insignificant. Moreover, when the investment rate is added as an explanatory variable in the growth equation, the coefficient on the real interest rate remains positive. As Gelb (1989) has noted, the real interest rate must proxy some growth effect different from those identified above. Thus the evidence does not support the view that positive real interest

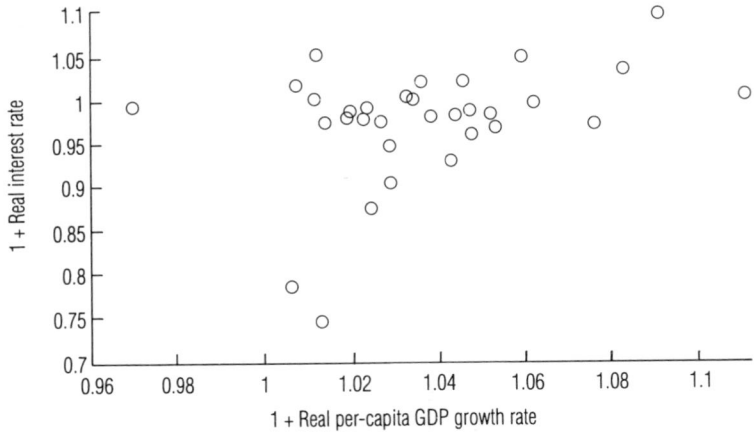

Note: Data are for the thirty-three economies listed in the note to Figure 2.9.

Figure 2.11 Real interest rates and growth, thirty-three economies, 1965–73. (*Source:* World Bank data.)

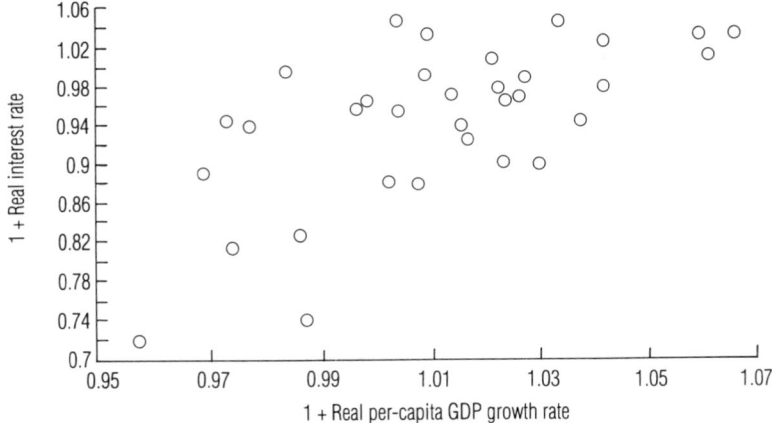

Note: Data are for the thirty-three economies listed in the note to Figure 2.9.

Figure 2.12 Real interest rates and growth, thirty-three economies, 1974–84. (*Source:* World Bank data.)

rates promote saving or that a linkage between real interest rates and investment raises the growth rate.

Financial intermediation—mobilizing saving and financing domestic investment—makes an important contribution to development. Specifically, for a given rate of saving, it can increase the share that is kept in the home country, and

Table 2.5 Effects of sporadic negative real interest rates on real per-capita GDP growth rates

Constant	r	DUM1	DUM2	I/Y	R^2
0.88	0.16	−0.007	−0.01		0.36
(44)	(2.63)	(−0.67)	(−2.24)		
0.88	0.12	−0.003	−0.002	0.16	0.49
(44)	(2.27)	(−0.26)	(−3.70)	(3.94)	

Note: DUM1 refers to cases in which there are more than three instances of very negative real rates; DUM2 is a dummy for the 1965–73 subperiod; r is the real interest rate on deposits; and I/Y is the investment rate. The t-statistics are reported in parentheses.
Sources: Author's computations based on World Bank (1989b); Polak (1989).

it can raise the efficiency with which the savings are allocated among alternative investment projects. Curiously, too much financial liberalization may be at cross-purposes with precisely these objectives. Insistence on a full range of capital flight products (such as dollar deposits in domestic banks) or on high real interest rates is likely to be destructive to financial stability and productive investment.

2.5   From stabilization to growth

The neoclassical growth models, or the modern versions that highlight externalities, focus on trend growth. They describe economies in which flexibility of relative prices ensures full utilization of resources along the path of potential output growth. Policymakers do face these issues, implicitly at least, because the policies they set determine in the long run an economy's incentive structure and hence performance. But the more obvious issue is the short run, in which lack of any growth, certainly in per-capita terms, is the most striking challenge.

Less than full resource utilization and slow growth, or no growth at all, has to do in part with the level of aggregate demand. After expansionary government policies cease driving an economy, it experiences great difficulty in shifting to a new regime in which growth in the traded goods sector and internal demand, including investment, become engines of growth. The difficulty in restoring growth—quite obvious in Bolivia or Mexico, for example—involves three sets of issues.

- Budget correction will have reduced real wages and hence internal demand. Without internal demand firms do not invest. Resources that are freed by fiscal austerity do not find their way automatically into exports or import substitution.
- If the exchange rate is highly competitive, this implies that the real wage is very low. Strongly competitive real exchange rates do ultimately support strong export growth. Chile after 1983 documents this, as does Turkey in the

Table 2.6 Index of economic indicators, Mexico, 1981–87

Indicator	1981	1983	1985	1987
Y	108	102	108	106
YPC	105	94	96	91
Manufacturing				
Y_m	106	96	106	105
W_m	103	75	71	61
E_m	105	91	92	85

Note: Index: 1980 = 100. Y = real GDP; YPC = per-capita real GDP; Y_m = real GDP in manufacturing; W_m = real product wage in manufacturing; E_m = employment in manufacturing.
Source: Banco de México data.

early 1980s. But in the short run, real depreciation does exert a contractionary effect on demand (see Lizondo and Montiel 1989 for a review).

- Firms' willingness to invest in export expansion or in domestic import substitution depends on their confidence that the regime will not revert to unsound economic policies. As discussed in the next section, if there is no front loading of incentives, the option to wait may be the best investment. Yet front loading of incentives is difficult because it involves still further redistribution of income.

Stabilization may be inevitable, but it is not a ticket for prosperity. Table 2.6, showing data for Mexico, documents these problems. The risk that stagnation will follow stabilization is thus very grave.

Although the problems of stabilization are being recognized, official institutions still offer an overly optimistic outlook. The IMF's rendition of stabilization and adjustment, for example, portrays a rosy scenario (Kahn and Knight 1985). But close inspection of the IMF model reveals that all the crowding-in problems discussed above are solved by assumptions: investment is assumed to rise spontaneously in response to structural adjustment; real depreciation drives growth immediately; and whenever the economy deviates from full employment the growth rate responds positively to the gap by an unexplained mechanism. In practice, of course, none of these assumptions hold. Unless the export sector rapidly becomes a strong, driving force, growth will not come. If domestic demand is the source of growth, then external constraints soon become binding (see Dornbusch and Edwards 1989).

Stabilization often fails, after a while, because of income distribution issues and recession, because the financing for supply-side policies that raise growth cannot be marshaled, or because the trimming back of credit growth and the devaluation produce a deep recession and no investment boom—not in the first year and not for many years.

If the private sector does not respond with investment and capacity expansion, and if confidence and inflation fears bar a public sector expansion, then the policymaker becomes the proverbial emperor without clothes. That is, although the policymaker has sharply increased profitability in the traded goods sector, the profits are expatriated, and there is neither growth nor equity.

A simplistic response to this problem is that policy is simply not credible, and that therefore, to no one's surprise, it fails to deliver on its promise. But that response is either tautological or foolish. One should not presume that the market automatically solves the coordination problems involved in the return of flight capital or the resumption of investment.

Ultimately, growth will return if the adjustment-induced pricing of resources is competitive by world standards and if incentives are present to save and to keep savings at home. Stabilization and adjustment have to accomplish this. The rest is a slow building of confidence that will develop the political will to go on and resist the (futile) temptation to change course and reverse policies. But there is some room to dampen the undesirable effects of adjustment in the short run, and there is critical room to think through the question of why the return of capital flows is so tricky. A cushion in the short run can be provided by well-designed public works. One form of such public investment is through emergency funds that finance local projects and thus provide a shock absorber to the income effects of real depreciation. If the projects are financed externally, and if they have, as they should, little direct import content, then they can help avoid the decline in internal demand. Such a project is being undertaken very effectively in Bolivia in the form of the Emergency Social Fund (see World Bank 1989a).

The other support for a return of confidence and thus growth has to come from the external side. Domestic production and investment have to become sufficiently safe for people to repatriate their assets and risk their wealth in production at home rather than keeping assets abroad. We now turn to this key problem.

2.6   The waiting option

The return of stability requires external resources to support confidence in the exchange rate and make available resources for growth. There are two sources of external resources, debt reduction and a return of flight capital. I concentrate here on the critical question of incentives for the return of flight capital. For some countries in Latin America external private assets are of extraordinary size, certainly more than sufficient to underwrite stabilization and growth if only they could be mobilized.

A common problem in the aftermath of stabilization is the lack of capital reflow (this section is based on Dornbusch 1990). Moreover, even if capital does return it is placed in liquid form in financial markets rather than in plant and equipment. Investors have an option to postpone the return of flight capital (see Table 2.7). They will wait until the front loading of investment returns is sufficient to compensate them for the risk of relinquishing the liquidity option of a wait-and-see position (the option value of the waiting approach has been used in

Table 2.7 Cumulative estimates of capital flight
(billions of dollars)

Years	Argentina	Brazil	Mexico	Peru	Venezuela
1978–82	5.8	25.3	n.a.	20.7	22.4
1983–87	24.8	35.3	3.3	18.9	6.8

n.a. Not available.
Sources: Cumby and Levich (1987); updated by the author from IMF data on balance of payment
statistics.

this context by van Wijnbergen (1985) and by Tornell (1988); Blejer and Isze
(1989) develop an argument similar to that presented here). Real investment is
slow to resume because of residual uncertainty whether stabilization can in fact
be sustained.

Assume that an economy (say, Mexico's) has two states of the world. In the
good state the return on an investment is r^a. In the bad state it is r^b. Investors have
the option to invest abroad (say, in Miami) at r^*, or at any time to make an
irreversible investment in Mexico. Their evaluation of states follows a Markov
process: in a bad state there is a probability q of persistence and $1 - q$ of a shift to
a favorable state. As a sharp simplification, once a favorable state prevails, it is
expected to last forever. Investors are assumed to be risk-neutral.

How much of a premium, ϕ, over the Miami return is required for an investor
to go ahead and invest in Mexico rather than to wait and see, maintaining the
option of investing only when the favorable state is verified? The required
front-end premium is

$$\phi = [q/(R^* - q)] (r^* - r^b) \tag{2.10}$$

where $R^* = 1 + r^*$. This formulation has two key features. First, it confirms
Bernanke's (1983) "bad news" principle that the option value of waiting depends
only on the bad news, not on the good news, because investors can take
advantage of good news situations by investing even late. Second, if bad states are
persistent, the premium nears the present value of the differential, $(r^* - r^b)/r^*$.
Thus, persistence translates into a sizable front-end premium required to bring
about immediate investor commitment.

The ideas can be carried a step further if we assume that there is a link between
the front-end premium and the extent of capital reflow. Such a relation can exist
either because a reflow reduces the probability of a bad state or because it raises
returns in unfavorable states and makes conditions more attractive. We assume
then that $\phi = \phi (K, \ldots)$ with a larger capital inflow, K, reducing the
premium—that is, $\phi'(K) < 0$.

The excess return on assets in Mexico, m, is taken to be exogenous to the
reflow. The criterion for the excess return in Mexico required to induce repatriation now becomes $m > \phi(K)$. It can be readily shown that there are two

equilibria. In one case, when the domestic rate of return is insufficient to warrant the risk of repatriation, no capital comes in. In the other case, because enough capital returns, the risk is low, and therefore the required excess return falls off to nothing. The question then is how to trigger this "good" equilibrium.

How can governments reassure investors? The common answer is, by bringing about a "credible" stabilization. If real depreciation is not sufficient to bring about investment, the government faces a very awkward position. Income is being redistributed from labor to capital, but because the real depreciation is not sufficient, the increased profits go the way of capital flight. Labor obviously will insist on reversing such a policy. Uncertainty is an important feature in understanding the relationships between real exchange rates and capital flight and in understanding post-stabilization difficulties. The options of postponing repatriation and of postponing investment in plant and equipment, in export markets, or simply in working capital are too valuable, and hence growth does not return.

The discussion of the option value of waiting (and the associated credibility issue) highlights one way in which the competitive model fails to address the transition from stabilization to growth. Stabilization by itself is not enough to trigger a virtuous circle. There is a need for a coordination mechanism that overcomes the competitive market tendency to wait.

The point can be taken a step further to bring in political-economic considerations. There are economic equilibria and there are political equilibria. Open economy issues must be modeled with both in mind. An extraordinarily large adjustment in real wages may set the economic incentives right, but in doing so it may also bring about a political situation that is not comforting for investors. Similarly, the direction and even size of required economic adjustments are understood, but politically these are not possible. What then?

What markets consider a sufficient policy action may simply be beyond the political scope of democratic governments. In fact, if governments went far enough to create the incentives that would motivate a return of capital and the resumption of investment on an exclusive economic calculation, the implied size of real wage cuts might be so extreme that on political grounds, asset holders might consider the country too perilous for investment. In the aftermath of a major macroeconomic shock, competitive markets by themselves may be unable to restore a good equilibrium.

The option value of a waiting approach highlights the critical leverage that developed countries can employ in underwriting (on a heavily conditioned basis, the more so the more effectively) stabilization loans. With such loans in place, private market participants feel comfortable in repatriating their assets. The repatriation in turn ensures that the loans will not effectively be drawn on (just as in the case of a bank run) and that growth resumes. A minimal step in that direction is for industrial countries to support the complete suspension of external debt service—to commercial banks and to official creditors—for a substantial period. Work by the League of Nations in the 1920s provided such programs, and the same are required today (see League of Nations 1926a; 1926b; 1946).

2.7 Conclusions

Countries that have experienced protracted high inflation, financial instability, and payments crises will not find their way back to growth easily. Their economies need to achieve not only fiscal reconstruction by thorough budget balancing but also a far-reaching institutional reconstruction that involves a financial system able to provide efficient intermediation and a regulatory and trade regime that helps allocate resources to maximize productivity. When external resources are in short supply, making the most of a country's resources through better allocation of resources is the only way of raising the standard of living. Fortunately, in the aftermath of mismanagement, the scope for such productivity enhancement is often substantial.

Economic reconstruction is the work of a decade or more. There are no greater dangers than complacency with an initial stabilization, which leads eventually to a reversal of sound exchange rate and fiscal policy. Chile's new democratic government seems to be keenly aware of the need to nurture and foster the stabilization in place today. In contrast, Turkey's government is allowing a dramatic slippage of progress achieved in the first part of the 1980s.

Reconstruction is necessary, but it is not sufficient. Public external support ultimately must become part of the effort. External support in the form of long-term stabilization loans, heavily conditioned on accomplishment and continuing effort, can help build the bridge by which flight capital returns and foreign direct investment is encouraged to take advantage of fresh opportunities.

Notes

1. The data for potential output come from Marfan and Artiagoitia (1989), as updated by the author.
2. The equation assumes a steady state where inflation is equal to money growth less real growth and a velocity equation that is linear in inflation: $V = \alpha + \beta\pi$ (see Dornbusch 1989).
3. Specifically, we now have $Y = AF(EXK, EXN)$, which, with linear homogeneity, becomes $Y = AEXF(K, N)$.
4. The distinction between GNP and GDP arises from net foreign assets. Capital formation, $\Delta K = S + \text{NICA}$, has as a counterpart national saving and noninterest current account deficits (NICA). The growth equation for GNP (Z) then can be written as $z = (1 - \kappa)(a + x + e + \alpha v) + rs + \kappa(r - r^*)\lambda$, where κ is the ratio of net foreign liabilities to GNP, λ is the noninterest current account deficit, and s the national saving rate. The rate of interest on net foreign liabilities is r^*, and the marginal return on home capital formation is r.

5. For simplicity we assume that the quantity of each intermediate good used in the final good is the same, so that $x_i = x$. This symmetry result would emerge if the production of each intermediate good had the same constant unit labor cost.
6. The regressions use all observations for the periods 1970–79 and 1980–86 reported in Okita and Faber (1989). The economies included in the sample are Bangladesh, China, Hong Kong, India, Indonesia, Korea, Malaysia, Nepal, Pakistan, Philippines, Singapore, Sri Lanka, Taiwan, and Thailand. Excluded because of lack of observations for real deposit rates were Burma, Fiji, and Papua New Guinea.

References

The word "processed" describes informally reproduced works that may not be commonly available through library systems.

Bernanke, Ben (1983) "Irreversibility, Uncertainty, and Cyclical Investment." *Quarterly Journal of Economics* 98(1): 85–106.

Blejer, Mario I., and Alain Isze (1989) *Adjustment Uncertainty, Confidence, and Growth: Latin America after the Growth Crisis*. International Monetary Fund Working Paper 89/105. Washington, DC.

Celasun, M., and Dani Rodrik (1989). "Debt, Adjustment and Growth: Turkey." In Jeffrey Sachs and Susan Collins, eds, *Developing Country Debt and Economic Performance*. Chicago: University of Chicago Press.

Chenery, Hollis, Sherman Robinson, and Moshe Syrquin (1986) *Industrialization and Growth: A Comparative Study*. New York: Oxford University Press.

Cumby, Robert, and Richard Levich (1987) "On the Definition and Magnitude of Recent Capital Flight." In D. Lessard and J. Williamson, eds, *Capital Flight and Third World Debt*. Washington, DC: Institute for International Economics.

De Melo, Jaime, and Sherman Robinson (1990) "Productivity and Externalities: Models of Export-Led Growth." World Bank Country Economics Department Working Paper WPS 387. Washington, DC. Processed.

Dervis, Kemal, and Peter Petri (1987) "The Macroeconomics of Successful Development." In Stanley Fischer, ed., *National Bureau of Economic Research Macroeconomics Annual 1987*. Cambridge, MA: MIT Press.

Dornbusch, Rudiger (1989) *Exchange Rates and Inflation*. Cambridge, MA: MIT Press.

Dornbusch, Rudiger (1990) "The New Classical Macroeconomics and Stabilization Policy." *American Economic Review* 90 (2, May): 143–7. (See also Chapter 3, this volume.)

Dornbusch, Rudiger, and Sebastian Edwards (1989) "Macroeconomic Populism in Latin America." National Bureau of Economic Research Working Paper 2986. Cambridge, MA.

Easterly, William (1989) "Policy Distortions, Size of Government and Growth." National Bureau of Economic Research Working Paper 3214. Cambridge, MA.

Fellner, William (1976) *Towards a Reconstruction of Macroeconomics*. Washington, DC: American Enterprise Institute.

Gelb, Alan (1989) "Financial Policies, Growth, and Efficiency." World Bank Country Economics Department Working Paper WPS 202. Washington, DC. Processed.

Helpman, Elhanan (1988) "Growth, Technological Progress, and Trade." *Austrian Economic Papers* 15(1): 1–12.

Khan, Mohsin, and M. Knight (1985) *Fund-Supported Adjustment Programs and Economic Growth*. IMF Occasional Paper 41. Washington, DC.

Layton, Walter, and Charles Rist (1925) *The Economic Situation of Austria.* [Report Presented to the Council of the League of Nations.] Geneva: League of Nations.

League of Nations [Sir Arthur Salter] (1926a) *The Economic Reconstruction of Austria.* Geneva.

League of Nations (1926b) *The Economic Reconstruction of Hungary.* Geneva.

League of Nations (1946) *The Course and Control of Inflation.* Geneva.

Lizondo, Saul, and Peter Montiel (1989) "Contractionary Devaluation in Developing Countries: An Analytical Overview." *IMF Staff Papers* 36, no. 1 (March).

Marfan, Manuel, and P. Artiagoitia (1989) "Estimación del PGB potencial, Chile 1960–1988." *Colección Estudios Cieplan,* no. 27 (December).

Molho, Lazaros (1986) "Interest Rates, Saving, and Investment in Developing Countries." *IMF Staff Papers* 33, no. 1 (March).

Murphy, Kevin, Andrei Shleifer, and Robert Vishny (1989a) "Income Distribution, Market Size, and Industrialization." *Quarterly Journal of Economics* 104 (August): 537–64.

Murphy, Kevin, Andrei Shleifer, and Robert Vishny (1989b) "Industrialization and the Big Push." *Journal of Political Economy* 97(5): 1003–26.

Okita, Saburo, and Michael L. O. Faber (1989) *The Asian Development Bank in the 1990s: Report of a Panel.* Manila: Asian Development Bank.

Polak, John (1989) *Financial Policies and Development.* Paris: OECD Development Center Studies.

Romer, Paul (1989a) "Capital Accumulation in the Theory of Long Run Growth." In Robert Barro, ed, *Modern Business Cycle Theory.* Cambridge, MA: Harvard University Press.

Romer, Paul (1989b) "What Determines the Rate of Growth and Technological Change?" World Bank Country Economics Department Working Paper WPS 279. Washington, DC. Processed.

Sareacoglu, R. (1987) "Economic Stabilization and Structural Adjustment: The Case of Turkey." In V. Corbo, M. Goldstein, and M. Khan, ed, *Growth-Oriented Adjustment Programs.* Washington, DC: IMF.

Schumpeter, Joseph (1934) *The Theory of Economic Development.* New Brunswick, NJ: Transactions Books reprint, 1983.

Song, Byung-nak (1990) *The Rise of the Korean Economy.* Oxford: Oxford University Press.

Tornell, Aaron (1988) "Credibility and Irreversible Investment and the Tobin Tax." New York: Columbia University Economics Department. Processed.

Uchitelle, Elliot (1989) "The Effectiveness of Tax Amnesty Programs in Selected Countries." *Federal Reserve Bank of New York Quarterly Review* 14(3, Autumn): 48–53.

van Wijnbergen, Sweder (1985) "Trade Reform, Aggregate Investment, and Capital Flight: On Credibility and the Value of Information." *Economic Letters* 19.

World Bank (1989a) "The Bolivian Emergency Social Fund." World Bank Population and Human Resources Department, Washington, DC. Processed.

World Bank (1989b) *World Development Report 1989.* New York: Oxford University Press.

3

The new classical macroeconomics and stabilization policy

The new classical macroeconomics (NCM) is not particularly useful in explaining stark episodes. To be successful, the new classical approach will have to be developed in a number of areas including coordination problems and political economy issues of stabilization. The modifications can in principle be worked into the NCM classical approach, but that will change the main thrust. So far, the message reads: markets clear, productivity shocks are the dominant source of fluctuations, intertemporal substitution in consumption and labor supply are the chief amplifying factors, and government policy is substantially irrelevant. On these key propositions, the evidence fails and the emphasis is misdirected. The issue is not whether markets work, but rather how they work, a concern rightly emphasized by the new Keynesian economics.

3.1   New classical economics

The NCM models the maximization problem of the individual rational and forward-looking agent.

Three implications follow from the methodology and are the distinguishing characteristic of this approach. The role of relative prices is pervasive once the proper distinctions are made between intra- and intertemporal terms of trade, and between price changes that are current and future, transitory and permanent, and anticipated and unanticipated. Next, because economic agents' policy environment is part of the information set and budget constraint, we can obtain informed answers to questions about the effects of policy realizations or changes in rules. Finally, the derivation of aggregate equations from basics constitutes the basis for "deep" as opposed to "opportunistic" or *ad hoc* analysis, including informed welfare judgments.

Financial support was provided by a grant from the National Science Foundation.

New classical economics in the open economy has no comprehensive statement. But a set of results and presumptions helps characterize what it is all about:

Rigorous insistence that markets work; individual self-interest ensures that relative prices adjust to ensure full resource utilization. Persistent involuntary unemployment is ruled out except when an explicit mechanism bars agents from pricing themselves into jobs. Variations in economic activity are not excluded by the approach, but they represent optimal adjustments of labor effort to the time path of productivity and real relative prices.

Governments optimally select spending and financing policy (see Lucas 1986). The tax rate is therefore intertemporally flat, and seigniorage is integrated in the optimal tax structure. Government spending is motivated by the optimal provision of public goods.

In the absence of capital controls, international capital markets are tightly linked so as to equalize *ex ante* rates of return adjusted for anticipated exchange rate changes and diversification considerations.

Nondistortionary tax changes are entirely neutral. Even in a Ricardian setting, government spending changes have sectoral demand effects (unless they are fully valued by households) and therefore affect relative prices over time and in the steady state. Because they affect relative prices, government spending changes do affect the current account whenever a distinction is made between traded and nontraded goods or between importables and exportables.

Monetary policy is entirely ineffective. Changes in the nominal money stock affect only prices and the exchange rate or translate into offsetting reserve changes. Real variables, specifically the real exchange rate, the real interest rate, or economic activity would be unaffected. Changes in the growth rate of money, with offsetting neutral reduction in taxation, would likewise have no real effects except to the extent that portfolio composition is shifted toward or away from external assets.

The behavior of the real exchange rate ought to be independent of the nominal exchange regime. Specifically, a shift from a fixed to a flexible exchange rate, or to a crawling peg should leave the real exchange rate unchanged in terms of its level or variability. A nominal devaluation does not imply a real devaluation.

3.2 The Mexican experience

A strong test of a theory is to expose it to a stark and discriminating body of facts. The NCM predictions have been tested extensively in regard to the relationship between budget deficits, debt, and consumption and the cyclical correlations properties of macro series. Few studies offer support for the NCM over more opportunistic models. Imaginative work on exchange rate regimes comes to the same conclusion (see Mussa 1986; and Stockman 1987).

A simple case study of Mexico (see Table 3.1) points in the same direction. How

Table 3.1 Mexico: economic indicators (1980 = 100)

	1981	1983	1985	1987
TOT	97	78	72	57
Y	108	102	108	106
YPC	105	94	96	91
Manufacturing:				
Y	106	96	106	105
W	103	75	71	61
E	105	91	92	85

Note: Y = real GDP, YPC = per capita real GDP, TOT = terms of trade; W = real product wage in manufacturing, E = employment in manufacturing.
Source: Banco de México.

does the NCM help explain the experience of Mexico? Per-capita income and employment fell significantly and the real wage declined by nearly 40 percent. A starting point for any approach is the recognition that the debt crisis of 1982, and the subsequent credit rationing, must be important influences, as should be the behavior of the real oil price.

In respect to the external balance, the NCM does not have a strong prediction—nondistortionary tax changes have no effect, but transitory government spending changes do affect the external balance. A regression with annual data for the period 1965–87 shows that the noninterest external balance ($NICA$) includes the primary budget (BUD), the log of the real price of oil (Oil), and the real exchange rate (REX) as significant explanatory variables.[1] An increase in the budget deficit by 1 percent of GNP worsens the external balance by a quarter of a percent. With budget changes reflecting at least in part changes in government spending, these results do not discriminate between the NCM and alternatives.

$$NICA = -68.0 \ - 0.25BUD + 2.24Oil - 14.1REX \qquad R^2 = 0.90$$
$$(-6.2)(-2.1) \qquad\quad (3.2) \qquad (5.8) \qquad\qquad \textbf{(3.1)}$$

Consider next real exchange rates. Figure 3.1 shows the real exchange rate measured as Mexican relative to competitors' manufactures prices expressed in a common currency. The NCM predicts independence of the real exchange rate (market-clearing relative prices) from the nominal exchange rate regime. That is not the case: the maxi devaluations of 1976, 1982, or 1987 show clearly in the data. Unlike in the case of floating rates, the timing of devaluations was discretionary and followed with a significant lag the accumulation of imbalances. Thus it cannot be argued that they reflect the timing of changes in equilibrium relative prices. This constitutes strong evidence against the NCM.

A strong case against the NCM comes also from the behavior of real wages and employment. The classical model does not help explain the large decline in real wages and employment in Mexico—just as it fails to explain the same facts in the Great Depression. A positive correlation of real wages and employment requires

Figure 3.1 The Mexican real exchange rate.

labor demand shocks. Suppose labor demand derives from a competitive industry with a CES production function. Using the observed data on output, employment, and real wages, this model implies that there must have been a *favorable* productivity shock of at least 20 percent between 1980 and 1987. Few observers would seriously assert that Mexican macroeconomic performance in the 1980s reflects a favorable shock.

Reality also departs from the new classical model in the area of government policy. The Mexican experience reflects U-turns in fiscal policy that are simply ruled out by the forward-looking, intertemporally optimizing model of government. In the 1970s, prior to the debt crisis, increased oil revenues translated into a boom in *current* spending by the government. In the 1980s, budget cutting became the rule. New classical theory would have predicted that, in response to the interest rate shock and oil price decline, the government would have responded with a permanent increase in tax rates; in fact, the government reduced subsidies and sharply cut back public sector investment and social spending. Moreover, stabilization has not been carried far enough to renew investment and growth.

I have listed a few inconsistencies and a careful study might harvest more. A model that explains the experience of Mexico or other Latin American economies today needs special features in several areas. One is that the treatment of investment and capital repatriation must be linked to the value of waiting, a point developed below. Another is that a theory of economic policy must explain why government stabilization is not carried to the point where the private sector carries on with substantial confidence.[2]

3.3 Capital repatriation and the waiting option

A common problem in the aftermath of stabilization is the lack of a stabilizing capital reflow. Moreover, when capital does return, it is placed in liquid form in financial markets rather than in plant and equipment. Investors have an option to postpone the return of flight capital. They will wait until the front loading of investment returns is sufficient to compensate them for the risk of relinquishing the liquidity option of a wait-and-see position. There is definitely little commitment to a rapid resumption of real investment—the reason being the residual uncertainty over whether stabilization can in fact be sustained.

I concentrate on a simple formulation that assumes that the economy (Mexico) has two states. In the good state, the return on an investment is r^g, and r^b in a bad state. Investors have the option to invest abroad (in Miami) at r^* or at any time to make an irreversible investment in Mexico. Their evaluation of states follows a Markov process: in a bad state there is a probability q of persistence and $1 - q$ of a shift to a favorable state. As a sharp simplification, once a favorable state prevails, it is expected to last forever. Investors are assumed risk-neutral.

How much of a front-end premium, Φ, over the Miami return is required for an investor to go ahead and invest rather than wait and see, maintaining the option of entering once the favorable state is verified? The required front-end premium is

$$\Phi_1 = [q/(R^* - q)](r^* - r^b) \tag{3.2}$$

where $R^* = 1 + r^*$. This formulation has two key features. First, it confirms Bernanke's (1983) bad news principle: that the option value of waiting depends only on the bad news, not the good news. The reason is that investors can avail themselves of good news situations by investing even late. Second, if bad states are very persistent, the premium approaches the present value of the differential, $(r^* - r^b)/r^*$. Thus persistence translates into a sizable front-end premium required to bring about immediate commitment.

The assumption that latecomers can obtain the same return as those who invested early is perhaps unrealistic. Suppose now that latecomers obtain in the year of investment only a fraction α of the good return, but thereafter participate equally. The formula for the front-end premium then becomes

$$\Phi_2 = \Phi_1 - [(1 - q)/(R^* - q)](1 - \alpha)r^g \tag{3.3}$$

The penalty for latecomers thus naturally reduces the front-end premium. But it is apparent that if bad states are expected to be highly persistent, this latter effect becomes small.

These ideas can be carried a step further if we assume that there is a link between the front-end premium and the extent of capital reflow. Such a relation can exist because either a reflow reduces the probability of a bad state, or it raises returns in unfavorable states. We assume, then, that $\Phi = \Phi(K, \ldots)$ with a larger capital inflow reducing the premium (i.e., $\Phi'(K) < 0$).

The return on assets in Mexico, m, is taken to be exogenous to the reflow. The criterion for the excess return in Mexico required to induce repatriation now becomes $m > \Phi(K)$. Figure 3.2 shows the schedule representing the return on assets in Mexico, m, and the required return $\Phi(K)$. There are two possible equilibria.pital repatriation is anticipated, then individual asset holders perceive a required return $\Phi(0)$ and see an actual return of m that is insufficient to cover their risk. As a result they do not repatriate, and hence the bad equilibrium prevails. Because no capital has returned, the equilibrium may be self-fulfilling in its assumption of a high probability of program failure.

In the other equilibrium, the individual investor expects at least K_0 to be repatriated. With so much repatriation, the risk assessment drops sharply and every investor repatriates. As a result, *all* capital comes back because the required return is below the actual payoff. The question then is how to trigger this "good" equilibrium.

How can governments reassure investors? The common answer is to bring about a "credible" stabilization. If real depreciation is not sufficient to bring about investment, the government faces a very awkward position: income is being redistributed from labor to capital, but because the real depreciation is not sufficient, the increased profits are taken out as capital flight. Labor will obviously insist that the policy be reversed. This uncertainty is an important feature in understanding the real exchange rate—capital flight relationships and the poststabilization difficulties. The options to postpone repatriation and to

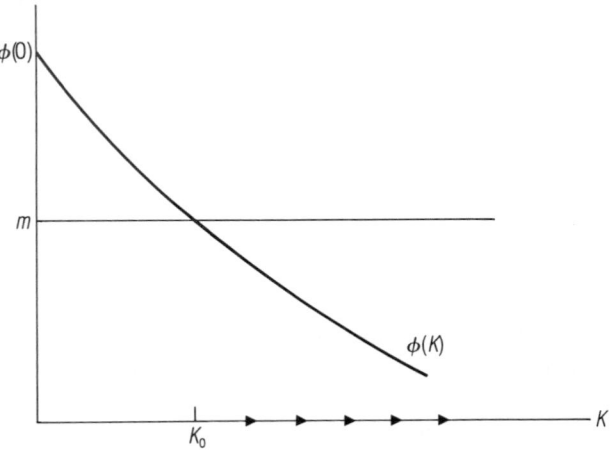

Figure 3.2 The capital repatriation problem.

postpone investment in plant and equipment, in export markets or simply in working capital, are too valuable, and hence growth does not return.

The discussion of the option value of waiting, and the associated credibility issue, highlights one way in which the competitive model of the NCM fails to address the transition from stabilization to growth. Stabilization by itself is not enough to trigger a virtuous circle. There is a need for a coordination mechanism that overcomes the competitive market tendency to wait.

The point can be taken a step further to bring in political economy considerations. There are economic equilibria and there are political ones. Open-economy issues must be modeled with both in mind. An extraordinarily large adjustment in real wages may set the economic incentives right, but it may bring about a political situation that is not comforting for investors. Similarly, the direction and even size of required economic adjustments are understood, but politically these are not possible. What then?

What markets consider a sufficient policy action may simply be beyond the political scope of democratic governments. In fact, if governments went far enough to create the incentives that would motivate a return of capital and the resumption of investment on an exclusive economic calculation, the implied size of real wage cuts might be so extreme that now, on political grounds, asset holders might consider the country too perilous a location. In the aftermath of a major macroeconomic shock, competitive markets by themselves may be unable to restore a good equilibrium.

Notes

1. *NICA* and *BUD* are measured as a percentage of GNP, and the real oil price and the real exchange rate are expressed as logarithms. The equation was corrected for second-order serial correlation.
2. See my 1989 working paper (Chapter 4, this volume) for a positive theory of stabilization.

References

Bernanke, Ben (1983) "Irreversibility, Uncertainty and Cyclical Investment." *Quarterly Journal of Economics* 98(1): 85–106.
Dornbusch, Rudiger (1989) "Credibility and Stabilization." Working Paper, MIT. (See also Chapter 4, this volume.)
Lucas, Robert (1986) "Principles of Fiscal and Monetary Policy." *Journal of Monetary Economics* 17, 117–34.
Mussa, Michael (1986) "Nominal Exchange Rate Regimes and the Behavior of Real Exchange Rates: Evidence and Implications," *Carnegie-Rochester Conference Series on Public Policy: Real Business Cycles, Real Exchange Rates and Actual Policies*, 25, 117–214.
Stockman, Alan (1987) "The Equilibrium Approach to Exchange Rates." *Federal Reserve Bank of Richmond Economic Review*, 16, 12–30.

4

Credibility and stabilization

Modern theories of stabilization policy typically focus on interaction between policymakers and the public, with imperfect information about the true intent or nature of the policymaker. The resulting strategic interaction involves reputation and punishment as central ideas, and the setting is one of a repeated game.[1] But this model does not seem to help greatly in explaining stabilization attempts and failures that involve one-time-only (though not always successful) stabilization.[2] Stopping hyperinflation in the 1920s or the famous 1926 Poincaré stabilization in France would be examples where strong performance of the policymaker does not yield reputation benefits in another round.[3] In this one-time-only context two important questions are just now being introduced in the literature: when do government ultimately try to stabilize? And when they do try to stabilize, why do they not undertake a program that is certain to succeed? Surprisingly, these questions are new, and there are no answers.

The timing and extent of stabilization are rather obvious questions in view of the fact that stabilization is often postponed until extreme conditions prevail, and that before stabilization actually succeeds, two or three attempts will have failed. The new political economy literature has started addressing these issues more formally. Alesina and Drazen (1989) discuss the question of when to stabilize in terms of a game between parties who are uncertain about who bears the costs of stabilization. Work by Fernandez and Rodrik (1990), although concerned with trade reform, can also be interpreted in these terms since they argue that it is not enough for a specific policy action to represent a positive-sum game for it to be undertaken. The timing and fact of stabilization are thus coming under investigation and offer a highly promising research area. The failure of stabilization programs—more than eight attempts in Argentina since 1982, several in Brazil, a handful in Israel before the successful one in 1985—remains

I am indebted to Jose deGregorio, Avinash Dixit, and Elhanan Helpman for helpful suggestions. The research for this paper was supported by a grant from the National Science Foundation.

largely unexplored. This is surprising because much of the informal discussion of stabilization is conducted as if it were known without much ambiguity what needs to be done to achieve stabilization, for a stabilization to be called credible.

In fact, a policymaker would have a hard time indicating how much of a fiscal adjustment is enough to ensure price stability and what exchange rate can be sustained without doubt. Even if the proper dosage could be determined, that might not be enough. Governments cannot create facts that are set once and forever, immutably. Any program can be undone, with more or less difficulty, by the next government. And this potential lack of persistence feeds back to the current policy actions required to make the program survive. Moreover, even a well-designed program may not be sturdy enough to withstand shocks such as a major, unexpected terms-of-trade deterioration. Thus, credibility is a relative term, and there is a need for a model of credibility. A stabilization is *ex ante* more or less credible. We need a theory to capture how the public forms a judgment of this credibility and how that judgment possibly interacts with the credibility.

There is, of course, an ample literature on credibility in models of repeated games and reputation, but their primary focus is on dynamics, learning, and dissimulation.[4] This strand of literature is particularly appropriate in analyzing the role of reputation in ongoing policy situations as the year-after-year performance of the Fed. It is far less interesting in those instances where an isolated stabilization takes place, say in the case of hyperinflation, and where success by definition implies that there is no repeat. Of course, to the extent that an isolated stabilization fails, there will be another one, but there is no reputation building at work. It is therefore useful to highlight the issues that arise in a one-shot game as is done below. This paper offers a first attempt to model the cost-benefit analysis of stabilization and give content to the notion of credibility. The result is a positive theory of stabilization that highlights the characteristics which make a stabilization more likely to succeed. The analysis, however, is incomplete in that it remains static and thus avoids the full issue linking timing and size of stabilization.

There are basically two reasons why a stabilization might fail. First, the wrong policies are undertaken: say, price controls rather than fiscal adjustment. We do not have a good theory why a rational, informed government might go this way and therefore leave it out of consideration. Even so, the prevalence of this reason for failure requires an explanation rather than a simple dismissal on the grounds of government ignorance. Second, programs might fail because, following the implementation of policy measures, the realization of certain variables relevant to the success of the program turns out to be unfavorable. Uncertainty may take two forms: the policymaker may be subject to instrument uncertainty, say, because the response of tax yield to tax rates or of trade flows to real exchange rates is random. Alternatively, productivity or the terms of trade may be random, and realizations adversely affect the performance of the program.

This paper deals with stabilization as a one-shot problem. This approach is used to ask what "credibility" might mean in a world where it is inconceivable that a program will succeed with probability one. A model is spelled out where the equilibrium program has some *ex ante* probability of failure so that credibility is always less than full. The model draws attention to the factors that raise or lower the probability of success of a stabilization program and thus offers a positive theory of stabilization.

4.1 A model of credibility

Consider an exchange rate stabilization. We think of the problem as a one-shot game where the policymaker must decide how much adjustment effort to exert. For the time being we disregard capital movements as well as any uncertainty associated with the policy instruments. The stabilization program is the solution to minimizing a loss function:

$$L = pK + \lambda A^2/2 \tag{4.1}$$

where p denotes the probability of program failure and A stands for adjustment effort. The government assigns a cost K to failure, and hence pK is the expected cost of program failure. The second term measures the cost of adjustment. Adjustment means real wage cuts or real spending cuts and as such is politically costly. More generally, as in Fernandez and Rodrik (1990) the cost may simply come from the fact that politicians do not know whether *their* constituency will bear the adjustment cost and hence will extract a price for cooperation in stabilization.

The adjustment effort A is one of the determinants of program success or failure. The model is completed by a realization from the stochastic process that influences foreign exchange revenues. Our attention now focuses on the construction of the *ex ante* probability of program success or failure.

The program fails if net foreign exchange disbursements F exceed available reserves R:

$$F = x - \alpha A > R \tag{4.2}$$

Net foreign exchange disbursements have two components. There is a random component x, and there is also the component that depends on adjustment effort (i.e., the real exchange rate). The more substantial the adjustment effort, other things equal, the smaller expected net disbursements. Specifically, a real depreciation (an increase in A) would reduce the trade deficit and hence the foreign exchange drain.

The probability of failure is the probability of net foreign exchange disbursements in excess of reserve holdings:

$$p = p(x > R + \alpha A) = \int_{\psi}^{\infty} f(x)\, dx; \qquad \psi = \alpha A + R \tag{4.3}$$

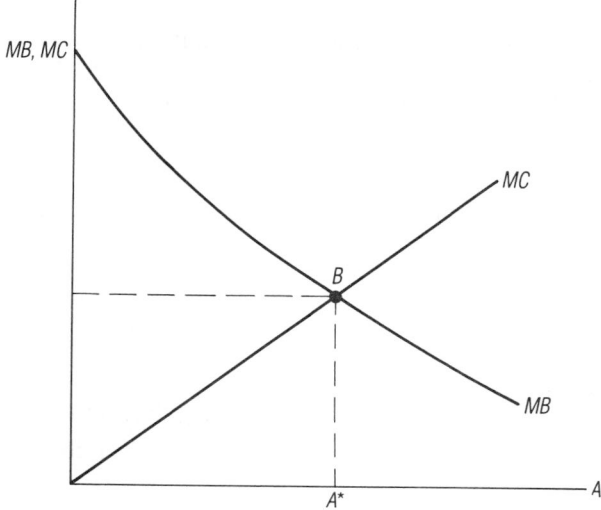

Figure 4.1 The equilibrium adjustment effort.

The government minimizes the loss function subject to equation (4.3). The first-order condition then is

$$Kf(\psi)\frac{\partial\psi}{\partial A} = \lambda A \qquad\qquad (4.4)$$

Figure 4.1 illustrates the solution. The marginal cost of adjustment ($MC = \lambda A$) is proportional to the level of adjustment effort λA. The coefficient λ is the parameter determining the marginal cost of adjustment. The marginal benefit $MB(= -K\partial p/\partial A)$ derived from the reduction in the expected cost of program failure is shown by the downward sloping schedule.

The optimization expressed in equation (4.4) yields an optimal adjustment effort A^* equal to

$$A^* = A^*(\alpha, K, R, \lambda, \sigma) \qquad\qquad (4.5)$$

where σ denotes the characteristics of the distribution of x. The equilibrium probability of program failure, substituting from equation (4.5) in equation (4.3), is

$$p^* = p^*(\lambda, K, \alpha, R, \sigma) \qquad\qquad (4.6)$$

As an example, suppose that the distribution of x is unimodal, and for concreteness let it be triangular. We are concerned with collapse arising from large positive realizations of x and hence look at the density $f(x) = (b - x)/b^2$ for the interval $0 \leq x \leq b$. The probability of collapse, with $a > \psi$, then is

$$p = \tfrac{1}{2} - \xi(1 - \xi/2); \qquad \xi = (\alpha A + R)/b \qquad (4.3a)$$

Using equation (4.3a) to derive the first-order condition yields an optimal adjustment effort and a probability of collapse given by

$$A^* = \frac{\kappa(b - R)}{\alpha}; \qquad p^* = \frac{1}{2} - \xi^* \left(1 - \frac{\xi^*}{2}\right), \qquad \kappa = \frac{1}{1 + \lambda a^2/Kb^2} \qquad (4.7)$$

where ξ^* is given by ξ evaluated at A^*.

The next step is to inquire what are the properties of this probability. Using the diagram or equations (4.5) and (4.6), it is straightforward to derive the following properties.[5]

1. Program failure is less likely the higher the initial stock of reserves R. Note that an increase in reserves brings about a reduction in adjustment effort since reserves provide a cushion. But the offset is less than complete since $-1 < \alpha \, \partial A^*/\partial R = -\kappa$.

The presence of reserves draws attention to the role of foreign loans in stabilization programs. Austria in the 1920s benefitted from League of Nations loans, and Israel in its stabilization could call on US aid. In much the same way Bolivia announced suspension of external debt service, which amounted to a self-administered external loan. In the literature on stabilization foreign loans are discussed as the *sine qua non*. In the present model they do play a role because they are to some extent a substitute for adjustment. In a model where the timing of stabilization also plays a role, unlike here, the arrival of a stabilization loan may be the occasion for stabilization because, in conjunction with adjustment, it creates a sufficient probability of success.

2. A higher marginal cost of adjustment (a larger λ) implies a higher probability of program failure. In societies that are politically highly polarized, adjustment is much more costly. As a result, adjustment effort will be less, and hence the probability of program failure will be larger. The coefficient λ could be interpreted in terms of the scope for cooperation between unions and the government: in Israel and Mexico such cooperation is possible and important; in Argentina it is excluded. Alesina (1988), Eichengreen (1988), and Dornbusch (1985) have emphasized the political costs in polarized societies of undertaking adjustment programs.

3. The higher the cost of program failure, K, the larger the adjustment effort, and the lower the probability of failure. One might conjecture that in a situation where there have been many previous failures the costs in terms of prestige or politics are small. Hence the investment in stabilization will be small, and in a self-fulfilling way, most programs will fail except if they were to experience unusually favorable (unexpected) conditions.

4. A higher responsiveness of the trade balance to adjustment effort implies in the case of a triangular distribution a reduced optimal adjustment effort A^*. But in combination with the effectiveness of adjustment, the impact of adjustment αA^* actually increases in the case of a triangular distribution so that program failure becomes less likely. More generally, as long as the distribution is unimodal, higher responsiveness of trade to adjustment effort implies a lower probability of program failure. But it is uncertain in general whether adjustment effort rises or falls.[6]

This responsiveness of trade flows can be interpreted as the extent to which an economy is open or closed. An open economy can achieve major trade improvements with relatively small real depreciation. Very closed economies have to achieve larger depreciation or expenditure cuts.

5. The impact of increased volatility on adjustment and collapse probabilities is ambiguous.[7] If reserves are relatively large ($a < 2R$), the possibility exists that optimal adjustment effort actually declines.[8] Moreover, since the probability of collapse rises for a given adjustment effort, the possibility then readily exists that increased volatility raises the probability of a collapse.

This set of predictions makes up a positive theory of adjustment. A test of the theory involves a cross-section of stabilization programs where the characteristics of countries ($R, \alpha, \lambda, \sigma, K$) are used to determine their *a priori* probability of success.

4.2 Supportive speculation

A critical aspect of stabilization may be supportive private speculation which is, of course, dependent on a program's credibility and influences it in turn. A proper model of stabilization must embody the endogeneity of speculation as a force that supports or weakens a stabilization effort. In part the role of speculation brings with it dynamic elements: if there is a risk that the reforms are not sustained, then speculation will not be supportive; and hence that stabilization may not occur. But before getting to the dynamic issues of reputation and precommitment, there is already some fruitful ground to be covered with a cost–benefit analysis of stabilization.

The most immediate complication is to consider a role for capital flows. Specifically, assume that private capital will return depending on the probability of program success or failure anticipated by the public, which we denote by p'. Our criterion for the probability of program failure now becomes

$$p = p(x > R + \alpha A + \beta(1 - p')) = \int_{\psi}^{\infty} f(x)\,\mathrm{d}x;$$

$$\psi = \alpha A + R + \beta(1 - p') \qquad (4.8)$$

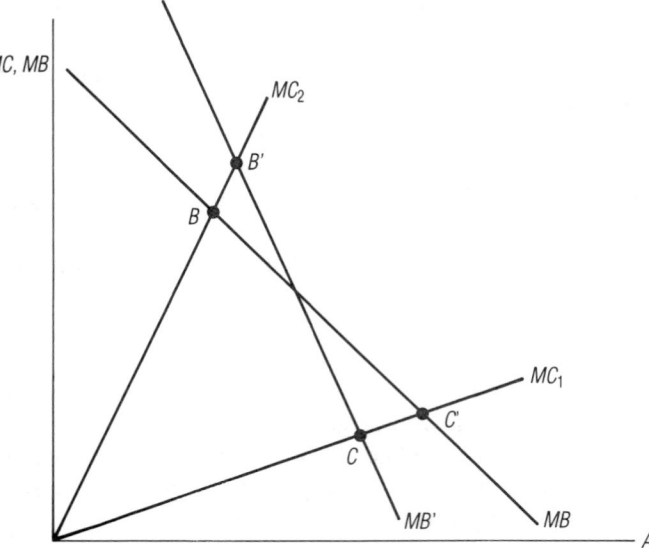

Figure 4.2 Adjustment effort and capital mobility.

where β measures the response of capital flight return to the perceived probability of program success.

We consider the case where the government selects its adjustment effort, followed then by the capital return decision of the public before the realization of the trade shocks is seen. In this case a Stackelberg solution is appropriate. The government recognizes that the public will evaluate the adjustment effort in the same way the government does and hence arrive at the same estimate of the probability of success. We therefore immediately set $p = p'$. The marginal benefit of stabilization becomes[9]

$$MB = -K\frac{\partial p}{\partial A} = \frac{\alpha K f}{1 - \beta f}; \qquad 1 - \beta f > 0 \tag{4.9}$$

so that stabilization benefits from a multiplier effect deriving from the supportive inward speculation associated with an increase in the probability of program success. The equilibrium adjustment effort and the probability of program failure will now depend on the degree of support derived from capital return.

The impact of supportive speculation on adjustment effort is uncertain. In the case of a uniform distribution, for example, both adjustment effort and the probability of success will rise. But, as shown in Figure 4.2, optimal adjustment effort may rise or fall depending on whether the economy moves from C to C' or from B to B' corresponding to different marginal cost situations. The impact of a higher β on equilibrium failure probability is

$$\frac{\partial p^*}{\partial \beta} = \frac{-f}{1 - \beta f}\left[(1 - p) + \alpha\frac{\partial A^*}{\partial \beta}\right] \tag{4.10}$$

It can be shown that with $f' < 0$, as assumed before, increased capital mobility will in fact reduce the equilibrium probability of default.

An interesting complication emerges when private speculators do not know the amount of reserves held by the central bank or when they do not know how much of a known stock of reserves will be sacrificed in a stabilization. Let R' be the reserves that speculators believe the central bank is willing to commit. Now it is no longer correct to assume that the policymaker's evaluation of the probability of failure equals that of the public. But even so, it remains true that the government can fully internalize the adjustment of speculators to adjustment effort. Specifically, it is readily shown that the marginal benefit of adjustment effort becomes

$$MB = -(\alpha f(\eta))/(1 - \beta f(\psi')) \tag{4.9a}$$

where η' is equal to η evaluated at R'.

The question we must now ask is whether the public can recover from the observed optimal adjustment effort uniquely what the government's planned reserve commitment in fact is. If so, then full internalization or a Stackelberg game is appropriate, and equation (4.9) applies. Since in fact optimal adjustment effort is a decreasing function of the level of reserves, given R', it is easy to establish that the public can determine the fixed point $R = R'$ from the observed adjustment effort and thus will in fact be able to estimate reserve commitments. Accordingly, the government must proceed immediately on that assumption and assume full information.

4.3 Instrument uncertainty

Consider next the case where there is uncertainty about the effectiveness of the policy multiplier α. The analysis here differs from Brainard (1967) not only with respect to adjustment costs but also in that overshooting the target is not penalized; this is appropriate in the context of fiscal or exchange rate stabilization unlike in the area of output stabilization.

We can again think of the foreign exchange stabilization studied above or, for example, of a fiscal stabilization. In this case A would represent the tax base or the tax administration effort, and α represents the uncertain yield coefficient. Stabilization involves the problem of putting in place an optimal tax administration or collection effort with an uncertain outcome.

The policymaker's loss function is the same as in equation (4.1), but now the probability of a program failure is given by

$$p = p\left(\frac{y}{A} > \alpha\right) = \int_0^v g(\alpha)\,d\alpha; \qquad v = \frac{y}{A}; \qquad y = x - R \tag{4.11}$$

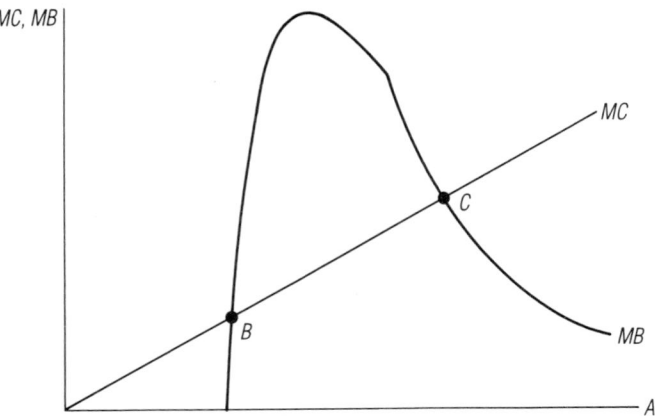

Figure 4.3 Instrument uncertainty.

where y is now deterministic.[10] Given the adjustment effort, program failure occurs if the multiplier turns out to be too small. Optimal adjustment effort must incorporate this uncertainty about the effectiveness of the policy instrument. The first-order condition accordingly becomes

$$(g(v)yK)/A^2 = \lambda A \tag{4.12}$$

Figure 4.3 illustrates another example for the case of a symmetric triangular distribution on the interval zero to unity. The equilibrium is at point C (point B is a local maximum of the loss function). In this case the equilibrium probability of program failure is simply[11]

$$p^* = \frac{x - R}{\sqrt{K/\lambda}} \tag{4.13}$$

Going beyond this simple case, the following properties are readily established for any distribution g.[12]

1. A higher cost of failure raises both adjustment effort and therefore the probability of success.
2. A higher marginal cost of adjustment reduces both effort and the probability of success.
3. Higher financing requirements x have an ambiguous effect on adjustment effort. But a higher level of x must raise the probability of program failure. Conversely, higher reserves (or, in this context, ability for debt finance) reduce the probability of program failure.

We note that they parallel the results already obtained for the case of uncertainty about net disbursements, thus reinforcing the generality of the earlier conclusions.

4.4 Extension

Consider now an extension to a two-period problem. Failure of a stabilization in the current period implies that the government carries into the next period the need to stabilize again, *m* with new adjustment costs, but also a loss of reserves and hence worse initial conditions. In planning the current adjustment effort, recognizing that it may not succeed, these future costs in case of failure are taken into account. The term K in the loss function in equation (4.1) becomes the vehicle to introduce these intertemporal aspects.

Now explicitly formulating the two-period problem, we have as a cost function,

$$L = p_1(F + J(R_2)) + \lambda A^2/2 \tag{4.14}$$

where J is the present value of the minimized second-period loss function that is conditional on the value of reserves R_2, carried into the second period. Assume next that if stabilization in the first period fails, the government loses a maximum of reserves Δ before abandoning the effort and restarting in the following period.

With these assumptions our problem now is to evaluate the marginal benefit of adjustment effort in the current period:

$$MB_1 = -(F + J(R_1 - \Delta))\frac{\partial p_1}{\partial A_1} \tag{4.15}$$

where F is a fixed cost of current failure.

The two-period model highlights the incentive to front-load adjustment effort. The payoff on the initial stabilization attempt involves not only avoidance of the current fixed cost of failure. An extra benefit arises from the fact that current success avoids the costs of renewed failure. Conversely, current failure carries the price of having to try again, but with the handicap of reduced reserves. Thus, policymakers have a strong incentive to do well on the first turn since every successive future attempt will involve higher adjustment efforts with a lower probability of success. Failure breeds failure because the declining reserves weaken the future chances, and hence credibility, of adjustment programs.

4.5 Concluding remarks

It is sometimes said that a stabilization failed because it was not credible. Either this represents a judgment in hindsight, with almost circular reasoning, or else it raises the interesting question of why a government might initiate a program that was less than fully credible. The model developed here explains why stabilization programs are less than fully credible. A number of characteristics of stabilization situations are identified and make up a positive theory of stabilization in that they help predict the *ex ante* probability or credibility of a program.

The model does not explain when stabilizations are undertaken. The fact that policymakers delay stabilization and increasing inflation, right up to mega- or hyperinflation, is not even uncommon. The model offered here does not help understand this propensity to delay. An extension has to consider the way in which deterioration of economic conditions affects the political costs of stabilization. There appears to be some evidence that when economic performance becomes appalling the political regime shifts from stalemate to a national unity government which, all of a sudden, appears to be able to accomplish a stabilization of the scope and ambition that eluded earlier governments. Thus, the cost–benefit analysis developed here must be combined with a political model of shifting costs of stabilization.

Notes

1. See Barro (1986) and Barro and Gordon (1983). For surveys of this approach see Persson (1988), Driffill (1988), and Blackburn and Christensen (1989).
2. For a different approach to one-shot stabilization, relying on information asymmetries between the private sector and the government, see Anderson (1989).
3. For the historical experiences see Sargent (1986). It is interesting to note that in 1924 Poincaré in fact had failed in a stabilization attempt.
4. See note 2 above.
5. The results in the text assume that $f' < 0$. They can be derived for any distribution by differentiating the first-order condition $\lambda A = Kf(\psi)$ and the definition of the probability of program failure $p = p(\psi)$.
6. Let $f(x)$ be the density function. From the expression for p^* we have $\partial p^*/\partial \alpha = -Af - \alpha f \partial A/\partial \alpha = -Af(1 + \Theta)$, where Θ is the elasticity of the adjustment effort. Differentiating the first-order condition $\alpha Kf = \lambda A$ with respect to α, we obtain $\Theta = (\alpha f K + \alpha^2 f' K)/(\lambda A - b^2 f' K)$. From the first-order condition $\alpha f K = \lambda A$ and $f' < 0$, it is readily shown that $-1 < \Theta$.
7. For the uniform distribution the MB schedule would be flat and shift down. In that case adjustment effort unambiguously declines.
8. Adjustment effort will fall if $2(1 - \kappa)(a - R) < a$.
9. We assume that $1 > \beta f(\psi)$.
10. We omit here explicit consideration of capital movements, but it is apparent that they can be introduced by writing $y = x - R - \beta(1 - p')$.
11. This solution holds for sufficiently low values of λ.
12. The proofs require using the second-order condition for a minimum of the loss function, $3\lambda + kg'y^2/A^4 > 0$.

References

Alesina, A. (1988) "The End of Large Public Debts." In F. Giavazzi and L. Spaventa, eds, *High Public Debt: The Italian Experience*. Cambridge: Cambridge University Press.

Alesina, A., and A. Drazen (1989) "Why are Stabilizations Delayed?" Mimeo, Harvard University.

Anderson, T. (1989) "Credibility of Policy Announcements." *European Economic Review* 33: 13–30.

Barro, R. (1986) "Reputation in a Model of Monetary Policy with Incomplete Information." *Journal of Monetary Economics* 16: 3–20.

Barro, R., and R. Gordon (1983) "Rules, Discretion and Reputation in a Model of Monetary Policy." *Journal of Monetary Economics* 12:101–21.

Blackburn, K., and M. Christensen (1989) "Monetary Theory and Policy Credibility: Theories and Evidence." *Journal of Economic Literature* 27:1–45.

Brainard, W. (1967) "Uncertainty and the Effectiveness of Policy." *American Economic Review* 57: 411–25.

Dornbusch, R. (1985) "External Debt, Budget Deficits and Disequilibrium Real Exchange Rates." In Gordon Smith and J. Cuddington, eds, *International Debt and the Developing Countries*. Washington, DC: The World Bank.

Dornbursch, R. (1989) "Stabilization, Credibility and Unemployment: The Experience of Ireland." *Economic Policy* 7: 174–209.

Driffill, J. (1988) "Macroeconomic Policy Games with Incomplete Information: A Survey." *European Economic Review* 32: 533–41.

Eichengreen, B. (1986) "Rational Expectations and Inflation: Book Review." *Journal of Economic Literature* 24: 1812–15.

Eichengreen, B. (1988) "The End of Large Public Debts: Comment." In F. Giavazzi and L. Spaventa, eds, *High Public Debt: The Italian Experience*. Cambridge: Cambridge University Press.

Fernandez, R., and D. Rodrik (1990) "Why is Trade Reform so Unpopular? On Status Quo Bias in Policy Reforms." NBER Working Paper No. 3269.

Persson, T. (1988) "Credibility of Macroeconomic Policy: An Introduction and a Broad Survey." *European Economic Review* 32: 519–32.

Sargent, T. (1986) *Rational Expectations and Inflation*. New York: Harper & Row.

Part II

Opening up and modernization

5

The case for trade liberalization in developing countries

In a broad swing of the pendulum, developing countries have been shifting from severe and destructive protection to free trade fever. Many of the notable examples are in Latin America. Mexico, after a major unilateral trade liberalization, is now negotiating a free trade agreement with Canada and the United States; Chile, traditionally a highly protected country, is a leading example of reducing trade barriers; Argentina and Brazil have entered free trade agreements. A free trade area for the Americas is becoming a serious possibility. The enthusiasm for more openness of the economy is not limited to Latin America; for example, Korea and Turkey are cases of highly successful liberalization. There are also cases in Africa—for example, Ghana and Botswana—to demonstrate the possibility and the benefits of opening up.

This new enthusiasm for freer trade stems from four overlapping sources:

Anti-statism. The world has seen a broad intellectual swing away from emphasizing the beneficial role of the state in the 1980s, and protection is seen as one of the manifestations of an overly intrusive state. Of course, a shift to a liberal trade regime has not always been the byproduct of a more democratic society: Chile under Pinochet or Korea in its liberalizing phase were under authoritarian rule. "Two cheers for the market, but not three," the saying goes; today the market gets at least three cheers, which may be at least one too many.

Poor economic performance. Many developing countries have suffered dismal economic performance and declining productive potential. Much of the reason can be traced to populist macroeconomic policies that engendered debt crises and hyperinflation. Of course, part of the reason was also a very adverse

I am indebted to Brian Aitken for valuable assistance and to the National Science Foundation for research support. The editors provided abundant, generous and thoughtful comments.

83

external environment. But since the days of plentiful external credit are gone, attention must shift to productivity gains as the source of growth. Trade may offer part of the solution.

Information. Citizens worldwide are exposed to more information about the opportunities available in other countries. It is no longer possible to conceal that goods in a country cost three or four times the world price or that they are not available. The elite want their BMWs, almost as a civil right; and the poor want cheap food and low-cost consumer durables that are available in world markets; firms know what technologies and inputs their competitors abroad can use and insist on the same access. It is no longer possible to assert that liberal trade policy must immiserize a country; on the contrary, many economic actors now see access to imports as a way of stretching their buying power.

World Bank pressure and evidence of success. Major research projects under the auspices of the NBER and the World Bank have documented the problems of inward-looking trade strategies and discerned the lessons from successful trade strategies (Balassa 1989; Bhagwati 1978; Bruton 1989; Krueger 1978; 1990; Michaely *et al.* 1991; Pack 1988; Thomas and Nash 1991a; 1991b). The research helped diffuse the black-and-white debate—free trade versus protection—to reach a more differentiated judgment involving the importance of neutral trade regimes as opposed to regimes that are biased against exports. The favorable performance of countries which adopted outward-oriented policies served to make trade liberalization, broadly understood, a central condition for World Bank lending.[1]

This paper next reviews the actual situation of protection in developing countries, to set the stage for a discussion of the prospective gains from liberalization. Three experiences with liberalization are then briefly sketched and the question is raised as to what can go wrong. The paper concludes by taking up two directions in which liberalization is now moving, regional free trade zones and liberalization of trade in services.

5.1 Protection in developing countries

Protection became the mode for most developing countries during the 1930s. During the Depression, industrial countries adopted restrictive trade policies, and commodity prices—a major source of earnings for developing countries—collapsed. Debt service problems loomed, as discussed by Eichengreen (1991). The pursuit of a policy of industrialization behind protective walls of tariffs and import quotas first took hold as a means of saving foreign exchange for debt payments, and then became viewed as a development strategy. The strategy was predicated on the assumption that primary producing countries would inevitably face a deterioration of the terms of trade; growth in demand for primary commodities was believed to be small because of low income elasticities for commodities and ongoing substitution toward alternative materials. At the same time, high rates of technical progress on the supply side would create a situation of excess supply and declining relative prices.

Trade policy changed little in the period immediately after World War II. Industrial countries continued for some time with highly restrictive trade policies, while many developing countries did not face foreign exchange problems due to their accumulation of foreign exchange reserves during wartime and subsequent boom in commodity prices during the Korean War. But then commodity prices collapsed again, and developing countries faced stark questions about the appropriate trade and exchange policies. As industrial countries moved gradually in the direction of trade liberalization and currency convertibility, should the developing world follow?

The prevailing view, especially in Latin America, was the doctrine from the United Nations Economic Commission for Latin America, more commonly known as ECLA. In this view, developing countries should pursue an import substitution industrialization strategy to avoid the problem of secularly deteriorating terms of trade (Prebisch 1959; 1984). Import substitution meant the development of domestic industry behind a high protective barrier of tariffs, quotas and licenses. That policy was pursued vigorously. Direct foreign investment helped industrialization proceed, in some cases with extraordinary success, as in Brazil.

There was an intellectual counter-current supporting the classical case for free trade, notably in Jacob Viner's (1952) Rio de Janeiro Lectures and Gottfried Haberler's (1959) Cairo Lectures (Meier 1963). The debate carried on into the 1960s when the protection doctrine became the main fare in the newly formed UN Conference on Trade and Development (UNCTAD), the intellectual forum in which developing countries shaped their views on trade and development strategy. Interestingly, while major progress was made in trade liberalization among industrial countries under the GATT, that same GATT allowed developing countries substantial leeway in maintaining trade protection (Finger 1991). This seems peculiar today, since poor countries especially ought to focus on making the best of their resources, but it fitted the prevailing ECLA doctrine that protection was a pathway to development.

In the late 1960s and 1970s, protection in developing countries softened in at least one direction. Many countries recognized that protection by tariffs and quotas did keep imports out, but that the resulting decline in demand for foreign exchange also led to an appreciation of the currency and hence a severe tax on exports of both traditional commodities and emerging industrial goods. Unstable real exchange rates added to the hazards of export activities. Moreover, duties on imported intermediate goods first implied a tax on export activities using these goods, and then helped cause a currency overvaluation which hurt export competitiveness of these products.

From an industrialization standpoint it made sense to avoid the anti-export implications of protectionist policies by reducing duties and pursing policies for stable exchange rates. The NBER studies mentioned earlier document that countries which adopted outward-oriented policies, at least to the extent of neutralizing anti-export bias, performed better than countries which failed to recognize the adverse effects of restrictions on their export potential.

It would be natural at this stage to offer a measure of the restrictiveness of the trade regime of various countries, and perhaps a time series portraying a protectionism index for developing countries. But even with great heroism, it is at best possible to create subjective, qualitative indices for individual countries.

Difficulties emerge from at least five sources. First, even if only tariffs were used, rates of duty differ widely across commodities. Hence one could measure at best weighted averages, but these may give a poor idea of the marginal protective effect of a tariff structure. Because of differing elasticities of demand and supply across goods, aggregate duty rates or total tariff revenue as a percentage of sales are a poor measure of restrictiveness.

Second, in the presence of intermediate goods the protective effect of a tariff structure depends on tariff rates on final goods relative to those on intermediate inputs. When intermediate goods enjoy lower tariff rates than final goods, as is usually the case, effective rates of protection can exceed statutory rates by a multiple.

Third, tariffs are not the only intervention by which trade might be hampered. The flora of common nontariff trade barriers include restrictive licenses; quotas; outright prohibitions; impediments to foreign exchange transactions (including required advance deposits for such transactions); customs valuation impediments, and more. Quantifying the effects of such restrictions on a common scale is even more difficult.

Fourth, the welfare cost of tariff rates and other impediments to trade depends on general equilibrium effects and market structure. For example, if substitution possibilities are moderate, then the welfare costs of distortions will be small. Similarly, restricted trade leads to imperfect competition, which may impose substantial economic costs.

Finally, restrictions on imports of one kind or another limit the quality, variety and the availability of technology.

While it is impossible to find a single representative number characterizing the restrictiveness of a trade regime, it is still possible to get an impression. An attempt to measure effective tariff rates, making appropriate adjustments for nontariff duties, has been made for the mid-1980s by Erzan and Kuwahara (1989). Table 5.1 presents some of their results. The first two columns show the effective tariff rates for various regions of the world on all sectors and on manufactures, while the third column shows that nontariff barriers are sometimes responsible for at least half of the protectionism impact. The table brings out that South and Central America and North Africa have had particularly high average tariff rates, and even more so in manufacturing. Within manufacturing, Erzan and Kuwahara also found that machinery and equipment receive significantly lower tariff rates than other manufactured goods.

Table 5.1 Protection in a sample of 50 developing countries

	Tariff Rate[a]		Non-Tariff Measures[b]
	All Sectors	Manufactures	
Caribbean	17	20	23
C. America	66	71	100
S. America	51	55	60
N. Africa	39	45	85
Other Africa	36	37	86
W. Asia	5	6	11
Other Asia	25	27	21

[a] Percent *ad valorem* tariff.
[b] Percent of tariff positions covered by non-tariff barriers.
Source: Erzan and Kuwahara (1989).

More recently, many developing countries have gone beyond compensation for anti-export bias to more radical reform. Quotas are being turned into tariffs, tariffs are being more tightly focused, and tariff rates are being reduced. Invariably, trade policy reform has also been part of a much broader program of policy reform including domestic stabilization and deregulation. Readers interested in the diverse experiences of many nations with such reforms might consult Papageorgiou, Choksi and Michaely (1990), Michaely, Choksi and Papageorgiou (1991), Thomas and Nash (1991b), Shepherd and Langoni (1991), Whalley (1989) and World Bank (1987; 1988).

5.2   Gains from liberalization

Measuring the benefits of trade reform has been a frustrating endeavor. Although the discussion of trade policy at times gives the impression that a liberal trade regime can do wonders for a country's economy, and most observers firmly believe that trade reform is beneficial, systematic attempts at quantification fail to single out trade policy as a major factor in economic growth. But then, of course, growth accounting has not come up with a satisfactory explanation for the residual which may be as much as 30 to 50 percent of growth. The channels through which trade liberalization could bring benefits are broadly these: improved resource allocation in line with social marginal costs and benefits; access to better technologies, inputs and intermediate goods; an economy better able to take advantage of economies of scale and scope; greater domestic competition; availability of favorable growth externalities, like the transfer of know-how; and a shake-up of industry that may create a Schumpeterian environment especially conducive to growth. This section will comment on each of these factors.

The static gains from improved resource allocation are the classical source of a gain from freer trade. Under perfect competition a small, price-taking country will gain by eliminating tariffs. Consumers are better off because their incomes stretch further, and resources are used more efficiently because they are no longer used to produce goods that could be imported at a lower price. As one early example of measuring these potential gains, Harberger (1959) estimated the welfare cost of protection in Chile to amount to 2.5 percent of GNP, as opposed to 10 percent for domestic distortions.[2]

While the traditional discussion often focuses on final, homogeneous goods, the case for freer trade is enriched by including the facts that trade liberalization increases the variety of goods, and raises productivity by providing less expensive or higher-quality intermediate goods. This aspect has been explored in some recent models of growth; for example, Romer (1989) emphasizes both the productivity of specialized resources and the limitations given by the size of the market. In a restricted economy, only a narrow range of specialized intermediate goods or capital goods can be profitably produced and therefore the full range of technological possibilities, which rely on a potentially broader range of inputs, cannot be exploited effectively. In this model, a greater variety of inputs does more for production than a greater quantity of a narrow range of inputs. Thus, access to a variety of foreign inputs at a lower cost shifts the economywide production function outward, which illustrates a concrete link between productivity and the trade regime.

The availability of imported intermediate goods and of technology, whether licensed or embodied in imported capital goods, is an important additional source of gain in shedding a restrictive trade system. If foreign exchange restrictions, for example, make it impossible to use a superior process, resources are wasted. They are similarly wasted if duties or prohibitions foreclose the import of key intermediate goods that may be extravagantly expensive or impossible to produce locally. If appropriate intermediate goods can be imported, a country may easily become an exporter of labor-intensive tasks such as assembly services; without such imports, that value-added opportunity is lost, along with the opportunity to graduate over time from assembly to tasks with higher value-added.

It is a well-known proposition that reducing certain tariffs, as opposed to eliminating all of them, is a more delicate issue. A partial tariff reduction is a second-best exercise, so welfare need not necessarily improve. However, it will generally be true that an equiproportionate cut in tariff rates will raise welfare. For more complicated situations of partial liberalization, computable general equilibrium models can (at least in principle) offer an answer as to the welfare effects.

Free trade leads to a more economically rational market structure. Gains from liberalization also result from scale economies and economies of scope that arise in wider markets. Moreover, markets in protected economies are narrow and lack of competitors from the rest of the world fosters oligopoly and inefficiency. Protectionism can create market power for domestic firms, where under free trade there would be none.[3] The casual evidence of these effects is striking. For example, when Mexico liberalized, firms put under pressure by import competition rationalized their activities to the point that they became export competitive. In fact, they looked to export markets to achieve a scale that would allow them to be competitive. Particularly in small countries where imports are restricted, quality is exceptionally low and variety falls far short of what is available in the world market. And prices are, of course, far above the world market, and more so the smaller and more protected the country.

An open trading environment is also associated with a transfer of know-how. Much is made, rightly, of the transfer of knowledge virtually by osmosis. Haberler (1959, p. 29) made the point this way:

> What J. S. Mill said 100 years ago is still substantially true. "It is hardly possible to overrate the value in the present low state of human improvement, of placing human beings in contact with persons dissimilar to themselves, and with modes of thought and action unlike those with which they are familiar. Such communication has always been, peculiarly in the present age, one of the primary sources of progress."

A similar argument underlies the discussion of the convergence of growth rates among countries in the world economy, as in Baumol *et al.* (1989) and the literature reviewed in Edwards (1991). However, the force of the Mill–Haberler argument is lessened once protectionism is taken into account. Multinationals can bring direct foreign investment, technology and knowledge, but under the cover of tariffs and quotas they may not do their best. Thus, today in Argentina, the 1964 Ford Falcon is still being produced with the US machinery of that time, without model change, as if the clock had stopped.

Beyond the general benefit of exposure to an advanced, competitive world market, the act of trade liberalization also carries the potential of dynamic benefits. In their systematic study of industrialization and development, Chenery *et al.* (1986) focused on the sources of growth in total factor productivity. Their work suggests that periods of trade liberalization also tend to be periods where total factor productivity growth is unusually high. Harrison (1991) and Salvatore and Hatcher (1991) discuss supportive evidence. The World Bank (1991, p. 100) shows for a large group of countries a positive association between trade liberalization and the residual in GDP growth after accounting for the growth in inputs. An aggressive trade opening may well qualify as a Schumpeterian change that triggers growth. As Schumpeter wrote (1934, pp. 64–6):

> Development in our sense is a distinct phenomenon. .... [I]t is spontaneous and discontinuous change in the channels of the flow, disturbance of equilibrium, which forever alters and displaces the equilibrium state previously existing. .... Development in our sense then is defined by the carrying out of new combinations.

In Schumpeter's analysis, the discontinuity of events and opportunities is the critical ingredient in promoting a new growth environment, it is *change* that is the source of increased productivity. Such a discontinuity involves, specifically, the introduction of a new good; the introduction of a new method of production; the opening of a new market; the conquest of a new source of supply of raw materials or half-manufactured goods; and the carrying out of the new organization of any industry. Together, deregulation and trade reform can shake an economy out of a slow-growth trap, toward an acceleration of growth which then develops its own dynamics and financing. Of course, there is no basis here for a *sustained* increase in growth. Rather, the model suggests a temporary acceleration of growth that need not be sustained indefinitely but will have shifted the economy to a higher growth path.

The Schumpeterian model has substantial theoretical support. For example, firms may well have available better techniques and good ideas, but they are unwilling to implement them except in the favorable setting of economywide, major and irreversible change. Once a program of liberalization is put in place, adaptation must take place and that is the occasion to implement major productivity improvements that had been on the shelves. The coordinated response to the change both acts to trigger externalities and it ensures thereby that a reversal becomes far less likely. High rates of investment and the associated increase in productivity are a natural byproduct of a successful break away from a trapped slow-growth economy. Trade liberalization is also a time when opportunities open up, because access to cheap inputs creates export opportunities, which carry rents and profits that can be invested in capital goods, which in turn yield further productivity gains. Although case studies of liberalization paint this picture, it is hard to capture in systematic measurements and cross-country comparisons.

It would be helpful at this stage to offer summary evidence on the proposition that outward orientation is beneficial, whatever the channels. But even though the case for these productivity gains is highly plausible, it has been hard to document in a clear-cut way. The comprehensive survey by Havrylyshyn (1990) does identify systematic evidence in support of the theory, but it is not overwhelming. The most plausible evidence comes from case studies. The other important source of quasi-evidence is the more novel work of modeling imperfectly competitive economies in computable general equilibrium models (for example, Norman 1990). These models highlight that in specific market structures or with specific scale economies, the gains from liberalized trade can be substantial. In fact, in some examples the gains are far larger than the static resource reallocation effects and come to more than 10 percent of GNP.

Recently, a number of studies have tried to investigate the link between growth performance and trade regime. The hypothesis, in line with the arguments above, would suggest that more open economies experience higher growth. Of course, without a satisfactory single and internationally comparable measure of openness and with so many other critical factors, investigations of this hypothesis start with a major handicap. The difficulty, of course, is in standardizing for all the factors impinging on growth performance. Edwards (1991) investigates the link to growth performance of a broad range of indicators of openness proposed

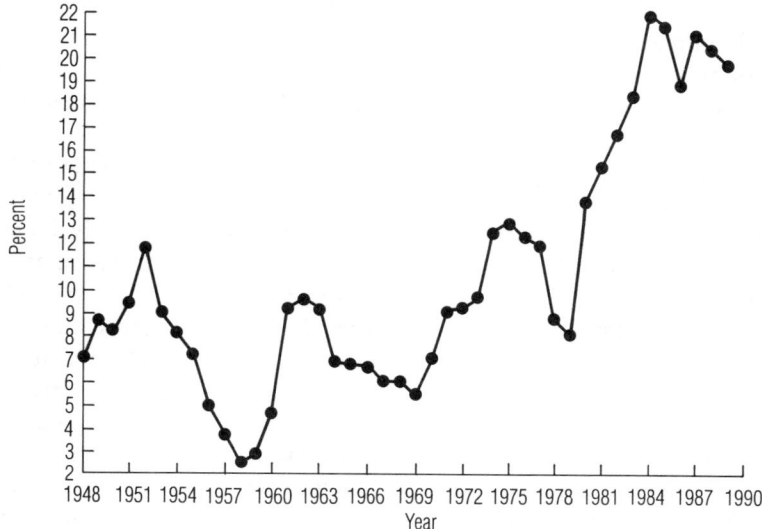

Figure 5.1 Turkey: import–GNP ratio.

in the literature and concludes that the sum of the evidence (though few individual pieces) amounts to persuasive evidence of the beneficial effects of an outward trade orientation.

5.3 Three examples: Turkey, Korea, and Mexico

In this section we sketch three examples of trade liberalization from three different parts of the world: Turkey, Korea and Mexico.

Following an earlier attempt, Turkish liberalization took place in the early 1980s. Compared to Latin America, Turkey had come early to face a debt crisis. Growth based on borrowing from abroad had been strong, but when financing disappeared, an adjustment of the economy became necessary (Sareacoglu 1987; Celasun and Rodrik 1989; Michaely *et al.* 1991; Papageorgiou *et al.* 1990). In the 1980–84 period, quotas were substantially eliminated, the exchange rate was depreciated, and the foreign exchange regime was liberalized. By the classification of a comparative World Bank study, the Turkish program was "major, strong and sustained."

The results of Turkish opening (and of accompanying domestic political and economic stabilization and reform) are altogether striking. Figure 5.1 shows the large increase in the import ratio, illustrating the radical change of trade orientation. During the late 1970s, Turkish imports had been growing about 2 percent per year, while exports were declining at 1 percent per year. But from 1979 to 1989, although Turkish imports grew by 10.4 percent per year, exports grew by 19.2 percent per year. Since overall growth in GDP was about 5 percent per year, this implies that trade became substantially more important to the Turkish economy. Interestingly, as Turkish imports and exports increased, manufacturing also grew from 22 percent of GDP in 1980 to 27 percent of GDP in 1989.

A second example is Korea, where trade reform occurred steadily in the 1970s. Here, the trade liberalization was selective. Major sectors of the economy were excluded, but the selection was accomplished in a manner that apparently did not interfere with productivity and growth. Korea made a point, in particular, of allowing capital goods and intermediate goods to be imported. For example, automobile engines were first imported, then produced under license and now under Korean design. By 1983, of some 10,000 product classes, 19.6 percent still contained import restrictions. By 1989 the fraction had declined to only 5.3 percent and most of these were primary commodities. Only 46 industrial products continue with import licensing or prohibition. The average tariff has been brought down from 24 percent to 11 percent for industrial products with the prospect under a new tariff law to lower them to 5 percent by 1993 (Young 1989).

Even though Korea liberalized only selectively, liberalization did take place. Korea's non-oil import–GDP ratio back in 1960 was less than 10 percent, similar to the figure today in Brazil or Argentina. But since 1975 or so, the figure has been in excess of 25 percent. With the help of a selectively liberal import strategy, Korea has been able to develop a highly competitive manufacturing sector that offers its own brand-name manufactures of increasing sophistication, ranging from cars to TVs and now high-technology goods. Interestingly, even though trade had been substantially liberalized in the 1980s, of the 12 percent import ratio for finished manufacturing, 1.3 percent was in consumer goods. Thus, liberalization was conspicuously concentrated on capital goods.

A third example of liberalization is Mexico. Until 1985 Mexico was totally protected: tariffs, quotas on top and licenses in addition, just in case. Table 5.2 gives an impression of the closeness of the Mexican economy. The result was a very poor productivity performance and an extraordinary degree of monopoly, which was strongly reinforced by domestic restrictions on entry and external restrictions on direct investment.

Starting in 1985, the economy was opened. The scheme first envisaged was a gradual opening, but as political pressures for delays and exemptions built up, the Mexican administration reacted by pushing ahead the timetable and opening radically. Although some areas like chemicals and automobiles have been substantially exempted so far, a great deal of liberalization has been accomplished. Import penetration increased already from an average of 11.3 percent in 1980–85 to 14.5 in 1986–90. By 1990 import penetration had already reached 17 percent. This sharp growth in imports, unaccompanied by an offsetting immediate gain in exports, gave rise to the free trade initiative with the United States which now is under discussion.

In the three countries considered here, the trade liberalization strategy is not

Table 5.2 Mexican trade restrictions (percent)

	1982	1990
Import license coverage	100.0	14.1
Tariff categories	16	5
Maximum tariff	100.0	20.0
Average tariff	27.0	13.1
Weighted average tariff	16.4	10.4

Source: United States International Trade Commission (1990) and Banco de México.

being questioned. Trade liberalization was part of a wider strategy of achieving stability and efficient resource allocation. As such, modernization and growth (and the resulting seeds for improved welfare) cannot be attributed uniquely to the trade strategy. But liberalized trade has so fundamentally shaken up the production structure, that more liberal trade is invariably credited with a good share of the performance. In Mexico's case, for example, output growth by 1989–90 was rising to above 4 percent, far exceeding the levels of the past five years. Even if there is no direct measure of the success of liberalization, indirect support comes from the fact that rolling back trade liberalization is simply not on the economic or political agenda.

5.4   What remains of the case for protection?

The case for protection rests on one of two pillars: externalities or learning effects. Externalities are, of course, the last recourse of scoundrels; they are invariably invoked as the case for intervention even though documenting them (as opposed to modeling them) is notoriously difficult. Externalities associated with a protection strategy would arise if the physical capital formation associated with industrialization or the formation of human capital carries spillover effects, pecuniary or real, that cannot be appropriated by the individual firm and industry. Learning by doing as an argument for protection, by contrast, does not rely on externalities but rather on capital market imperfections that make firms reluctant to engage in the development of the productivity bonus even though from the social point of view it is warranted. Labor market imperfections may also stand in the way of a warranted industrialization if the training of labor that yields the productivity benefits cannot be captured by the investing firm and cannot be borne (for capital market or information reasons) by the workers who will be vested with the benefits. In either case, it is clear that protection is never the first-best strategy. Targeted subsidies are always better, although considerations of feasibility and political economy will always be brought in favor of protection.

Against the massive evidence that small countries will wither behind protective barriers, there is some evidence that protection can also yield success. Korea, Brazil and Japan would be the parade cases. These countries are among those with the highest growth rates of GDP and total factor productivity in the 1965–80 period and none of them is a free trader. Brazilian growth averaged 7.7 percent over the period and that of Korea was 6.7 percent per year; industry grew at 10 and 16 percent per year, respectively.

Essential ingredients of the strong performance were three. First, exchange rate policy was carefully designed to avoid overvaluation and with it macroeconomic bottlenecks. Second, external credit played a key role, as did foreign investment and foreign technology. Third, the trade regime was sufficiently selective so that intermediate goods and capital goods were not excluded. Care was taken, in particular, not to tax exports implicitly.

Even though we portray the experience as a success, the interpretation might be open to challenge. Brazil did crash in the 1980s and is now seeking trade liberalization as a means to growth. In Korea, the massive investment in the heavy industry was seen in the early 1980s as a major blunder. Today, with lower oil prices, even that judgment is no longer true. While the discussion remains open, the fact is that under the cover of significant (though porous) protection both countries developed in the 1960s and 1970s a world-class manufacturing sector. It remains to discern exactly what makes the difference between an Argentine experience where protection was a disaster and these very positive cases.

It is perhaps the experience of Korea and Brazil, where industrialization under the cover of protection led ultimately to highly competitive export industries, that accounts for the interest in the export sector as an engine of growth and the locus of government intervention. One direction is to focus on targeted liberalization that does not interfere with the nurturing of infant industries; infants have to grow up at home, they cannot start off as exporters. Another is to shift the focus to export strategies. For example, de Melo and Robinson (1990) develop a model of such a process and find that, in a computable general equilibrium model calibrated to the typical developing country experiencing export-led growth, policies that support export externalities yield significant growth effects.[4]

The potential gains from liberalization strategy and the successful nurturing of infant industries by selective protection and subsequent export policies must be qualified in one important dimension. If developing countries as a group open up, there is every reason to believe that their terms of trade will be adversely affected. Flooding the world market with their manufactures, while their market access to industrialized countries remains the same, cannot fail to reduce the prices at which they will export (Faini *et al.* 1990). But for the individual country, that is not a reason to shy away from liberalization. Even for developing countries as a group, the benefits from the various sources discussed above are likely to outweigh substantially the costs of worsened terms of trade.

Even when there is a case for protection, the Korean experience suggests that the strategy works best when used selectively. In this manner the country will not devote resources to accomplishing the impossible and as a result lower productivity economywide. Rather, selective protection (even on a wide basis) serves to capture the learning benefits while minimizing the resource cost. That involves inevitably guessing where the areas of learning and externalities are likely to lie, it involves the risk of double-guessing markets, and it often fails. But in Korea and a handful of other cases, it has helped improve growth or at the least it seems to have done no harm to a stellar performance.

5.5   What can go wrong?

One problem for trade reform is political. Too long a phase-in period with too many safeguards for those who might be adversely affected is an invitation to disruption and reversal. The other risk comes from the exchange rate. The elimination of obstacles to trade invariably creates an immediate increase in imports. But although inputs become more readily available and technology improves, the beneficial rise in exports does not happen immediately, even if a real depreciation is undertaken. For example, when Chile first liberalized imports almost fully in the late 1970s (but overvalued its managed exchange rate) import levels exploded and the exchange rate collapsed. Another stabilization had to be undertaken. Without a real depreciation, exports will scarcely help pay for the higher imports.

Because of balance of payments problems, comprehensive trade reform requires one of two conditions: either the country must be politically in a position to have a major real depreciation of the exchange rate (to help boost exports) or else it must have access to foreign exchange for a substantial period of time. Real depreciation is a problem because it means a fall in real wages unless offset by the improvement in the standard of living that stems from reduced protection. If reserves are not available and depreciation is impractical, the only realistic option for trade policy is to approach liberalization more gradually.

A gradual path to trade liberalization should occur in two steps. In a first round, the country should move from quotas and licenses and other nontariff barriers to a uniform, high tariff of (say) 50 percent. Later, as the economy grows and the external balance can support liberalization without the risk of a foreign exchange crisis, tariffs can be taken down to (say) 10 percent. This more moderate policy still opens the economy, because even tariffs at high rates allow competition at the margin, while quotas and licenses are there to prevent it. But at the same time it avoids the grave risk of an exchange crisis.

A drastic example of liberalization at the wrong exchange rate comes from the recent unification of Germany. Prior to unification East Germany had traded mostly with the Soviet Union, and little with nonsocialist economies. When consumers faced unification and free trade with West Germany, they turned overnight from domestic goods toward West German merchandise. In economies left out of world progress, "opening up" translates into a situation where domestic goods become lemons that cannot be sold virtually at any price. The result in East Germany was a decline of industrial production of 50 percent and, for a time, mass unemployment. Joint ventures and western brand names on improved eastern products are seen as the answer.

Of course, the East German experience is special in that the exchange rate conversion made West German goods expensive, but not astronomically so. However, even in a situation where exchange rates are set so that foreign goods are clearly far more expensive than domestic brands, say by a factor of two or three, rapid and pervasive import penetration is likely to occur. Liberalization in Chile and Mexico has made that clear.

The East German experience will be repeated, although on a lesser scale, as other countries open up, whether in Eastern Europe or in the Third World. One response is to try and avoid such disruptions by continuing protectionism or traditional trade agreements. But the right answer is to recognize that the adjustment ought to happen, because consumers and producers do want better and more varied goods. Countries should bite the bullet by adopting highly competitive exchange rates, even if that means that imports are relatively quite expensive. Only when there is massive support from abroad and coordinated direct investment (as in the case of East and West Germany) can there be an expectation of avoiding a sharp real depreciation.

5.6   New directions in trade strategy

In concluding this paper, we draw attention briefly to two new directions in trade strategy: service trade liberalization and regional free trade agreements.

Most of the discussion of trade liberalization in the past has focused on merchandise trade and until recently almost no attention and certainly no empirical work has paid attention to trade in services. The Uruguay Round of trade negotiations now under way changes that. Trade in services is a major issue for developed countries who see themselves as exporters, but also for developing countries who expect some export opportunities, but also recognize the role of services in promoting productivity.

Most of the recent attention has focused on financial services (banking, underwriting, insurance) where there are obvious gains from scale economies and competition. Financial markets in developing countries (and in Europe) operate far less competitively and with far larger spreads and fees than in the United States. Hence the case for liberalizing financial service trade. But the interest in service trade liberalization extends to other areas: accounting, consulting, legal services, construction planning, design, telecommunications and others. It is clear that the case for liberalized trade in services is no different from that for trade in merchandise. The fact that services have not been much traded in the past draws attention to a stark omission in the traditional assessments of the cost of protection.

The second new direction is even more sweeping: developing countries are looking for free trade arrangements with developed countries. Previously, the issue of market access and preferential access to the markets of developed countries had been a chief item on the agenda of UNCTAD. The General System of Preferences, under which industrial countries gave developing countries privileged market access for a broad range of goods, was a way of implementing that objective. What is new is the willingness to practice free trade as a two-way street. Mexico has taken that route in asking for free trade negotiations with the United States and Canada and, following an acrimonious debate before the US Congress, negotiations are now under way. The United States may take the NAFTA (North American Free Trade Agreement) as a blueprint to allow other countries to adhere to a conditional most-favored-nation basis. If that turns out to be the case, the Americas may become a free trade area in the next decade or two.

Notes

1. These factors apply even more forcefully to Eastern Europe and the Soviet Union. As these economies shed central planning, a wide-open trade regime is seen as a critical measure. Nothing could more dramatize the belief in the promises of openness than the advice to drop from one day to the next all and any obstacles to international trade (Sachs 1991; Dornbusch 1991). Nor could any policy have a more drastic immediate effect; when East Germany liberalized totally in its union with West Germany, industrial production fell within a year by 50 percent and unemployment skyrocketed.
2. There are the famous Harberger "triangles." See Harberger (1959).
3. See Helpman (1989) and Helpman and Krugman (1989) for a broad analysis of the many issues emerging under imperfect competition. See also Baumol and Lee (1991).
4. Going beyond liberalization, de Melo and Robinson (1990, pp. 30–1) conclude: "If there are externalities to be exploited, policy makers should pursue them aggressively and not worry overmuch about getting the instruments just right . . . [W]hen there are rectangles to be gained, an economy can easily afford some triangles along the way."

References

Balassa, B. (1989) "Outward Orientation." In H. Chenery and T. N. Srinivasan, eds, *Handbook of Development Economics*. New York: North Holland, Vol. 2, pp. 1645–90.

Baumol, W., S. A. Batey Blackman and E. Wolf (1989) *Productivity and American Leadership: The Long View*. Cambridge, MA: MIT Press.

Baumol, W. and L. S. Lee (1991) "Contestable Markets, Trade and Development." *World Bank Research Observer* 6(1), 1–18.

Bhagwati, J. (1978) *Foreign Trade Regimes and Economic Development. Anatomy and Consequences of Exchange Control Regimes*. Cambridge, MA: Ballinger.

Bruton, H. (1989) "Import Substitution." In H. Chenery and T. N. Srinivasan, eds, *Handbook of Development Economics*. New York: North Holland, Vol. 2, pp. 1601–44.

Celasun, M. and D. Rodrik (1989) "Debt, Adjustment and Growth: Turkey." In J. Sachs and S. Collins, eds, *Developing Country Debt and Economic Performance*. Chicago: University of Chicago Press.

Chenery, H., S. Robinson and M. Syrquin (1986) *Industrialization and Growth*. Oxford: Oxford University Press.

de Melo, J. and S. Robinson (1990) "Productivity and Externalities. Models of Export-Led Growth." Working Papers WPS 387, World Bank.

Dornbusch, R. (1991) "Priorities of Economic Reform in Eastern Europe and the Soviet Union." Centre for Economic Policy Research, Policy Paper No. 5, London. (See also Chapter 7, this volume.)

Edwards, S. (1991) "Trade Orientation, Distortions and Growth in Developing Countries." Mimeo, University of California, Los Angeles.

Eichengreen, Barry (1991) "Historical Research on International Lending and Debt." *Journal of Economic Perspectives* 5(2): 149–69.

Erzan, R. and K. Kuwahara (1989) "The Profile of Protection in Developing Countries." *UNCTAD Review* 1(1): 24–49.

Faini, R., F. Clavijo and A. Senhadji-Semiali (1990) "The Fallacy of Composition Argument: Does Demand Matter for LDC Manufacturing Exports?" Center for Economic Policy Research, Discussion Paper No. 499, December.

Finger, M. (1991) "Development Economics and the General Agreement on Tariffs and Trade." In de Melo, J. and A. Sapir, eds, *Trade Theory and Economic Reform. Essays in Honor of Bela Balassa*. Cambridge, MA: Basil Blackwell, pp. 203–23.

Haberler, G. (1959) "International Trade and Economic Development" (The Cairo Lectures). Reprinted in *International Trade and Economic Development*. Washington, DC: American Enterprise Institute, pp. 17–54.

Harberger, A. (1959) "Using Resources at Hand More Effectively." *American Economic Review* 40(1): 134–46.

Harrison, A. (1991) "Openness and Growth: A Time-Series, Cross-Country Analysis of Developing Countries." Mimeo, World Bank.

Havrylyshyn, O. (1990) "Trade Policy and Productivity Gains in Developing Countries: A Survey of the Literature." *World Bank Research Observer* 5(1): 1–24.

Helpman, E. (1989) "The Noncompetitive Theory of International Trade and Trade Policy." In *Proceedings of the World Bank Annual Conference on Development Economics*, pp. 193–216.

Helpman, E. and P. Krugman (1989) *Trade Policy and Market Structure*. Cambridge, MA: MIT Press.

Krueger, A. (1978) *Foreign Trade Regimes and Economic Development. Liberalization Attempts and Consequences*. Cambridge, MA: Ballinger.

Krueger, A. (1990) "Comparative Advantage and Development Policy Twenty Years Later." In Krueger, A., ed, *Perspectives on Trade and Development*. New York: Harvester Wheatsheaf, 49–70.

Meier, G. (1963) *International Trade and Development*. New York: Harper and Row.

Michaely, M., A. Choksi and D. Papageorgiou (1991) *Liberalizing Foreign Trade. Lessons of Experience in the Developing World*. Cambridge, MA: Basil Blackwell.

Norman, V. (1990) "Assessing Trade and Welfare Effects of Trade Liberalization." *European Economic Review* 34(4): 725–45.

Pack, H. (1988) "Industrialization and Trade." In H. Chenery and T. N. Srinivasan, eds, *Handbook of Development Economics*. New York: North Holland, Vol. 1, pp. 333–80.

Papageorgiou, D., A. Choksi and M. Michaely (1990) *Liberalizing Foreign Trade in Developing Countries. The Lessons of Experience*. Washington, DC: The World Bank.

Prebisch, R. (1959) "Commercial Policy in the Underdeveloped Countries." *American Economic Review* (Papers and Proceedings), 40: 261–4.

Prebisch, R. (1984) "Five Stages in My Thinking on Development." In G. Meier and D. Seers, eds, *Pioneers in Development*. Oxford: Oxford University Press, pp. 175–191.

Romer, P. (1989) "Capital Accumulation in the Theory of Long Run Growth." In R. Barro, ed, *Modern Business Cycle Theory.* Cambridge, MA: Harvard University Press, pp. 51–127.

Sachs, J. (1991) "Sachs on Poland." *The Economist*, January 19th.

Salvatore, D., and T. Hatcher (1991) "Inward Oriented and Outward Oriented Trade Strategies." *Journal of Development Studies*, 27(3): 7–25.

Sareacoglu, R. (1987) "Economic Stabilization and Structural Adjustment. The Case of Turkey." In V. Corbo, M. Goldstein, and M. Khan, eds, *Growth-Oriented Adjustment Programs.* Washington, DC: IMF and World Bank, 119–139.

Schumpeter, J. (1934) *The Theory of Economic Development.* Reprinted by Transactions Books, New Brunswick, NJ, 1983.

Shepherd, G. and C. Langoni (1991) *Trade Reform Lessons from Eight Countries.* San Francisco: ICS Press.

Thomas, V. and J. Nash (1991a) "Reform of Trade Policy." *World Bank Research Observer*, 6(2): 153–72.

Thomas, V. and J. Nash, eds (1991b) *Best Picture in Trade Policy Reform.* Oxford: Oxford University Press.

United States International Trade Commission (1990) *Review of Trade and Investment Liberalization Measures by Mexico.* USITC Publication 2275, Washington, DC.

Viner, J. (1952) *International Trade and Economic Development.* Glencoe, IL: The Free Press.

Whalley, J. (1989) "Recent Trade Liberalization in the Developing World: What is Behind It and Where Is It Headed?" NBER Working Paper, No. 3057, August.

World Bank (1987) *World Development Report.* New York: Oxford University Press.

World Bank (1988) *Adjustment Lending. An Evaluation of Ten Years of Experience.* Policy and Research Series No. 1.

World Bank (1991) *World Development Report.* New York: Oxford University Press.

Young, K. (1989) "Trade Reform in Korea," Korea Development Institute, mimeo.

6

Investment in developing countries

Five principal ingredients make up the setting in which investment will flourish: opportunities; prosperity; coordination; firm governance and rules of the game; and finance. I will comment on the role of each.

6.1   Opportunity

Some regions are blessed, others barely present any opportunities however hard they might try. Some regions of Africa fall into the latter category and so do parts of Latin America—for example, Bolivia. They once offered opportunities, when their primary commodities benefitted from attractive world prices. Ruled by oligarchies or colonial administrations that single-mindedly fostered respect for property and the established order, they offered plausible outlets for foreign capital. Today the commodities are not worth much in world markets, and politics is unstable. It is hard to make up for the lack of a God-given opportunity. Scale economies favor production in industrial centers, transport costs are not extreme, and the result is that an economy may lack attraction for investment in a quite radical fashion. It will become depressed and there is not much that can be done about it. Frankly, emigration may be the best answer. Note that this used to be said even of Ireland.

One might argue that there is a wage in dollars low enough to make production for the home and world market profitable. I doubt that is true because the wage being that low turns into a political problem and with that new difficulties arise which get in the way of investment. I may exaggerate my point about opportunity, but I believe we should advance with far more caution the view that with the right policies any place can be a place in the sun. There simply may not exist an economic *and* political equilibrium in parts of the world that had their good day but now are economically deserted. Ghost towns in the Far West give an example of what I have in mind and dirt-poor countries may present the same phenomenon except for the ability to leave.

6.2   Prosperity

The next ingredient for investment is prosperity—the feeling that things are going well, that they will continue to do so. Prosperity is mostly in the mind of investors, but even so or for that very reason, it is the chief driving force of a broad-based investment boom.

Prosperity is made easily, even populists can do it. García in Peru is a good example. Two years of spending and he received a standing ovation from the business community and a healthy dose of investment. Three years later the experiment crashed (see Dornbusch and Edwards 1990). That is the danger with prosperity: it may be built on sand and turn out to be very ephemeral, as it did in Peru. Prosperity is in the nature of passion and unreason, fear of losing out on a good thing, not the Swiss-style prosperity based on centuries of wise, moderate and steady accumulation.

A good description of this atmosphere of prosperity comes from Hyndman (1967, pp. 153–4):

> Buenos Ayres surpassed every other city in its luxury, extravagance, and wholesale squandering of wealth. There was literally no limit to the excesses of the wealthier classes. While money, luxuries and material poured in on the one hand, crowds of immigrants from Italy and other countries flocked in to perpetuate the prosperity of the new Eldorado of the South. Railways, docks, tramways, waterworks, gasworks, public buildings, mansions, all were carried on at once in hot haste ...

The commercial real estate experience of Massachusetts in the late 1980s presents yet another example of the same phenomenon. Prosperity is a powerful engine, but often for a risky trip.

6.3   Coordination

The profitability of an individual investment is almost inevitably dependent on what happens elsewhere in the economy. This situation creates a serious problem for investment: like two Germans at the door, everybody says "After you, please!" and if nobody will be first, then nothing happens in the economy (see Dornbusch, 1990). Everybody keeps saying the fundamentals are right and yet they wait, holding off investment except of the most liquid kind.

Even though coordination is central to generating investment, often little can be done. Occasionally there are extraordinary opportunities, as is the case today in Mexico. The large amount of flight capital waiting abroad, if returned, would easily cement economic stability. The capital is waiting for the message to start the stampede. The creative use of a free trade agreement may well become the coordinating device that sends the message that all is well, that it is safe to come home. When that message spreads, coordination is a done deal and prosperity will take off.

6.4 Rules of the game

Luigi Einaudi, Italy's celebrated postwar finance minister and president, said of investors that they have the memories of elephants, the hearts of lambs and the legs of hare. Institutions are there to assure investors of stability in property rights and in economic management. Without an institutional setting principal-agent problems cannot find a satisfactory resolution and if they go unresolved opportunities dry up.

6.4.1 *Institutions*

Decentralization of responsibilities and decisions, specifically between lenders and producers, calls for property rights that secure the interest of lenders without unduly interfering with the ability of managers to carry out long-term decisions. When property rights become insecure capital markets dry up and the horizon of firms shrinks to a year, a month or a day.

In many places in Latin America property rights are in question. There is no way of securing equitable judgments in court and stockholders are routinely deprived of their return by majority owners. Extremely low price–earnings ratios on stock often are a signal not of a country without opportunity but of a country without an effective legal system. Venezuela and Brazil are striking examples.

Rules of the game also apply to macroeconomic management. If real interest rates, real exchange rates, and inflation rates are violently unstable the horizon inevitably shrinks. And with the shrinking horizon goes the decline in profitability and the reduced incentive to invest. Of course, real interest rates and real exchange rates are not the only variables that count. Even so, a comparison of Argentina and Chile is revealing. With three times the variability of Korea (see Table 6.1), it is hardly surprising that investment in Argentina is not only

Table 6.1 Variability of the real exchange rate (coefficient of variation)

	Argentina	Korea
1970–79	18.1	9.9
1980–90	29.2	10.8

low—negative in net terms—but also too short-horizon and too defensive from a social point of view.

Interventionist policies, particularly the recurrent use of price controls and discretionary interference in firms' production and pricing plans, add to the instability of real exchange rates.

6.4.2 *Continuity*

Investors abhor transitions. Unresolved issues, in the way discussed by Bernanke (1983), stand in the way of investment while continuity supports commitment.

The sound rule in banking states "never lend in a transition." This rule applies with equal relevance to investment decisions. Governments, therefore, must make every effort to move quickly to the sustainable regime and to put in place mechanisms that reassure asset holders against abrupt moves. Governments must have a *policy*, not a day-to-day discretionary reaction to events. This idea is fundamental to what is called *Ordnungspolitik* in Germany— stability of rules (see Stutzel *et al.* 1982).

The critical missing link in many Latin American countries today is governance. Mexico exemplifies the critical role of purposeful government in fostering confidence, growth and the return of flight capital. And Argentina or Brazil show how the melting, or the outright wrecking of economic institutions, ultimately undermines the willingness of citizens to invest. The ensuing decapitalization ultimately undermines a country's ability to pay yesterday's wages. Standards of living decline and make politics increasingly difficult because distribution rather than growth is at the center. Workers call for reactivation as the answer to their plight, but in fact the country's ability to sustain past standards of living has been dissipated.

6.5 Finance

The last but not least determinant of investment is finance. Here the focus is on three issues: the initial debt overhang; the government budget as a source of national saving; and finally the structure of financial intermediation.

6.5.1 *The overhang*

Unresolved debt problems, not debt *per se*, are an obstacle to investment. It is hard for a man to establish a relationship with a lender if the estranged wife keeps barging in claiming alimony. Mexico has demonstrated that getting debt out of the headlines and off the front page, however good or disappointing the deal, is a critical first step to focusing discussion on the far more important task of restructuring and growth. The Brady Plan may not solve the debt problem, but it certainly is a first-rate way to push the problem to the sidelines where it belongs. Ultimately, after reconstruction, debt can easily be serviced in many countries. The chief issue is to take away its nuisance value today.

6.5.2 *Stability and the budget*

Anyone who invested in nominal assets in Argentina in the mid-1980s today would have in real terms less than 5 cents on the dollar. Even if people save, nobody can expect them to invest their saving in a financial system that robs them systematically. No surprise, then, that capital flight is endemic in an environment of protracted financial instability. In the area of finance the first priority must be the establishment of financial normality. The essential ingredients for this are budget balance and a stable exchange rate policy.

When rules are stable and prosperity abounds, so does saving. Feldstein and Horioka (1980) show that what is saved tends to be invested in the country. Thus, unless instability drives the savings out, shortage of resources should not be the issue. Moreover, if the opportunities abound and stability of rules is not in question, external savings will be available for the asking.

Feldstein and Horioka found in their investigations of international saving–investment linkages that savings tend predominantly to be invested in the country where the saving occurs. We must thus conclude: if what is saved is available for investment it must follow that if the government saves more, then more is available for private investment. Taxation is the most effective means of increasing public sector saving. More attention should be focused on creating broad-based efficient tax systems and thus reduce deficits in the budget. This would promote stability and make more resources available for private investment.

6.5.3 *Intermediation*

All this would suggest that there is no issue. But there are questions to be asked about intermediation. Financial institutions are in the business of intermediating between ultimate lenders and final borrowers (see Goldsmith 1969 and Dornbusch 1991). How well do they do their job? Recurrent crises in markets for sovereign debt, the savings-and-loan scandal and the fragility of commercial banks in the USA, and the same problem in many countries that have "opened up," suggest that the intermediation structure must be an area of extreme suspicion and the most thoughtful regulation.

A key consideration is to achieve an intermediation system that focuses on lending to small and medium-sized firms for whom the agency costs of the capital market are prohibitive. Unfortunately banks do not find these businesses the most attractive and rather favor large projects like less developed country debt or vast real estate development projects. History is not on their side.

In the area of finance two other considerations apply. The first is to create an institutional structure that makes it possible to have a broad equity market. Equity markets are essential to avoid an economy that is overindebted. There are problems with equity, but they fall short of the risks of an overly leveraged economy (see Tirole 1991).

References

Bernanke, B. (1983) "Irreversibility, Uncertainty and Cyclical Investment." *Quarterly Journal of Economics* 98(1): 85–106.

Dornbusch, R. (1990) "The New Classical Economics and Stabilization Policy." *American Economic Review* 80(2, May): 143–7. (See Chapter 3, this volume.)

Dornbusch, R. (1991) "Policies to Move from Stabilization to Growth." *Proceedings of the World Bank Annual Conference on Development Economics 1990*. Washington, DC: World Bank. (See Chapter 2, this volume.)

Dornbusch, R., and S. Edwards (1990) "The Macroeconomics of Populism in Latin America." *Journal of Economic Development* 32: 247–77. (See Chapter 13, this volume.)

Feldstein, M. and C. Horioka (1980) "Domestic Savings and International Capital Flows." *Economic Journal*, 90 (June): 314–29.

Goldsmith, R. (1969) *Financial Structure and Development*. New Haven: Yale University Press.

Hyndman, H. (1967) *Commercial Crises of the Nineteenth Century*. Reprints of Economic Classics. New York: Augustus M. Kelley.

Stutzel, W. *et al.* (1982) *Standard Texts on the Social Market Economy*. Ludwig Erhard Stiftung. New York: Gustav Fischer.

Tirole, J. (1991) "Privatization in Eastern Europe: Incentives and the Economics of Transition." *NBER Macroeconomics Annual*, 6: 221–59.

Part III

Reform problems after communism

7

Priorities of economic reform in Eastern Europe and the Soviet Union

Socialist planners ruined the economies of Eastern Europe. The new policy-makers face economies that are overmanaged, where output is overburdened with claims, and politics is overwhelmed by unrealistic expectations of progress. Markets must be introduced with great urgency to decentralize decisions and depoliticize much of the economic sphere. Progress will inevitably be slow, but it will not start unless restrictions on activity and pervasive controls give way to far more freedom and decentralization.

The experience of East Germany in the past six months shows that even under the most favorable conditions Eastern Europe's economies may disintegrate. Foreign support may mitigate the extent of collapse, but foreign support will be very limited. Eastern Europe will have to find its own way. Moreover, there is only little guidance to be derived from historical precedent. Germany in 1948 offers some answers and so does the experience of Latin America. These precedents must not be overlooked out of an exaggerated perception that Eastern Europe's problems are entirely special; but clearly the tasks to be accomplished are far larger and the prospects for rapid achievement moderate at best.

7.1   The agenda

The need for reform is pervasive and little can be said about sequencing other than to assert four principles:

- The government must focus on what is important, not on what is urgent. The

I would like to acknowledge helpful discussions with Olivier Blanchard, Peter Diamond, Michael Piore, Richard Portes and John Williamson. I have also benefitted from the recent literature, notably Arriagada (1990), Hinds (1990), Fischer and Gelb (1990) and Portes (1990).

Table 7.1 The agenda

Day 1	Rules of the game and an economic model
Day 2	Institutions: fiscal, legal, pensions, social-safety net
Day 3	Macro balancing
Day 4	Privatization
Day 5	Decontrol, convertibility and protection
Day 6	Integration: trade not aid
Day 7	Finance

administrative and political capacity is very small; it must be devoted to achieving essentials.

- The sequencing of reforms must avoid widening the vacuum. Reforms should create opportunities to be filled by individual initiatives, not open gaps that require further and more encompassing government action.
- Wherever possible, the government should organize an immediate and full retreat from responsibility for production and distribution of goods. The market provides an effective means of decentralizing and depoliticizing decision-making.
- The government cannot protect the entire population from the burden of restructuring. It must target the small group that gets a parachute. The rest must fall on their feet, somehow.

Accompanying these principles is a warning: there must be no illusions in two respects. First, Western governments do have an interest in stability and prosperity in the East. But their commitment of resources will be limited. Beyond an initial effort little can be expected; Eastern Europe must find its own way. Second, policymakers in the new democracies must not fool themselves about their ability to phase in change gradually. The walls are down and citizens are impatient; radical change is the only realistic option.

Within these guidelines, one possible view of the agenda is set out in Table 7.1. In many discussions there is relatively little emphasis on the first two issues. But they are critical items in building up a functioning market economy. Before discussing details of reform, one prior issue must be resolved: rapid or gradual reform?

7.2 How fast?

Gradualism or jump, how fast should reform proceed? Policymakers, because they are intrinsically interventionist, favor gradualism and controlled transition. How persuasive is gradualism? A quotation from the memorandum of the Gorbachev–Yeltsin working group gives the flavor. Under the Heading "Man, Freedom and the Market" we are told:[1]

> Only when the people see that all the possibilities and resources currently
> devoured by the giant state machine have been channeled to serve the people,

will the leadership of the country be in a position to appeal to the people to be patient, to take up another heavy load in the name of the Motherland and of their own future and the future of their children.

We must not fool ourselves: there is little patience left and even less disposition for sacrifice. Why sacrifice, and for whom and with what prospect of improvement? A mere beginning of change, at this stage, is just not enough.

Gradualism opens the door to an unstructured free-for-all: consumers will go to the black market, firms will produce for the black market. Households will turn to Deutschmarks and dollars and thus provoke hyperinflation, workers will privatize firms spontaneously. Those who are left out or fall behind will radicalize. The common experience is that economic disintegration takes much longer to come than one thinks, but that it ultimately happens much faster than one would have thought. Economies collapse because of a structural problem: they operate with a high division of labor. But this division of labor cannot continue in an institutional vacuum as it exists today. Therefore a flight forward, to a full-blown market economy, has to be the right answer.

Gradualism may seem a low-risk strategy in that, day to day, events seem under control. But the realistic answer is immediate, radical reform, not the mirage of a phased-in move to a market economy. Temporary collapse may be inevitable one way or the other, but in the context of radical reform it may at least be the seed for reconstruction.

The administrative capacity for *successful* gradual reform simply does not exist: after all, communism, even with the advantage of repression, could not handle the task of allocating resources. Nothing has changed with new and highly committed, talented personnel joining the ranks. They, too, will be unable to mastermind an economywide soft landing. The lesson of the postwar period is that those countries that pushed reform most aggressively soon showed the best results, even if the transition period was very hard. The market is already there; the only choice is whether to work *with* the market or to lose out in a fight *against* the market.

In Eastern Europe the case for gradualism might be that it avoids collapse: jumping all at once into a capitalistic, unplanned system with open markets breaks up existing economic structures from one day to the next. Firms cannot sell their goods because imports from the West take away customers both at home and in former trading-partner markets. Even in those instances where goods might be sold, the large decline in consumption and in investment further reduces employment and demand. If the real disorganization were not enough, macroeconomic imbalances are exacerbated by a currency crisis as households and firms flee onto the safe ground of hard currencies and goods. Moreover, the economic crisis would immediately destabilize the political transition; for many the way back may seem shorter than the way forward. In China that was the case; why would it be inconceivable in some parts of Eastern Europe or the Soviet Union?

In the gray area between a control economy that no longer functions and a market economy that is not fully accepted, economic collapse is inevitable. Collapse occurs because the cooperation required by a high division of labor does not arise spontaneously; it requires either the coercion of a repressive regime or else the incentives of a market economy. That was apparent in the collapse of production in postwar Germany and it is apparent today in Eastern Europe and the Soviet Union.

How to get from here to there? The answer must be that the transition needs to be accomplished extremely fast because the ice is melting, the distance is great and the task is overwhelming. The illusion that transition could be managed over years to come is just that. The pace will be determined by the market, which is already operating on the back stage. Countries that move fast will draw resources from abroad and stand a better chance to retain scarce human capital and political reserves; countries that drag their feet risk falling into deep poverty where even the unsatisfactory living standards of the past decade can no longer be mustered because the organization of the economy has vanished.

Gradualism offers superficial appeal because it seems to take away the harshness of adjustment and puts a better face on the inevitable restructuring. But gradualism is only appropriate if going slowly promises better results—not only getting there ultimately but also at lower cost. Gradual withdrawal may be the cure for some addictions, but it does not apply when the central problem is the shortage of mechanisms that ensure output is supplied to the market of a kind and at a price that people will buy. The entire problem arises because of the demonstrated inability of the government to handle the economic problem. The risk of a collapse is real, and the notion that gradualism helps control events is overly optimistic.

A gradualist solution is appropriate when a market economy is in place and the issue is how to improve the use of resources *at the margin* even if the required changes are substantial. If most firms can survive by adapting their activities to the changed market opportunities, it makes sense to support that outcome by a transition period in which restructuring can take place. Because this is not the case in Eastern Europe, radical and rapid reform is the right medicine.

A major tension arises between the concern to maintain existing employment patterns and standards of living, on one hand, and the recognition that drastic changes are required and time is short, on the other. An approach that is overly cautious and protective along the lines of a *dirigiste* welfare state risks handling the adjustment poorly. A case can be made that rapid, radical reform offers the best bridge to a market economy. The Germany of 1948 offers a precedent. The drastic cut with the past in the form of monetary reform and radical deregulation was the key step. Unemployment, fed by refugees from the East, increased to nearly a million and a half by early 1950; but with strong growth unemployment then fell during the 1950s (see Figure 7.1). Cumulative growth of real GDP in 1950–55 amounted to 57 percent. In the United Kingdom, by contrast, unemployment was always below 2 percent but growth was very modest—a cumulative growth of only 13 percent. Practicing the welfare state clearly had its costs (see Table 7.2).[2]

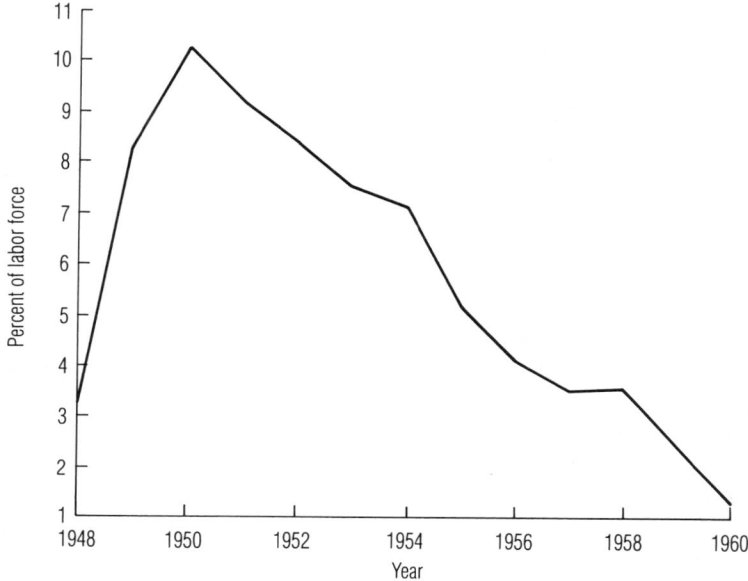

Figure 7.1 West German unemployment rate, 1948–60.

Table 7.2 Comparative performance, 1950–59 (percent)

	Growth	Unemployment rate
Germany	7.9	6.7
UK	1.9	1.5

7.3 Rules of the game

On day one of the reform the government must create the preconditions for a market economy. Specifically two actions are required: first, the acceptance of unlimited and unrestricted private property; second, the acceptance of full economic freedom to carry out all and any activity the individual sees fit to pursue.

Economic freedom includes freedom of transaction, freedom to enter any kind of activity and produce any kind of good for any kind of customer. These rights should be pervasive and unrestricted, overriding any existing restrictions. Rather than gradually developing a legislative program that opens opportunities now closed, the process should be radically reversed: everything is permitted, unless specifically ruled out by *new* legislation.

The acceptance of property rights is essential if private initiative is to be pointed to creating new firms and organizations. Unless property is accepted, economic activity will be hand-to-mouth. If people are to work and invest today for benefits to be reaped tomorrow and beyond, their right to property must be firmly accepted. If property is not accepted the train cannot leave; assets would be stripped and consumed, capital would be eaten or "privatized" in unrecoverable forms that enhance personal welfare but do so at a large social cost.

The property issue has been dramatically mishandled in some Eastern European countries where the rights of very remote owners have been revived. As a result, great uncertainty has been introduced into any transaction and delays have been put in the way of investment. This is perhaps the best example of how *not* to proceed.

The right to unrestricted economic activity, including specifically the right to open any kind of business and to enter any activity, fills, at least partially, the extraordinary void as government firms collapse. Unless private businesses open and mushroom, there is no place for workers to go as large government firms close down or raise productivity. Small and medium-sized business has, potentially, the flexibility to absorb substantial amounts of labor, fast. If regulation stands in the way, there is not even the prospect that unemployment will be short-lived.

Striking the balance between unrestricted economic freedom, competition and social goals requires a reference framework. The right model might be Germany's "social market economy".[3] The acceptance of economic freedom must ultimately be mitigated in two ways. First, *laissez-faire* liberalism does not ensure competition, because the incentive to cartelize will be too obvious and the impediments to monopoly too few. Ultimately legislation in support of competitive markets must come into play; for most questions that issue is fairly remote since the distance from the early one-man-one-truck mode to a distribution or production monopoly is huge. But in the context of privatization with foreign firms of major public utilities or industries the consideration applies. The government must resist the temptation of trading short-run employment gains deriving from a rescue operation by foreign capital for long-lasting high levels of market protection.

Second, *laissez-faire* liberalism also fails in the social area and hence needs to be supplemented by specific measures. These should go in two directions. The fiscal system ultimately must strike the right balance between redistribution and efficiency. There is no ready answer, but the experience of the West suggests that excessive progressivity is a mistake: it brings too little revenue and costs too much in efficiency.

More immediately, the government needs to put in place a targeted social emergency program that shelters the poorest groups and the helpless old from the inevitable rigor of the adjustment phase. A program must be put in place because without it, opposition to adjustment is overwhelming. Unfortunate half-hearted attempts make matters worse because subsidies become even more pervasive. But the program must be highly targeted because fiscal resources are extraordinarily scarce.

A difficult but essential part of the rules of the game applies to the labor market. Eastern European productivity levels are very low relative to those in advanced countries and thus labor-shedding will be essential to ensure the survival of firms. It must therefore become possible to fire workers as firms are restructured. Moreover, this must be achieved in the transition period without incurring delays and burdens so large that they endanger the economic viability of firms that *are* potentially rescuable. The counterpart of a flexible labor market, of course, should be social institutions that dampen the hardship of unemployment.

A market economy with rules of the game is then a first, vital step, without which there would be chaos. With rules of the game there is at least the prospect of vigorous reconstruction after the initial collapse. This was the German experience in 1948. Müller-Armack (1948), who created the concept of the "social market economy", noted at the time that the key problem was not the physical destruction of capacity; rather he observed that "the missing of a genuine cooperation between productive factors is at the core of our current economic problems". The determined turn toward a market economy, with free initiative and full rights, to resolve the formidable organizational task of putting factors of production to work with each other is thus a first priority.

7.4   Institutions

A market economy does not function in an institutional vacuum. Specifically, to thrive it requires an abundant, well-functioning institutional infrastructure. Among the key elements is a functioning legal system that protects the right to conduct economic transactions and provides the possibility of sanctions and redress. The most suitable way of handling this issue is to adopt wholesale and without question the entire civil code, including corporate law, of a well-functioning legal system, say the Netherlands or Finland. There is absolutely no merit in trying to create a new one; time is too short and this clearly is not an area where originality will have large payoffs.

The institutional infrastructure also encompasses mundane issues such as an accounting system. Without standardized, modern accounting the economy cannot function: economic profitability cannot be assessed, public finance cannot function and major privatization is altogether implausible. Thus the import of a ready-made accounting system is mandatory. Once again, it does not make much difference from where. Above all, governments should avoid spending time and resources in "reinventing the wheel" in this area. It is obvious that the existing massive bureaucracy should find its way into the accounting profession; training programs should be started immediately. These programs have the payoff that government employment can ultimately be cut much more easily.

The need for institutional reform does not end with accounting, a legal code and the introduction of courts. For example, a key program to implement is a pension system. In the short run there is no question that the old will be immediately dependent on the state, whatever their work history or their contributions. But the transition has to be made as early as possible to define the conditions of entitlement and the contributions required. Again, importing an existing reasonably functioning system cuts down on scarce administrative resources.

A further institutional reform concerns the tax system. A tax system appropriate to a market economy cannot view profits as the prime target and full equality as a mandate. A simple, high-yield tax system is critical. Such a system should involve very few taxes, and rates should be moderate so as not to interfere with incentives. A comprehensive 20 percent value-added tax might be a useful backbone of such a tax system. There should also be significant taxes on capital gains and profits: in the transition period capital gains will be extravagant. They should not be discouraged by any means. But the government must secure a good share both to make capital gains socially legitimate and also to have a source of revenue for the social emergency programs.

The list of items to fill the institutional vacuum is very long and it includes an efficient system of unemployment compensation. At the same time there is a need to create an effective bankruptcy mechanism. Inefficiency cannot be put in the budget on an open-ended basis. Without a bankruptcy mechanism there is too little incentive to adjust.

These issues are often not on the priority list of reform, but they do belong there. Their effective implementation takes much time; for that reason they ought to be initiated very early. Fortunately, this is made easier by the existence of ready-made systems abroad. Moreover, this is one of a few areas where technical assistance is not useful and readily available.

7.5   Macro balance

Macroeconomics becomes harder as political repression becomes less effective. In economies with large public sectors, politicized wage-setting, a printing press and new democracy, macroeconomic instability is endemic. For Eastern Europe and the Soviet Union today much is to be learned from the vast costs of inflation as experienced in Latin America. But there are also important lessons to be gathered from the European experience in the aftermath of World War II.

Bulgaria seems poised to experience extreme inflation once decontrol of prices, the monetary overhang and a large budget deficit have their rendezvous. And in the Soviet Union, monetary overhang and huge budget deficits financed by money creation also set the stage for a potentially serious inflation. The overhang built up over half a decade of monetary expansion is now beginning to slide: shortages are pervasive and black markets increasingly spring up to satisfy the demands remaining unfulfilled on the official market. No relief is to be found on the budget side: the data show persistent and increasing deficits. As comprehen-

Table 7.3 Monetary reforms in the 1940s and 1950s

Country	Date	Write-down	Blocking	Capital levy or forced loan
No monetary reform				
Italy				
UK				
Confiscatory reform				
Austria I	Jul 1945		*	
Austria II	Nov 1945		*	
Austria III	Nov 1947	*		
Belgium	Oct 1944		*	*
Bulgaria I	Mar 1947		*	*
Bulgaria II	May 1952	*		
Czechoslovakia I	Oct 1945		*	*
Czechoslovakia II	Jun 1953	*		
Denmark	Jul 1945		*	*
Finland	Dec 1945		*	*
France	Jan 1948		*	*
Germany (East)	Jun 1948	*	*	
Germany (West)	Jun 1948	*	*	
Hungary I	Dec 1945	*	*	
Netherlands	Sep 1945			*
Norway	Sep 1945			*
Poland I	Dec 1944			*
Poland II	Oct 1950	*		
Romania I	Aug 1947	*	*	
Romania II	Jan 1952	*		
USSR	Dec 1947	*		
Yugoslavia	Apr 1945	*	*	*
Hyperinflation stabilization				
Greece	Nov 1944			
Hungary II	Aug 1946			

Source: Dornbusch and Wolf (1990).

sive price controls remain in effect and output is, at best, stagnant, the monetized part of the deficit adds directly to the overhang.

As market forces are unleashed and controls are lifted, the removal of the monetary overhang becomes crucial. Monetary adjustment can be accomplished in two ways: either by a big, possibly one-shot, inflation, or else by a reduction of effective nominal money balances. Money balances can be either written off, consolidated as debt or retired by asset exchanges or budget surpluses. Of course, monetary reform is not enough; it attends at best to the *stock* issue, the monetary overhang, but it does not solve the *flow* problem, which is the budget deficit. The flow problem calls for the conventional budget cutting. Table 7.3 provides a summary overview of the reforms of the 1940s.

Most monetary reforms of the 1940s were differentiated according to the type and magnitude of asset holdings in respect to the write-off ratio. The differentiation recognized the political objective of targeting groups that had gained, illegally or otherwise, in the war, or simply reflected the desire to share burdens on the basis of the ability to pay. An investigation of the distribution of monetary assets was therefore always an important aspect in designing monetary reform.

Two arguments are commonly cited against the alleged need for a monetary reform. The first is to note that the ratio of monetary assets relative to income is so high because there are no other assets available. That argument may well be true, but it does not address the question of what happens when inflation starts. There will be a flight to the dollar, precisely because there are no other assets available. It is to avoid this destabilizing portfolio shift that a monetary reform is necessary.

The second argument notes that the overhang is not so high, and very moderate compared to the 400 percent or more of Germany in 1948. That argument also fails to ask the right question: what ratio of money to income will the public be willing to hold if inflation gets under way? A ratio of 60 or 70 percent would be extremely high by the standards of Western Europe or Latin America. With an inflation rate of 50 or 100 percent, a money/income ratio of 30 percent would be far too high.

If this reasoning is correct, some kind of monetary reform is appropriate. The wrong kind, quite decidedly, is a conversion of money into interest-bearing debt. The budget problem is already serious in many countries and thus the need to add extra charges is perilous. Another option is a "blip" in the price level that reduces the real value of money. Conceptually that is a possible solution. In fact, it is extremely hard to avoid the single blip becoming an inflationary process which, once it gets under way, raises velocity and turns into a fully-fledged and substantial inflation.

The remaining options are a freeze, a write-off or a conversion. A freeze tries to avoid an answer to a serious question. Leaving the overhang frozen risks financial instability down the road. Conversion into assets is an attractive solution except for one problem: the timetable for monetary reform is radically short and the plausible timetable for privatization seems drawn out under the most optimistic conditions. Thus conversion is difficult except in the following form. The money overhang is converted *today* into shares in the future privatizations. The desirable feature of such a mechanism is that it puts more interest behind privatization.

An outright write-off is equally attractive; it reduces the risk of macroeconomic instability and creates an opening for a new financial system. But we emphasize once more that without budget balancing extreme inflation is totally unavoidable. There is no room for debt finance as yet and access to external capital is very limited. In these circumstances there is a direct road from deficits to high inflation. Inflation in turn creates a formidable political and economic obstacle to economic reform.[4]

7.6 Privatization

Property rights can be used as a driving force in promoting an efficient and accountable use of resources. It is essential here to strike the right balance between technical simplicity, fairness and incentives. Furthermore, while it is easier to privatize residential structures, priority must go to reorganization of firms. Unless firms are functioning with a view to the market they cannot keep up employment. One coherent solution involves the following steps:

1. All government assets are allocated to a few funds, say five.
2. All citizens receive shares in each of these funds, on a per-capita basis. Beyond distribution to citizens there needs to be a provision for the financing of pension funds and possibly a participation of the regular budget in the dividends.
3. The funds are required to distribute earnings and pay taxes.
4. The shares are transferable and freely tradable, with restrictions applying over time to avoid instant liquidation and disappointment.
5. The funds can sell off enterprises to individuals who may be financed by investment banks, domestic or foreign.
6. The funds are structured so as to be liquidated altogether or broken up into smaller funds over an eight-year period.
7. The performance of the funds will be monitored by public pressure, and this will serve as a crude incentive device to get capitalism moving.

The purpose of these mechanisms is strictly to achieve privatization. It is another and separate issue to put in place a legal and economic structure that ensures that the ultimate firms, once privatized, will be well managed. The issue that is of interest here is how privatization can be achieved.

The lesson from Germany today, somewhat overstated, is that it is more important to do it fast than to do it well. The statement makes the point that if privatization does not happen, collapse of economic activity may be inevitable. The operation of a number of competitive privatization funds responds to the experience in East Germany where the process was concentrated in a single agency (the Treuhand) and became highly cumbersome and political. A multiplicity of funds offers the best chance of some competition in designing new ideas and methods in this largely unexplored region.

Implementation must go far beyond accepting the principle of privatization. It requires legal institutions, an ability to monitor compliance and more than rudimentary accounting to go along. If these are not available the privatization experience risks being needlessly messy, corrupt and socially controversial or even unacceptable.

The government urgently needs capital for reconstruction and the economies need dollars for survival and growth. In this context, foreign direct investment becomes a potent source of economic development. The USA, Canada, Latin America and Australia were developed by foreign direct investment, as was Central Europe. The argument that assets are "too cheap" and therefore foreigners should be kept out for the time being is fallacious. Assets are so cheap (in dollars or Deutschmarks) because there is such an acute uncertainty about the economic prospects of the region and no legal protection whatsoever.

A good case can be made for a capital gains tax to allow society to participate in windfalls, by exclusion of foreign investment from privatization is unjustified. Capital gains taxes are an effective way for society to share windfall profits or "unfair" gains of people who know better, move faster or have privileged access to capital.

Foreign direct investment brings the two bonuses of technology and know-how as well as market access abroad. Both are in desperately short supply today. It is doubtful whether Eastern Europe and the Soviet Union can afford even to think twice about a massive move into joint ventures. The experience of import penetration in East Germany, special of course but a warning nevertheless, suggests that consumers will simply turn away from traditional domestic goods. Therefore joint ventures that put foreign brand names on domestic products may be the cheapest way, and perhaps the only one, to maintain employment in the years to come.

Foreign direct investment will ultimately play a key role in rebuilding Eastern Europe. But policymakers need to be aware that even with very strong reform programs foreign direct investment may be slow to come. The reason is that investors do not suffer large costs in holding off their commitments until the current uncertainty is substantially resolved. The costs of coming a bit later are very small relative to the costs of entering only to find out that reforms are not implemented or simply fail. Investors' ability to hold off and wait means that governments have to work far harder to make their programs of stabilization both persuasive and lasting.[5]

7.7 Decontrol, convertibility, and protection

Convertibility for trade transactions plays a critical role for three reasons. First, the rest of the world provides an immediate reference system of prices. The ability to trade freely therefore ensures that resource allocation is driven into conformity with the alternative cost of resources. Second, trade provides competition and opportunity. It creates alternatives to the home market and it brings onto the market goods competitive with those supplied at home. While coming as a cultural shock to domestic firms, this is the shock consumers have in mind when they turn to imports. Third, ability to trade brings a country in touch with superior technology, processes and products. These in turn can enhance the competitiveness of domestic factors of production. The case for open trade cannot be made more dramatically than by the example of Eastern Europe, where product availability, quality and design are years behind the level of many less developed countries including Korea and Brazil.

All this argues for an immediate and unrestricted access to foreign markets, both for exporters and for importers. But it is important to put this reform in tune with domestic adjustments to avoid a vacuum. Clearly domestic price liberalization must go hand-in-hand with opening trade, since otherwise the highly distorted price structure leads to irrational trade patterns. Second, one must ask whether progress on the import and export side can be expected to be in lock-step. If not, and if imports rise sharply while exports only grow sluggishly, a major fall of economic activity could easily result. That occurred in East Germany.

7.7.1 *Protection*

In the aftermath of World War II, Western European countries delayed full convertibility until 1958. In some countries exchange controls lasted even longer than that, although European multilateral clearing started as early as 1950 with the European Payments Union. A similar scheme has been suggested as a means for slowing down the break-up of Comecon trade.

Economic planning has failed miserably; it is more than questionable, therefore, that new planning schemes should be introduced to keep alive a trade and production system that has demonstrated its failings beyond any doubt. But a case might be made in a large and relatively closed economy like the Soviet Union, to accompany full access to world markets with a high, uniform tariff. The tariff would ensure that for a while domestic firms enjoy some protection even though, at the margin, they will have to compete. It is far better to go this route than to postpone trade opening altogether on the argument that it leads to a loss of jobs.

7.7.2 *Countertrade*

The experience of East Germany suggests that import opening leads to an immediate, extreme displacement of domestic products by imports. It would seem that domestic products become "lemons"—goods for which there is no market price at which customers will buy them.[6] One answer is that domestic firms must immediately make arrangements to market those products (with whatever repacking that might be required) under foreign brand names. But there is also a case, in the context of convertibility and unrestricted trade, to engage in some countertrade transactions within the former Comecon.

Firms could make agreements for a year or two, at world prices, to trade with each other those goods which are of reasonable quality but would risk falling out of favor in the general stampede toward Western brands. Public sector procurement should work in this direction.

Countertrade must remain very minor and cannot change the basic reality of a need to adapt rapidly; in isolated cases, however, it can avoid the unnecessary collapse of firms.

7.7.3 *Capital account convertibility*

There is no reason whatsoever to liberalize the capital account completely for resident outflows. Unfortunately, however, the control of capital outflows is administratively hard. Rather than practicing multiple exchange rates or black markets, governments should grant full convertibility But they should not go overboard and encourage dollar deposits in the domestic banking system in those countries where a monetary breakdown has not occurred.

These considerations apply to countries that have not experienced a hyperinflation. With the risk of high and unstable inflation the ability to create money becomes a severe handicap and use of a foreign currency becomes a reasonable strategy.[7] In countries where inflation has become extreme and the currency is broken down it becomes plausible to make a very radical shift to using the dollar or the Deutschmark as the national currency.

7.7.4 *Exchange rate policy*

A common mistake in Latin America has been to use exchange rates as a means of controlling inflation, and the mistake is now emerging in Eastern Europe. Of course, in the short run a fixed exchange rate helps control inflation. But already in less than a year or two such a policy becomes a source of financial crisis. Realistic exchange rates, if necessary, crawling pegs, are the *sine qua non* of a successful open trade policy.

What can be said about the level of exchange rates? It is difficult to believe that any Eastern European country, or the Soviet Union, would have a chance in world trade if its wages were anywhere near the East German level. Once successfully integrated into the world market, with well-established brand names and stable markets, a country's wage level can be high. But at the beginning, without any stature, wages in dollars have to be extremely low. Table 7.4 offers a comparison of the main manufacturing countries. In looking at these data it helps to focus on Korea: what can Eastern Europe or the Soviet Union do better than South Korea? If there is little to show then the wage in dollars cannot be as high as that of South Korea.

7.8 Trade not aid

Industrial countries and specifically Western Europe have an important stake in the success of economic and political transition in the East. The response has been to provide money. That is desirable but ultimately will not be enough. A $50 billion subsidy to Eastern Europe and the Soviet Union in the next year or two does not go far enough to make a dramatic mark, yet it is a relatively large amount in the eyes of taxpayers.

The discussion about just how much to contribute and on what conditions obscures a far more basic point: if reform fails, citizens of Eastern Europe will

Table 7.4 Hourly compensation in manufacturing (1989 wage in US dollers; index: USA = 100)

United States	100	Korea	25
West Germany	123	Taiwan	25
Italy	92	Hong Kong	19
Japan	88	Singapore	22
France	89	Mexico	16
United Kingdom	73	Brazil	12
Spain	64		
East Germany[a]	40		

[a] Estimate by the author.
Note: The US compensation in 1989 was $14.3 per hour.
Source: US Department of Labor.

start migrating west *en masse*. We might see migration waves as dramatic as those of 1945. The experience of West Germany gives a foretaste. Time works against gradualism. Unless the success of reform becomes more and more plausible, literally by the month, selective migration will gain momentum. The West has basically only one possible response to offer, unrestricted free trade. That, in combination with economic reform, may draw the capital and expertise to turn Eastern Europe into a viable production location where reasonable wages can be paid.

The industrialized countries have not focused on this issue, hoping that it simply will not arise. But their reluctance to face it squarely and early works to the detriment of successful reform. The end of communism is rightly seen as one of the two most dramatic events in this century. It would be naïve to believe that there should be no repercussions in the economic sphere. Free trade is hard to swallow for the West, but the prospect of massive, unstoppable immigration should lead to a second thought.

A major economic integration with Europe opens the doors not only for goods. It also brings Eastern Europe culturally and politically back to the center. This integration in turn ensures a far easier flow of resources—technology, education and capital—and it becomes an important vehicle for political stability. The experiment worked extremely well in the case of Spain; it stands the same chances for Poland or Hungary and other countries in the East.

7.9 Finance

The first priority of financial reform is to clean out the balance sheets of firms and banks. The government implicitly or explicitly guarantees deposits in banks and owns both the creditor (banks) and the debtor (firms). An outright cancellation of domestic debts does not have any effects whatsoever on outside actors not does it pose moral hazard problems. This clearing of balance sheets ensures that companies can now be privatized without the encumbrance of debt and therefore can command higher prices. Even if they were not to generate higher prices there is still an advantage: in the next few years Eastern European interest rates will be high in real terms because stabilization will remain precarious. Hence there is a serious risk of bankruptcies for firms that carry high debt burdens. Moreover, even when debt burdens are not high, debt service interferes with the private ability to raise resources for investment in the prospective capital markets or abroad.

This clearing of balance sheets is all the more important in that debt burdens presently have no relation to a firm's assets. They may reflect a history of political pricing below cost rather than real assets. From this perspective, even the most attractive firm might be unprofitable simply because of its debt burden. The service of past debts should in no way become an obstacle to prospective profitability.

Debt cancellation is also essential for the banking system. If the banks are to compete with foreign entrants they need a clean balance sheet to start with. Otherwise the grave risk emerges that domestic banks have to charge high interest rates to cover their non-performing loans while foreign banks can compete with low rates. Foreign banks which charge lower rates could, of course, attract the best loan customers. Over time domestic banks would therefore worsen and in a vicious circle become ultimately the holders of most non-performing loans. Ultimately the government budget inherits the banking system since deposits will be insured. There is ample precedent for this process; examples are Chile, Turkey and even the US savings and loans crisis.

The next question is what kind of assets the financial system should be allowed to supply. Offering a wide range of financial products is *not* an early priority in economic reform.[8] If anything, we are finding out that this has been largely overdone in the West. But there is a need to create the basic vehicles for saving and intermediation. If savers do not have access to convenient and value-stable assets they will not save or they will find a way of taking their assets into dollars or abroad. Thus a financial system must be created from scratch, without time bombs in the balance sheets. The counterpart of deposit taking, of course, is lending. There is little expertise and the right response is to spread lending widely. The mistake to be avoided is that most of the resources go to keep alive large firms long beyond solvency. On the contrary, severe credit rationing might be a better strategy to help create new small and medium-sized firms that can create unemployment and growth.

Regulation of the financial system is critically important. Without regulation, but with *de facto* deposit insurance, financial instability becomes a very strong risk. Regulation must aim to avoid any substantial exposure of the banking system to foreign risk or the concentration of its lending on a few large firms or industries.

One other problem emerges on the financial agenda, namely to take a realistic view of external debt (see Table 7.5). One thinks here particularly of Hungary, where the government, for reasons that are hard to understand, serves debt fully

Table 7.5 Eastern Europe and the USSR: debt in 1987

	Debt[a]	Debt/Exports[b]	Price[c]
Bulgaria	7.6	205	20
Czechoslovakia	5.1	59	
East Germany	19.9	98	
Hungary	17.3	310	80
Poland	38.9	427	13
Romania	2.7	19	
Yugoslavia	22.5	113	54
USSR	40.0	48	

[a] Convertible currency debt, billion US dollars.
[b] Ratio of net external debt to exports to the market economies.
[c] Secondary market, cents per dollar
Sources: UN, World Bank and Salomon Brothers.

and punctually even though arrears with commercial banks are the cheapest and only source of external credit.

Few believe—given the exposure—that there will soon be new, unsecured commercial bank lending. Even for purposes of maintaining credit ratings, the case here looks as uncompelling as it does in Latin America. This is not to argue in favor of frivolous default, but rather that the West has a greater interest in the ultimate political stability and economic prosperity of the East than in the punctual service of relatively minor debts. The most plausible chance of debt service some time in the future is to use these resources now for reconstruction, building an economy that ultimately may be able to sustain the existing debt.

It is hard for political leaders in the West to encourage debt delinquency, but they should seriously assess this step for Eastern Europe. There is much talk today of the need for a Marshall Plan for the East. It would be mistaken use of official Western resources to use scarce foreign exchange to sustain debt service rather than make a major advance on reconstruction. Costa Rica's debt strategy, not that of Romania in the 1980s, ought to be the appropriate precedent for Eastern Europe today.

7.10 Concluding remarks: The great leap forward

Policymakers in Eastern Europe and the Soviet Union should not sacrifice priorities in trying to "manage" a soft landing. They now have to introduce the key changes that let economic agents look after most of the decisions. Markets must be allowed to spring up and solve the central task of creating employment and some standard of living. It is assumed that government can handle this better than the market, but why, then, are these countries so much of a mess, and why are they collapsing? The new leaders have a hard time allowing change to proceed; they rightly fear that there will be hardship. But they wrongly believe that they can avoid it by exercising discretionary controls and restrictions on production, employment, trade and property. These tools were discredited under communism; they should be thrown overboard immediately.

The no man's land between the market and repressive controls makes it impossible to carry forward an economy organized around the division of labor; economies will simply collapse as no signals are around to give direction as to the key questions: what to produce, for whom, and how. The worst scenario is that of a mixed economy: capitalism without profits and socialism without planning. There are two ways to go: backward to repressive control of politics and economics, as in China, or a great leap forward to the market.

With the great commitment to democracy in some countries, we can fortunately rest assured that communist repression will not be the answer. But democracy, with the initial conditions existing in Eastern Europe, is not enough to let markets function. Governments must implement without delay *pervasive* privatization of the economy and liberalization in respect to property and economic decisions. First let markets function, then decide whether and where some restraints are in order. Economic agents must be able to look ahead and decide what to do with their lives; unless the government steps out of their way the whole process cannot even begin. If reform proceeds hesitantly, economic collapse is certain and the market economy experiment becomes discredited before it even starts.

Notes

1. See Working Group (1990), unpublished manuscript, Brookings Institute, p. 1.
2. See Denton, Forsyth and Maclennan (1968), Sohmen (1959) and Dow (1964).
3. See Watrin (1979).
4. See Dornbusch, Sturzenegger and Wolf (1990) on the dynamics of extreme inflation.
5. See Dornbusch (1990) on the option value of waiting in the context of foreign investment.
6. See Akerlof (1970) for this problem.
7. See Dornbusch, Sturzenegger and Wolf (1990).
8. See the discussion in Polak (1989) and Dornbusch and Reynoso (1989).

References

Akerlof, G. (1970) "The Market for 'Lemons.' Quality Uncertainty and the Market Mechanism." *Quarterly Journal of Economics* 84: 488–500.

Arriagada, G. (1990) "Socioeconomic Transformation in Eastern Europe." Mimeo, Wilson Center, Washington, DC.

Blanchard, O., R. Dornbusch, P. Krugman, R. Layard, and L. Summers (1990) "Reform in East Europe and the Soviet Union." Mimeo, Wider.

Borenzstein, E. and M. Kumar (1990) "Proposals for Privatization in Eastern Europe." Mimeo, International Monetary Fund.

Corbo, V. and J. de Melo (1987) "Lessons from Southern Cone Policy Experiments." *World Bank Research Observer*, 2: 111–43.

Denton, G., M. Forsyth, and M. Maclennan (1968) *Economic Planning and Policies in Britain, France and Germany*. London: George Allen & Unwin.

Dornbusch, R. (1990) "The New Classical Macroeconomics and Stabilization Policy." *American Economic Review* 80(1) 143–7. (See Chapter 3, this volume.)

Dornbusch, R. and A. Reynoso (1989) "Financial Factors in Economic Development." *American Economic Review* 79: 204–9.

Dornbusch, R., F. Sturzenegger and H. Wolf (1990) "Extreme Inflation: Dynamics and Stabilization." *Brookings Papers on Economic Activity* 2: 1–84.

Dornbusch, R., and H. Wolf (1990) "Monetary Overhang and Reforms in the 1940s." CEPR Discussion Paper No. 464.

Dow, J. (1964) *The Management of the British Economy: 1945–1960*, Cambridge: Cambridge University Press.

Edwards, S. (1989) "On the Sequencing of Economic Reforms." NBER Working Paper No. 3138, October.

Fischer, S. and A. Gelb (1990) "Issues in Socialist Economy Reform." Mimeo, World Bank.

Hinds, M. (1990) "Issues in the Introduction of Market Forces in Eastern European Socialist Economies." Mimeo, World Bank.

McKinnon, R. (1982) "The Order of Economic Liberalization: Lessons from Chile." Carnegie Rochester Conference Series.

Müller-Armack, A. (1948) "Das Grundproblem unserer Wirtschaftspolitik: Rückkehr zur Marktwirtschaft." *Finanzarchiv* 11(1): 57–78.

Polak, J. (1989) *Financial Policies and Development*. Paris: OECD.

Portes, R., ed. (1990) "Economic Transformation in Hungary and Poland." *European Economy* No. 43, March (special issue).

Prust, J. *et al.* (1990) "The Czech and Slovak Federal Republic: An Economy in Transition." IMF Occasional Paper No. 72.

Richter, R., ed. (1979) "Currency and Economic Reform: West Germany after World War II." *Zeitschrift für die Gesamte Staatswissenschaft* 135(3), September (special issue).

Sohmen, E. (1959) "Competition and Growth: The Lesson of West Germany." *American Economic Review* 49(5).

Tumlir, J. and L. LaHaye (1981) "The Two Attempts at European Reconstruction after 1945." In R. Richter and W. Stolper, eds, "Economic Reconstruction in Europe: The Reintegration of Western Germany." *Zeitschrift für die Gesamte Staatswissenschaft* 137(3), September (special issue).

Urrutia, M. and S. Yukawa (1988) *Development Planning in Mixed Economies*. Tokyo: United Nations University.

Watrin, C. (1979) "The Principles of the Social Market Economy: Its Origins and Early History." In R. Richter, ed., "Currency and Economic Reform: West Germany after World War II." *Zeitschrift für die Gesamte Staatswissenschaft* 135(3). September (special issue).

8

A payments mechanism for the Commonwealth and Eastern Europe

Until recently, the United States and most of Western Europe strongly supported the existence of a united Soviet Union and actively discouraged a break-up. But the break-up has now occurred and the new Commonwealth structure is becoming a reality. For the time being it guarantees free trade and a common ruble area. But that may not last. In fact, Ukraine is thinking of introducing new coupons and may plan to require the use of these coupons in the purchase of goods. The introduction of national currencies has been postponed so far because of the sheer physical lack of new money. But it presumably remains a strong point on the political agenda of the new nationalism. Thus, if in a few months another round of disunion emerges, with new frontiers and new monies, an Eastern Payments Mechanism (EPM) might help avoid unnecessary trade collapse.

There are two reform options: one is that each and every country move immediately to convertibility, the other is to develop a mechanism such as the European Payments Union of the postwar period. Full and early convertibility is the preferred answer of economists and officials in the West, but politicians in the East are reluctant to go immediately all the way. They fear the loss of control just as Europe did in the postwar period. But as each country seeks control of its foreign exchange outlays or of its underpriced and hence scarce exports by itself and without thinking about the systemwide consequences of its policies, risks of a trade collapse increase sharply.

The payments mechanism proposed here is not a new idea by any means, nor is it a panacea (see, for example, van Brabant 1991; Havrylyshyn and Williamson 1991; Bofinger 1990; 1991a; 1991b; Gros 1991; and Kenen 1991). By itself, without complementary reforms it will do virtually nothing to improve the

I am indebted to George Soros, John Flemming and to participants at an IMF seminar for helpful suggestions. An earlier version of this paper was presented at a meeting with officials of the former USSR organized by the European Commission in Brussels, January 16–18, 1992.

outlook. But as part of a reform effort, and if full convertibility is not acceptable immediately and by all, it can help maintain trade among the republics and revive some of the trade with Eastern Europe that vanished needlessly. Trade between Cuba and the USSR was high almost exclusively for political reasons, but trade among the members of the CIS certainly has an important geographic motivation. There is no presumption that most of this trade should go overboard in favor of a dominant new trade orientation toward industrialized countries.

8.1 The problem and the risks

The breakdown of internal trade among various republics of the former Soviet Union is happening for a number of reasons. Each reason is enough to disrupt trade; together the effect is likely to be devastating. Just what can happen is made clear by a precedent.

First, Eastern Europe, in the transition from communist rule, is already witnessing a massive fall of trade within the region (Table 8.1). It might be argued that some trade should disappear, being based on plans rather than markets, but it is equally clear that *some* of the trade made perfect sense—Polish potatoes for Russian gas—but fell victim to some malfunction.

Second, the extraordinary degree of specialization of the republics makes each of the economies far more vulnerable to trade disruption than would be the case in the West. Massive reliance on scale economies led to the creation of firms so large that less than a handful supplied the entire Soviet market in a particular commodity group.

Belorussia offers perhaps the most extreme example of the degree of interdependence: more than 75 percent of the country's NMP is represented by foreign trade, nine-tenths of which is with other republics (Table 8.2).

The specialization brings with it the potential for an extraordinary chain reaction: with so much specialization, if deliveries fail anywhere, the entire chain of production in an industry can break down. The failure to have these final goods on hand for trading further widens the inability to import and produce.

Third, the lack of a price system makes it extremely unattractive to trade goods for rubles; barter is more attractive because at least there is a counterpart in

Table 8.1 The collapse of Eastern bloc trade: percentage decline in dollar exports, 1987–90

From/To	USSR*	Czechoslovakia	Hungary	Poland	E. Germany
USSR*	−46	−42	−41	−35	−53
Czechoslovakia	−43	–	−23	−32	–
Hungary	−46	−18	–	−52	–
Romania	−53	−70	−52	−82	–

USSR* denotes the USSR, Albania, Bulgaria, Cuba, E. Germany, Mongolia, and N. Korea.
Source: IMF, *Directory of Trade Statistics*.

Table 8.2 Trade dependence: percentage of net material product

	Exports		Trade balance[a]	
	Inter-republican	Total	Inter-republican	Total
Russia	18.0	36.8	28.5	41.3
Ukraine	39.1	45.8	−3.9	−5.4
Belorussia	69.6	76.1	−0.2	−2.5
Kazakhstan	30.9	33.8	−1.1	−7.7
Uzbekistan	43.2	50.5	0.1	−4.4

[a] In millions of rubles at world market prices.
Source: IMF *et al.* (1991).

goods received. But barter is hard to arrange and there is now a proliferation of competing authorities in different republics who might assert their claim to certain goods. This threat alone is cutting off trade.

Fourth, nationalism is emerging as an issue. From the republican perspective, sending goods to Moscow is being questioned, certainly if it is for rubles. Moscow is looking skeptically at delivering underpriced goods like oil or other tradable goods to the republics, as the opportunity cost of the implied subsidies is becoming crystal clear.

Fifth, lack of trust is the newest problem, a luxury that did not exist under central communist rule. With central control and enforcement gone, an institutional vacuum has opened up. If, for seasonal reasons or otherwise, a barter deal involves delays between receipt and shipment of goods, who is to know whether the quid pro quo will actually arrive? Without a guarantee mechanism, fewer trade risks will be taken, especially if nobody has any idea who might be responsible or liable for failure to deliver on a contract.

Sixth, the ruble is no longer an effective medium of exchange for the entire CIS. This situation has arisen in part because of the lack of internal convertibility (i.e. there is no price system) and in part because of its deteriorating quality as an asset (i.e. the black market purchasing power of the ruble in terms of goods and foreign exchange is vanishing). But even the limited usefulness of this currency is being put in question by the possibility of imminent monetary reforms which will introduce new moneys and freeze or just write off old ones.

Seventh, with an opening to the West, captive markets for goods are disappearing and alternative sources of supply are growing. Because of a desire to take advantage of the new markets, dollars could assume an entirely special quality because they can allow direct access to *any* good *now*. Rubles, it is feared, will get you nothing now and less later. Given this perception, a dollar shortage might emerge. If this happens, settling inter-republican imbalances in hard currency will seem less unattractive than cutting down on imports to save scarce foreign exchange for trade with the West. Of course, trade restriction is a two-way street; if one country contracts, the other experiences larger imbalances and will have to cut down in turn.

Eight, bilateral barter is an extraordinarily primitive way of conducting trade. People can become experts at these deals, but this form of trade is still unquestionably inefficient. Moreover, with strategic goods such as oil or food in the balance, there is a grave risk that countries might be forced into bargains far away from the market. In fact, the focus on strategic goods makes countries try and exert control even more fully over goods at their command in order to take more chips to the bargaining table. As a result, trade tends to shrink.

8.2   Essentials

An ideal economic system to facilitate trade has the following characteristics: in each country there exists an operating price system; no restrictions on the right to trade; no obstacles to trade such as tariffs, permits or quotas; a fully convertible (i.e. no exchange control or licenses) and stable currency; and a well-functioning system of trade credit. Such an economy is not in place now and there is little prospect of creating it overnight. It is tempting to maintain an uncompromising insistence that reformers go for nothing less than this, but there are few examples in history to encourage that position. To be fair, in the succession to the Austro-Hungarian empire Czechoslovakia went far in fulfilling the conditions, but who else did?

Even if certain republics managed to implement the complete set of reforms, unless all do, their interaction will pose difficulties. Trade problems emerge as much from the best performer, who can exercise choice, as from the worst, who can only react to the external effects of internal mismanagement by increasing degrees of trade restriction. A pessimistic view of the chances of reform, in extent and timing, therefore aims at a system that incorporates countries at various stages of reform where some are far behind others.

Price reform is the only *absolute* prerequisite to maintain trade. The role previously played by plan and coercion, and now weakly sustained by sheer inertia, has to be augmented by a price system. Without price reform goods will not move, at least not in official hands. In the West, sellers send Christmas cards to buyers. In the Soviet Union, the cards go to the sellers since, with goods underpriced in terms of rubles, the latter are in command. For goods to move, sellers have to be willing to part with them. Without effective coercion (administration), prices are the only way to accomplish this.

If the government were unusually able and effective, a gradual and strategic decontrol might be possible. But the cruel fact is that the government is not in a position to administer an ambitious program of staged decontrol. The absence of both *command* and *prices* leaves economic actors without a blueprint on how to keep afloat an immensely specialized economy. Precisely because the economy is so specialized, because scale went hand-in-hand with command, the vulnerability today is extreme and the need for prices acute. Prices and markets are an effective means to decontrol decisions. In the no man's land between coercion and a price system with markets and institutions decentralized economies simply cease functioning.

One argument for price controls is their use as a means of maintaining an affordable supply of food to the people. However, postponing price liberalization for food risks major distribution problems, including the threat of unrest as troops help themselves, republics refuse to give up goods, and others have no means but coercion to get access. In the same way, mispricing of raw materials and intermediate goods leads to their hoarding or diversion to world markets with the result that final goods production grinds to a standstill. The extreme degree of specialization at the final goods stage makes this problem particularly threatening.

Recognizing the parallel with Poland is appropriate (for an account of the Polish experience, see Sachs 1991). The radical price liberalization in Poland makes one thing certain—nobody is talking about famine. In Poland, unlike in the Soviet Union, goods are available in the shops. Of course, for most people, the perception is that the goods are there, but who can afford them? But even that question understates the progress. The availability of goods has become a powerful engine in motivating people to work harder, take initiatives, and find ways to earn the incomes which represent the tickets for goods. In the USSR, Poland's performance is often viewed with horror and portrayed as the one course that is unacceptable. A more mature view is that only in the most optimistic scenario can the Soviet Union make the required adjustments as effectively as was done in Poland.

It is neither necessary that there be a single money nor that the various monies that come into existence are particularly hard. In each country government can regulate as they wish who can participate in foreign trade and what incentives or disincentives they might be offered. Even so, by joining a payments mechanism they all stand to benefit. Before developing the specific advantages, we briefly review the EPU which can serve as a prototype for the mechanism that might be created.

8.3   The European Payments Union[1]

Western Europe emerged from World War II with price control, demilitarization problems, soft and inconvertible currencies, and massive trade restrictions that were meant to conserve the very scarce foreign exchange. Bilateral barter trade was the rule. But the inefficiency of bilateral balancing quickly became burdensome.

Two problems in particular needed attention. One problem was the need for some "swing", i.e. short-term credit lines that would allow countries to avoid the need for strict balancing of bilateral trade each month. The other problem was the inability to use a multilateral offset mechanism which would allow a country to use its net balance with one European country as a means of settling a bilateral deficit with another.

In postwar Europe every country tried to run surpluses in bilateral trade and acquire in settlement dollars which then could be used for trade with countries like the USA. The strategy used to earn surpluses was, of course, a sure way to lead to trade contraction via restrictions. The Intra-European Payments and Compensation System (IEPS) made some headway in introducing multilateral clearing. But not until the establishment of the EPU was a comprehensive mechanism developed.

The basic provisions of the EPU were as follows. First, the system operated by the BIS interacted with the central banks in each member country. Once a month the central banks would report their total *net* claims on each member. These claims would be calculated on the basis of the declared dollar parity of the respective members. The agent would undertake multilateral clearing, offsetting surpluses with one country and deficits with another to arrive at the net position. A country would be credited for the total net dollar balance, or debited if there was a total net deficit.

Second, the extent of credit in the system was determined by quotas and cumulative creditor or debtor positions. Each country would receive a quota based on its "turnover," defined as exports plus imports. This quota would determine, according to a system of "tranches," the access to credit.

The financing of imbalances proceeded according to the criterion of *cumulative* imbalances of a member with the Union since the beginning of the EPU. The first 20 percent of the quota could be used without restrictions. But if a country built up further imbalances, a portion had to be settled in gold or dollars and only the remainder was financed by credit. The exact share to be settled in hard currency was 50:50 (with some variation over time). Once a quota was exhausted, the settlement of imbalances had to be made fully in hard currency.

Creditors received a portion of their cumulative balances settled in hard currency and agreed to extend credit for the rest.

Third, countries progressively liberalized trade among the membership.

Fourth, the United States politically supported the establishment of the EPU and helped capitalize it. A strong and unified Europe was seen as the strongest defense against communism.

Fifth, the EPU functioned from 1950 until 1958, when most members took their currencies to full current account convertibility. The initial agreement provided for a two-year, renewable operation. Subsequent renewals were for one-year periods. A simple majority of members (as represented by quotas) could ask for dissolution and final settlement.

Sixth, the EPU was managed by a board that would make recommendations when payments problems emerged. And, although difficulties did emerge at the outset, peer pressure proved highly effective in bringing about adjustment.

Table 8.3 Quotas and cumulative EPU balances (millions of US dollars)

	Quota	1950	1951	1952
Austria	70	−37.4	−130.6	−108.8
Belg.-Lux	360	21.8	604.3	761.3
Denmark	195	−38.4	−33.5	−27.3
France	520	212.4	−196.9	−625.7
Germany	500	−356.7	431.4	366.0
Greece	45	−70.8	−186.7	−229.0
Iceland	15	−3.3	−8.5	−12.5
Italy	205	−30.9	195.2	104.9
Netherlands	355	−107.9	−53.1	266.3
Norway	200	−51.1	−70.1	−76.9
Portugal	70	36.8	97.4	66.7
Sweden	260	0	177.2	208.8
Switzerland	250	−12.6	141.0	195.6
Turkey	50	5.3	−98.9	−218.1
UK	1060	433.0	−469.0	−682.2

Source: Patterson and Gunn (1952).

Table 8.4 An EPU history, 1950–58 (figures in billions of US dollars)

Total bilateral positions[a]	46.4
Settled by:	
Multilateral compensation	20.0
Compensation through time	12.6
Gold and dollars	10.7
Special settlements	0.5
Credit balance outstanding[b]	2.7

[a] Sum of monthly surpluses and deficits.
[b] The credit balance in 1958 was settled by special arrangements between net debtors and creditors, primarily France and Germany.
Source: Yeager (1966).

Table 8.3 gives an impression of persistence and reversals of cumulative creditor positions. Since quotas were set at 15 percent of 1949 turnover, the imbalances were substantial. Where they exceeded quotas special arrangements had been made.

The entire history of the EPU can be summarized by examining the data presented in Table 8.4. The total sum of imbalances (double-counting) was $46.4 billion. Somewhat less than half was immediately cleared by multilateral offsetting. This fact supports the claim that multilateralism *does* take away the strain of bilateral balancing. About a third ($12.6 billion) was settled by credit and subsequent reversal of imbalances. Thus a country would borrow from the union for some time and then run a string of surpluses that would extinguish the debt. Settlement in hard currency amounted to just under a quarter, so clearly there was hard currency discipline in the system which increased in the late 1950s.

8.4   The relevance of an EPM: Questions and answers

What is the advantage of the mechanism?
Multilateral clearing and limited credit avoid a state of siege on the trade front. It allows fewer restrictions designed to save hard currencies for trade with the outside world.

Even if there is a case for a payments mechanism, why not go all the way to convertibility? In fact, is a payments mechanism not really an obstacle to full reform?
Full convertibility is desirable at the earliest possible stage. In Europe it took until 1958 and it is clear in hindsight that the slowest countries were using the convenience of the mechanism to slow down those which could have moved faster. But the EPU also created an important trade zone which might not have arisen if countries had moved individually, made mistakes and simply rolled back convertibility.

It is essential today to maintain an open internal market in the East. With competitive restraints on exports and limits on imports arising from exchange shortage, the Soviet Union's successor countries would experience a catastrophic decline in their standard of living. The payments union helps build the common market and can evolve increasingly to full convertibility—say, in three or four years, or even in two— by simply increasing the portion of imbalances that has to be settled in hard currency. If that portion is 100 percent, that corresponds to full convertibility.

Can an EPM be used even when countries have different currencies?
Yes. The point of the mechanism is to use the offsetting of balances so that no hard currency is used for settlement. The credit mechanism (with discipline) is another means to save on foreign exchange.

How can one be sure that a country is not cheated by the system?
The member countries jointly guarantee the credits. It is (barely) conceivable that a country might walk out, but the remaining ones would still be guarantors of the shared balance. Of course, it also gives group sanction to raise the cost of upsetting the system. And if the West supports the system, then Western sanctions in the form of reduced aid will be an effective way to give the system confidence.

What discipline does the system create to cope with large cumulative deficits?
Hard currency settlement for a fraction of the cumulative imbalance ensures that deficits are not free—they have to be settled in dollars. As countries will run out of dollars and reach their quota ceiling they will have to make adjustments or reach the point where they settle 100 percent in dollars.

After price reform some republics could have large deficits because they import vital goods such as oil. How can the payments union help?

The payments mechanism can only help bring about multilateralism and limited credit. It is not primarily a mechanism for transfers or aid. Countries which import oil will want to set prices at world levels and bring about conservation. Russia may or may not decide to make transfers, but it cannot afford to misprice oil or any other tradable good for very long.

The settlement of imbalances on the basis of *cumulative* imbalances implies that a country which runs a deficit month after month moves quickly into upper tranches of the credit line and has to settle increasingly in hard currency.

How do firms in one country trade with those in another if their currency is inconvertible?
In each member country there will probably be exchange control regulations that will specify the transactions for which firms can make contracts abroad. With a payments union, the set of goods that is liberalized for intra-union trade tends to be wider than what is liberalized for trade with countries outside the union. Firms pay their central bank in local currency (at the official exchange rate) for their imports or they receive from their central bank the local currency equivalent of their exports.

Price reform and realistic exchange rates imply that countries can afford to liberalize aggressively and to be quite free in the allocation of foreign exchange. It would be desirable, as a condition of membership, that countries maintain the same (dollar) exchange rate for trade in the union and with third countries.

Isn't there a risk that the system will not last very long? Structural deficit countries will quickly exhaust their reserves and that is the end of the mechanism.
Not so. When a country has used its full credit quota that simply means no further credit is available and all imbalances must be settled in hard currency. It still leaves for this country the benefit of multilateral offsetting and for everyone else that benefit plus the credit mechanism. In analogy with credit cards, people who have used their credit line can still use their card, they just have to pay the bill at the end of the month.[2]

Does a payments mechanism free foreign exchange reserves?
Yes. Since, for intra-system use, there is no need to settle in hard currency (except in higher tranches). As a result, foreign exchange can be used rather than held. Precisely because foreign exchange needs are reduced and a temporal credit cushion is in place, countries do not need to play overly defensive strategies as they would in a reserve shortage situation.

The reserve issue is particularly important for two reasons. First, when countries do not have access to external credit (and this is patently the case for the CIS), reserve holdings are the only buffer. If reserve levels are low then trade and payments policies will be highly defensive and thus the uncoordinated system is forced into a low-trade mode. Second, intra-CIS trade is very high relative to external trade. Thus the gains from a regional payments mechanism are substantial.

Can countries pick their own exchange rate? What if they pick the wrong one?
Countries must learn to select an exchange rate at which their trade balances
(except for transfers from the West). When they have deficits, spending must be
reduced and competitiveness increased. There may be some room for temporary
trade restrictions to achieve balance, but the discipline of the settlements
mechanism will force countries to have exchange rates at which they can
maintain external balance.

*How can the mechanism start to work if the new countries do not even have hard
currency reserves?*
The West, in funding the system, can put into the mechanism a starting pot.
Participating countries will then discipline each other so that nobody overuses
the endowment.

*After so many years under the domination of Moscow, now that they are finally
independent, should the new states not seek immediately a link with the West and get
away from inter-republican trade? Is that not what Czechoslovakia and Poland did?*
Trade with the West will certainly be an important feature of the emerging foreign
trade pattern. But why sacrifice productive inter-republican trade? Instead,
much of that trade can continue, once it is based on market prices rather than
planners' mistakes. Eastern Europe will certainly make a serious mistake if it
sacrifices opportunities in the East to narrow-minded nationalism. It is certainly
better to have a prosperous neighbor than one whose collapse of trade leads to
economic difficulties and political risk. The West will insist on economic
cooperation as the quid pro quo for economic aid. It can accept limited trade
discrimination (including Eastern Europe) as a way of establishing a viable
economic zone in the East.

*The multilateral offsetting of balances and the credit mechanism are obviously
attractive, but should there not be the same trade policy applied to other republics
and the rest of the world? Why favor members in the system?*
In the case of the EPU, trade barriers were erected to protect scarce foreign
exchange. Dollars were scarce since they represented access to capital goods and
raw materials. In the Soviet Union, just as in Eastern Europe, there will be a
shortage of foreign exchange unless real exchange rates are set at outright
impoverishing levels. Some protection against the outside helps save at least part
of the economic structure.

If the exchange rate is uniform and trade is open, what protects domestic
economic activity? The first answer is that a highly competitive exchange rate
will. Imports will be very expensive and exports will be very profitable. Thus
domestic production will be favored. But there is also a case for going further. In a
transition period, while agents learn to interact with the world economy, a
protective tariff is appropriate. The case for a tariff lies in the experience of East
Germany, where domestic goods were uniformly treated as "lemons"—everything from the West was better, even eggs. To avoid a wholesale collapse of

demand for domestic goods a competitive, uniform exchange rate can be supplemented with a uniform tariff which declines over a five-year period from 50 to 10 percent.

The argument for a tariff used here is a variant of that used to protect infant industries. It applies to the supply side, where learning about enhancing product design and quality will make domestic products increasingly desirable over time. It also applies to the consumer where the initial instinct to go all out for Western goods creates an externality since it involves a far more competitive exchange rate and lower real wage than would apply if a "buy-CIS" effect is induced by a tariff. But it is important to use a uniform tariff rather than quotas or licenses because the CIS needs competition, even if it is only at the margin where a tariff ceases to offer protection.

Could countries with convertible currencies participate in the mechanism? Specifically, could and should Poland or Czechoslovakia be a member?
There is no reason for countries like Poland not to join and use the multilateral offsetting mechanism and the credit mechanism. Polish firms would take advantage only if it were profitable and the same is true of the republics. The advantage is this: countries that would run deficits with Poland if trade is settled in dollars would be reluctant to let trade flourish even if they had surpluses in the system with other countries. Trade restrictions would needlessly kill off trade while, with a clearing mechanism, the imbalances could be offset multilaterally. On the trade front, too, broadening the free trade area to include Eastern Europe would be in everybody's interest.

Is there any evidence from the experience of the EPU in the 1950s that a payments union slows down the progress toward convertibility?
Current account convertibility was achieved gradually in the 1950s. Countries with a persistently strong external balance, such as Germany, moved ahead with trade liberalization. Other countries followed more gradually. It is clear that convertibility could have been achieved earlier, but it is not clear whether that would not have occurred at the price of a less rapid and pervasive trade liberalization. The annual renewal of the EPU was at least a mechanism to keep an eye on the target of convertibility. Moreover, Switzerland was a member even though the currency was fully convertible. The EPU experience brings out the connection between trade and payments liberalization; trade restrictions may come off more rapidly if a payments arrangement makes countries less vulnerable to external balance swings.

Why does the IMF seem so ambivalent, if not downright hostile, toward such a system?
The same was true in the 1950s. The IMF adopted a hands-off policy with respect to the EPU which was seen as a competing forum for policy discussion and surveillance. As a result, the IMF lost its effectiveness with respect to Western Europe. An extra factor might be this: the IMF is anxious to avoid the creation of

new, bad monies. Of course, a single and very bad money (which is the current situation) might be even worse.

8.5   Conclusion

As central management weakens there is need to define national independence on the economic front. If the republics do not take the initiative in reforming, trade will inevitably collapse. And with the trade collapse may come a dramatic fall of all economic activity and public order. If they introduce new money which turns out to be soft and thus inconvertible, trade problems will emerge almost immediately. Reserve shortages will soon lead to competitive trade restrictions.

Among the urgent priorities of a newly independent country is price liberalization to bring goods back to the market and into production. The price reform includes the choice of a realistic exchange rate. Another immediate step is the creation of a coordinating mechanism that bridges the borders and facilitates to the maximum the exchange of goods. Third in priority is monetary reform, including balancing the budget and dealing with the ruble overhang.

Most reforms have to do with the operation of the domestic economy—price liberalization, property rights, etc.—where there is little role for outsiders. But the West *can* play an important role in the setting up of a payments union. The help of the West can come in three areas. First, in designing the technical set-up and using utmost pressure (as the United States did in the creation of the EPU) to push the scheme ahead and get it implemented. This impetus is necessary because each internal party will seek modalities that meet their short-run situation and there is not much room to do this.

Second, the West can capitalize and guarantee the mechanism. This does not take much since most of the credit (except for special arrangements) is extended by the members. In the case of the EPU, the United States contributed capital of $270 million.[3]

Third, the West can administer the mechanism. This might be done by the BIS, as in the case of the EPU, or by a central bank such as the Bank of Sweden. But the agent would only keep the books. Just as in the case of the EPU, the burden of liberalizing and dealing with crises falls on the members, who must learn how to live with one another.

Economic efficiency will thrive in a regime where convertibility comes soon. But, if the margin for error in an immediate move to convertibility is very high, it is better that the change happens more slowly. Full convertibility in three years is better than a reaction against quick action which leads to trade restrictions and inconvertibility for a long time to come. Moreover, there are strong economic arguments in support of the proposition that the CIS, and preferably all the countries of Eastern Europe, become a vast free trade zone. However, members of such a free trade area might want to maintain temporary restrictions on imports from the West. Of course, the economics is quite clear on the most efficient form of such restrictions, namely a uniform tariff at a moderate rate. Just to give a benchmark, some have argued 40 percent. This protection would help to offset the extraordinary advantages of the West along the lines of the infant-industry argument.

Notes

1. See Milward (1984), Kaplan and Schleiminger (1989), Yeager (1966), and Patterson and Gunn (1952).
2. I owe the analogy to Michael Mussa.
3. James Boughton of the IMF estimates that an equivalent funding today would require $1.8 billion.

References

Aghion, P., J. Flemming, and J. Pisani-Ferry (1991) "A Framework for a Multilateral Clearing Scheme." Mimeo, European Bank, London.

Bofinger, P. (1990) "A Multilateral Payments Union for Eastern Europe?" Discussion Paper No. 458. London: Center For Economic Policy Research.

Bofinger, P. (1991a) "Options for the Payments and Exchange Rate System in Eastern Europe." *European Economy* (special issue: "The Path of Reform in Central and Eastern Europe") No. 2: 243–62.

Bofinger, P. (1991b) "The Difficult Path to Convertibility in the Soviet Union." Mimeo, Landeszentralbank Baden-Württemberg.

Collignon, S. (1991) "A Proposal to Create an ECU Zone to Assist Eastern Europe's Transition to a Market Economy." Mimeo, Paris: Association for the Monetary Union of Europe.

Greene, J. and P. Isard (1991) *Currency Convertibility and the Transformation of Centrally Planned Economies*. IMF Occasional Paper No. 81. Washington, DC: International Monetary Fund.

Gros, D. (1991) "A Soviet Payments Union?" Mimeo, CEPS, Brussels.

Havrylyshyn, O. and J. Williamson (1991) *From Soviet DisUnion to Eastern Economic Community?* Policy Analysis in International Economics No. 35. Washington, DC: Institute for International Economics.

International Monetary Fund *et al.* (1991) *A Study of the Soviet Economy*, Washington, DC: International Monetary Fund.

Kaplan, J. and G. Schleiminger (1989) *The European Payments Union*. Oxford: Oxford University Press.

Kenen, P. (1991) "Transitional Arrangements for Trade and Payments Among the CMEA Countries." *IMF Staff Papers* 38(2).

Milward, A. (1984) *The Reconstruction of Western Europe 1945–51*. Berkeley: University of California Press.

Patterson, G. and J. Gunn (1952) *Survey of the United States International Finance 1952*. Princeton, NJ: Princeton University Press.

Sachs, J. (1991) "The Economic Transformation of Eastern Europe. The Case of Poland." Mimeo, Harvard University.

Soros, G. (1991) "An Interrepublican Payments System." Mimeo, New York: The Soros Foundation.

van Brabant, J. (1991) "Key Problems in Creating a Central European Payments Union." *Banca Nazionale del Lavoro Quarterly Review* No. 177 (June): 119–50.

Williamson, J. (1991) *Currency Convertibility in Eastern Europe.* Washington, DC: Institute for International Economics.

Yeager, L. (1966) *International Monetary Relations.* New York: Harper & Row.

9

Monetary problems of post-communism: Lessons from the end of the Austro-Hungarian empire

The transition experience of the former Soviet Union seems to offer almost unrivalled challenges: if the politics is difficult, the economics seems almost unsurmountable. Yet, for many of the transition issues faced by Russia and other republics of the CIS today, there is in fact precedent. The break-up of the Austro-Hungarian empire from 1919 to 1924 brings up many of the same questions and it is therefore interesting to review that experience and to ask what lessons might be learned from the 1920s that have relevance for the CIS experience today.[1]

All too often, it is argued that a country's experience is so unique that outsiders cannot possibly understand exactly what the problem is and what good solutions might exist. And more importantly, analogies from other countries, past or present, are invariably rejected as irrelevant or at best superficially similar but failing in essential ways. It is all too common to be told "you don't understand, this country is different." But, more often than not, the similarities with other experiments are striking, the mistakes are the same, and one cannot help commenting on this with some cynicism: even the rationalization for radically wrong strategies is the same.[2]

The case of the CIS does have a claim to novelty and perhaps for that reason might not lend itself to parallels. After all, the transition from a full-fledged command economy to the market is a totally new experiment and certainly has an important bearing on events and remedies to be prescribed. And there is another difference: Moscow is not Vienna. They may be comparable in the concentration of bureaucracy and intellectual talent in the capitals, but Moscow

---

Expanded version of a lecture delivered at the Institute of World Economics, Kiel, on the occasion of being awarded the Bernhard Harms Prize at the Kiel Institute on June 27, 1992. Thanks go to Horst Siebert, the president of the Institute, and his colleagues for the warm hospitality at the Institute and the lively discussion. Guy Debelle provided helpful research assistance.

is rich in resources, notably oil, while Vienna had nothing to offer on its side of a bargain and by 1919 had lost everything except its debts and bureaucrats. Yet, in the area of macroeconomics, and beyond, analogies do apply and thus I propose here to explore what is relevant in the 1920s experience.

The case of the Austro-Hungarian empire is a profitable analogy for three reasons. First, many of the issues connected with the emergence of new states and the problems of nationalism were present at the time. Second, a major upheaval occurred with questions about the appropriate economic regime—socialism or communism then, the market today. Finally, there was a major role to play in stabilization and normalization for the winners of the time, by analogy the West today.

Among, the most interesting lessons are those concerning monetary arrangements and external intervention. The current IMF strategy of favoring a ruble zone, despite the lack of any structure for controlling deficits across new national borders (or even within) can only end in the uncontrolled disarray that was witnessed in 1919–20 in the former empire. Moreover, the appropriate intervention is more likely than that which ultimately occurred in Austria and Hungary— League of Nations resident Commissioners, rather than timid IMF missions tendering $1 billion, more with a mind to elections in the United States than the determined and forceful reform and reconstruction of Russia.

Another lesson is the grave effects of a nationalistic break-up and the role the outside world can play in supporting constructive policies that recognize the new sovereignty of the parts but also keep in perspective their interdependence. And there is a grave risk that Russia has learnt all too quickly from Brazil; an IMF agreement need not mean more than a temporary good advertisement and a key to some helping of money and then, soon, another one. There is also a lesson which is relevant for the industrial countries as a group: effective assistance should come early, with a high level of engagement and with strong commitments on the part of recipient parliaments.

9.1   The curses of post-communism

A pessimistic, although accurate description of the present problems is captured by the five curses of post-communist societies: unstable politics; budget deficits; nationalism; lack of economic institutions; and the withering interest of the West.

9.1.1   *Unstable politics*

Any young, active democracy has to find a center of gravity. Invariably that task is difficult to achieve quickly. Argentina had a hard time, the Philippines are witnessing their difficulty, Brazil has been in a lingering crisis for a decade, Weimar Germany had its trouble and Russia today is no different.

In the CIS, there are pervasive remnants of the communist elite who hold power in the parliaments and even in the administration. In Ukraine the same communist president rules now as then, Belorussia has not seen much change, and in Russia's parliament conservative forces represent a hefty weight. The mix of the forces of reaction and a broad, divided group of parties ranging from nationalists to entrepreneurs makes it difficult to build a political coalition. In such a situation, reform measures that carry a heavy dose of discomfort or represent threats to the status quo are difficult to deliver. Far easier is populism—promise the sky, full steam ahead.

9.1.2 *Budget deficits*

Budget deficits are large and perhaps extremely large—5 percent of GNP, 10 percent or more. The deficits are predominantly financed by money. Previous experience with extreme inflation shows that sooner or later deficit finance does translate into accelerating inflation. From there, it is often a short step to uncontrolled inflation: erosion of the real yield from taxation, exchange collapse, indexation, and dollarization are the accelerating forces that make it a short step from 500 percent inflation to 1,000, 10,000 percent and beyond.

But for the time being, warnings fall mostly on deaf ears. "Politically impossible" has become the international vocabulary for dismissing out of hand the need for early and firm budget balancing. Because inflation has not exploded to phenomenal levels (yet), complacency seems almost warranted. But there is an old truth in this business: explosion of the economy takes much longer to come than one thinks; but when it does come, it happens much faster than one would have thought.

9.1.3 *Nationalism*

The repressive empire organized by Stalin and his successors left no room for dissent. With the breakdown, new republics have emerged and as they define themselves, nationalism is the central theme. To some extent that is normal and perhaps even good. But clearly, it is being carried to extremes in many places. Minorities are locked up in enclaves and want to assert their self-determination; religious minorities want to give expression to their individuality. The communist elite is among the chief driving forces of this nationalist movement; putting themselves at the head has given them an extra lease on political and economic leadership.

Nationalism in some places has exploded into civil war, with its obvious destructive consequences. In these regions it will take decades to repair the damage and perhaps much more since these feelings have been simmering underground for decades. But even in more moderate cases, economic nationalism—turning away from Moscow dominance and from trade—is costly enough. The breakdown of intra-CIS trade and the risk of tariff walls and quotas is a real possibility. Administrative disarray and backwardness are one reason we have not seen more. The other is that Russia has much to offer—cheap petroleum—and the other republics have much to lose.

9.1.4 *Lack of economic institutions*

The former Soviet economy is trapped between a command economy that no longer functions and a market economy that functions at best sporadically. Institutions are missing pervasively: there is no basic economic law that entitles people to pursue economic profit in any way not specifically denied; there are few, if any, legal institutions, and the ability to seek remedies under the law is more than limited. In fact, it is even hard to set free people who are in jail for having pursued profitmaking too early or too successfully. While championing the free market, the government has not understood the basic message of free market economics, namely that it offers decentralization. Policymakers desperately hang on to control. There is no shortage of decrees, but there is a gaping shortage of commitment to letting a market economy actually come into being at the cost of political power and control.

Marz (1991, p. 102) comments on the lack of revolutionary preparedness of the new policymakers who came to power in Vienna in 1919: "the socialist economic constitution of the future was defined by the empty notion of the 'socialization of the means of production', which could be filled with co-operative, syndicalist, or Utopian ideas depending on individual attitudes." There is some of this same lack of revolutionary preparedness in the indecisiveness in burning the bridges with communism, that is apparent in the republics of the former Soviet Union. The issue is not that the blueprints have not been prepared, it is much more that the notion of a market economy is acceptable only as a principle, but not in the details. In Vienna of 1919, socialization was a foregone conclusion, except it never happened because nobody could agree on the details.

9.1.5 *The withering interest of the West*

The interest of the West was intense while daily events dominated the news and while the nuclear risk seemed large and plausible. But by now the interest of the West is waning. The risk of nuclear accidents is diminished—either in reality or at least in wishful thinking—and the risks of conventional warfare from the East have all but vanished.

Now that the novelty and fear have worn off, the West is losing interest. By now it is already impossible to marshal the enthusiasm for a large program. The IMF is being moved to the center of the stage so that political leaders can move away before the bad news arrives. There is no surprise in this disengagement. After all, Russia is no larger than Brazil and once the threat is gone, the excitement also vanishes and with it the willingness for major international action.

Against this background, what can be learned from the Austro-Hungarian experience, following World War I?

9.2 The Austro-Hungarian transition

The empire was made up of a number of different ethnic groups, dominated by Austria and by Hungary. Austria and Hungary had some separation in the conduct of their affairs, but for the regions and minorities there was a strong subordination to Vienna and Prague, respectively. As Pasvolsky (1928) and Seton-Watson (1962) report, the political integration was precarious and the suppression of ethnic minorities vigorous. (Between Austria and Hungary the agreement was: "You keep a lid on your Slavs and we'll watch ours.")

Economic integration of the various groups was complete. For our purpose there are three decisive points:

- There was a monetary union with full control vested in the Austro-Hungarian bank in Vienna.
- The empire was run as a joint fiscal operation, with the separate budgets in Austria and Hungary contributing to the common imperial expenditures and the debt service.
- The various parts of the empire formed a free trade area with substantial economic integration as a result of the distribution of resources.

Starting in 1916–17, Austria increasingly lost control of the economic integration. In the face of food shortages and price controls, various regions increasingly held back supplies, thus reducing Vienna to near-famine conditions. Political integration, too, broke down. In fact, in the last phase of the war, Czech troops sided with the Allies and some other ethnic groups did much the same. Political control was lost as the role of the monarchy and the entire political system were put in question by the communist revolution in Russia and the spread of radical political ideas to Central Europe and the West.

9.2.1 *The disintegration*

In the fall of 1918 came both the armistice and with it the end of the empire. Walre de Bordes (1924, p. 7) offers a vivid picture of the accumulated hatreds and of the special disdain for Vienna:

> With the disruption of the Monarchy the barriers of all the longstanding national, political and economic jealousies had been broken. The Czechs, the Yugoslavs, the Poles and Hungarians hastened to seal up the issues of their new frontiers ...
> Vienna was regarded as a gigantic parasite, the city of lotus-eating idlers.

In rapid succession, there were revolutions in various regions, declarations of independence, a brief attempt to sustain the monarchy in Austria and then the declaration of the Austrian Republic. Provisional governments took over and tried to establish a new order.

Table 9.1 The dismemberment of the Austro-Hungarian empire

	Austrian empire		Hungarian kingdom	
	territory[a]	population[b]	territory[a]	population[b]
Prewar status	300.0	28.6	324.4	20.9
Ceded to:				
Austria	79.6	6.6	5.1	0.4
Hungary	—	—	92.7	7.9
Czechoslovakia	77.8	9.8	62.9	3.6
Romania	10.4	0.8	102.8	5.3
Yugoslavia	29.3	1.7	66.5	4.1
Poland	80.3	8.4	—	—
Italy	22.6	1.5	—	—

[a] Square kilometers.
[b] Population in millions.
Source: Pasvolsky (1928).

By November 1919 there were *de facto* independent countries, even though it would take another year for them to be recognized by the peace treaties of St Germain and Trianon.[3] In Austria the Republic was proclaimed with the avowed objective of joining Germany in a union. The ultimate redistribution of territory and population is shown in Table 9.1. Czechoslovakia and Poland emerged from the war as new countries, Austria and Hungary were radically cut back, while Yugoslavia, Romania, and Italy each gained some parts of the former empire.

Austria fared worst in the redistribution, being left without industry, without primary commodities, and without the rich agricultural lands. Of course, trade would have been a way to get access to all of these goods, but what did Austria have to offer? Vienna was called the *water head* of the empire; it had the bureaucrats and the banks, and not much else. Moreover, the nationalism of the surrounding new nations, as already noted, led them to close Austria off and out. The question "Can Austria Survive?" would continue for years, even after stabilization (see Layton and Rist 1925).

9.2.2 *The monetary problem*

During the war years money and prices had grown in a massive way. But while prices increased more than by a factor of 28, the exchange rate did not even quadruple (Table 9.2). Note, this is the free market rate in Zurich, not the controlled rate in Vienna. Exchange control and the sheer physical obstacles to both capital flight and trade must account for the very large discrepancy between price inflation and currency depreciation.

The political separation of 1918–19 and the creation of borders did not change the fact that the Austrian crown was the currency in use throughout the region. It was held by the public and there was no other currency except in Poland where rubles and German marks were circulating along with crowns.[4] Thus it was

Table 9.2 Wartime finance (index July 1914 = 1)

	Money[a]	Prices	Crown[b]
July 1914	1.0	1.0	1.0
July 1916	3.2	4.0	2.5
July 1917	5.2	8.2	2.6
Nov. 1918	13.2	16.4	3.0
Jan. 1919	14.3	28.4	3.5

[a]Notes in circulation.
[b]Crowns per Swiss franc in Zurich.
Source: Walre de Bordes (1924) and Schweizerische Nationalbank (1944).

Table 9.3 Distribution of Austro-Hungarian notes
(estimated percentage share in total issue)

Czechoslovakia	31.1	Austrian Poland	2.6
Austria	20.8	Russian Poland and Ukraine	2.6
Hungary	18.2	Trentino and Istria	1.3
Yugoslavia	11.7	Foreign markets	6.5
Transylvania	5.2		

Source: Walre de Bordes (1924, p. 42).

essential to find a way of reconciling the sovereign conduct of fiscal policy with the holding of a foreign managed money. Table 9.3 shows an estimate of the distribution of money in various regions of the former empire.

To complicate matters, the immediate monetary problem of 1919 was this: budgets were unbalanced and money creation was the routine. However, there was an important difference between Austria and the rest. The Austro-Hungarian Bank, which had the monopoly on note issue, was located in Vienna and was operating for the benefit of Austria. Note issue was used to finance the government and discounting war loans substantially near par, despite their depressed market price. As a result, note circulation was expanding rapidly and prices were rising. Austria was effectively imposing seigniorage on the new countries, which were on the crown standard but did not have access to note issue nor to discounting.

The temporary solution to the problem was found in an agreement between Austria and Czechoslovakia: the Czechs would be represented on the board of the bank, and the bank would not finance the government nor discount war loans. But predictably, the agreement did not work. Note issue continued at a rapid rate. Whether for nationalistic reasons or out of a genuine economic concern, Czechoslovakia pulled out in February. The plan was put in effect to create monetary autonomy by stamping the crowns in the hands of residents on Czech territory, thus effectively creating a new and separate money.

Czechoslovakia was a new country and hence had to make some decisions on how to handle its monetary affairs. The situation was different in countries that already had an established currency and needed to resolve the currency situation in newly acquired territories. Yugoslavia was the first to act in this regard.

Table 9.4 Stabilization

	Stamping	Stabilization	Level[a]
Austria	12–14 March 1919	11/1922	14,000.0
Czechoslovakia	3–9 March 1919	3/1919	6.5
Hungary	18–27 March 1920	6/1924	14,500.0

[a] Level of final exchange rate index: June 1914 = 1.
Source: Kerschagl (1929) and League of Nations (1946).

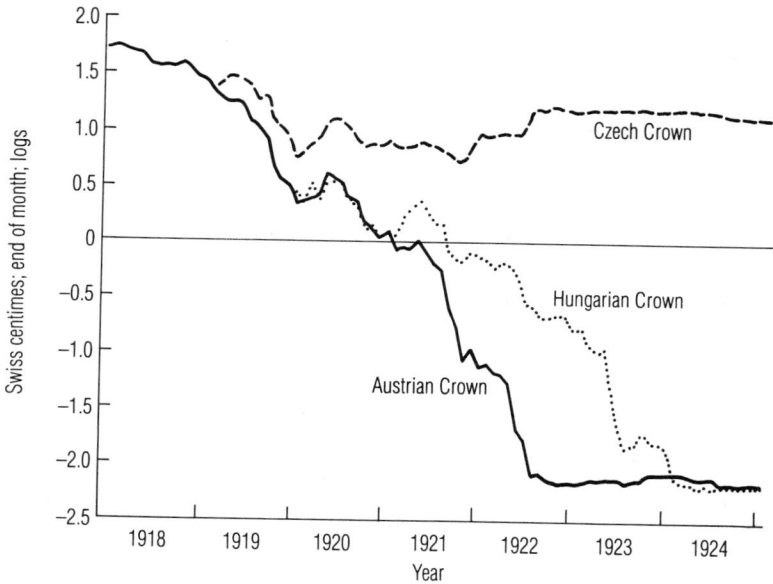

Figure 9.1 Successor currencies in Zurich.
(*Source*: Schweizerische Nationalbank (1944) and Hantos (1925).)

Already on January 8, the kingdom of Serbs, Croats, and Slovenes ordered the stamping of crown notes on its territory. Following Czechoslovakia and Yugoslavia, every country sooner or later proceeded to stamp notes or replace them with national issue, more or less systematically, with or without capital levy or forced loan in the process. This process was not complete until 1920. Moreover, simply the introduction of a national money was, of course, not tantamount to stabilization.

Rather than examining the Austro-Hungarian notes in all regions, we concentrate here on the three main countries—Austria, Czechoslovakia and Hungary. Table 9.4 shows their very different experiences in the immediate postwar years. Figure 9.1 offers an overview of the experiences in terms of the three currencies' performance in Zurich.

9.2.3 *Stabilization in Czechoslovakia*

Czechoslovakia is the outstanding example of a country that upon entering statehood and democracy avoided hyperinflation.[5] The leadership of Rasin was an essential part of that experience. Foreign assistance played some role, particularly in the earliest phase, but it was in no way the defining characteristic of the experience. Central to the success were three factors identified by Rasin (1923, p. 77)—a balanced budget, no unnecessary spending, and: "That we must all work and save. We must save, save, and produce, otherwise our Czech crown will lose its value just as the Austrian crown did . . ."

Czechoslovakia stopped inflation before it even started. With mounting disagreements over the management of the Austro-Hungarian Bank, Czechoslovakia moved rapidly to monetary independence. The government refused to give its consent to special Austro-Hungarian credits to Austria and then to Hungary but to no avail; the government denied legal tender status to an issue of 25, 200 and 100,000 crown notes that were being introduced by Vienna to counter the currency shortage. They were easily recognizable since in the rush they were poorly executed, being imprinted only on one side.

Under finance minister Rasin, Czechoslovakia moved to monetary reform and stabilization in the first few months of 1919. The key steps in the consolidation were:

- Stamping of all notes on the territory and retention of 50 percent of these notes (and of deposits) withheld against payment of a future wealth and war gains tax.
- Creation of a national "banking office" (in the finance ministry, with an independent board) with the strict obligation not to issue credits to the government over and above an initial allocation implicit in the remaining note issue. The bank could discount private bills without restriction.
- Exchange control and surrender of external assets, including gold and silver coins and foreign exchange. Residents had to sell external assets to the "Devisenzentrale" at the current (Prague) rate or else lend them to the government at 4 percent, reimbursable in the initial currency after 4 years.[6]
- A drastic wealth tax with top rates of 30 percent on wealth and 40 percent on wartime gains, payable over 3 years with an immediate first installment.
- Pursuit of currency appreciation and deflation to kill off and roll back the potential inflation.

Rasin had planned to go much further. His initial plan was for an 80 percent withholding of notes and a major appreciation forced with an external loan to back the currency. He felt that price and currency instability meant a lasting disease and a state of steady fever leading to recurrent wage fights which would be more dangerous for a young republic than an outright operation (see Rasin 1923, p. 29).

Table 9.5 Czechoslovakia: dollar price level and unemployment (index Jan. 1921 = 100)

	Dollar price level	Unemployment
1920	126	n.a.
1921	96	101
1922	164	179
1923	151	291
1924	155	135
1925	158	69

Source: Chanal (1929).

The actual plan was drastic enough. The stamping of notes proceeded with order and deliberation. Borders had been closed and an elaborate program put in place to effect the stamping in just a few days. When the Czech currency appeared for the first time on the Zurich exchange market it opened with a premium of more than 60 percent over Austrian notes. Austria was considered to be the least likely state to achieve stability; Czechoslovakia looked a lot better (see Rasin 1923; Schmidt-Friedlaender 1929; and Chanal 1929). A decisive US loan of $50 million helped support the currency. And for a while the crown held a stable level, but then was pulled down (though with a widening margin) by the pervasive bad news from Central Europe. Further budget tightening and credit reduction were put in place.

The way to stability was very arduous and Rasin himself became a victim of it when he was assassinated in January 1923. In an effort to break inflation, the government practiced *de*flation (Table 9.5). In fact, Rasin had planned to restore the prewar parity but had to give up the goal in the face of a very costly deflation (see the discussion in Englis 1937).

Following a low of the currency in November 1921, the government intervened to push the crown up and then let it fly. Tight money reinforced the nominal appreciation, and real appreciation ensued (see Figure 9.2).

The result of the hard money strategy—reinforced by hyperinflation in Austria and then in Germany—was a massive appreciation and overvaluation, notably in 1922–23, with a rapid and strong increase in unemployment. High-powered money was actually declining during this period (Table 9.6). The government drastically reduced discounts so that despite reserve inflows the *nominal* quantity of money was declining.[7] In this sense, a conscious policy of deflation was practiced.

Fiscal policy reinforced the monetary measures of stability. The deficit was small throughout—less than $50 million—and was financed by domestic debt and external borrowing (Table 9.7).

By 1925, the "stabilization crisis" had passed, unemployment had returned to moderate levels and a stable exchange rate and price level were in place. But even though the risk of inflation had completely subdued, in hindsight, the deflation experience was not considered successful even by the Central Bank. Thus Englis

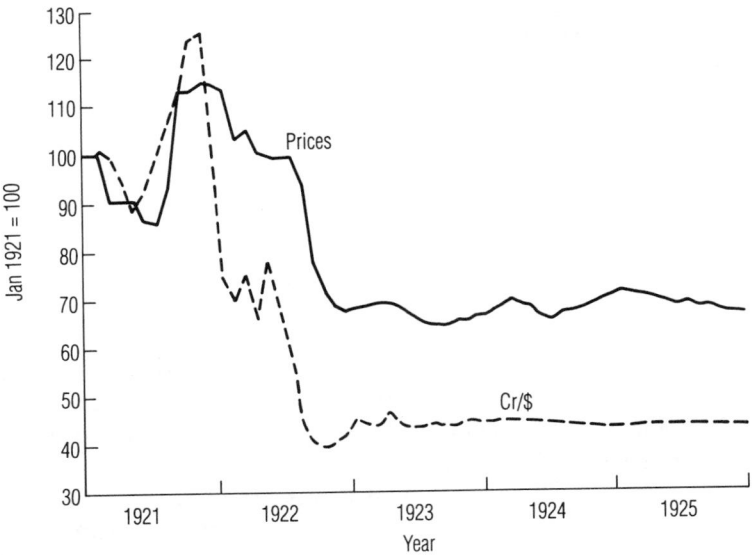

Figure 9.2 Czech prices and currency.
(*Source*: Chanal (1929).)

Table 9.6 High-powered money and reserves in Czechoslovakia
(millions of Czech crowns)

	Money	Foreign assets	Domestic credit
1919			0.6
1920	12.4	0.9	4.3
1921	12.8	1.1	4.2
1922	10.6	1.5	2.2
1923	10.6	2.3	2.0
1924	10.0	1.6	2.5

Source: Schmidt-Friedlaender (1929, pp 110–14).

(1937, pp. 50–1), a former governor of the Central Bank, launched a stinging
attack by noting:

> The situation was thus one of great difficulty. There was a crisis in industry, a
> banking crisis, unemployment, a financial crisis. . . . In making a critical survey of
> this period we cannot avoid coming to the conviction that the policy of deflation
> was a mistake. It was supported by the most varied arguments of an unscientific
> nature.

In summary, the Czech case makes the point that it is possible to establish
stability even in a new democracy and under difficult circumstances. The case
also shows that it is not easy. Czechoslovakia started in 1919 with a series of bold
moves. But because of lack of stability in the region and genuine questions about

Table 9.7 The Czech budget and trade balance (millions of Czech crowns)

	1920	1921	1922	1923	1924
Budget*	−2.0	2.1	−1.6	−1.8	−0.8
Trade balance	4.2	4.9	5.4	2.4	1.2

*Excluding investment.
Source: Chanal (1929).

its ability to stick to this policy (in Hungary Hegedus looked much like Rasin, for a while, and then failed) credibility was not complete and hence the costs of stabilization were very large.[8] But within five years the task was accomplished.

9.2.4 Austrian hyperinflation and stabilization[9]

Austrian monetary affairs were overshadowed by political instability. Early attempts to maintain a monetary area with the various successor countries failed, mostly because Vienna could not halt the printing press. The Yugoslav and Czech stamping of notes forced Austria's hands. To avoid an inflow of unstamped notes from the various countries, it proceeded in March 1919 to execute its own currency exchange, replacing the tendered notes with stamped bills. But, of course, the mere stamping of bills did not do anything to establish price and exchange stability. The budget deficit was large and it was covered by money issue. Not surprisingly, exchange depreciation and inflation were the counterpart.

The facts of the Austrian inflation are well known.[10] Of interest here is to mention the brief role of Joseph Schumpeter who was finance minister for six months in 1919.[11] Schumpeter recognized the need to bring public finance under control and, specifically, the overriding necessity of ending money creation in the financing of the state. His stabilization plan, published after he was forced out of office, opens this way (see Seidl and Stolper 1985, p. 344):

> The leading principle of financial policy must be that no bank note or state note must be forthwith issued, directly or indirectly, to finance the needs of the State. German-Austria has doubtless reached that limit where further issue of uncovered paper money must lead to a complete anarchy in economic life. Productive activity in the economy will only resume when a stop is put to the depreciation of money and the resulting economic demoralization.

There was another point on which Schumpeter was emphatic—external credit was the key to stabilization (Seidl and Stolper 1985, p. 346):

> Without external assets there can't be a stabilization of currency and hence no order in the public finances. The reverse sequence, first to establish internal order and then to seek external credit, is a path of desperate dissipation [*Verblutung*] which has been taken all too often in financial history. The fateful vicious circle:

no external credit, no internal order but without internal order no external credit, must be solved. The State must find external credit, however severe the burdens that must be imposed on the citizens.

Schumpeter failed to convince the cabinet of his position. The main point of the plan was to faithfully continue debt service and to rely on a large external support to rebuild stability. The external support was to come through a major wealth tax that was to be instituted (65 percent at the top!), but wealth holders could obtain advantages if they collaborated by mobilizing foreign credits in their own name and made them available to the government. The project was smart, but not practical. Moreover, Schumpeter's position conflicted with that of the cabinet on a number of issues: he opposed the union with Germany, he opposed major socialization, and he plotted with foreign investors. The difficulties accumulated and soon he was out of office without having made much of an impression.

Marz (1991, p. 156) reports another scheme of Schumpeter in which he sought contact with Sir Francis Oppenheimer, the British financial expert, to discuss a reform project that would lead to a major external loan. As part of the agreement, the Western powers would manage the Austrian central bank "with the proviso that the sensibilities of the Austrian people be duly considered." By 1922, niceties such as the sensibilities of the Austrian people no longer mattered.

For the period 1920–21, much of the currency story is one of failed stabilizations, hopes for external loans and squandering of credits when they did come. In the process, the economic conditions in Austria deteriorated sharply. Starting in mid-1921, a major collapse of the currency set off hyperinflation and, following a brief period of stability at the end of the year, another bout of depreciation moved Austria to the final phase.

The central partner in Austria's stabilization in 1922 was the League of Nations. Throughout 1919–22, Austria had pleaded with the Supreme Council, major countries and the League of Nations to get support for external loans to stabilize the currency. Nothing was forthcoming, which increasingly undermined any expectation of stabilization. A critical step in promoting external support was political: Austria had to make the tour of the capitals to secure agreements on the removal of the lien put on Austrian assets to secure reparations so that these assets might serve as collateral for a new loan. But that was not enough. In August 1922, Austria's minister in London appealed to Lloyd George and the Council of the Allied Powers for an immediate loan guarantee. Should no such guarantee be forthcoming, the minister warned, the Austrian parliament would be convened to be told that neither this nor any other government was capable of continuing to govern. Moreover, the powers of the Entente would be blamed, in Austrian and in world opinion, for being responsible for the destruction of one of the oldest centers of civilization in the heart of Europe. The fate of Austria would be put in the hands of these powers. The appeal failed, the crown collapsed even further.

Weary of a sequence of loans to Austria each of which had failed to change the situation, the Allied Powers did agree to refer Austria to the League of Nations (1926a, p. 15) to explore a program of reconstruction

> containing definite guarantees that further subscriptions would produce substantial improvement and not be thrown away like those made in the past. The representatives of the Allied Powers have reached the above decision with much reluctance and from no lack of sympathy with the Austrian people, but they have been obliged to take into consideration the crushing taxation which their respective countries already support in consequence of the war.

A direct and desperate appeal by the Austrian chancellor, Monsignor Seipel, before the League was publicly credited with the change of fortune. But the real work was done behind the scenes: the monsignor had gone to Italy to offer that Austria become part of a Greater Italy. For Yugoslavia and Czechoslovakia, and for the Allied Powers, this was viewed as a great threat to whatever stability there was in Central Europe (see Bauer 1923). The League agreed through its Financial Committee to participate directly in the reform program and raise guarantees for a stabilization loan. The pace quickened; within a month, three key protocols were signed in October 1923. One provided for political and territorial integrity of Austria and an agreement of signatories not to seek special advantages. For Austria this political agreement meant abandoning the idea of seeking a union with Germany or Italy. Another provided for loan guarantees. The key though was the third protocol which described Austria's responsibilities.[12]

In the agreement, based on a preliminary report of the Financial Committee, Austria committed itself to elaborate with the Financial Committee a detailed stabilization program. Central to the program would be a multi-year budget stabilization plan. The plan would include not only limits on the deficit but also a spending ceiling. An independent Bank of Issue was to be created and it was to have a foreign adviser. The parliament would be required to grant the government full powers in the execution of this plan. A commissioner appointed by the guaranteeing country would supervise Austrian public finance.

Specifically, the language of the protocol stipulated (League of Nations, 1926a, p. 192):

> The Austrian Government will forthwith lay before the Austrian Parliament a draft law giving, during two years, to any Government which may then be in power, full authority to take all measures, within the limits of this programme, which in its opinion may be necessary to assure at the end of the period mentioned the reestablishment of budgetary equilibrium without there being any necessity to seek for further approval by Parliament.

But even though a loan was forthcoming, the League's Financial Committee left no illusion about the need for Austria to reform (see League of Nations, 1926a, pp. 26–7):

> At best, the conditions of life in Austria must be worse next year, when she is painfully reestablishing her position, than last year, when she was devoting loans intended for that purpose to current consumption without reform.

The alternative is not between continuing the conditions of life of last year or improving them. It is between enduring a period of perhaps greater hardship than that she has known since 1919 (but with the prospect of real amelioration thereafter—the happier alternative) or collapsing into a chaos of destitution and starvation to which there is no modern analogy outside Russia.

There is no hope for Austria unless she is prepared to endure and support an authority which must enforce reforms entailing harder conditions than those at present prevailing, knowing that in this way she can avoid an even worse fate.

The League's Financial Committee took a direct and active part in developing the reform program. The prospect of the League loan, and more importantly the reconstruction law which gave the government full powers, led to an immediate end to the depreciation. And with a stabilized exchange rate, real tax collection quickly increased. Moreover, on the strength of the forthcoming loan and the stable currency, the government was able to raise a domestic loan to finance the budget deficit. The printing press was immediately stopped. The new Bank of Issue started in January 1923.

Of course, not everything was that easy. Unemployment increased sharply and budget cutting was hard (see Heilperin 1931; Wicker 1986; and Kniebock 1925). For example, employment in government and public sector enterprises was cut by fully 30 percent. The League's commissioner did play an important role even if he was never forced actually to use his authority to block expenditures. By 1923 Austria was already well within the targets of the budget, by 1924 the budget was balanced and in 1925 there was a surplus. The financial stabilization had been accomplished even if the question "Can Austria survive?" continued.

In summary, the lesson from the Austrian example is clearly that stabilization needs the right political conditions. Austria endured the complete disillusion of extreme inflation and misery. At that point it became possible to trade full powers to the government and the commissioner in exchange for the prospect of stability and perhaps an improvement in living standards. There can be little doubt, judging from Bauer (1923), that without external support and enforcement, fiscal control on a lasting basis would not have happened. The socialists' idea of fixing the budget involved an emergency capital levy and a forced loan. As we will see in the case of Hungary, such measures cannot fill the place of a lasting fiscal correction.

The second point is to note just how tough the League was: not only did it draw up the stabilization plan and require full powers for the government, it even required a resident commissioner who controlled the budget and had the last word. No wonder, then, that the plan worked, and that it worked so fast.

9.2.5 *Hungarian hyperinflation and stabilization*[13]

In its final stages, Hungary's stabilization paralleled that of Austria, but the way there was far more colorful. As seen in Figure 9.1, Hungary's stabilization came only in 1924. Early in 1919, a Soviet regime (the Red Terror) took over Hungary.

The objective of the regime was to install a full-fledged communist economy and link up with the Soviet Union. Printing money was an important means of achieving this.

Hungary continued, *de facto*, to be in a monetary area with Austria. The Austro-Hungarian notes circulated in Hungary as legal tender. Moreover, the Soviet regime found the plates of certain Austrian notes which happened to be in the subsidiary of the Austro-Hungarian Bank in Budapest. The Soviet government immediately proceeded to issue money. But lacking the Austrian blue note paper, they printed on white paper. They also used photomechanical processes to fake lower-denomination Austrian notes (see Kerschagl 1920: and Nagy 1931). Issue of money in the name of the Soviet government did not succeed, even when the death penalty was threatened for people who refused acceptance. A third means of issuing money was linked to the postal savings system which issued small-denomination notes.

The actual issue by the Soviet government of Austrian money was probably less significant than the general appearance of a breakdown of normal monetary relations. Of course, there was not much normality with the Red Terror in the streets. The next act of the Hungarian drama was an invasion by Romanian troops which overthrew the Soviet government and occupied Budapest for three months. Upon evacuating the city, they took with them much of the capital stock. Finally, a royalist government came into office and, in late 1919, normalized monetary conditions. The easily recognizable fake Soviet notes were demoted to one-fifth of their face value.

Starting in January 1920, Hungary's currency was separately quoted in Zurich (see Nagy 1931, p. 9). Only in March 1920, however, was a stamping of the currency executed on Hungarian territory. Fifty percent of the tendered notes were withheld as a forced loan that carried 4 percent interest. There had been a general expectation, following the end of the Soviet regime and the Romanian occupation, that stability would come and with it a strengthening of the currency. Hungary, it was believed, had far better prospects than Austria.

If weak government was the chief reason for failure to stabilize in Austria, the same cannot be said of Hungary. As the League (1926b, p. 9) notes in discussing the period after 1919, following the Red Terror and the Romanian invasion "the Right resumed power, and Hungary has since had a strong, stable and drastic government." In fact, however, Hungary's currency depreciated, though not quite on the scale of the Austrian money.

By 1921, there was a brief attempt at stabilization. Hegedus, a banker, became finance minister and was given full power. In public discussions of the time the point was made that a depreciating exchange rate increases budget deficits and thereby feeds money creation. Hence a strong currency was part of the package as much as the control of money issue. A wealth tax and consolidation of the debt which reduced interest burdens helped reduce the budget deficit and the currency rose by nearly 200 percent in Zurich. Money creation was actually brought to a halt and a note issue institution was created with the obligation not to make advances to the state.

The budget improvement did not last long and the administration of the wealth tax was inefficient. Moreover, the strengthening of the currency did not bring the lasting fiscal bonus that had been expected. Disappointed with domestic and external politics and with the difficulty of carrying forward his stabilization, Hegedus resigned in the fall and another exchange collapse ensued. With continuing budget deficits, further rounds of money creation and depreciation soon followed (see Siklos, 1993; Graz 1935; Kerschagl 1929; and Fellner 1924).

Why, in the face of a clearly successful Czech stabilization, did bouts of depreciation and inflation linger on in Hungary? Boross (1984, p. 206) offers a simple political interpretation:

in a country such as Hungary where during the past three years two revolutions and a counterrevolution had taken place, and where the ruling regime's consolidation was far from accomplished, where instead of solving old social tensions even more were created (see the plight of 300,000 refugees from territories lost to Hungary) those responsible for the financial policy of the country—especially with the Czechoslovak example highlighting the difficulties—were reluctant, even unwilling to pursue a deflationary policy. The very potent "real-political" consideration having been that the price of deflation in terms of unemployment, social unrest, political instability was far greater to the country than that of inflation.

In the League's (1926b, p. 10) autopsy:

Hungary at last presented a problem which in its main features was the same as Austria's—a rapidly depreciating currency and an unbalanced budget; an inability in the financial, economic and political forces of the country to achieve unaided restoration.

Inflation and depreciation continued in Hungary, after the successful stabilization in Austria. In the face of increasingly rapid exchange depreciation, in April 1923 Hungary took its turn to approach the League of Nations. The reparation commission waived its lien and by early 1924 the protocols for a Hungarian loan were signed.

The stabilization in Hungary proceeded on the basis of the following principles set out by the League Committee report (see League of Nations 1926b, p. 18): stoppage of inflation with a view to the stabilization of the crown, this being assisted by an independent Bank of Issue which could not finance the government; budget balance by June 30, 1926; a reconstruction loan; control through a Commissioner General.

Just as in the case of Austria, a condition for the loan was the ratification by parliament of full powers for the government to execute the agreed program, including specifics for the increase in taxes, cuts in spending and five half-yearly budgets for the period to 1926.

By June 1924 currency stabilization had taken place. Just as in Austria, money creation to finance the government stopped from one day to the next, although full convertibility had to wait for a while. A domestic loan covered the brief transition and by July 1924 the budget was already balanced.

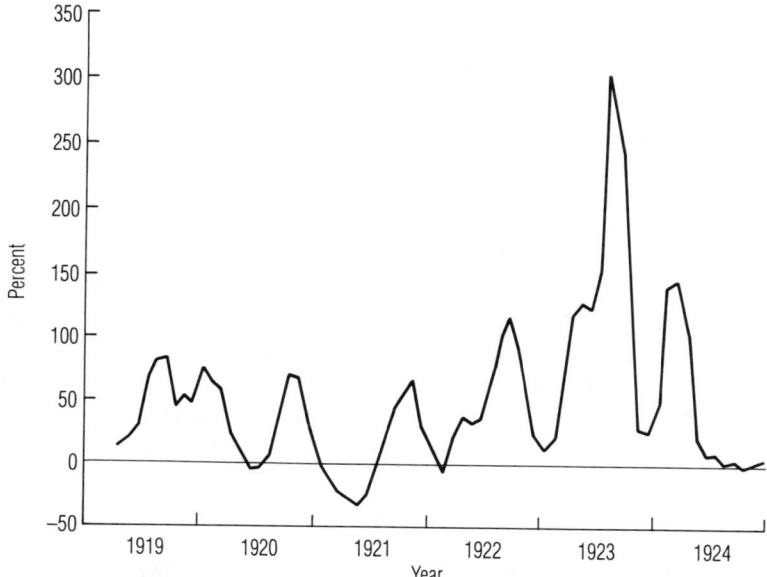

Figure 9.3 Hungarian inflation (percent over past three months).
(*Source*: Boross (1984).)

In summary, the case of Hungary illustrates three points. First, that the erosion of a country's public finance over time is gradual and cumulative. Initially Hungary did not manage to cut loose from Austria because of domestic turmoil. Then it tried to stabilize but failed to follow this up with fiscal balance. Progressively more and more bouts of depreciation occurred until the big explosion of 1923 ultimately created the political conditions for complete reform. There is no single event or mistake that led to the great inflation; rather, it was a process of erosion and increasing sensitivity of the budget and of inflation of the exchange rate (see Figure 9.3).

The second message overlaps with that of Austria. Once external loans flow in and the budget achieves credibility through the League's firm surveillance, stability quickly follows.

Third, an independent central bank with a limitation on financing the government, creates an automatic block to any link between budget deficits and money and hence between deficits and the exchange rate. Therefore stability is more likely.

9.3   Coordination problems

So far we have looked at stabilization in three countries separately, disregarding the effects of interdependence that might have been there. But there are clearly three areas where interdependence does matter.

9.3.1 *Economic and political confidence*

The most immediate spillover effect arises from contamination. In the 1920s, each successor country was valued in the market in part on the strength of its own policies, but in part also for being in Central Europe, exposed to the same risks and those countries who were not doing well. In fact, if one country was doing poorly in economics or politics, it became plausible to project that very same scenario onto the adjacent countries. In currency markets this meant a strong common factor, however different the policies.

The fact is illustrated by the Czech currency. It is affected, for example, by Bolshevism in Hungary and by the declaration of the monarchy and the return of King Charles to Budapest. Likewise, when Germany, Hungary and Austria collapse, Czechoslovakia is the place where hot money flees. The interdependence effect is of significance because stabilization is already hard enough without the extra bad news that comes from a neighbor's poor economics or politics.

9.3.2 *Unstamped notes, faked notes, and monetary chaos*

A large problem in the break-up of the Austro-Hungarian empire was the uncoordinated if not chaotic handling of notes. The peace treaties required countries to stamp notes on their territory and turn over any amount withdrawn from circulation (say, by capital levy) to the reparation commission. The risk then was not the deliberate and organized attempt to use Austrian notes to buy Austrian goods—i.e., to recover the seigniorage implicit in the notes. Rather the problem was that the dates and details of note stamping were not synchronized and not handled with equal efficiency. As a result, unstamped notes were floating around from one country to another in search of the most favorable exchange rate. Moreover, once a multitude of notes were already circulating, with various kinds of stamps, it became attractive to avoid capital levies or take advantage of favorable exchange rates by faking the stamps, the notes or both.

Table 9.8 gives an impression of the variety of arrangements ranging from very large capital levies—enforced by dramatic sentences, for example in Czechoslovakia—to conversion rates into existing currencies. The picture is further complicated by the fact that 1 and 2 crown notes, because of their quantities, were not stamped and hence became an important foreign exchange arbitrage vehicle. Finally, certain Austrian notes printed against the protests of successor states were excluded from legal tender status—for example 10,000 crown notes in Czechoslovakia—and therefore were excluded from stamping altogether.

Impediments to travel and border controls may have hampered the open arbitrage in notes among various countries. In fact, however, there was a thriving market in unstamped notes. Both stamped and unstamped Austrian crowns were quoted in Berlin, and Figure 9.4 shows the premium or discount at various times on unstamped crowns.[14]

Table 9.8 Stamping and levies, forced loans, or conversion

	Date	Levy/Forced loan/Conversion
Czechoslovakia	3.1919	50%
Austria	3.1919	
Hungary		
first	8.1919	Write-down of Soviet notes
second	3.1920	50%
Romania		
first	6.1919	2 : 1 to lei
second	8.1920	40% + 5% premium
Poland	12.1919–12.1921	100 : 70 to Polish mark
Italy	11.1919–12.1921	10 : 4; 10 : 6 to lira
Yugoslavia		
first	1.1919	–
second	11.1919	4 : 1 to dinar

Source: Kerschagl (1920; 1929) and Schmidt-Friedlaender (1929).

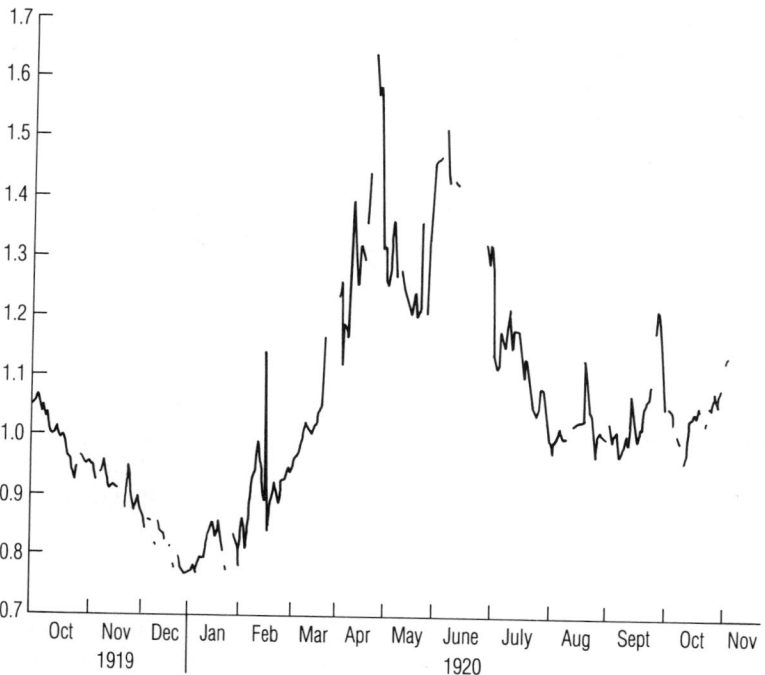

Figure 9.4 Ratio of unstamped to stamped Austrian crowns.
(*Source*: Diesen (1922).)

The reason to withhold notes from stamping was quite apparent at the outset. In Czechoslovakia, for example, 50 percent of the notes were withheld against a future capital levy. Presenting the notes withheld in Prague for stamping in

Vienna was not so attractive because the Austrian stamped crown traded in Zurich at a rate much below that of Czechoslovakia. Holding on to the notes offered the possibility of getting something better, ultimately, in Hungary. This prospect became far more attractive once the Red Terror was gone and Hungary seemed to move toward stability. But for those who had missed out on a stamp in the three countries there seemed to be trouble—unstamped notes went to a 40 percent discount. But there were still possibilities in Poland, Romania and, for a long time, Italy.[15] Better yet, for a while the Austro-Hungarian bank accepted unstamped notes at par to pay off pre-October 1918 debts.

It is doubtful that the confusion and trafficking arising out of the disorganised stamping arrangements materially contributed to the hyperinflation of some countries or the deflation of Czechoslovakia. More likely it was merely a headache and a moral affront. The same is true to a lesser extent of forgery, which created genuine uncertainty as to which money was or was not genuine. Walre de Bordes (1924, p. 236) reports an Austrian weekly:

> Our only hope—however absurd it may sound—is that the Hungarian and Polish crowns will soon rise higher than the Austrian crown, and that the Hungarian and Polish stamps can be counterfeited just as easily as the Austrian stamp, so that it will become again more profitable for the forgers to counterfeit them (just as was formerly the case with the Yugoslavian and Czechoslovakian stamps) and that we no longer be the victims of their favor.

In fact, the pressure of forgery was such that at one point Vienna issued notes that carried the designation *echt österreichisch* (genuine Austrian)!

9.3.3 Nationalism

The most serious problem in the dissolution of the Austro-Hungarian empire was no doubt nationalism. Tariffs, quotas, exchange control and transport barriers were all put in place to break the established trade linkages and develop the new economies to become far more autarchical (see Pasvolsky 1928; and Graz 1935). Moreover, the trade in services that had been the livelihood of Budapest and Vienna was basically cut off. In fact, "nostrification" policies called for corporations which had their head offices in Vienna but the plants in Czechoslovakia to move there or else risk their assets.

In a wide open trading system with stable real exchange rates, the division of the empire into successor states would not have made much difference. But with trade impediments abounding and unstable currencies, the arbitrary division created both economic and political problems. Pasvolsky (1928), for example, notes that the textile industry was broken up, with the spindles in Czechoslovakia and the looms in Vienna, with tariffs and quotas between the two.

Layton and Rist (1925, p. 25) in their analysis of Austria's economic problems highlight precisely the trade issue.

> Post-war commercial policy ... has largely been based upon the idea of economic self-sufficiency, and has sought to make the new national units independent, not

merely in the political but also the economic sphere. The attempt to carry out this policy naturally produced chaotic results in an area such as Austria-Hungary, which had hitherto enjoyed complete freedom of trade.

Specifically, tariff rates on Austrian goods ranged between 21 and 31 percent in Czechoslovakia; 28 to 40 percent in Hungary; and 49 to 67 percent in Poland. Layton and Risk (1925, p. 27) estimated that restrictive commercial policy caused a 40 percent decline in Austrian and Czech exports to Hungary. Another conclusion was that the new protection created trade diversion: while exports increased, the new exports were to distant markets, not predominantly to the neighboring countries. The share of intra-Danubian trade in the regions' exports fell sharply.

An early attempt to overcome these problems was the Portorose conference and protocol of 1921. Plans of a Danubian economic union were under discussion and the conference was an attempt to turn these into concrete moves to phase down restrictions. The key agreement provided for the removal of import restrictions and prohibitions by July 1922. In fact, the agreements were not ratified and hence this ambitious trade liberalization never came into its own. More conferences were held, but no progress was made.

The only progress that did materialize was on a bilateral basis under the pressure of the League of Nations in connection with the stabilization plans of Austria and Hungary. Central Europe had the worst of all worlds; the countries opened up neither on a regional basis nor on a multilateral basis. They remained substantially closed; industrialization was seen as the only means to provide a reasonable standard of living for an overcrowded region and no country was willing to sacrifice its own industrial project. But there was not only economic opposition to an integration project. Equally important was the reluctance of the successor states to see Vienna regain a central and powerful role in the economic future of the region.

9.4   Lessons

What can be learned from the Austro-Hungarian experience that can be useful in guiding policies in the former Soviet Union? The lessons fall into three groups: how to stabilize; what economic relations to foster among the new countries; and how the outside world can best assist stabilization and reform.

9.4.1   *Stabilization*

In this area the lessons are abundantly clear:

- Large, unbalanced budgets sooner or later lead to extreme inflation. It may take time, the march toward inflation may not be a steady acceleration, but ultimately it comes. Moreover, once inflation reaches a significant level of around 20 percent per month, going back will become extremely difficult.

- Stabilization requires three steps: fixing the exchange rate; balancing the budget; and ensuring the independence of the central bank. Each of these three steps is indispensable. Fixing the exchange rate establishes immediately a stabilizing force and inertia with beneficial effects for expectations, the budget and politics. Balancing the budget provides the fundamentals that warrant fixing the exchange rate. Finally, the independence of the central bank acts as an insurance against relapse and thus helps improve expectations.

  All three conditions may not be achievable at the outset. Specifically, budget balancing may not be immediately possible or convenient, at least not fully. The answer then is for it to be financed not by money but by debt—domestic or preferably external—with a clear limitation on the deficits. Still, exchange rate fixing and the creation of central bank independence can and should go ahead.[16]

- Exchange rate overvaluation is a grave risk. The risk may stem either from insufficient inflation control or from an overly ambitious nominal exchange rate policy. Overvaluation may help cool inflation, but it invariably leads to real and financial crisis. Overvaluation is not only a risk that arises in the context of an insufficiently conservative program; as the case of Hungary (Hegedus) and especially Czechoslovakia (Rasin) demonstrates, it can also happen to the overly zealous. The solution is that when overvaluation becomes an issue, however painful the choice, one must move to a crawling peg.

- Exchange control is a contentious issue. Notwithstanding the Brussels conference recommendation favoring unfettered exchange markets, Austria, Hungary, and Czechoslovakia all maintained exchange controls well into their stabilizations. There may be a case for controlling capital flows (if administratively possible), but there is no plausible case for controlling commercial transactions. Given the administratively overburdened and backward situation in the former Soviet Union, all kinds of exchange control should be avoided.

9.4.2 *Cooperation*

The analogy with the end of the Austro-Hungarian empire provides two conclusions in this area:

- It is a quite awful idea to maintain a currency area between sovereign nations based on an *un*stable center currency. Continued use of a depreciating crown strained relations after the break-up of the empire, and the same is the case today. Moscow is at the center and may control the note issue, but there is clearly no control of what might be printed elsewhere.[17]

  A clean break is far better, and the sooner it is done the better. The right answer, of course, is to base a currency area on a stable currency, i.e., the

Deutschmark or the dollar. There is no conceivable reason why countries should not immediately adopt a Western currency as their money and thus avoid a few years of high inflation or hyperinflation and the resulting destitution.

- In the trade and payments area, the case of the former Soviet Union quite strikingly matches the Austro-Hungarian story. The same misdirected policies are being put in place under the force of nationalism and in search of autarchy.

There is an urgent need to create an explicit free trade area in the region. As the European Payments Union (EPU) has demonstrated amply, freeing regional trade and discriminating somewhat in favor of the region is a good development policy. It is natural to worry whether a regional trade and payments mechanism slows down the move to convertibility or whether, on balance, it advances trade. The experience with the EPU is still being evaluated, notably the question whether it delayed the transition to convertibility! Presumably one will conclude that while it may have slowed down the fastest members, it speeded up the slower ones. But at least the Institut für Weltwirtschaft (1954) is firmly on record in support of the European Payments Union as a trade creating device (see also Williamson 1992; and Dornbusch 1992b).

9.4.3 What the West can do

The Austro-Hungarian story is most striking in its relevance to the role of the outside world. Stabilizing these countries became ultimately a very important issue, because stability of the region was at risk. Driven by the force of this political motive, the League of Nations overcame its inertia and developed an important program. Four aspects of the League program deserve mention:

- A requirement for League of Nations loan guarantees was the removal of the lien of the reparation commission. No fresh money will come if old money (dead money) has a prior claim. The liens were removed and reparations became subordinate to the need for stabilization. The present-day analogy is, of course, the external debts of the East. Even as late as last fall, the West was trying to collect loans, not recognizing that Russia was bankrupt and in clear need of a major support program.
- The reform program included a substantial stabilization loan; the loan was to be *used*, not held for decoration. Specifically, the stabilization plan involved a multi-year progression toward budget balance with the external loan supplying both resources for the budget and the external gap. Here is the League's (1946, pp. 79–80) own analysis of what these loans can accomplish:

> Given a strong and competent administration, there is no doubt that inflation can be controlled by domestic measures alone. Reliance on foreign help may

undermine a country's determination to set its house in order. .... Yet it cannot be denied that foreign loans can help. ... Foreign loans may help, firstly, in a technical way in checking the monetary mechanism of inflation; and they may help, secondly, in a more fundamental way by meeting the real capital needs of reconstruction and so relieving the underlying conditions which give rise to inflation.

- The program came with exceptionally stiff *political* conditionality. This is something that has literally disappeared, but was clearly decisive at the time. The League required *full powers* for the government and, on top, installed a commissioner with significant discretion.[18] The foreign supervision of Austria's public finance, for example, lasted for four years, until financial stability was assured. It is no surprise, then, that the political deadlock was cut and stabilization could move ahead. The chief problem in stabilization is *not* technical, the problem is political and the League overcame these problems with a vast sweep.
- The League participated in the stabilization at an extremely high level of personnel and with high visibility. The League's Financial Committee which developed the actual program included senior officials and the Committee's reports went to the Council of the League.

In each of these areas we are failing today in the most radical fashion. Loans are given without programs; political support is nonexistent and no effort has been made by the West to mobilize it; political and economic representation of the West is made at a modest level. The West, plainly, is trying to limit the exposure.

The League was aware that the stakes were high—Austria had offered herself to Italy with dramatic consequences should such a deal occur. Today the stakes are at least as high, but the vision is not there to match. More forgivable, but equally unwise, is the lack of foresight of the Eastern countries which practice inflationary policies that inevitably lead to crisis.

We are still at a very early stage in the disintegration phase; hyperinflation is not in sight and pervasive demoralization has not set in. Yet it is clear that there is a grave risk that things are going wrong. It is thus a good time to reflect on the League of Nations' (1946, p. 84) conclusions about its inter-war stabilization efforts: "International financial assistance would have been much more effective, and would in the end have cost much less, had it been given in 1919 instead of, say, 1924. Only under the pressure of desperate necessity was it given at the later date."

Successful stabilization, reform and reconstruction are always painful. That was the case in the 1920s, and it also was the case in Europe and in Japan in the 1940s.[19] The former Soviet Union cannot escape from the fact that it will, under the most favorable conditions, look ahead to a decade of austerity. The more the political system recognizes and accommodates the need, the more hard work, saving and investment are the rule, the more fertile the contribution from the West can be.

Notes

1. The Austro-Hungarian experience has, of course, been studied already from the perspective of hyperinflation. See notably Cagan (1956), Sargent (1982) and Dornbusch and Fischer (1986). Dornbusch (1992a) and Dornbusch, Sturzenegger and Wolf (1990) review extreme inflation and its stabilization. Independent work by Flood, Garber and Spencer (1992) explores many of the points raised in this paper. There is also precedent in the monetary history of Latvia, Lithuania and Estonia as well as Poland that has relevance to what is happening today in these countries. See League of Nations (1945; 1946).

2. In Dornbusch and Edwards (1991) this theme is presented in the context of the Latin American macroeconomic populism paradigm.

3. See Kerschagl (1920; 1929) and Zeuceanu (1924) for a discussion of the peace treaty provisions.

4. See Namier (1922) for a vivid picture of the monetary chaos and the prevailing sophistication.

5. See Rasin (1923), Cakrt (1926), Jack (1927), Chanal (1929), Schmidt-Friedlaender (1929), Hantos (1925), Englis (1937), Nogaro (1924), Pasvolsky (1928), Piot (1923), Rist (1924), Young (1925) and Sargent (1982). Wolf (1992) compares Czechoslovakia in the 1920s and the 1990s.

6. The valuta loan yielded $11.5 million. See Rasin (1923, pp. 48–9).

7. Rasin rejected categorically the notion of the quantity theory of money, but he did practice it with a vengeance. Both Cakrt (1926, p. 71) and Schmidt-Friedlaender (1929) note that Rasin had been a student of Fisher.

8. Some put an interesting positive light on it: "Crises are selection processes. They teach industry to calculate with each fraction and prepares them for world market competition" Cakrt (1926, p. 47). Also, Cakrt (1926, p. 69) notes of Rasin that "his principle 'per aspera ad astra' enables him to easily endure the painful consequences of his policies because he sees that this moves his people tangibly close to a better future."

9. See Kniebock (1925), Heilperin (1931), Gaertner (1923), Walre de Bordes (1924), Pasvolsky (1928), League of Nations (1926a) and Kerschagl (1920; 1929).

10. See Walre de Bordes (1924), Cagan (1956), Sargent (1982) and Dornbusch and Fischer (1986).

11. See Marz (1991) for an account and Seidl and Stolper (1985; 1992) for Schumpeter's speeches, transcripts of cabinet meetings and the stabilization plan.

12. See League of Nations (1926a), which gives the actual text of the agreements as well as a narrative drafted by Sir Arthur Salter, and League of Nations (1945).

13. See Fellner (1924), League of Nations (1926b), Graz (1935), Hantos (1925), Heilperin (1931), Kerschagl (1920; 1929), Pasvolsky (1928), Young (1925), Seton-Watson (1962), Sargent (1982), and Siklos (1993).

14. The data are reported in Diesen (1922) and are calculated from cross rates of German marks per stamped and unstamped crowns.

15. In those regions where conversions were offered at a fixed rate that was out of line with the Zurich cross exchange rate, there was also an incentive to either flood in or withhold depending on the gain or loss from the arbitrage.

16. Schweickert, Nunnenkamp and Hiemenz (1992) come out strongly against fixed exchange rates.

17. A foretaste was given by a recent press report. The *Financial Times* (Lloyd and Volkov 1992, p. 2) quotes Mr Yunosov, Uzbekistan's central bank chairman, to the effect that his country will have to issue coupons to make up for the ruble deficiency.

18. Bauer (1923) notes that in Austria's case the full powers were actually vested not in

the government but rather in a cabinet council which thus maintained the democratic control of the parliament.
19. See Giersch, Paqué, and Schmieding (1992) and Dornbusch *et al.* (1992).

References

Bauer, O. (1923) *Die Österreichische Revolution.* Vienna.

Boross, Elizabeth A. (1984) "The Role of the State Issuing Bank in the Course of Inflation in Hungary Between 1918 and 1924." In Gerland D. Feldman *et al.* eds, *The Experience of Inflation.* New York, pp. 188–227.

Braun, Martha S. (1923) "Die Doppelnote. Währungspolitische Projekte der Nach-kriegszeit 1918–1922." In Melchior Palyi, ed., *Geschichte der Stabilisierungsversuche.* Schriften des Vereins für Socialpolitik, Vol. 165, Berlin, pp. 105–65.

Cagan, Phillip (1956) "The Monetary Dynamics of Hyperinflation." In Milton Friedman, ed., *Studies in the Quantity Theory of Money.* Chicago, pp. 23–117.

Cakrt, Jan (1926) *Rasin als Währungsreformer.* Mährisch-Ostrau.

Chanal, A. (1929) *Monnaie et économie nationale en Tchécoslovaquie.* Montpellier.

Diesen, E. (1922) *Exchange Rates of the World.* Christiania.

Dornbusch, Rudiger (1992a) "Lessons from Experience with High Inflation," *World Bank Economic Review* 6: 13–31. (See also Chapter 1, this volume.)

Dornbusch, Rudiger (1992b) "*A Payments Union for the Former Soviet Union.*" Massachusetts Institute of Technology. Mimeo, Cambridge, MA.

Dornbusch, Rudiger, and Sebastian Edwards, eds, (1991) *The Macroeconomics of Populism in Latin America.* Chicago: University of Chicago Press.

Dornbusch, Rudiger, and Stanley Fischer (1986) "Stopping Hyperinflations: Past and Present." *Weltwirtschaftliches Archiv* 122: 1–47.

Dornbusch, Rudiger, R. Layard, W. Nolling, eds, (1992) *Postwar Economic Reconstruction.* Cambridge, MA.

Dornbusch, Rudiger, Federico Sturzenegger and Holger C. Wolf (1990) "Extreme Inflation: Dynamics and Stabilization." *Brookings Papers on Economic Activity* 2: 1–84.

Englis, Karel (1937) "Outline of the Development of Czechoslovak Currency." In National Bank of Czechoslovakia, *Ten Years of the National Bank of Czechoslovakia.* Prague, pp. 37–69.

Fellner, F. von (1924) "La situation financière de l'État Hongrois." *Revue Economique Internationale* 3: 48–70.

Flood, Robert P., Peter M. Garber, and M. Spencer (1992) *The Dissolution of the Austrian-Hungarian Empire: Lessons for Currency Reform.*" Mimeo, International Monetary Fund. Washington, DC.

Gaertner, Friedrich (1923) "Die Stabilisierung der Österreichischen Krone." In Melchior Palyi, ed., *Geschichte der Stabilisierungsversuche.* Schriften des Vereins für Social-politik, Vol. 165. Berlin, pp. 47–77.

Giersch, Herbert, Karl-Heinz Paqué, and Holger Schmieding (1992) *The Fading Miracle: Four Decades of the Market Economy in Germany.* Cambridge.

Graz, G. (1935) "Die Wirtschaft Ungarns." *Zeitschrift für Politik* 24: 95–107.

Hantos, Elemér (1925) *Das Geldproblem in Mitteleuropa.* Jena.

Heilperin, Michel A. (1931) *Le Problème Monétaire d'Après-Guerre et sa Solution en Pologne, Autriche et en Tchécoslovaquie.* Paris.

Institut für Weltwirtschaft (1954) *Zur Frage der Koexistenz von Konvertibilitätsländern und Inkonvertibilitätsländern im Raum der EZU.* Kiel.

Jack, D. (1927) *The Restoration of European Currencies.* London.

Kerschagl, Richard (1920) *Die Währungstrennung in den Nationalstaaten.* Vienna.

Kerschagl, Richard (1929) *Die mitteleuropäischen Währungen und Notenbanken.* Vienna.
Kniebock, V. (1925) *Das Österreichische Sanierungswerk.* Stuttgart.
Layton, Sir Walter T., and Charles Rist (1925) *The Economic Situation of Austria.* Geneva: League of Nations.
League of Nations (1926a) *The Financial Reconstruction of Hungary.* Geneva.
League of Nations (1926b) *The Financial Reconstruction of Austria.* Geneva.
League of Nations (1945) *The League of Nations' Reconstruction Schemes in the Inter-War Period.* Geneva.
League of Nations (1946) *The Course and Control of Inflation.* Geneva.
Lloyd, J., and D. Volkov (1992) "Russia Cracks the Whip over Rouble Zone." *Financial Times,* July 31, p. 2.
Marz, Edward (1991) *Joseph Schumpeter.* New Haven, CT.
Mitzakis, Michel (1925) *Le Relèvement financier de la Hongrie et la Société des Nations.* Paris.
Nagy, Tibor (1931) *Die Ungarische Nationalbank.* Munich.
Namier, Lewis B. (1922) "Currencies and Exchanges in an East Galician Village." *Manchester Guardian (Reconstruction Supplements),* April, pp. 36–7.
Nogaro, Bertrand (1924) "La Signification de l'Expérience Monétaire Tchécoslovaque." *Revue Economique Internationale* 2: 49–77.
Pasvolsky, Leo (1928) *Economic Nationalism of the Danubian States.* New York.
Piot, André (1923) *La Couronne Tchécoslovaque Jusqu'à la Mort de Rasin, 1918–1923.* Paris.
Pommery, Louis (1926) *Changes et monnaies.* Paris.
Popovics, Alexander (1925) *Das Geldwesen im Kriege.* Vienna.
Rasin, A. (1922) "Currency Conditions in Czechoslovakia." *Manchester Guardian (Reconstruction Supplements),* April, pp 39–41.
Rasin, A. (1923) *Die Finanz- und Wirtschaftspolitik der Tschechoslowakei.* Munich.
Rist, Charles (1924) *La Déflation en pratique.* Paris.
Sargent, Thomas J. (1982) "The Ends of Four Big Inflations." In Robert E. Hall, ed., *Inflation: Causes and Effects.* Chicago, pp. 41–97.
Schmidt-Friedlaender, Reinhard (1929) *Die Währungspolitik der Tschechoslowakei.* Reichenberg.
Schweickert, Rainer, Peter Nunnenkamp, and Ulrich Hiemenz (1992) *Stabilisierung durch feste Wechselkurse: Fehlschlag in Entwicklungsländern - Erfolgsrezept für Osteuropa?* Kieler Diskussionsbeiträge, 1881. Kiel.
Schweizerische Nationalbank (1944) *Statistisches Handbuch des Schweizerischen Geld- und Kapitalmarktes.* Zurich.
Seidl, Christian, and Wolfgang, F. Stolper, eds, (1985) *Joseph A. Schumpeter. Aufsätze zur Wirtschaftspolitik.* Tübingen.
Seidl, Christian, and Wolfgang F. Stolper, eds, (1992) *Joseph A. Schumpeter. Politische Reden.* Tübingen.
Seton-Watson, Hugh (1962) *Eastern Europe between the Wars, 1918–1941.* Hamden, CT.
Siklos, Pierre L. (1993) "Interpreting a Change in Monetary Regimes: A Reappraisal of the First Hungarian Hyperinflation and Stabilization: 1921–28." In Michael Bordo and F. Caprie, eds, *Monetary Regimes in Transition.* Cambridge, MA: MIT Press.
Tinbergen, Jan, ed., (1939) *International Abstract of Economic Statistics.* London: International Conference of Economic Services.
Urschitz von Usszich, Alois (1928) *Die Entstehung der Österreichischen Nationalbank.* Charlottenburg.
Walre de Bordes, J. (1924) *The Austrian Crown.* London.
Wicker, Elmus R. (1986) "Terminating Hyperinflation in the Dismembered Habsburg Monarchy." *American Economic Review* 76: 350–64.

Williamson, John (1992) *Trade and Payments after Soviet Disintegration*. Institute for International Economics, Policy Analyses in International Economics No. 37. Washington, DC: Institute for International Economics.

Wolf, H. (1992) *"Transition in Czechoslovakia: Then and Now."* Graduate School of Business, New York University.

Young, John P. (1925) *European Currency and Finance*. US Senate, Foreign Currency and Exchange Investigation Serial 9. Washington, DC.

Zeuceanu, A. (1924) *La Liquidation de la Banque d'Autriche-Hongrie*. Vienna.

Part IV

Developing country debt problems

10

Our LDC debts

The United States has a major stake in the world debt problem because it affects the profitability and even the stability of our banking system. But it also matters because debt service requires trade surpluses for debtors. We are now experiencing the reverse side of the coin from collecting debt: debtor countries, having made their goods extra competitive, are selling in our market and are competing with our exports. The debt problem is therefore a part, though perhaps a small part, of the US trade crisis. Finally, we have a major foreign policy stake in the debt crisis because debt collection brings about social and political instability.

This paper reviews these various aspects of the debt problem. Section 10.1 sets out debt facts, followed in Section 10.2 by a brief look at the origins of the debt problem. That issue is important in laying the groundwork for solutions that involve sharing the adjustment. The "transfer problem" in Section 10.3 is the general framework in which we discuss the problem of debt service for the debtor countries. Section 10.4 deals with bank exposure and the quality of less developed countries' (LDCs) debts. The US trade implications of the debt crisis are briefly addressed in Section 10.5. The paper concludes with an overview of alternative proposals for solving the debt problem.

10.1 Debt facts

In this section I provide an overview of debt facts: in the aggregate and in country detail of who owes whom how much, with what maturity, and in which currency.[1]

10.1.1 *An overview*

Table 10.1 shows aggregate debt data for selected years in both current and

The author is indebted to Eliana Cardoso, Martin Feldstein, Stanley Fischer, and Simon Johnson for many helpful comments and suggestions.

Table 10.1 Capital-importing LDC debt (billions of US dollars; 1980 prices)

	1978	1980	1982	1984	1986	1986 % Share
Total	399	570	763	849	967	100.0
Africa	72	94	117	128	144	14.9
Asia	93	135	180	212	265	27.4
Europe	48	68	77	82	101	10.4
Non-oil Middle East	30	43	56	68	75	7.8
Western Hemisphere	156	231	333	359	383	37.5
Total (1980 Prices)[a]	523	578	822	974	987	—

[a]Deflated by industrial countries' unit export value.
Source: IMF, *World Economic Outlook*, and *International Financial Statistics*.

Table 10.2 Debt–GDP ratios (percentages)

	Africa	Asia	Europe	Non-oil Middle East	Western Hemisphere
1978	32.2	15.9	23.7	52.9	31.8
1982	36.3	21.5	30.8	66.6	43.5
1986	44.3	30.0	40.0	63.2	47.0
Cumulative real GDP growth, 1982–86	4.2	31.1	11.4	−0.3	5.5

Source: IMF, *World Economic Outlook*.

constant dollars. There is a problem in finding a suitable deflator for the world economy. Possible candidates are the US GNP deflator, or either import or export prices for LDCs. I select instead the price (export unit value) of industrial countries' exports as a broader price index of trends in the world economy. World trade prices since 1980 have declined and even in 1986 are below their 1980 level. Accordingly, this index behaves very differently from, for example, the US deflator, which has been steadily increasing.

Since 1978, LDC debt has increased by 142 percent in nominal terms and 88 percent in real terms. In these aggregate data we observe the slowdown of debt growth since 1982 and the effect of changing trends in world prices with inflation in the early period and deflation since 1980.[2]

A second perspective is provided by looking at debt relative to some scale variables. The most common scale variables are exports of goods and services and GDP. Table 10.2 shows debt relative to GDP.

The most interesting point made by these data is that differences, at least at this aggregate level, are minor. Latin America is normally singled out as *the* problem case. But on a debt-income basis, non-oil Middle East countries stand out as carrying an even larger burden. The other point to note is the deterioration in debt ratios since 1982. This is surprising when one sees banks today rationing credit. The explanation lies primarily in the fact that GDP in US dollars has declined for most debtor countries as a result of large real depreciation.[3]

There is another interesting presentation of debt–income ratios in singling out different groupings of countries. Interestingly small, low-income countries have a higher debt–GDP ratio (64.0 percent) than net oil importers (35.3 percent) or the group of problem debtors (46.6 percent). Thus countries in a group with Afghanistan and Bangladesh have higher debt ratios than the group including Brazil and Mexico. We shall see below that this does not translate into higher debt *burdens* since much of the poor countries' debt is concessional.

10.1.2 *Short, long, official, and private debt*

The maturity structure of the debt is primarily medium term. Throughout 1978–86, the share of short-term debt (less than one-year maturity) in total debt of all capital-importing LDCs never exceeded 20 percent. But, of course, there are significant differences between countries. The larger the borrowing from commercial banks, the shorter the maturity of debt. In the period to 1982 there was an increase in the share of short-term debt, reflecting the increasing recourse to commercial bank financing. But since then, with rescheduling and increased official lending, the share of short-term debt has declined from 20 percent to only 13 percent. Since most debtors are not in a position to amortize their debts, the distinction between short- and long-term debt is becoming increasingly irrelevant.

Table 10.3 shows the share of debt to official creditors in total debt. The table reports the data for various regions.

The differences among country groupings in their funding is quite striking. Latin America stands out as borrowing a very much larger share from private sources than the remaining countries. But there is also an interesting difference in behavior over time. For Latin America and Africa, the absolute and relative increase in official credit since 1982 is much more substantial than for other regions. In 1985, for example, commercial bank exposure declined in absolute terms, while official exposure, especially of multilateral agencies, increased.

10.1.3 *Debt service burdens*

The burden of debt service is made up of interest payments and amortization. As such it is affected by three factors:

Table 10.3 Share of long-term debt to official creditors in total debt (percentage of total)

	Africa	Asia	Europe	Non-oil Middle East	Western Hemisphere
1978	34.0	54.9	27.6	57.6	15.9
1982	38.9	42.5	30.7	58.5	12.4
1986	48.6	43.5	33.3	58.5	20.3

Source: IMF, *World Economic Outlook.*

Table 10.4 LDC interest payments, 1986

	Africa	Asia	Europe	Non-oil Middle East	Western Hemisphere
Percent of debt	6.8	5.8	8.0	7.3	8.4
Percent of GDP	3.0	1.7	3.2	4.6	3.9
Percent of exports	14.1	6.1	10.8	17.0	27.7

Source: IMF, *World Economic Outlook*.

1. The maturity profile of debt, which dictates the amount of amortization in a given year. Any bunching of maturities would translate into large year-to-year fluctuations in debt service.
2. Interest rates on the debt. This factor depends on the private–official composition of the debt. Official debt may be concessional and long term while private debt typically involves floating-rate interest payments.
3. Debt service measured relative to some benchmark such as exports or GDP. The benchmark is affected by the country's real exchange rate. Real depreciation, as already noted, will reduce real GDP in dollars and hence raise the debt–income ratio. Measuring debt relative to exports implies that changes in the value of exports—say, as a result of exchange rate policy or as a consequence of changes in world commodity prices—will affect the debt–export ratio.

The distinction between long- and short-term debt, in an environment of universal rescheduling, is becoming uninteresting. I thus focus only on interest payments. Table 10.4 shows debt service measured by interest payments as a fraction of debt, GDP, and exports. I again focus on the geographical distribution.

The first row makes apparent the difference in effective interest rates paid. Africa and Asia have a significantly larger share of concessional loans, and, accordingly, interest payments as a fraction of debt are in excess of two percentage points less than for Latin America. As a benchmark we can compare the effective interest rate with the LIBOR (London Interbank Offered Rate), which in 1985–86 averaged 7.8 percent. Divergences of the effective rate for LIBOR reflect concessional loans and the spreads above LIBOR on commercial bank loans.

The interest burden as a fraction of GDP shows Africa and Europe in the middle range, a low figure for Asia, and a high indebtedness for Latin America and the non-oil Middle East. Differences between the GDP and export-based comparisons reflect economic structure. Europe is wide open while Latin America is much more closed. Latin America's export-to-GDP ratio is much lower than that for Asia, for example.

The difference between debtors with commercial as opposed to concessional debt becomes particularly apparent when comparing effective interest payments. While the effective interest rate for small, low-income countries in 1986 averaged 3.4 percent, for the remaining groups it was between 6.9 percent and 8.7 percent.

10.1.4 *Currency denomination*

The currency composition of lending to LDCs is not well documented. There is little doubt that the major part of loans, perhaps 60–70 percent, is in US dollars. The denomination issue is very important since large fluctuations of real exchange rates between the United States, Europe, and Japan involve changing burdens of real debt and changing bank exposure.

Since February 1985 the dollar has declined in world markets by more than 50 percent relative to key currencies. Over the same period, prices of industrial countries' exports, which we might use as an index of prices in world trade, have fallen only 5 percent while prices of commodities exported by LDCs fell 7 percent over 1982–86. The movement of the dollar thus did not carry significant consequences for debtor countries if they were entirely denominated in dollars. If, however, a significant part was denominated in yen or in European currencies, the vast exchange rate movements would have meant an increase in real debt burdens.[4]

10.1.5 *Major problem debtors*

We conclude the review of facts with a listing of major *problem* debtors. This group of countries corresponds to the fifteen heavily indebted countries shown in Table 10.5, along with their total debts, interest payments, and debt per capita.

In this table, Chile, Peru, and Bolivia are shown as having the highest debt–GDP ratio, while Chile, Argentina, and Mexico show the highest per-

Table 10.5 Fifteen heavily indebted countries

Country	Debt[a]	Debt per capita[b]	Interest–GDP ratio[c]	Share of debt to private creditors
Argentina	50.8	1,662	7.9	86.8
Bolivia	4.0	622	10.0	39.3
Brazil	107.3	791	5.8	84.2
Chile	21.0	1,740	12.9	87.2
Colombia	11.3	395	3.3	57.5
Ecuador	8.5	906	6.0	73.8
Ivory Coast	8.0	846	8.7	64.1
Mexico	99.0	1,261	6.3	89.1
Morocco	14.0	842	8.2	39.1
Nigeria	19.3	210	1.9	88.2
Peru	13.4	680	10.8	60.7
Philippines	24.8	456	6.2	67.8
Uruguay	3.6	1,204	9.8	82.1
Venezuela	33.6	2,000	8.1	99.5
Yugoslavia	19.6	848	n.a.	64.0

[a]Billions of US dollars.
[b]Thousands of US dollars.
[c]Interest payments on the external debt as a percentage of GDP.
Sources: *Fortune*, December 23, 1985; *The Economist*, September 27, 1986; *International Financial Statistics*; and World Bank (1986).

capita debt figures. Bolivia and Morocco are interesting in that their debts are predominantly to official creditors. Finally, Nigeria is of interest because of the relatively low per-capita debt by comparison with the other countries.

10.2 The origins of the debt problem

In this section we review the origins of the debt problem. Three facts combined to produce the debt crisis of 1982. The proportions vary from one case to another, but in almost all instances there is a combination of the following factors: (1) poor macroeconomic policies of debtor countries, including overvaluation of their currencies; (2) the downturn in the world economy, involving sharply higher interest rates and lower growth; (3) initial overlending and subsequent credit denial by commercial banks.

10.2.1 *Domestic mismanagement*

In the late 1970s, debtor countries worldwide, with rare exceptions, embarked on policies inducing currency overvaluation. The policies were motivated by a single purpose: to contain and reduce stubborn inflationary pressure. The popularity of the policy, in the short term, stems from the fact that real wages increase. The increase in real wages translates only gradually into lower employment. Hence there is a period of euphoria as standards of living are artificially inflated by the real appreciation while the resulting external imbalance is financed via reserve depletion and external borrowing.

Each of the countries in Table 10.6 showed some real appreciation in 1979–82, indicated by an increase in the real exchange rate index. For example, in Argentina the real exchange rate moved from a value of 73 in 1976–78 to 116 in 1980. Not all cases were as extreme, and the annual averages conceal some of the even higher peaks. But the basic point is that most debtor countries, sometime in 1979–82, experienced real appreciation of some degree.

The exact timing of real appreciation differs but the story is invariably the same. There are, however, significant differences in the magnitude of overvaluation. Argentina, Chile, Mexico, and Venezuela had much more extreme

Table 10.6 Real exchange rates (index 1980–82 = 100)

	Argentina	Brazil	Chile	Mexico	Venezuela	Korea
1976–78	73	116	75	98	95	92
1979	101	96	79	98	94	95
1980	116	85	95	104	93	96
1981	107	103	108	114	100	101
1982	76	112	97	82	110	103
1983–85	74	85	86	86	98	96

Source: Morgan Guaranty, *World Financial Markets*.

experiences than Brazil or Korea. Brazil is interesting because its policy of using (normally) a crawling peg geared to the United States–Brazil economywide inflation differentials ensured that high-productivity growth in tradables translated into a steady real depreciation. Dollar depreciation reinforced the gain in competitiveness in the late 1970s, but when the dollar strengthened in the 1980–82 period, competitiveness was lost. In Korea's case the real appreciation was very short lived and in fact quite minor compared to, say, Argentina.

The particular details of mismanagement differ between countries. For example, we look at Argentina, Brazil, Chile, and Mexico.

Argentina

Under Finance Minister Martínez de Hoz in the post-Peronist military government, inflation was reduced from more than 600 percent in 1976 to less than 200 percent in 1978. But further inflation reduction was hard to achieve. A large budget deficit was an obvious reason, yet the government preferred to focus on the inflation–depreciation spiral and the role of expectations.

Appealing to the law of one price, and the critical role of expectations, the government implemented in December 1978 a policy of preannouncing the rate-of-exchange depreciation. The preannounced *tablita* showed a steady deceleration of the rate of depreciation, and this was actually implemented. But inflation reduction was very slow, hence the real exchange rate became steadily overvalued.[5] Even so the policy was continued until March 1981 when it finally broke down.

The consequences for debt of overvaluation came primarily from the side of the capital account. Argentina had liberalized international capital flows entirely. As a result, residents, aware of the growing overvaluation, could freely shift into foreign assets ranging from dollar bills to foreign deposits and securities or real estate. The extreme overvaluation, reaching more than 40 percent, led to large-scale capital flight. The government borrowed in New York, using the proceeds to sustain the exchange rate along its preannounced path. The public bought dollars and redeposited them in the very same banks from which the government had borrowed. And that process continued, in the fullest knowledge of all concerned, until a change in the military government led to a collapse of the policy.

My estimate of Argentine capital flight in 1978–82 is $23 billion, not counting unrepatriated interest earnings which would raise the figure to well above $30 billion.

Chile

The Pinochet government instituted free market reforms and fiscal orthodoxy in Chile. These included elimination of tariffs and quotas and a balancing of the budget.[6] But inflation, while sharply reduced from the near hyperinflation levels of 1972–74, would not disappear. By 1979, with inflation the only major economic problem, the government fixed the exchange rate. The rate was fixed at 39 pesos/$ even though inflation was still near 30 percent, way above world inflation, and wages were indexed in a backward-looking fashion.

Not surprisingly, the exchange rate became increasingly overvalued. Wage increases far outpaced world inflation and thus the real exchange rate appreciated steadily. In the short run the policy was popular since it raised living standards. But it became increasingly apparent that an unsustainable overvaluation was accumulating. By 1981 the system started to unravel. The public responded in their accustomed way. Taking advantage of what was perceived to be a very transitory "sale" of imports, the entire country participated in the flight into imports (in particular, durables).

The real exchange rate appreciated by more than 25 percent between 1978 and 1981. The value of imports increased by 50 percent. Import volume indexes tell an extraordinary story: breeding stock +328 percent, automobiles +226 percent, electro domestic equipment +156 percent. The Chilean example highlights that, especially in the case of producer and consumer durables, a transitory exchange rate overvaluation has major effects on the timing of purchases. The government was not deterred by these developments. Steadfastly, the authorities maintained the exchange rate and asserted that the exchange rate policy was visibly successful, as evidenced by the declining rate of inflation.

As in all other cases, the policy ultimately broke down. Tariffs are back today and so are quotas. Inflation is back to the point where the adventure started. The lasting difference is an extraordinary debt burden and extremely high unemployment. We return to these issues below.

Mexico

The large increase in oil prices during 1978–79 would lead one to expect that Mexico should have done well. But even with sharply increased revenues from oil, the current account deteriorated in 1979–81 from $5 billion to $13 billion. At the same time there was a major outflow of capital.[7]

An estimate by Morgan Guaranty places the amount of capital flight during 1976–82 at $36 billion, while a World Bank estimate for 1979–82 gives $26.5 billion (*World Financial Markets*, March 1986; *World Development Report*, 1986). The extent of capital flight is associated with a peculiarly Mexican institution: the sixth and final year of the presidency. Such a year was 1982, and people expected, correctly, that overvaluation and an excess of spending would ultimately lead to a balance of payments crisis. Under these circumstances, capital flight became extreme.

Brazil

The Brazilian case is special in that the policy mistakes may well have been minor. Brazil certainly ran very large budget deficits. Oil price increases and increased world interest rates were absorbed by the public sector deficit, and the resulting external deficit was financed by increased borrowing abroad. But much of the earlier borrowing by state enterprises, especially in 1972–78, financed a massive national investment effort (Cardoso 1986).

In Brazil's case, tight restrictions on imports and the near absence of capital flight made for an experience very different from that of Argentina, Mexico, or Chile. The chief source of debt accumulation was the public sector, which meant that the damage was much more limited than was the case in the other countries. Indeed, by early 1985 it seemed that lower interest rates and a sharply reduced oil price helped solve Brazil's debt problems for the major part. Since then the current account has once again deteriorated, in part as a result of an overly expansionary policy. But even so, Brazil is among the debtor countries that are more likely to be able to sustain growth and debt service.

10.2.2 *The world macroeconomy*

A major part in the origins of the debt crisis was played by the sharp downturn in the world economy during 1979–81. In the 1970s, partly as a result of the oil shocks, but also because of overexpansionary policies, the United States had experienced increasing inflation. In 1979–81, under the pressure of the collapsing dollar, US policies changed sharply. The full-employment budget was cut by nearly 1.5 percentage points of GNP. Nominal interest rates were allowed to rise from 9 percent in 1978 to 17 percent in 1981, and real interest rates increased sharply.

The sharp change in the world economic environment is shown in Table 10.7, which compares the early 1970s and the period preceding the debt crisis. The early 1970s favored debtors: strong growth, high inflation, and low interest rates. By comparison, in 1980–82 inflation was low, interest rates were extraordinarily high, and growth was stagnant.

It is particularly important in this context to see the *real* interest rate issue. For debtor LDCs the US real interest rate is hardly appropriate. An alternative is provided by the inflation rate in world trade. Manufactures prices were declining by 2.4 percent while commodity prices fell by 13.3 percent per year. Any realistic estimate of real interest rates cannot fail to come up with extraordinarily high rates.

Table 10.7 Key macroeconomic variables of the world economy (annual percentage rates)

	LIBOR	Inflation[a]		OECD growth
		Manufactures	Commodities	
1970–73	7.6	12.4	14.4	5.9
1980–82	14.7	−2.4	−13.3	0.9

[a] Inflation rate in world trade.
Source: IMF, *IFS*; and World Bank, *Commodity Trade and Price Trends*.

Table 10.8 Terms of trade changes, 1978–82 (cumulative percentage change)

Fuel exporters	15 heavy debtors	Small low-income countries	Non-oil LDC exporters	Net oil importers
54.5	7.9	−27.8	18.2	−20.1

Source: IMF, *World Economic Outlook.*

Commodity price developments have different effects depending on whether a particular debtor is a net exporter or a net importer of commodities. The point is important in a comparison of Korea and Latin America. Korea (like Japan, for example) is a net importer of commodities. As a result, the collapse of commodity prices in 1979–81 helped offset in part the oil price increase. Brazil, by contrast, is a net exporter of commodities and has a production structure that makes the country vulnerable to oil price increases and commodity price decreases. Table 10.8 shows terms of trade changes and highlights the very different experience of various debtor groups.

These world economic developments meant that most LDCs experienced a sharp deterioration in their current account. Reduced export revenues, on account of the decline in commodity prices and world recession, were reinforced by sharply increased nominal debt service burdens. Thus debtors were made illiquid. To continue on the accustomed course, external financing needed to increase sharply. The lack of smooth financing in the case of Mexico then brought on generalized credit rationing.

10.2.3 *Overlending and credit rationing*

In the period to mid-1982, reckless lending was the rule. It is possible today to search the 1980–81 discussion of debt problems for warnings of the crisis to come. The Bank for International Settlements had expressed concern at least since 1978. A Group of Thirty inquiry in 1981 sought to uncover whether banks felt debt was a major issue and failed to find dominant concern (Group of Thirty 1981a; 1981b; Kraft 1984). In a survey of one hundred banks the question was posed, "Last time no serious debt defaults arose. This time do you think that a general debt problem affecting countries is likely to emerge?" In response, 72 percent of the banks questioned expressed the view that a debt crisis was not likely, 13 percent thought it might possibly happen, and only 15 percent replied in the affirmative (Group of Thirty 1981b).

If there were some concerns, they were certainly not enough to stop a final lending boom. Table 10.9 shows Latin America's current account deficit and its financing. Between 1979 and 1981, private lending to Latin America exactly doubled. It is unclear how these credits were justified at the time. There were two arguments. One was the need for recycling, which had worked well at the time of the first oil shock. The other was the lack of information on country exposure. Neither, of course, is a reasonable explanation.

Table 10.9 Latin America: current account imbalances and financing (billions of US dollars)

	Current account	Borrowing	
		Official creditors[a]	Private creditors
1978	19.4	2.2	25.8
1979	21.8	2.7	27.4
1980	30.2	6.1	35.9
1981	43.3	6.5	54.1
1982	42.0	14.6	28.8
1983	11.4	17.7	2.0
1984	4.9	10.7	7.0
1985	5.9	5.1	−0.6

[a]Including reserve-related liabilities. Private capital flows (flight) and errors and omissions make up the difference in the row sums.
Source: IMF, *World Economic Outlook*.

Subsequent to overlending was credit rationing following the Mexican moratorium of August 1982. As shown in Table 10.9, private lending fell off dramatically and in 1985 even turned negative. The credit rationing phenomenon is not surprising; faced with a country's inability to meet debt service, each individual lender is reluctant to put up money that would only serve to pay other banks' claims. Hence without a cartel there is no lending. But if there is no lending then, of course, debt service is impossible and hence debtors will default.

The problem in 1982 was therefore to develop a system that would organize creditors. They would have to provide the part of debt service that could not be extracted by improvements in debtor-country external balances. At the same time the cartel would serve, much as the occupation of customs houses in the old days, to extract a maximum of debt service by a lien on the debtor countries' macroeconomic policies. The IMF, having been ignored in the 1970s, eagerly (and skillfully) assumed the task of orchestrating debt collection, fiscal discipline, and forced lending.

10.3 The transfer problem and debt service fatigue

We now ask why debt service appears to be such a major problem. In one sense the answer is quite straightforward: countries that used to spend, borrowing the resources from official and private creditors (with little thought of how to service or even less repay the loans), now no longer command these resources—they are limited to spending (this section draws on Dornbusch 1985b; 1986b; 1986c). The adjustment is complicated by two facts. The first is the macroeconomics of earning foreign exchange; the second is the political economy problem of finding extra budget resources for debt service. These issues are familiar from the discussion of German reparation payments following World War I.[8] Exactly the same issues arise in the context of the involuntary debt service now under way.

Table 10.10 Latin America: investment and the external noninterest surplus (percentage of GDP)

	1977–82	1983–85	Change
Gross investment	24.3	18.5	−5.8
Noninterest external surplus	−0.6	4.7	5.3

Source: IMF, *World Economic Outlook.*

10.3.1 *The reduction in spending*

The first issue is how a country adjusts to a reduction in its spendable resources. Before the debt crisis, foreign loans supplemented domestic income, enlarging the resources that could be spent. Interest payments on loans were automatically provided in the form of new money, and the principal on debts was automatically rolled over. With managing the debt so easy, and with ready access to resources beyond what was required to service the debt, spending ran high. After credit rationing began in 1982, spending had to be limited, and absorption fell below the level of output as interest now had to be paid out of current production. Interest payments now had to be earned by noninterest surpluses in the current account.

Table 10.10 shows the debt service process at work. In the post-1982 period of involuntary lending, debtor countries achieved a shift in their noninterest external balance of nearly 5 percent of GDP. This external balance improvement served to make net transfers of interest to the creditors. It was matched by a nearly equal reduction in investment in the debtor countries.

This perverse resource transfer, of course, came at the expense of living standards in the developing countries. But more important, the transfer had as a counterpart a sharp decline in investment. Interest payments thus were really financed by a mortgage on future standards of living and on the debtors' growth potential. In countries where population growth is high and income distribution is appalling, such a policy may turn out to be very shortsighted.

But there remained the issue of how to distribute the cut in spending between its various components: government, consumption, and investment. As we saw above, a large part of the cut took the form of reduced investment. There was, of course, also a decline in consumption. A fall in investment was not enough due to two special features of the adjustment process. First, cutting total demand has macroeconomic multiplier effects that translate into a reduction in output, income, and hence private spending. Second, at the same time as involuntary debt service started, there also occurred a deterioration in the world economy that required an extra downward adjustment in spending.

10.3.2 *The foreign exchange problem*

The second macroeconomic issue in adjusting to debt concerns the fact that the country needs to earn dollars, not pesos. In other words it needs to generate a trade surplus. The cut in spending will, of course, reduce import demand and also free exportables for sale abroad, but for two reasons that will not be enough. First, a sizable fraction of the expenditure cut will fall on domestic (nontraded) goods, not tradables. The spending cut thus creates directly unemployment rather than potential foreign exchange earnings. Even for those goods that are directly tradable it is not necessarily the case that increased supplies can be sold. Often there is the problem of obtaining market access, and, if the goods are not homogeneous commodities like cotton or copper, a cut in their price is required to realize increased sales. Even then, unless demand is sufficiently responsive, total earnings may not increase.

To translate the spending cut into foreign exchange earnings, a gain in competitiveness is required. The gain in competitiveness draws resources into the tradable goods sector and in the world market makes it possible to sell the increased production of tradable goods. Of course, the only way to gain competitiveness is by reducing the wage in dollars by a real depreciation. But the real wage cut also generates increased unemployment, at least in the short run, as the spendable income of workers is cut. The size of the required cut in real wages is larger, the larger the share of traded goods in income and the smaller the share of wages in GDP.

The overwhelming difficulty in the adjustment process is that external adjustment via a gain in competitiveness reduces employment. The dominant effect on employment is from the reduction in real wages and the resulting reduction in domestic demand. The positive employment response that would be expected in the tradable goods sector from the gain in competitiveness is often very weak and slow. One reason is that expectations of a *sustained* change in competitiveness do not take hold immediately. The traded goods sector thus adopts a wait-and-see attitude, which makes real depreciation a highly precarious policy tool. The Mexican experience in this respect is particularly instructive.

A second important difficulty arises from the worldwide adjustment to forced debt service. Since most debtor countries were overspending in the early 1980s and are now under a forced debt service regime, they all had to resort to real depreciation to enhance their competitiveness. But that means they are competitively cutting their wages relative to each other, and not only relative to those of the creditor countries. As a result, an isolated country, cutting its dollar wage, say, to 50 percent, will gain much less in terms of increased dollar revenues because all the competing LDCs are doing much the same.

10.3.3 *The budget problem*

The third macroeconomic problem in the adjustment process involves the budget. Much of the external debt is public or publicly guaranteed. Of the part that was not initially public, much has wound up in the public sector in the aftermath of the crises, as a result of bank failures. The government thus must service a debt that before was either in private hands or automatically serviced by new money. The problem, of course, is where to find the extra 3 or 4 percent of budget revenue that will pay these new interest costs.

There are basically four avenues: raising taxes and public sector prices; reducing government outlays; printing money; or issuing domestic debt. Raising taxes is notoriously difficult since most of the taxes are already levied in the form of social security taxes on workers. An easier solution is to raise public sector prices or to eliminate subsidies. The elimination of subsidies is particularly cheered by creditors and international agencies since it means moving closer to efficient resource allocation.[9] Of source, the imposition of extra taxes or the withdrawal of subsidies is inevitably inflationary from the price side unless the tax increase or subsidy cut is offset by a reduction in other prices or wages. Of course, from the revenue side it reduces the growth in money and hence, in combination, leads to a recession with inflationary pressure sustained by prevailing inflation.

Cutting government spending is another option. Attention here focuses on the often extreme inefficiency of the public sector. The public perceives that there must be a way to pay the bills out of increased efficiency, rather than reduced private absorption. The fact is, of course, that there is little room for public sector improvements in the short term. Large-scale firing of redundant workers would create an overwhelming political problem. Plant closings are of the same kind, and selling inefficient, overunionized firms runs into the obvious problem that the potential buyers might need to be paid to take over the liability. Perhaps the best advice may be that public sector firms should be simply given away. The problem is that the workers might oppose even that.

The most common adjustment is a cut in or freeze of public sector wages. This has happened in most of the debtor countries, and in some cases on a very large scale. It does help the budget, but it presents its own problems. The reduction in relative wages for the public sector promotes an exodus of the wrong kind. The efficient workers leave and only those with little alternative stay in the public sector.

In many of the debtor countries the answer to forced debt service has almost inevitably been to increase government budget deficits and to finance this by issuing debt or printing money. Money finance brings with it the problem of high and often extreme inflation. It is no accident that Argentina and Brazil experienced extraordinary inflation rates in the aftermath of the debt crisis. When deficits are financed by debt, while the imminent inflation problem may be absent, there is still the issue of excessive debt accumulation which ultimately poses the risk of an inflationary liquidation or a repudiation.

There is an interaction between the foreign exchange problem and the budget problem. The need to devalue to gain competitiveness implies that the value of debt service in home currency increases. A given payment of, say, $1 billion now amounts to more in pesos, produces a larger peso deficit, and hence gives rise to the need for increased inflationary finance. Thus devaluation is a source of inflation not just directly via the increased prices of traded goods and any accompanying indexation effects. It works also indirectly by raising the required inflation tax. In the classical hyperinflations, major movements in the exchange rate were the prelude to the outbreak of uncontrolled inflation; there is some evidence that exactly the same process is at work in the debtor countries today (see Dornbusch and Fischer 1986; Fischer 1986; 1987).

The budget is also adversely affected by the problem of capital flight. To stem capital flight, provoked by the inflationary consequences of debt service or perhaps by an impending tax reform, the country will have to raise real interest rates to very high levels. These high real interest rates in turn apply to the domestic debt, causing it to grow more rapidly, and thereby raising future budget deficits and hence the prospect of instability. That in turn feeds more capital flight and yet higher rates. There is thus an extraordinary vicious circle surrounding the sudden need to service debt and the inability to do so through ordinary taxation.

It is worth recognizing an important tradeoff in the adjustment process. To earn foreign exchange, the real wage must be cut in terms of tradable goods, thus enhancing competitiveness. But to balance the budget it is often necessary or at least recommended to cut subsidies for such items as food or transportation, and that also means a cut in real wages. There is thus competition between two targets—a cut in the dollar wage or a cut in the tortilla wage. A choice must be made because there is only so much one can cut. Because of the lags with which the trade sector adjusts, this suggests that the competitiveness adjustment should take precedence and that budget balancing should follow once the economy's resources are reallocated. Since the real depreciation by itself is already bound to produce slack, there is no risk of overheating in this sequence of adjustment.

A final point is the link between budget cutting and the extraordinary fall in Latin American investment. In the category of government spending, the easiest cuts are in investment. Postponing investment and maintenance is much easier than firing workers. The resulting impact on aggregate investment is so large because the public sector, in the form of public sector enterprises, accounts for a large part of total investment and because the public sector was in the forefront of adjustment. This is a very ineffective means of adjustment because it fails to recognize the distinction between the public sector's current and capital accounts.

10.3.4 *Case study: Mexico*

Mexico illustrates in a striking way many of these issues. The least noted fact, apparent in Table 10.11, is the dramatic shift in the budget over the past three years. The *noninterest* or primary budget has improved by more than 7 percent of GDP. From a deficit of nearly 4 percent of GDP in 1982, the noninterest balance has shifted to an estimated surplus of 3.2 percent in 1986. The improvement is all the more impressive in view of the large decline in oil revenue in 1986. Note that the whole improvement in the noninterest budget went to finance increased interest payments on the domestic and foreign debt.

Table 10.11 Mexico's budget (percentage of GDP)

	1982	1983	1984	1985	1986[a]
Budget deficit	17.1	8.9	7.7	8.4	15.8
Primary deficit	3.7	−5.2	−5.4	−4.2	−3.2
Operational deficit	n.a.	−0.2	−0.7	−0.9	−2.1
Public investment	9.3	6.6	6.5	6.1	5.1

[a] Estimate.
Source: Mexico, Presidencia de la República and Sectetaria de Hacienda y Crédito Público.

Table 10.12 Mexico: macroeconomic indicators

	1970–81	1982	1983	1984	1985	1986[a]
Per-capita growth	3.5	−2.8	−7.5	1.4	0.4	−6.3
Inflation	17	99	81	59	60	100
Investment/GDP	23.6	21.1	16.0	16.3	16.9	14.9
Real wage (1981 = 100)	n.a.	105	76	73	67	64
Current account/GDP	−3.5	−3.8	3.8	2.5	0.3	−2.6
External interest/GDP	n.a.	7.5	7.1	7.0	6.0	6.4
Price of oil ($US/barrel)	12.4	28.6	26.4	26.8	25.4	11.2

[a] Estimate.
Source: IMF, and Sectetaria de Hacienda y Crédito Público.

The total budget recorded a deficit of nearly 16 percent of GDP for 1986. The increase in interest payments is largely a reflection of inflation. Inflation and the accompanying exchange rate depreciation raise the nominal interest rates required to make Mexicans hold the depreciating asset. These interest rates in turn translate into a large interest bill in the budget. There is a budget deficit because there is inflation, not the other way around.

Table 10.12 shows further details on the Mexican macroeconomic situation. We already saw the cut in public sector investment. The table indicates that total investment shows a sharp decline, leaving little *net* investment.

Consider next the current account. There is a striking turnaround, from the deficits prior to the crisis to surpluses afterward. In 1983–84 the surpluses were enough to help finance capital flight and also meet the interest payments. In 1985, interest was paid out of these surpluses by attracting a reflow of private capital via very high interest rates. But with the oil price decline the external financing problem returned, forcing a choice between further real depreciation and an alteration in the terms of debt service.

The real exchange rate and the real wage have both declined sharply in the past few years. Real wages today are 40 percent below their 1980 levels, and the external competitiveness has improved by 40 percent. These are extraordinary adjustments for any country to make. Finally there is the employment story. The labor force is growing at 3.5 percent per year, but employment, after an initial decline, has been entirely stagnant over the past four years. The informal sector and migration to the United States were the main shock absorbers in employment. Thus unemployment is growing and so, too, is social conflict. The lack of employment growth, even after so extreme a real depreciation, is an issue

Table 10.13 Brazil: Macroeconomic indicators

	1982	1983	1984	1985	1986[a]
Inflation	99	142	197	227	65
Per-capita growth	−1.3	−5.5	2.3	6.1	6.8
Budget deficit[b]					
Actual deficit	16.7	19.9	22.2	27.1	10.9
Operational deficit	6.5	3.0	1.6	3.5	5.1
Current account deficit[b]	8.5	3.5	—	0.1	−0.1
External interest	6.5	5.3	5.4	4.7	3.7
Noninterest deficit	2.0	−1.8	−5.4	−4.6	−3.6

[a] Estimate.
[b] Percentage of GDP.
Source: Banco Central do Brasil.

of major concern. It suggests that depreciation reduces employment for quite a while before the substitution takes over.

Early results for trade were disappointing. More recently, Mexico has started to build up a strong non-oil export growth, but that has turned out be be a mixed blessing. US trade concerns have spilled over to Mexico in the form of more than one hundred countervailing duty cases!

10.3.5 *Case study: Brazil*

Brazil, just like Mexico, started off her adjustment with a large decline in per-capita income and with a sharp acceleration of inflation. The inflation acceleration is largely due to the real depreciation required to generate a noninterest surplus. The presence of indexation translated exchange depreciation into an increase in inflation. The higher inflation in turn showed up in a sharply larger budget deficit (see Table 10.13).

The noninterest external balance improved sharply. This is seen in Table 10.13 in the shift of the noninterest current account from a deficit of 2 percent of GDP in 1982 to a 3.5–5 percent surplus in 1984–86. In contrast to Mexico, the Brazilian budget has not improved sharply, which has meant more stimulus to growth and to recovery.

The difference between the case studies of Mexico and Brazil, in 1986, is in both oil and macroeconomics. Lower oil prices in Brazil's case more than compensate for the adverse conditions of the boom in the external balance. But the external balance is certainly also improved by the import substitution and export capacity expansion made possible by the investments of the early 1970s, which came on line just in time to help service the debt.

10.4 Bank exposure and the quality of debts

In this section we review the debt problem from the side of commercial bank creditors by looking at the extent of exposure and at the quality of debts.

Table 10.14 US bank claims on nonindustrial countries (billions of dollars)

Year	OPEC	Non-OPEC	Eastern Europe
1977	14.3	45.0	7.0
1982	23.2	101.9	6.6
1985	20.4	100.9	5.1

Source: Federal Reserve.

Table 10.15 US bank claims on non-OPEC LDCs

	All banks	9 major	15 major	All other
Total claims ($ billion)				
1978	52.5	33.4	9.9	8.9
1982	101.9	61.5	20.6	19.8
1985	100.9	63.5	19.8	16.9
Percentage of capital				
1978	110	163	107	57
1982	154	227	162	75
1985	99	156	99	41

Source: Federal Reserve.

10.4.1 *Exposure*

Table 10.14 gives a broad overview of loans by US banks to regions other than the industrial countries or offshore banking centers. In these categories, Nigeria and Venezuela are included among the OPEC countries while Mexico is part of the non-OPEC countries.

Between 1977 and 1982, claims on non-OPEC countries more than doubled. By contrast, since then there has been a complete standstill in lending. The table shows that loans to Eastern Europe are small and relatively stable in size. Exposure to OPEC countries is more sizable and has declined since 1982.

Table 10.15 looks at lending to non-OPEC developing countries, this time disaggregating by size of bank. We also show how these claims have evolved relative to equity capital.

Three conclusions emerge from Table 10.15. First, debt is a "big bank" problem. More than 60 percent of total debt is owed to the major money center banks, and nearly 85 percent to only twenty-five major banks. Second, small banks have managed to reduce their claims over the past three years by 15 percent. Third, all banks and in particular the money center banks have been able to reduce their exposure measured as a percentage of capital. The exposure reduction has occurred primarily via a build-up of capital, in part by issuing equity commitment notes. But in part the exposure reduction is due to sell-off of loans, writedowns, and a slowdown or actual halt in new money commitments.

To judge the implications of LDC problem debts for the banking system, we look at the group of most heavily indebted countries (Table 10.16). For simplicity we take all of Latin America (including Venezuela) plus Nigeria, the Philippines,

Table 10.16 US bank exposure to problem debtors, 1985

	All banks	9 major	15 major	All other
Total exposure ($ billion)				
Latin America	80.4	60.5	16.0	15.2
Other debtors	12.6	8.8	1.9	1.2
Percentage of capital				
Latin America	78.9	148.6	80.0	36.9
Other debtors	12.3	21.7	9.5	2.9

Source: Federal Reserve.

Table 10.17 Market price of problem debt, December 1986 ($ billions)

Country	Total debt	Debt to US banks	Price[a]
Argentina	50.8	8.4	66.0
Bolivia	4.0	0.1	7.5
Brazil	107.3	22.2	75.5
Chile	21.0	6.5	68.0
Colombia	11.3	2.2	86.5
Ecuador	8.5	n.a.	65.5
Ivory Coast	8.0	0.4	77.0
Mexico	99.0	24.2	56.5
Morocco	14.0	0.8	69.5
Nigeria	19.3	0.9	39.0
Peru	13.4	1.5	19.0
Philippines	24.8	5.1	73.5
Uruguay	3.6	0.9	66.5
Venezuela	33.6	9.7	74.5
Yugoslavia	19.6	2.2	79.0
Weighted average			67.1

[a] Average of bid and offer price in cents per dollar debt.
Source: Dealer information.

Morocco, and Yugoslavia. The total exposure in 1985 was close to $100 billion and approximately 90 percent of bank capital. Thus, in the extreme situation of all these debtors repudiating their debts completely, bank stockholders would be largely, though not altogether, wiped out, while depositors would be left fully intact. That picture is more favorable than much of the public discussion of the "LDC debt bomb" might lead one to believe. Of course, this point holds only in the aggregate and thus is not very revealing. The more revealing comparison disaggregates by bank size. In this case it becomes apparent that their exposure is far in excess of their equity. Brazil, Argentina, and the Philippines alone (to take the 1987 major confrontation cases) account already for more than half of the capital of major banks.

Even Latin America's debt is to a large extent held by non-US banks. The Bank of International Settlements reports Latin American debt to banks in the reporting countries of $160 billion in 1985. Table 10.17 shows that only about half of that debt is owed to US banks. For the remaining problem debtors, the BIS total is $37 billion. In their case the US loans are thus only one-third of the total of exposure to banks in the United States and elsewhere (Bank for International Settlement 1986).

There is an important difference, though, between European and US banks. During the period of dollar appreciation, European banks were forced to increase their reserves against dollar loans. Furthermore, these loan provisions were facilitated by tax advantages. Since 1985 the dollar has depreciated significantly, and this has worked to increase European loan loss reserves further relative to their claims. As a result, European banks are said to have been able, in some instances, to set aside loan loss reserves to cover problem debts in full. This, of course, is far from the case for US banks.

10.4.2 *The quality of debts*

In the nineteenth century and until World War II, LDC debt mostly took the form of bonds traded on organized markets and widely held by the public. The postwar debt, by contrast, is owed to official institutions and commercial banks. Accordingly, there are no good price quotations that might be used as a measure of the quality of debts. Very little of claims on debtor LDCs takes the form of bonds.[10] But for some time, bank claims on various LDCs have been swapped between banks, sold outright between banks, and are now even being sold to nonbanks. The market has become central to discussions of debt-equity swaps. In these transactions, further discussed below, purchase of discounted debt is the starting point for a foreign investment in a debtor country.

Table 10.17 shows the average of the bid and offer price in the secondhand market. It would be a mistake to believe that all debts are actively traded, but even so the prices provide some indication of market valuation.

There are quite extraordinary divergences in prices, Bolivia, Peru, and Nigeria have low valuations, but perhaps more interesting is the difference between Mexico and Brazil. Why is Brazil thought to be so much better a credit risk than Mexico? The major difference would have to be between being an exporter and an importer of oil. The average price of problem debts is 67 cents per dollar. Discounts of 25 percent and more suggest that these are indeed problem debts and that the prospect of a return to voluntary lending might be very remote.

However, the story is not that simple. Consider the case of Uruguay. The country's debt stands at a discount of 33.5 percent, suggesting that the debt is poor. Yet in the fall of 1986, Uruguay issued a long-term public sector bond at the same rate as the US Treasury. This suggests that the large discounts reflect above all a market that is too narrow, so it is illiquidity of banks that dominates in depressing the prices.

10.5 US trade effects of the debt crisis

There is considerable difficulty in allocating the deterioration of the US external balance between competing causes: the overly strong dollar, the rapid domestic

Table 10.18 US trade with South America (billions of US dollars)

	Exports	Imports	Trade balance
1979	13.6	13.2	0.4
1980	17.4	14.4	3.0
1981	17.7	15.5	2.2
1982	15.3	14.4	0.9
1983	10.5	16.0	−5.5
1984	11.0	21.0	−10.0
1985	11.0	20.9	−9.9

Source: Survey of Current Business.

Table 10.19 Latin America's bilateral trade balance with various groups (billions of dollars)

	USA	Japan	EEC	Industrial countries
1980	−3.4	−2.4	2.8	−4.2
1985	10.8	0	7.7	18.7
Change as percentage of exports	42.9	54.8	20.8	35.1

Source: IMF, Directions of Trade Statistics.

growth relative to that abroad, the budget deficit, and the turnaround forced on debtors' trade balances by the need to service external debts.

Table 10.18 gives some indication of the shift in our trade with Latin America. Not all of the shift can be attributed to the debt crisis since our loss in competitiveness must certainly account for some part of what happened. Also, the trade figures of the early 1980s are inflated by Latin America's overvaluation and spending spree. But even so, there was a major shift in the bilateral balance amounting to $10–12 billion from 1979 to 1985.[11]

Table 10.19 compares the evolution of Latin American trade with different countries, showing a substantial shift toward bilateral surpluses with respect to each of these groups. While the surplus with the United States is far larger in absolute terms, this is not the case when the change is expressed relative to exports. This is a crude way of illustrating that the dollar appreciation may not be so dominant in this bilateral trade balance swing.

If $10 billion is taken as the change in the bilateral trade balance, even attributing it to the debt crisis, one does not come up with much damage to the United States. After all, this change is less than one quarter of 1 percent of US GNP! Of course, this does not exhaust the damage, and GNP is not the proper scale variable. Other damage to US trade and investment interests occurs via the depression of demand and profitability in the debtor countries. US multinationals that produce in those countries have sharply reduced sales and profits. Similarly, there are declines in US exports of services (other than interest) to debtors. There are no ready estimates of losses in service exports.

In judging whether a $10 billion deterioration in the trade balance is large, one must bear in mind two points. The swing in the trade deficit helps facilitate a noninflationary absorption of our budget deficit. Switching lending from LDCs to the US Treasury helps finance our own deficits under better (short-term) macroeconomic conditions. But there is clearly a cost for the affected industries. A large share of the trade deterioration, for example, is in the capital goods sector as Latin America's decline in investment reduced our exports. For this sector the trade deterioration with Latin America is, of course, far above the one-quarter of 1 percent of income. Even so, it would be difficult to make the debt crisis the main reason for our $150 billion trade problem.

10.6 Solutions to the debt problem

The ordinary aftermath of imprudent borrowing and adverse international conditions, as in the 1920s and 1930s most recently, is debt default.[12] Debts are normally written down or simply not serviced for many years. When servicing is ultimately resumed, it occurs without full payment of arrears and often at reduced interest rates.

The major differences in the present debt crisis are two. First, commercial banks and governments, rather than bondholders, are the main creditors. A more significant difference is that the governments of the major industrialized countries have insisted on debt service and have managed a system of debt collection, with the IMF as the chief coordinating agent. The system avoids illiquidity by making available essential "new money" at profitable spreads over the cost of funds to banks, and it enforces the debts by behind-the-scenes political pressure. The creditors are efficiently organized in this case-by-case approach, while debtors have been unable to put up a united front.[13]

The debtors' problem, especially in the case of Latin America, is how to gain debt relief or additional credit, so as to make available resources for investment and develop speculation in support of the government's ability to promote growth policies without risking financial instability. Tax reform and improved tax enforcement are certainly of overriding importance in this. Improved efficiency in the public sector is important, but measures to attract capital or secure relief on the external debt seem the most desirable or practicable alternatives. We review here five possible directions of change: an improved world macroeconomy; a facility; debt-equity swaps; a reversal of capital flight; and Bradley-style debt relief.

10.6.1 *The world macroeconomy*

In 1982 the prospects of strong growth in the industrialized countries, lower interest rates, a weaker dollar, and stronger real commodity prices were the central scenario that encouraged the "muddling-through process." This favorable scenario implied that by the end of the decade, debt–export ratios would have declined significantly. Some of these developments have in fact occurred, and for some countries they have even been reinforced by an unexpectedly large decline in oil prices. But the expected benefits in terms of enhanced creditworthiness have not in general appeared. It is true that South Korea is at present not a problem debtor, but Brazil is and so are many other countries.

Looking ahead to the next few years, what macroeconomic developments can be expected and how will they affect the debt situation? The most important development for the world economy is US budget balancing. There are basically three scenarios. In one case, rapid budget cutting is accommodated by monetary expansion in the United States and in the rest of the world. In this setting, interest rates decline sharply, growth is sustained, and the main exchange rates between industrial countries remain unaltered. This is a highly favorable scenario for LDCs in that much lower interest rates implicitly transfer to them resources in amounts far in excess of what can be expected from creditor-country taxpayers.

The second scenario envisages the same budget cutting, perhaps more spread out in time, but without monetary accommodation. In that case, interest rates decline somewhat, but there will be a world recession. Most debtors would not benefit, or would benefit very little, since the lower interest rates are offset by slack in their export markets.

A third scenario envisages a hard landing: budget cutting and a flight from the dollar that forces the Federal Reserve to *raise* interest rates to stem the inflationary impact of depreciation. Such a development would bring about systemwide illiquidity and likely default.

The world macroeconomy does hold out some promise. A Gramm–Rudman–Hollings budget cut, soon and with worldwide monetary accommodation, would make a major advance toward solving the debt problem. But for the time being there is not much of a sign of either the budget cutting or the monetary accommodation.

10.6.2 Debt–equity swaps

The debt problem has two aspects. The first is that debtors cannot service their debts as contracted. Moreover, the interest they pay comes largely at the expense of much needed investment in their economies. Thus debtors have a resource and investment shortage. On the lenders' side, small banks are tired of the acrobatics involved in debt collection. They want to avoid yet another round of rescheduling. But there is no money in the debtor countries to pay them off, nor can the large banks do so, given their already extravagant exposure. These twin problems strain the skills of regulators, accountants, and policymakers worldwide.

The poor quality of LDC loans can be judged by the discount at which they trade in the emerging secondhand market. The large discounts suggest that an imminent return to voluntary lending is highly unlikely. Creditors' attention is therefore shifting to new ways of liquidating debts without taking outright and massive losses on the entire portfolio. But if banks are to get out, who will get in?

Debt–equity swaps have emerged as a seemingly attractive solution to the debt problem—clearly not *the* solution, but a sound contribution with all the rings of free enterprise.[14] Their apparent merit is in solving two problems at once: they allow banks to sell off loans without a massive decline in loan prices, and debtors can reduce their external debt and at the same time pull in foreign investment. All things considered, the swaps appear to be a good idea. But there are reasons for skepticism.

Before turning to these objections, a qualification is important. There should be no doubt that debt–equity swaps agreed to between private firms and their commercial bank creditors (without government intervention or subsidies) are entirely appropriate. Likewise, there can be no objection to direct foreign investment. On the contrary, there should have been more in the past, and the more there is in the future the better. The objections raised here concern exclusively the use of already strained debtor budgets to grease the wheels.

The basic difficulty is that debt–equity swaps amount to a budget subsidy by debtor countries that will allow banks to get out and foreign investors to get in. Here are the mechanics: First Regional Bank sells Brazilian government bonds at a discount to Dreams, Inc., a US firm specializing in services. Dreams, Inc. presents the debt to the Banco Central do Brasil to be paid off in cruzados. The proceeds are used for the purchase of a Brazilian firm. It seems that everybody gains: the bank has found a way of selling some of its illiquid portfolio without depressing the secondhand market; the investing firm gains the advantage of buying cruzados at a discount; and Brazil gains because she can pay the foreign debt in local currency rather than dollars. Moreover, much needed investment takes place.

The debtor government will have to finance the repurchase of debt from the foreign investor. One cannot simply print local money to pay. In fact the government will issue domestic debt and use the proceeds to buy back its foreign debt as it is presented by the foreign investor. Hence, when everything is done, the government has a reduced external debt, but a matching increase in domestic debt. The country owns less of its capital stock, since the foreign investor will have bought some, and in return has redeemed some of its external debt.

Is there any advantage for the budget? In the budget there will now be reduced interest payments on external debt offset by increased domestic debt service. There is a net reduction in interest if the debtor country can appropriate most of the discount at which the external debt is traded and if the real domestic interest rate (in dollars) is not too high relative to the cost of servicing the external debt. The net result is likely to be an increase in debt service because real interest rates in debtor countries are exceptionally high.

On the balance of payments side, however, swaps might seem to be good news: foreign debt is reduced and as a result burdensome interest payments to abroad come down. But the reduced external interest payments are matched, at least potentially, by increased remittances of dividends or profits by the new foreign owners of the national capital stock. Hence, on the payments side the trick also does not do much good. In fact, the country becomes less liquid since it is much easier to control the service of bank debt than the remittances of multinationals. The massive outflow of remittances from Brazil in 1986 makes this point.

Debt–equity swaps are primarily a balance sheet operation, not a net resource transfer. One might argue that the government could target deals to make them less a transaction in existing assets and instead be directed toward new, extra investment. More likely, financial intermediaries will look for firms, domestic or foreign, that are already investing. They will approach the firms with a new kind of financing package involving debt–equity swap that, because of an implicit subsidy by the government, turns out to be less costly than alternative sources of finance. Thus debt–equity swaps will finance investment, but they finance at the budget cost of a subsidy investment that would have taken place anyway. This explains the reluctance of debtor countries to plunge into the scheme.

Debt–equity swaps bring together, with the glue of budget pesos, two entirely separate operations that would arise in a free, unregulated market. To solve the banks' problems, marking to market of LDC debts would occur and hence debts could be sold to the nonbank public. To cope with the resource problem, debtor countries would set up investment funds in which nonresidents can invest in the private economy with liberal facility for repatriation of dividends. The two separate steps ensure that old, bad debts do not prevent new investment. The bad debts are distributed more widely, though at a possible loss to all the banks' stockholders. The debtor countries gain extra resources which they may use to expand investment or to buy back their debt, whichever appears more profitable. This is the market solution. Debt–equity swaps, by contrast, are a way of nationalizing the transaction, pushing budget subsidies to bank stockholders rather than to extra investment.

Balance sheet tricks are not a substitute for gaining extra real resources for investment. Improved government budgets in the debtor countries, increased private saving, increased efficiency in their public sector, and net resource transfers from abroad are the only way for investment and growth to return. Of course, debtor countries should open all doors to foreign direct investment—the sooner and wider, the better. But there is no justification for subsidizing such investment.

10.6.3 *Reversal of capital flight*

Wishful thinking turns to the $100 billion or more of Latin American assets that have fled from financial instability and taxation to the industrial countries, especially the United States. Reversing these capital flights, primarily in the case of Mexico or Argentina, would make it almost possible to pay off the external debt; much of the debt was incurred in the first place to finance the exodus of private capital.

Estimates of the amount of capital flight in the 1970s and early 1980s differ widely. But whatever the methods by which the magnitudes are estimated, the fact of at least a $100 billion capital flight from Latin America is not in question. Estimates are particularly large for Mexico, Argentina, and Venezuela and much smaller for Brazil and Chile. For both Argentina and Mexico, estimates of $25 billion to $35 billion are not uncommon, hence the suggestion that reversing the mammoth outflow could help pay off the debt without tears.

The idea that private capital could be the main solution, or at least provide an important contribution, is naïve. There is little historical precedent for a major reflow, and when it does happen it is the last wagon of the train. Einaudi once observed that savers "have the memory of an elephant, the heart of a lamb, and the legs of a hare." Capital will wait until the problems have been solved; it will not be part of the solution and is even less likely to provide a bridgehead.[15]

It is often argued that if only countries adopted policies guaranteeing savers a stable positive real rate of interest, there would be no capital flight problem. But that argument is not very realistic in three respects. First, in the context of adjustment programs, devaluation is often unavoidable. Compensating savers for the loss they would have avoided by holding dollar assets would place a fantastic burden on the budget, which in turn would breed financial instability. Second, maintaining high real interest rates poses a serious risk to public finance. The public debt that carries these high real rates snowballs, and that in turn is a source of instability. Third, raising the return on paper assets above the prospective return on real capital is terrible supply-side economics; it ultimately erodes the tax base and deteriorates the financial system by souring loans. A country in trouble simply cannot make its chief priority keeping the bondholders in place.

Capital controls, where feasible, are a better strategy for restoring order in public finance than papering over extreme difficulties for a while using extraordinarily high real interest rates. The latter strategy was, indeed, at the very source of the mess in Argentina under Martíinez de Hoz and explains some of the difficulties in Mexico today.

The capital flight problem is encouraged by the fact that the US administration no longer withholds taxes on nonresident assets. For with this tax-free US return, anyone investing in Mexico (and actually paying taxes there) would need a yield differential, not counting exchange depreciation and other risks, of several extra percentage points.

There is much talk about the problems of banks putting in new money only to see it used by debtors such as Mexico to finance capital flight. Of an extra dollar of new money conceded by creditors, 70 cents are said to leave in extra capital flight. This indicates the need for a cooperative approach where debtor-country governments, the tax authorities in creditor countries, and the commercial banks cooperate in stopping capital flight and tax evasion. Of course, none of the three parties can succeed alone.

10.6.4 *The facility*

A number of proposals have been made over the past four years by academics, business leaders, and politicians in an attempt to drive a wedge between old, bad debts and the recognized need for new investment in debtor countries. Old debts are seen in this context as oversized mortgages on the debtor countries that impede the free and voluntary flow of new funds. The means to achieve such a flow is a facility that buys up LDC debts from banks and reduces debt service costs for debtors.[16] Lightening the burden of old debts and using an international fund with its diversification possibilities and possible credit standing provides important opportunities for passing on benefits to the debtors, without destructive effects on the solvency of banks or the asset position of their stockholders.

The details of such facility schemes vary. Invariably they are administered by the World Bank and involve allusions to the Marshall Plan, recycling, and the sharing of international burdens by strong currency countries or countries with significant external surpluses. On the basis of a capital subscription to be made by an as yet undesignated donor, leveraged by significant borrowing in the world capital market, the facility would take LDC debts over from banks or buy these in the secondhand market. Benefits to the LDCs occur because the facility will have a lower cost of capital than the individual LDC, both because of diversification and guarantees. The benefit of the reduced cost of capital and of the facility's purchases at discount of debts from banks would be passed on to debtors in the form of more favorable interest rates or debt reduction.

The concept of a facility draws attention to an important practical problem in credit markets. The higher the interest rate charged on credit, the less likely that it can and will be paid. Hence a policy of risk premiums is exactly that—it makes loans risky. Thus the facility would avoid this problem by charging a common interest rate, but it would reward countries for performance by writing down outstanding debt.

Such a facility would introduce a new party into debt negotiations. Concerned with the solvency and productivity of the facility, the management could take positions on rescheduling agreements to ensure that the value of the assets it carries is not impaired by extortionary settlements or unreasonable adjustment programs. One might imagine that the facility makes available a long-term reconstruction loan to a particular country, say Mexico, and in exchange secures from the banks extraordinary reductions in spreads or maturities. Of course, to perform this function aggressively would require that the manager of the facility have stature and independence beyond the immediate reach of the US Treasury.

The main question about the facility, the issue of the donor aside, is who the beneficiaries should be. The facility must, ultimately, involve taxpayers' money, although this may occur in a highly remote, off-budget, and leveraged fashion. The use of taxpayers' money makes it reasonable to ask whether the facility should benefit starving African debtors, middle-income Latin America, or winners such as Korea. Assigning the use of the fund primarily to Latin America rather than to Africa, whose debt is mainly to property authorities, is politically attractive.

10.6.5 *Debt relief*

Debtor countries have failed to form an effective cartel that could impose debt relief in the form of a writedown, sharply reduced interest rates, generous grace periods, or the consolidation of debt into perpetuities. On the contrary, debtor countries have competed with each other and, as a result, have wound up with poor terms and a short leash.

So far, only two attempts have been made to turn debt service into a major political issue. One is the case of Peru, where the government unilaterally limited its debt service to a specified fraction of export revenue. The other is the Mexican case of 1986. In each instance the large domestic costs of debt service and the destructive effects on investment, inflation, and growth potential led the governments to try and limit the damage. It is hard to believe that Peru got very far, but it is certain that Mexico initiated an important change in policies and procedures. The Mexican success suggests to some observers that with enough determination (and a favorable geographic location), debtors can in fact secure reduced spreads, contingency funds, and even an underwriting of growth.

At the same time, the debt problem is starting to become a political issue. Henry Kissinger, Lord Lever, Sen. Bill Bradley, and an increasing number of policymakers and policy economists are advocating a more political approach to the debt problem. This is the case in part for reasons of foreign policy. But poor US trade performance is also starting to be seen as a reflection of debtor countries' need to earn foreign exchange for debt service. This point has been emphasized especially by Bradley (1986a; 1986b). The Bradley debt plan accordingly emphasizes the need to create a vehicle for trade-debt discussions. Focusing explicitly on the link between trade concessions by debtor countries and targeted, limited debt relief, this approach consciously makes debt a political issue. Besides adapting the regulatory system to facilitate writedowns agreed between debtors and creditors, the proposal also calls for reduced interest payments, extra money, and debt writedowns.

Several negative responses to the Bradley proposal have been voiced, suggesting that the plan is impractical or undesirable. One argument is that the particular details—for example, the annual debt summit—are implausible, complicated, or useless. The trade issue, viewed from the perspective of the US external sector and growth, is small—there has been only a $12–15 billion swing in the bilateral balance with South America. Moreover, the writedowns are felt to be insufficiently conditioned on performance of the debtor countries and hence not worth making. Another criticism is more basic. It amounts to the assertion that any and all kinds of debt relief reduce or even destroy the beneficiaries' ultimate chances of renewed access to the international capital market. Countries that accept debt relief, it is argued, will be tainted. Only those that service humbly will see the day of voluntary lending. Historical precedent for all of Latin America suggests the opposite.

Political solutions to the debt problem are likely to be close to the arrangement Mexico secured and far away from the ambitious Bradley Plan. Resistance to writedowns might soften, even if there is no indication of this at present, and terms might become more flexible. But even so the debt problem will remain an overwhelming burden on the growth prospects of Latin America. Taxpayers are unwilling to underwrite Latin American growth, and politicians are unwilling to underwrite the banks. Growth in Latin America will therefore depend in equal parts on a solution to the US deficit problem with generous monetary accommodation and on the introduction of reasonable public finance in the debtor countries. With these two conditions met, and excepting extreme episodes such as the 1986 Mexican oil decline, growth can start again, although the losses of the 1980s will not be made up.

Debt relief can come from direct government intervention, but it can also come if governments withdraw from organizing the debt collection process. Meltzer (1984) has advocated this course and Milton Friedman (1984, p. 38) has observed: "So I think the way you solve the LDC 'debt bomb' problem is to require the people who make the loans to collect them. If they can, fine, and if they can't, that's their problem." There is little doubt that a withdrawal of governments (and the IMF) from the debt collection process would lead to a rapid disintegration of the creditors' cartel and a reduction of debts to levels more congenial to debtors.

10.6.6 *Moral hazard*

Solutions to the debt crisis involving debt relief encounter one apparently overwhelming objection: Latin America's debt reflects to a large extent mismanagement and capital flight. Granting debt relief to Latin debtors, but not to countries where management was more careful, amounts to rewarding poor policy performance and thus invites repetition.

But the moral hazard argument can also be made in two other ways. First, not giving debt relief means that the governments of creditor countries enforce bad loans. They thus encourage poor lending policies on the part of commercial banks, which now expect their governments to help collect even the poorest sovereign loans. Second, in the context of capital flight it is frequently argued that amnesty for tax fraud and illegal capital transfers is an effective and desirable policy for encouraging a reflow. Of course, the same moral hazard argument applies, as future tax morality would be undermined.[17]

The major weakness of the moral hazard argument in cases such as Mexico and Argentina results from capital flight: those who pay are primarily workers whose real wages are cut. Owners of external assets are rewarded by capital gains and thus turn out to be net beneficiaries of the debt crisis. The moral hazard argument thus can be turned around to support the case for debt relief.

Notes

1. There is a lot of flux in debt data. A good survey of the problems can be found in Mills (1986). We use here the IMF data, data reported by Morgan Guaranty *World Financial Markets*, and the US country exposure survey, except where otherwise noted.

2. The classification of countries follows the IMF. See *World Economic Outlook* (October 1986): 31–4.
3. Note that real GDP and dollar GDP behave very differently. A real depreciation may raise real GDP but is certain to lower dollar GDP.
4. This increase in real debt burdens would have outpaced any advantages from cumulatively lower interest rates on nondollar debt. As is well known, exchange rate movements have far exceeded the depreciation implicit in international interest differentials.
5. See Dornbusch (1985a; 1986a) on the Martínez de Hoz experiment.
6. On the Chilean experiment, see Edwards and Edwards (1987) and Ramos (1986).
7. On the Mexican case, see Cardoso and Levy (1986).
8. See especially Fraga (1986) for a comparison between Germany in the 1920s and Brazil in the 1980s. See also Dornbusch (1985b).
9. The fact that it is often food subsidies that are eliminated, without the proverbial neutral lump-sum tax to compensate the losers, does not seem to limit the case for the policy recommendation.
10. There are a few public sector bonds outstanding. Edwards (1986), and Dornbusch (1986b; 1986c) look at the yields of Mexican, Argentine, Venezuelan, and Brazilian bonds.
11. The change in the bilateral trade balance in manufactures is more significant than the change in the total bilateral trade balance because declining oil and commodity prices reduce our import bill and hence are reflected in a smaller change of the total balance.
12. For an extensive discussion of solutions, see Lessard and Williamson (1985).
13. The Mexican settlement forced the commercial banks to put up an unexpectedly large contribution. The settlement has demonstrated that the debt problem is not dead, but also that government involvement might boomerang.
14. For a strong statement of support for debt–equity swaps, see the Morgan Guaranty *World Financial Markets* issue of September 1986.
15. The public opinion survey on Mexico reported in the *New York Times* on November 16, 1986, makes most apparent just how pessimistic nationals of debtor countries are about the chances of economic recovery.
16. The most recent proposals are the editorial by David Obey and Paul Sarbanes in the *New York Times*, November 9, 1986, and the suggestion for a Japan Fund made in various speeches by Jim Robinson of American Express.
17. There is an interesting difference in public finance ideology: government debt writedowns in the form of a capital levy are said to undermine the very foundations of government credit, but tax amnesty is viewed as a practical response.

References

Bank for International Settlement (1986) *Annual Report.*

Bell, Geoffrey L., and John G. Heimann (1982). *Risks in International Bank Lending.* Group of Thirty.

Bergsten, Fred C., William R. Cline, and John Williamson (1985) *Bank lending to developing countries: The policy alternatives.* Institute for International Economics. April.

Bradley, B. (1986a) "Defusing the Latin debt bomb." *Washington Post*, October 5.

Bradley, B. (1986b) "A proposal for Third World debt management." Paper presented in Zurich, June.

Cardoso, E. (1986) "What policy makers can learn from Brazil and Mexico." *Challenge,*

September/October.

Cardoso, E., and R. Dornbusch (1987) "Brazil's tropical plan." *American Economic Review* (papers and proceedings), May.

Cardoso, E., and S. Levy (1986) "Mexico." In R. Dornbusch and L. Helmers, eds, *The open economy: Tools for policy makers in developing countries.* World Bank.

Cline, W. (1983) "International debt and stability of the world economy," Institute for International Economics, Washington, DC, September.

Cohen, D., and J. Sachs (1986) "Growth and external debt under risk of repudiation." *European Economic Review*, June.

Cooper, R. N., and J. Sachs (1985) "Borrowing abroad: The debtor's perspective." In G. Smith and J. Cuddington, Eds, *International debt and the developing countries.* World Bank.

Dale, Richard, and Richard P. Mattione (1983) *Managing global debt.* Washington, DC: Brookings Institution.

De Grauwe, P., and M. Fratianni (1984) "The political economy of international lending." *Cato Journal*, Spring/Summer.

Delamaide, D. (1985) *Debt shock.* New York: Anchor Press/Doubleday.

Dillon, Burke K., Maxwell C. Watson, Russell G. Kincaid, and Chanpen Puckahtikom (1985) *Recent development in external debt restructuring.* International Monetary Fund. October.

Dornbusch, R. (1985a) "External debt, budget deficits, and disequilibrium exchange rates." In G. Smith and J. Cuddington, eds, *International debt and the developing countries.* World Bank.

Dornbusch, R. (1985b) "Policy and performance links between LDC debtors and industrial countries." Brookings Papers on Economic Activity, No. 2.

Dornbusch, R. (1986a) "The Bradley Plan: A way out of the Latin debt mess." *Washington Post*, August 27.

Dornbusch, R. (1986b) "Impact on debtor countries of world economic conditions." In *External debt, investment and growth in Latin America.* International Monetary Fund.

Dornbusch, R. (1986c) "International debt and economic instability." In *Debt, financial stability and public policy.* Federal Reserve Bank of Kansas.

Dornbusch, R., and S. Fischer (1986) "Stopping hyperinflation." *Weltwirtschaftliches Archiv*, April.

Eaton, J., M. Gersowitz, and J. Stiglitz (1986) "The pure theory of country risk." *European Economic Review*, June.

ECLA (1985) *External debt in Latin America.* Denver, CO: Lynne Rienner Publishers; published in cooperation with the United Nations.

ECLA (1986) *Debt, adjustment, and renegotiation in Latin America.* Denver, CO: Lynne Rienner Publishers; published in cooperation with the United Nations.

Edwards, S. (1986) "The pricing of bonds and bank loans in international markets: An empirical analysis of developing countries' foreign borrowing." *European Economic Review*, June.

Edwards, S., and A. Cox-Edwards (1987) *Monetarism and Liberalization. The Chilean Experiment.* Cambridge, MA: Ballinger.

Eichengreen, B., and R. Portes (1986) "Debt and default in the 1930s: Causes and consequences." *European Economic Review*, June.

Feldstein, M. (1986) "International debt service and economic growth: Some simple analytics." NBER Working Paper No. 2076.

Fischer, S. (1986) The international debt problem and the Baler plan. Testimony before the Joint Economic Committee, January 23.

Fischer, S. (1987) "Sharing the burden of the international debt crisis." *American Economic Review* (papers and proceedings) Vol. 77.

Fishlow, A. (1985) "Lessons from the past: Capital markets during the 19th century and the interwar period." *International Organization*, Summer.

Fraga, A. (1986) *German reparations and Brazilian debt: A comparative study*. Princeton Essays in International Finance, No. 163. September.

Friedman, M. (1984) *Politics and tyranny*. Pacific Institute for Public Policy Research.

Gersovitz, M. (1985) "Banks' international lending decisions: What we know and implications for the future." In G. Smith and J. Cuddington, eds, *International debt and the developing countries*. World Bank.

Group of Thirty (1981a) *The outlook for international bank lending*. New York.

Group of Thirty (1981b) *Risks in international bank lending*. New York.

Guttentag, Jack, and Richard Herring (1983) *The lender-of-last-resort function in an international context*. Princeton Essays in International Finance, No. 151. May.

Guttentag, Jack, and Richard Herring (1986) *Disaster myopia in international banking*. Princeton Essays in International Finance, No. 164. September.

Hakim, P. (1986) "The Baker Plan: Unfulfilled promises." *Challenge*, September/ October.

Kaletsky, Anatole (1985) *The costs of default*. 20th Century Fund.

Kenen, P. (1983) "A bailout for the banks." *New York Times*, March 6.

Kindleberger, C. P. (1982) "The cyclical pattern of longterm lending." In M. Gersovitz *et al.*, *The theory and experience of economic development*. London: George Allen & Unwin.

Kraft, J. (1984) *The Mexican rescue*. Group of Thirty.

Krugman, P. (1985) "International debt strategies in an uncertain world." In G. Smith and J. Cuddington, eds, *International debt and the developing countries*. World Bank.

Lessard, D., and J. Williamson (1985) *Financial intermediation beyond the debt crisis*. Washington, DC: Institute for International Economics, September.

Lever, H., and C. Huhne (1986) *Debt and danger*. Boston: Atlantic Monthly Press.

Maddison, A. (1985) *Two crises: Latin America and Asia, 1929–38 and 1973–83*. Paris: OECD.

Maddison, A., ed. (1986) *Latin America, the Caribbean and the OECD*. Paris: OECD.

Mehran, Hassanali (1985) *External debt management*. International Monetary Fund.

Meltzer, A. (1984) "The international debt problem." *Cato Journal*, Spring/Summer.

Mendelsohn, M. S., ed. (1981) *The outlook for international bank lending*. Group of Thirty.

Mills, R. H. (1986) "Foreign lending by U.S. banks: A guide to international and U.S. statistics." *Federal Reserve Bulletin*, October.

Moreira-Marques, M. (1986) *The Brazilian quandary*. New York: 20th Century Fund.

Niehans, J. (1985) "International debt with unenforceable claims." Federal Reserve Bank of San Francisco. *Economic Review*, No. 1.

Nowzad, B., and R. C. Williams (1981) *External indebtedness of developing countries*, International Monetary Fund. May.

Obey, D., and P. S. Sarbanes (1986) "Recycling surpluses to the Third World." *New York Times*, November 9.

OECD (1986) *Financing and external debt of developing countries: 1985 survey*. Paris: OECD.

Posner, M., ed. (1985) *Problems of international money, 1972–85*. International Monetary Fund.

Ramos, J. (1986) *Neoconservative economics in the Southern Cone of Latin America, 1973–83*. Baltimore, MD: Johns Hopkins University Press.

Reiffel, A. (1985) *The role of the Paris Club in managing debt problems*. Princeton Essays in International Finance, No. 161. December.

Sachs, J. (1983) "LDC debt in the 1980s: Risk and reforms." In Paul Wachtel, ed, *Crises in the economic and financial structure*. Lexington, MA: Lexington Books.

Sachs, J. (1984) *Theoretical issues in international borrowing.* Princeton Essays in International Finance, No. 54. July.

Sachs, J. (1985) "External debt and macroeconomic performance in Latin America and East Asia." *Brookings Papers on Economic Activity*, No. 2.

Sachs, J. (1986) "Conditionality and the debt crisis: Some thoughts for the World Bank." Harvard University. Typescript.

Simonsen, M. (1985) "The developing country debt problem." In G. Smith and J. Cuddington, eds, *International debt and the developing countries.* World Bank.

Sjaastad, L. (1983) "International debt quagmire: To whom do we owe it?" *World Economy*, September.

US Senate Committee on Finance (1932) *Sale of foreign bonds or securities in the United States.* January.

Watkins, Alfred J. (1986) *Till debt do us part.* Roosevelt Center for American Policy Studies. Washington, DC: University Press of America.

Watson, M., D. Mathieson, R. Kincaid, and E. Kalter (1986) *International capital markets.* International Monetary Fund. February.

Weinert, R. (1983) "Banks and bankruptcy." *Foreign Policy*, Spring.

Winkler, M. (1933) *Foreign bonds.* Philadelphia: Roland Swain Co.

World Bank (1986) *A strategy for restoration of growth in middle-income countries that face debt-servicing difficulties.* Development Committee.

11

Debt problems and the world macroeconomy

11.1 Introduction

This paper discusses the role of world macroeconomic factors in contributing to the debt crisis. I investigate what role these factors—interest rates, commodity prices, growth—played in bringing on the debt crisis, and how they facilitated or complicated the first five years of adjustment. I also ask whether and in what way the world macroeconomy is likely to contribute to the solution of the debt problem in the next five years.

The paper begins with the presentation of a conceptual framework and a review of the behavior of key macroeconomic variables in the past quarter of a century. I then proceed to a discussion of the origins of the debt crisis and a description of the adjustment period, 1982–87. The following part reviews alternative scenarios for the period 1987–90 and their bearing on debt questions. I also ask what contribution to expect from commercial policies. The paper concludes pessimistically that for many debtors sufficient improvement cannot be expected from a good performance of the world economy. This makes it necessary to find mechanisms that would make it possible to reverse resource flows.

11.2 External debt and the debt crisis

In this part of the paper I set out a conceptual framework in which to discuss debt problems and present the macroeconomic background to the debt crisis of 1979–82.

11.2.1 *A conceptual framework*

The balance of payments and national income accounts give us a basic framework for analysis. The identities and relations they contain, which are true by accounting definition, provide an objective conceptual setting.

There is a debt problem when a country cannot service its debt on the contracted schedule. Debt service difficulties may either be an inability to pay the principal of a maturing debt, as is the case for Colombia or Venezuela today, or an inability to pay both interest and principal. We focus here on debt difficulties of the more serious kind where interest cannot be paid. The reason is that difficulties in paying principal, when interest is regularly paid, should not present any problem since rolling over is a routine operation. The only reason difficulties with principal can become debt problems is if creditors wish to limit their regional exposure and hence insist on payment of principal even from those countries which are good debtors.

Focusing on interest payments, the current account of the balance of payments can be separated into two components: the noninterest current account (NICA), which includes trade in goods and in all services except interest payments on the external debt, and interest payments. Interest payments can be financed by noninterest surpluses or by net capital inflows:

$$\text{Interest Payments} = \text{Noninterest Current Account} + \text{Net Capital Inflows} \tag{11.1}$$

The category "net capital inflows" includes four components: reserve decumulation, direct foreign investment inflows, long-term portfolio inflows, and short- or medium-term borrowing abroad which is often called "new money." In the debt problems of the interwar period or the period preceding 1914, new money took the form of a "funding loan." Today it is concerted or involuntary lending by the commercial bank creditors and multilateral institutions.

Table 11.1 shows these current account components for problem debtor countries in the 1978–87 period.[1] It reveals the turn in the noninterest current account from a string of deficits until 1982 to a series of surpluses. In the period up to 1982 both interest payments and the noninterest deficit need financing and hence are reflected in a rapidly rising debt. After 1983 a large part of interest is

Table 11.1 The current account deficit and external debt: countries with recent debt-servicing difficulties ($ billion)

	Noninterest current account deficit (resource transfer)	Interest payments	Current account deficit	External debt
1978	17.1	14.8	31.9	242
1979	10.1	21.8	31.9	292
1980	5.0	34.3	39.6	356
1981	20.2	47.5	67.7	430
1982	5.4	57.5	63.1	494
1983	−30.2	52.1	21.9	514
1984	−48.6	57.2	8.6	534
1985	−50.2	53.6	3.1	553
1986	−32.7	50.2	17.5	573
1987	−27.8	45.7	17.9	586

Source: IMF, *World Economic Outlook*.

Table 11.2 Financing of problem debtors' imbalances ($ billion)

	1979–82[a]	1983–86[a]	1987
Current account deficit[b]	39.5	7.8	14.8
Non-debt-creating inflows	7.1	4.6	5.1
Net borrowing	49.4	11.6	16.3

[a] Period average.
[b] Deficit on goods, services, and private transfers.

paid by noninterest surpluses and hence the increase in debt is sharply reduced. But debt is still rising, reflecting the financing of the remaining interest payments not met by the surplus and the financing of capital flight and reserve build-up.

$$\text{Interest Payments} = \text{Noninterest Current Account} \\ + \text{New Money} + \text{Other Net Capital Inflows} \qquad \textbf{(11.2)}$$

The category "other net capital inflows" is typically very small. There is little room for reserve decumulation, and long-term capital flows tend to be small. The only time other net capital inflows assume importance is in the case of capital flight or, less frequently, a repatriation of capital.

The discrepancy between the current account on one side and the sum of net borrowing plus non-debt-creating inflows (chiefly direct foreign investment and official aid) represents reserve changes and capital flight (Table 11.2).

The noninterest deficit is often called the net resource transfer since it measures the net imports of goods and services (other than interest) over which a country acquires command. Noninterest deficits are the normal pattern for developing countries in which saving is low relative to investment. Noninterest deficits are the channel through which resources are transferred from rich to poor countries to support capital formation and growth in the developing world. Private and public lending forms the financial counterpart. Using the national accounts identities we can represent the financing of investment from the resource point of view as follows:

$$\text{Investment} = \text{Saving} + \text{Real Resource Transfer from Abroad} \qquad \textbf{(11.3)}$$

Table 11.3 shows the real resource transfers and the investment rates for Latin America. The table brings out strikingly the decline in investment as a counterpart of the real resource transfer abroad. The shift in resource transfers is almost exactly matched by a decline in investment.

Table 11.3 Resource transfers and investment as a percentage of GDP

	1973–82	1983–85
Gross investment	24.3	18.5
Noninterest surplus	−0.6	4.7

The essential distinction between pre-crisis and post-crisis is the turn of the net resource balance, with debtor countries now making net resource transfers to creditor countries.

11.2.2 *Debt crises*

Any debt crisis involves the inability of debtors to meet timely payments of interest and principal. Thus the gap between interest payments that are due and the noninterest current account is the chief characteristic of a debt problem. Four factors then can be identified as leading to a debt problem:

1. With an unchanged willingness to roll over debt and provide a given flow of new money, an increase in real interest rates raises the financing requirement. The imbalance between new money requirements and credit voluntarily supplied brings about a debt crisis.
2. A deterioration in the noninterest current account, because of domestic macroeconomics or because of a worsening in the terms of trade or a fall in export demand, opens a financing gap.
3. An increase in world inflation leads to an increase in nominal interest rates and hence to an early *real* amortization of the external debt. Although real interest rates are unchanged there is a cash flow problem for debtors.
4. With an unchanged interest rate and noninterest current account, creditors decide that exposure is excessive and therefore limit new money commitments and require that maturing principal be paid off.

I now proceed to identify the impact of world macroeconomic events on debtor countries. Specifically, given policies such as the real exchange rate and fiscal policy, how has the world macroeconomy been one of the factors leading to the debt crisis; how has it influenced the evolution of the debt problems since 1982; and what implications can be anticipated from alternative scenarios of the world economy in the coming years? World interest rates, growth, and commodity price trends are at the center of the discussion.

A special interest, however, attaches to their joint behavior. For example, what if the interest payments a country owes increase but the noninterest deficit also increases? And at the same time creditors become unwilling to increase their exposure? The financing equation then no longer adds up and something must give. When a debt crisis occurs and outright default or arrears are not the answer, creditors are often coerced into involuntary lending and debtors undergo adjustment programs to turn their noninterest deficits into surpluses. Creditworthiness must be reestablished. Now debtors have noninterest surpluses that finance the interest payments. But there may still be a part of interest payments financed by net capital inflows or "new money."

With this background in mind we can turn to the main world macroeconomic variables that had an influence in creating the debt crisis.

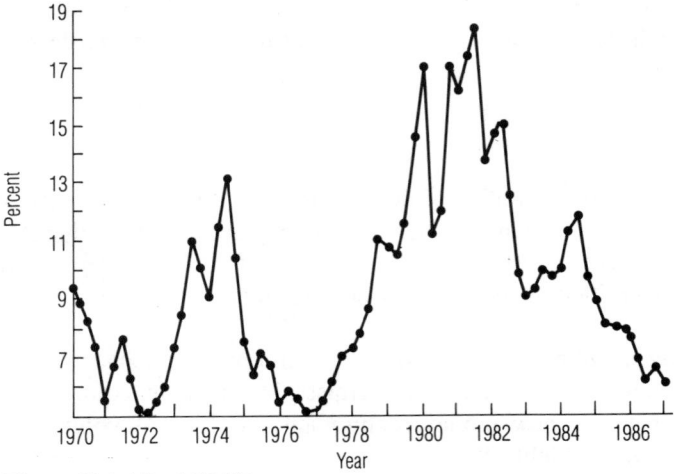

Figure 11.1 The LIBOR rate.

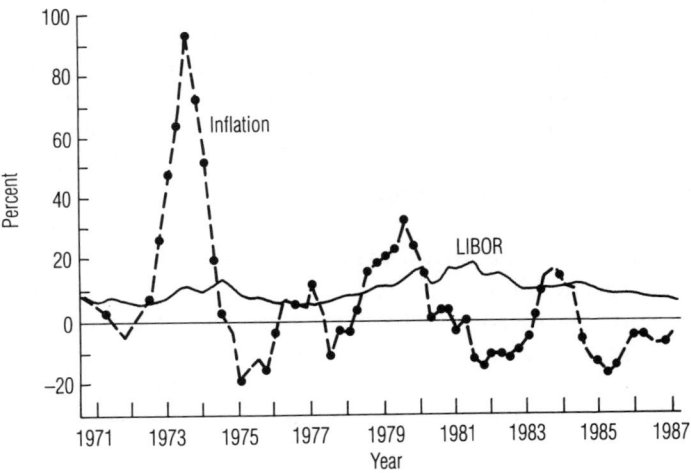

Figure 11.2 Interest rates and commodity price inflation.

11.3 The world macroeconomy: An overview

Figures 11.1 to 11.4 highlight the chief external variables for debtor countries: the interest rate, the real interest rate, the real price of commodities, and world economic activity. Figure 11.1 shows the London interbank offer rate for dollar deposits (LIBOR). The contribution of interest rates to the debt crisis is shown by the peak level of an interest rate in excess of 18 percent in late 1981.

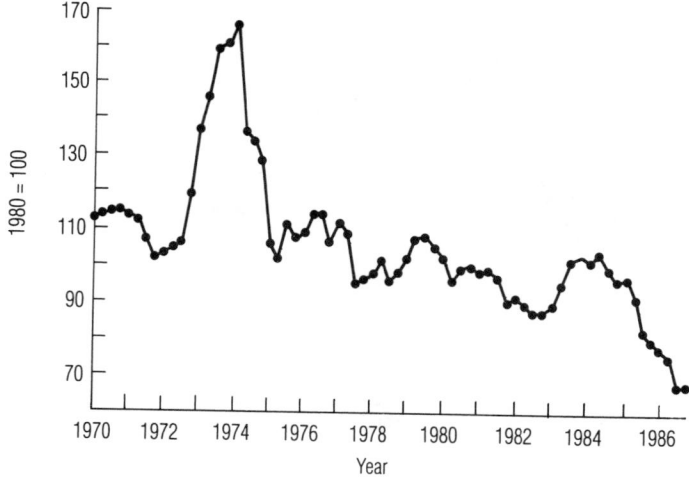

Figure 11.3 Real commodity prices.

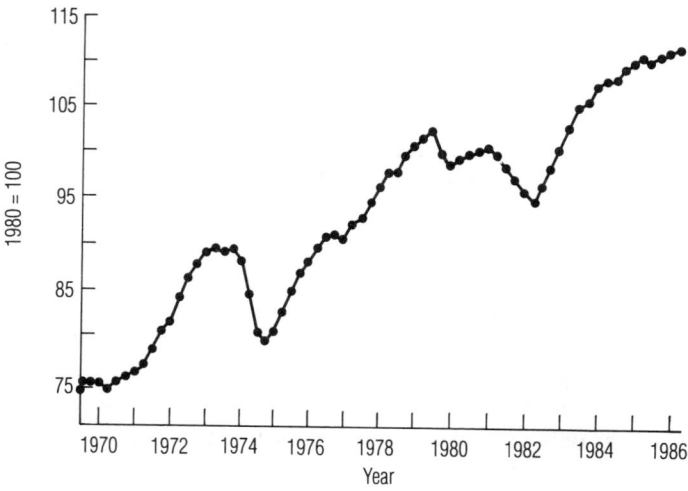

Figure 11.4 World industrial production.

The interest rate effects appear through two separate channels. One is associated with the level of nominal rates, given the real rate of interest. When higher inflation increases the nominal interest rate the effect on debtors is a shortening of the effective maturity of the debt. The *real* value of the debt is amortized at a faster pace. As a result debtors may experience liquidity problems.

Interest rates also, of course, hurt debtors when real rates increase. In this

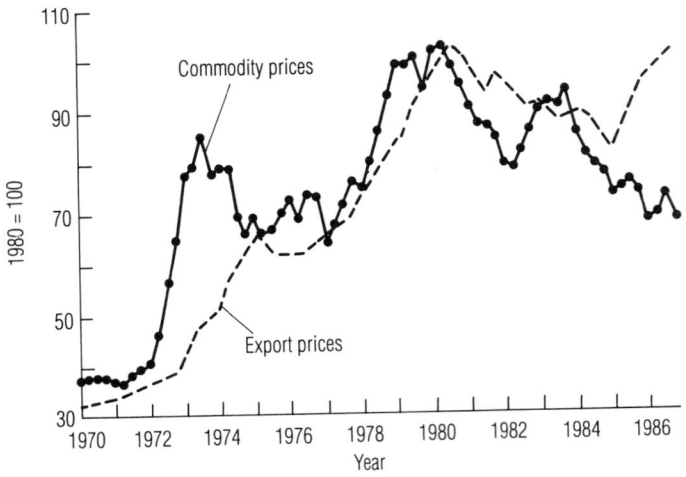

Figure 11.5 Commodity prices and industrial countries' export prices.

context it must be decided in terms of at which rate of inflation the real interest rate should be assessed, and there is considerable difficulty in identifying the correct inflation rate. Alternative candidates might be the debtor countries' GNP deflator in dollars or the rate of inflation in world trade. We chose here the latter series, and it is shown in Figure 11.2 together with the LIBOR rate. The behavior of the real rate is, of course, striking in that the sharp increase in nominal rates was accompanied by a falling level of prices in world trade. The combination implied that the real interest rate facing debtor countries was much higher than 20 percent per year.

Figure 11.3 shows the price of commodities. The series shown here is the IMF index of all (non-oil) commodities deflated by the export unit value of industrial countries. Commodity prices show a steady decline since their peak levels in 1973–74. By late 1986 they had fallen to only 40 percent of the peak level. But in the early 1980s, when the debt crisis first occurred, the real price of commodities did not show a dramatic deterioration. Commodity prices thus were not an immediate source of the crisis, but they did become relevant later in raising the costs of adjustment for several debtor countries.

Figure 11.4 shows world economic activity measured by the index of industrial production in the industrialized countries. The behavior of the index is relatively smooth. The events of the early 1980s do not appear striking even though there was a decline of about 5 percent. Figure 11.5, finally, focuses on the divergent behavior of nominal prices in world trade (the industrial countries' unit export value) and nominal commodity prices.

Table 11.4 shows data for these aggregate indices. The table reports the

Table 11.4 Aggregate world macroeconomic indicators

	Real commodity prices (1980 = 100)[a]	LIBOR (%)	Inflation[b] (%)	World activity[c] (1980 = 100)
1960–69	115	5.2	1.0	56
1970–79	115	8.0	11.4	86
1980	100	14.4	13.0	100
1981	96	16.5	−4.1	100
1982	89	13.1	−3.5	96
1983	98	9.6	−3.3	99
1984	101	10.8	−2.5	106
1985	88	8.3	−0.4	110
1986	72	6.9	13.7	110
1987	63	6.8	12.8	112

[a] Measured in terms of manufactures export prices of industrial countries.
[b] Rate of inflation of industrial countries' unit export values.
[c] Industrial production.
Source: IMF and Economic Commission for Latin America.

averages for the 1960s and 1970s and more detailed information on the period of the debt crisis.

In addition to interest rates, real commodity prices, and economic activity in industrial countries, a fourth external factor influences the noninterest current account. This is commercial policy in developing countries and its influence on market access and hence export performance. There are no good aggregate indicators of market access or of changes in market access. But there is also no suggestion that this factor would have been an important element in provoking the debt crisis. Of course, that does not mean that protectionism did not increase the costs and difficulties of debtor countries once the crisis had started.[2]

11.4 Examples of the effect of the world macro shock

The overview of external factors gives little guidance as to what was the impact on individual debtors. Their common factor is only to be debtors and hence to be hurt by an increase in world interest rates. But even that exposure differs significantly across countries depending on their share of floating-rate debt. At one end of the spectrum are poor debtors with most of their debt at concessional rates; at the other end are Brazil and Mexico, for whom almost the entire debt has interest rates linked to market rates.

But differences in trade structure also matter, and these imply differential effects of the movement of commodity prices in debtor countries or of economic activity in industrial countries. Korea, for example, imports commodities while Brazil and Argentina are net commodity exporters. To investigate the differential impacts of the 1980s external shock, the experiences of a number of individual countries will be examined.

11.4.1 *Brazil*

Brazil exports both commodities and manufactures. In the early 1980s the country had just become a predominant exporter of manufactures. Of a total of $24 billion in exports in 1981, nearly 38 percent were primary commodities (coffee, iron, soya, sugar) and the remainder manufactures. But much of manufactured exports had a high import content—for example steel or orange juice. On the import side, a striking 51 percent was oil. Of the external debt of $50 billion, 80 percent was at variable interest rates and more than 80 percent was dollar-denominated.

For Brazil, therefore, oil prices and the world money market rate were the chief variables of interest. Being a net exporter of (non-oil) commodities, Brazil would on balance be hurt by a decline in real commodity prices. The concentration in exports on coffee, orange juice, soya, and iron ore is, however, important to note.

The external balance problem, of course, originated in the oil price increase of 1978–79. Oil imports increased from $4.5 billion in 1978 to $11.4 billion in 1981. This increase in the oil bill was automatically financed both in the budget and in the current account by the borrowing of the state enterprises in the world capital market.

The increase in world interest rates in 1979–81 added to the interest bill. In 1979 net interest payments amounted to $4.2 billion. By 1981 they had risen to $9.2 billion and in 1982 to $12.6 billion. At the end of 1978 the external debt was only $44 billion; by the end of 1981 it had risen to $61 billion and by the end of 1982 to $70 billion. The increase in LIBOR from 8.9 percent in 1978 to 12, 14, and 17 percent over the next three years added a cumulative $7 billion to the external debt. The combination of higher interest rates and higher oil prices "explains" almost the entire increase in debt between the end of 1978 and the end of 1981.

The fact that higher interest rates and higher oil prices explain the increase in debt can also be read to say that the failure to adjust to these external shocks, and the ability to borrow in world markets, meant that external debt was the means by which the country financed the impact of the external shock.

11.4.2 *Mexico*

The second oil price increase in 1978–79 provided an apparently sound basis on which to engage in a growth strategy. Petroleum export revenue increased from only $1 billion in 1977 to $14 billion in 1981. But spending increased far ahead of the increased revenues. The noninterest budget deficit, oil revenues notwithstanding, increased from 2 to more than 8 percent of GDP (see Table 11.5). The current account deteriorated even though oil revenues doubled every year.

The strong domestic expansion, combined with a fixed exchange rate, encouraged overvaluation. The extent of overvaluation at no point became as extreme as it had been in Chile or Argentina. But even so it led to significant deterioration in the trade balance and to massive capital flight.

The capital flight was concentrated in the period 1981–82, in the final phase of

Table 11.5 Mexico's macroeconomy, 1977–81

	1977	1978	1979	1980	1981	1982
Current account deficit (% of GDP)	2.3	3.1	4.1	4.4	5.8	3.8
Real exchange rate (1980–82 = 100)	93	94	98	104	114	83

Source: Morgan Guaranty Trust and Banco de México.

the López Portillo government. The deterioration in the external balance and the increasing difficulty in financing the deficit made it apparent that an exchange crisis was around the corner. Large wage increases led to an expectation of a sharp increase in inflation altogether incompatible with the maintenance of a fixed exchange rate. With no restrictions on capital flows there then occurred a massive flight into the dollar. In fact, the capital flight would have been much larger had it not been for the existence of domestic dollar deposits in the banking system. These Mex-dollar accounts absorbed a good part of the speculation, although their holders ultimately did much worse than those who bought the real thing.

Estimates of the amount of capital flight from Mexico in 1978–82 differ. A recent study by Cuddington (1986) estimates a total of more than $25 billion, whereas Morgan Guaranty Trust (1986) gives the higher number of $36 billion. Whatever the exact number, there is no question that somewhere between 10 and 15 percent of GDP went abroad in these critical years. And the reason is exclusively mismanagement since, unlike in the case of Argentina or Chile, there was no deterioration in external conditions until interest rates increased. On the contrary, the oil price increase had provided an extraordinary gain in real income and a potential improvement in the external balance.

11.4.3 *Argentina*

The Argentine external debt problems were largely due to a mismanagement of the exchange rate. The overvaluation of 1978–81, combined with the liberalization of capital flows, brought about massive capital flight.

Table 11.6 shows the basic data. Note the large real appreciation in 1978–80 and the terms of trade improvement up to 1981. The oil price increase, which was

Table 11.6 Argentine macroeconomic variables, 1978–82

	1978	1979	1980	1981	1982
Debt/GDP	23.9	30.2	37.3	48.1	60.3
Current account as % of GDP	4.0	−1.0	−7.6	−7.4	−3.8
Terms of trade[a]	84	88	100	114	99
Real exchange rate[a]	65	84	100	70	49

[a] Index 1980 = 100.

Table 11.7 Korean macroeconomic variables, 1978–82

	1978	1979	1980	1981	1982
Terms of trade[a]	118	115	100	98	102
Net exports of goods and nonfactor services[a]	−3.0	−7.3	−7.8	−5.4	−2.6
Net factor payments from abroad[b]	−1.3	−1.5	−3.3	−4.0	−4.1

[a]Index 1980 = 100.
[b]Percentage of GDP, national income accounts.

important for Mexico, Brazil, and Korea, had no effect on Argentina's terms of trade since the country is self-sufficient in oil.

The increase in external debt in Argentina far exceeds the cumulative current account. Therefore interest rate and terms-of-trade shocks cannot account for the major part of the debt problem before 1981. On the contrary, overvaluation and capital flight are the chief problems in this period. As we shall see below, this is no longer the case after 1982 when the terms of trade deterioration become an important issue.

11.4.4 *Korea*

As an oil importer Korea experienced a major deterioration in the terms of trade (see Table 11.7). The interest rate shock reinforced the external balance deterioration. Even so, by 1982 the external balance had already turned around and the deficit had become more moderate. In part this is a reflection of the real depreciation which restored competitiveness in the years following the crisis of 1980. In part it reflects a successful policy of exporting labor services to the oil-producing countries.

11.4.5 *Chile*

The Chilean case, just as that of Argentina and Mexico, reflects until 1982 primarily a mismanaged exchange rate rather than a predominance of external shocks. As shown in Table 11.8, the terms of trade initially improve and the

Table 11.8 Chilean macroeconomic variables, 1978–82

	1978	1979	1980	1981	1982
Terms of trade[a]	94	106	100	86	77
Real exchange rate[b]	91	100	120	136	122
Trade balance[c]	−0.4	−0.4	−0.7	−2.7	0
Current account[c]	−1.1	−1.1	−2.0	−4.7	−2.3

[a]Index 1980 = 100.
[b]Index 1981–82 = 100.
[c]Billions of US dollars.
Sources: CIEPLAN, Santiago, Chile, and Morgan Guaranty Trust.

deterioration of the external balance is above all due to the extraordinary overvaluation.

Only in 1981–82 do international factors take over and cause the deterioration of the external balance by means of increased interest burdens. In 1981 the overvaluation and the external factors combine to yield record deficits. But by 1982 exchange rate adjustment and domestic restraint already compensate on the trade side and the current account deterioration only reflects increased interest rate burdens.

11.4.6 *Conclusion*

The examples illustrate that external factors were by no means the only influence in the debt crisis. On the contrary, domestic policies were an important, often the main, influence in bringing about a large accumulation of debt. External factors reinforced the impact of these debts in 1981–82 via the interest rate shock.

11.5   The period 1982–87

This section investigates how the world macroeconomy influenced the debt problem in the period after 1982. I start with a review of the beliefs of 1982, namely that favorable trends in the world economy would significantly facilitate debt service. From there I go on to a more detailed consideration of the actual evolution of the world economy to ask whether world macroeconomic conditions in fact facilitated debt service or added to the burden.

11.5.1 *The beliefs of 1982*

When in 1982 Mexico, and shortly afterwards a host of other Latin American countries, encountered acute debt service problems, the process of concerted or involuntary lending started. The basic philosophy of that process had three ingredients:

1. To ensure an ultimate return to voluntary lending it was essential that debtor countries service their debts to the maximum extent possible, on commercial terms and without significant concessions other than with respect to the maturity of the debt principal.
2. Adjustments in debtor countries, specifically in the budget and exchange rates, would go far toward bringing about a swing in the noninterest balance so as to service debt.
3. The world macroeconomy would make a substantial contribution in reducing the burden of debt servicing. From the vantage point of 1982 the macroeconomy could only improve. Debtor countries could anticipate higher growth in demand for their exports, lower interest rates, and improving terms of trade.

The question of adjustment in debtor countries is beyond the scope of this paper and has been amply dealt with elsewhere.[3] The issue of interest here is the contribution of the world macroeconomy. Certainly in 1982 the outlook must have been favorable:

1. The world economy was in the deepest recession since the 1930s. In the recovery period there had to be, accordingly, an expectation of growth significantly above trend. This growth would bring about two results. First, it would mean an increase in demand for manufactures exports from debtor countries. Second, it would translate into a cyclical upturn of real commodity prices. These stylized facts were quite beyond doubt, given the ample empirical evidence on the cyclical behavior of real commodity prices and export volumes.[4]
2. With respect to interest rates the outlook also had to be outright favorable. The short-term interest rate was at record high levels in American history. These high levels of interest rates were an immediate result of a deliberate attempt to use monetary policy to stop the sharply accelerating US inflation of the late 1970s and early 1980s. With the success of disinflation, interest rates would decline and hence the extraordinary debt service burdens of 1982 would come down.
3. Even though the dollar had appreciated already for more than a year there was not much discussion on this issue. The reason was presumably that dollar appreciation started from a very low point so that overvaluation was not yet a relevant notion. Nor was there an expectation of significant further appreciation. Discussion of a contribution of dollar depreciation to the debt crisis only occurred over the next three years as dollar overvaluation became increasingly apparent.

The framework for analysis of debt problems rapidly became the Avramovic–Cline model of debt dynamics, which focuses on the ratio of debt to exports, b. The key question was whether the evolution of the world macroeconomy made declining ratios of debt to exports likely. The evolution of the debt–export ratio over time can be developed in terms of several determinants, specifically interest rates, i, the growth rate of export prices, p_x, and the growth rate of export volume, x:

$$\dot{b} = b(i - p_x - x) - v \tag{11.4}$$

where v denotes the noninterest current account surplus as a ratio of exports.

Equation 11.4 highlights the debt problem in the sense of an ever rising debt to export ratio. Such a course is unlikely if the real interest rate, defined as nominal rates less the rate of inflation of export prices, is less than the growth rate of export volume and if there is a noninterest current account surplus. Table 11.9 shows the long-term averages for some of these variables for use as a benchmark.

With the data for problem debtors, and assuming a spread over LIBOR of 2.2

Table 11.9 Long-term average growth rates, 1969–78

	LIBOR	Export prices	Export volume	Debt ratio[a]
Asia	7.8	10.1	10.8	75.7
Western Hemisphere	7.8	13.9	1.7	197.7
Problem debtors	7.8	12.1	2.3	164.3

[a]Ratio of debt to exports of goods and services in 1979.
Source: IMF.

percent, we observe that the debt–export ratio would be declining unless there was a noninterest current account deficit in excess of 7 percent of exports. Of course, in 1978–82 the deficits were in fact much larger.

The expectation of declining nominal interest rates and cyclically rising nominal and real export prices for debtor countries implied an expectation of low real interest rates. Recovery and sustained growth in the industrial countries were expected to translate into significant growth in export volumes.

Adjustment in debtor countries, in terms of both expenditure cutting and real depreciation, was expected to translate into significant export growth and into an increased noninterest current account surplus. Thus for every element in the debt dynamics equation a favorable scenario could easily be predicted. And if there was any pessimism on real interest rates and growth in export volume, the fact of noninterest current account surpluses provided the necessary leeway to make a trend reduction in debt burdens plausible.

Cline (1983) in particular expressed the view that the debt problem was largely under control. Using simulations for the major debtor countries, and assuming alternative scenarios for the world economy, he showed that for most debtor countries there was an expectation of declining debt–export ratios. Moreover, the gain in creditworthiness implied by a reduced debt–income ratio in several cases could be accompanied by significant growth in the debtor countries. Brazil, for example, could in Cline's simulations achieve both an average growth rate of 6 percent and a reduction in its debt–export ratio. The Cline analysis rightly emphasized the crucial role of oil prices in determining the relative performance of Mexico and Brazil. With the assumption of declining oil prices Mexico was a problem country and Brazil's prospects were relatively bright.

Table 11.10 shows a medium-term scenario developed by the IMF in 1982 as well as the actual outcome for the key variables. The IMF scenario assumed a strong internal adjustment in the debtor countries, continued inflation fighting in the industrial countries, a constant real price of oil at the 1982 level, and a sharply declining real LIBOR rate. Table 11.10 reports three scenarios: the baseline scenario is labeled A; scenario B is a pessimistic and hence imposes extra adjustment requirements on debtors; and scenario C is optimistic. The optimism and pessimism are judged in terms of the growth–inflation mix in industrial countries. There was apparently no recognition at the time of the real interest rate consequences of rapid disinflation and of the US monetary–fiscal mix. The other

Table 11.10 The 1982 IMF scenarios for non-oil developing countries (average annual rates for 1984–86 except as noted)

	A	B	C	Actual
Industrial country growth	3.2	2.2	4.3	3.1
Industrial country inflation	5.5	8.0	4.5	3.8
Real LIBOR rate[a]	2.0	2.0	2.0	5.4
Net oil importers				
Export volume	7.6	5.9	9.2	8.1
Terms of trade	−0.5	−1.7	0.9	0.7
Net oil exporters				
Export volume	5.0	4.0	6.0	3.6
Terms of trade	0	−1.0	1.0	−10.0
1986 Current account[b]				
Net oil importers	−13.7	−19.4	−9.0	−1.4
Net oil exporters	−20.6	−27.0	−17.5	−16.8

[a]Using the US GNP deflator.
[b]Percentage of exports of goods and services.
Sources: IMF, *World Economic Outlook*, 1982 and April 1987.

respect in which the scenario is interesting is that there was a quite explicit confidence that current account imbalances could be financed.

11.5.2 *The actual experience since 1982*

The actual outcome shown in Table 11.10 differs from the IMF scenario in the following respects:

1. Real interest rates continued to be far higher than expected. The US monetary–fiscal mix thus had strong implications for the performance of countries with high debt ratios and a high ratio of floating rate debt.
2. The real oil price fell dramatically and hence the relative performance of net oil exporters was due more to their adjustment efforts than to favorable terms of trade.
3. The assumption that debtor countries could afford to run significant current account deficits was overly optimistic. Financing constraints in fact limited these deficits.

Table 11.11 gives further details on commodity prices, nominal interest rates, and real oil prices, which were only addressed in the terms of trade category of Table 11.10. Nominal interest rates did, indeed, decline significantly from their peak levels, and OECD growth showed somewhat above the 3 percent threshold that had been set as a benchmark for solving debt problems. The significant difference from the 1982 outlook was in respect to commodity prices. Rather than showing a recovery in nominal and real terms they in fact continued to decline. The decline was so significant that in 1986 they were at a lower level than at any time in the preceding quarter of a century, as already shown in Figure 11.3. In nominal terms they had fallen back to the level of 1977.

Table 11.11 Commodity prices, oil prices, and interest rates (average annual percent)

	Commodity prices	Interest rates[a]	Real oil[b]
1969–78	9.8	7.8	
1980–82	−4.1	14.8	100
1983–86	−3.4	8.9	80

[a]LIBOR.
[b]Deflated by manufactures prices: index 1980–82 = 100.
Source: IMF.

Table 11.12 The deterioration of creditworthiness (percentage)

	Debt/GDP			Debt/exports			Debt service		
	1978	1982	1986	1978	1982	1986	1978	1982	1986
All debtor LDCs	26	34	40	132	151	180	14	20	22
Problem debtors	31	43	49	180	254	282	28	40	38

Source: IMF, *World Economic Outlook*.

Creditworthiness

The belief that debt and debt service ratios would decline has not in fact been borne out, as is shown in Table 11.12. On every measure of creditworthiness debtor countries today look worse than they did in 1982, excepting the debt service ratio. The reduction in interest rates since 1982 clearly helped reduce the service ratio, as did the long-term restructuring of debts. But even though there is a marginal reduction in the debt service ratio, the extent of decline falls short of the 1982 expectations.

Favorable conditions in the world economy and the beneficial effects of adjustment programs on the part of debtors were expected to show in time an improvement in creditworthiness sufficient to warrant a return to voluntary lending. That remains the expectation, but the process is not on schedule. Abstracting from the oil shock, which improved the situation of Korea and Brazil while dramatically worsening that of Mexico, there has been as yet no improvement as dramatic as had been anticipated. Standard indicators of creditworthiness such as the ratio of debt to GDP or debt to exports have in fact worsened since 1982.

The return of voluntary lending was predicated on countries restoring their credit standing. While creditworthiness is a broad and vague idea, the operational concept was a reduction of ratios of debt to GDP and debt to exports. Table 11.12 shows that since 1982 creditworthiness measured by these benchmark ratios has worsened or at least not improved, making the current adjustment effort of debtor countries entirely open-ended.

Table 11.13 Cline projections and actual 1985 outcomes ($ billion)

| | Argentina | | Brazil | | Mexico | |
	Cline	Actual	Cline	Actual	Cline	Actual
Exports	10.4	8.4	29.5	25.6	23.6	21.9
Imports	6.4	3.8	18.2	13.2	16.0	13.5
Oil			7.0	5.7		
Interest	6.2	5.3	13.0	9.6	10.7	9.9

Source: Cline (1983) and various government publications.

The Cline projections

While the preceding discussion focuses on groups of countries, it is also of interest to see how forecasts fared in specific country cases. The analysis by Cline (1983) provides that possibility for the year 1985. Table 11.13 shows the results for Argentina, Brazil, and Mexico.

Three points stand out in these comparisons. First, that export revenues fall short of those predicted by Cline. Second, that import spending is much lower than Cline had predicted. Third, that interest payments are somewhat lower than predicted by Cline. Note, though, that the Brazilian current account surplus of 1985 was correctly predicted by Cline. Of course, by 1986 the differences are much more pronounced because of the vast influence of the decline in oil prices from $28 to $15 per barrel.

Extreme cases

There are some countries that are outliers in the adjustment period since 1982. On one side are countries which are predominant exporters of commodities and borrow primarily from official sources. They would experience the large and continuing decline in commodity prices without the advantage of reduced interest burdens. Among the countries that come to mind in this category, Bolivia stands out. Their interest payments have been as much as 70 percent at fixed rates, so the fall in world interest rates did not bring major benefits. But the terms of trade deteriorated over the period 1981–86 by 14 percent. The value of exports declined in 1984–86 cumulatively by 40 percent!

On the other side, the most striking improvement in the external debt position during the adjustment period has been made by Korea. Korea benefitted from every one of the factors characterizing the 1982–87 period: lower commodity prices, lower oil prices, and lower interest rates. Each of these factors exerted a very significant impact on the external balance, and hence the combined effects—in conjunction with an aggressive exchange rate policy—produced a dramatic improvement in the external balance. The shift in the current account represents nearly 10 percent of GNP by 1986 and is still widening.

11.6 The outlook

In this section I ask whether there are important shifts in the world macroeconomic outlook, and in the outlook for trade policies and the capital market, that promise to help overcome the debt problem or threaten to make its solution much more difficult. On the side of macroeconomics there is certainly a possibility of quite different scenarios depending on the way in which the US budget problem is solved and the response of interest rates and the dollar to budget cuts when they do take place.

11.6.1 *The 1987 IMF scenario*

A useful frame of reference for the world economic outlook is the 1987 IMF medium-term scenario shown in Table 11.14. The central assumption of this scenario is a continued high real interest rate compensated by sustained growth in the world economy and in debtor country exports. There is an expectation of moderately rising real oil prices and no change in the terms of trade.

In terms of equation (11.4) above, the IMF outlook places major reliance on continued large noninterest current account surpluses and on export volume growth to help contain or reduce debt problems. The scenarios allow for growth

Table 11.14 The 1987 IMF world economic outlook

	1987	1988	1989–91 average
Industrial countries			
Growth	2.3	2.8	2.9
Real LIBOR	3.6	3.0	3.4
GDP deflator	2.9	3.4	3.2
World economy			
Manufactures prices	11.0	3.1	3.0
Oil prices	8.7	3.1	3.0
Nonoil commodities	−4.9	5.1	4.7
Problem debtors			
Real GDP	4.4	4.7	5.0
Terms of trade	−2.1	−1.0	—
Export volume	5.4	5.9	5.6
Import volume	2.5	3.6	5.7
Current account[a]	−1.5	−0.6	−0.6
Interest payments[a]	6.3	5.9	5.4
Latin America			
Real GDP	3.3	4.7	4.8
Terms of trade	−4.7	−0.6	0.2
Export volume	0.1	7.2	5.1
Import volume	−0.8	2.4	5.4
Current account[a]	−14.3	−9.3	−5.7
Interest payments[a]	25.3	23.1	20.5

[a] Percentage of exports of goods and services.
Source: IMF, *World Economic Outlook*, April 1987.

in imports at roughly the same rates as those of exports, which is possible because the starting point is a large noninterest surplus. Hence maintaining equal growth rates, with unchanged terms of trade, ensures that noninterest surpluses are maintained. In other words, the IMF assumes that in the period to 1991, problem debtors will continue to make real resource transfers to their creditors at present rates.

11.6.2 *US adjustment: Implications for debtor countries*

It is interesting to go beyond the IMF outlook and focus on the central development in the world economy in the next few years, namely US adjustment of the twin deficits. Table 11.15 shows the US macroeconomic data for the recent years. It is quite apparent that the large size of the US external deficit is at least to some extent a counterpart of the ability of debtor countries to service their debts by noninterest surpluses. The extent to which debtor countries were able to shift their trade balance with the United States is apparent from Table 11.16 which focuses on all goods and, specifically, on manufactures.

Table 11.16 shows that while the bilateral balance has not shifted when one considers all goods, the same is not true for manufactures where there is a shift of more than $50 billion. The difference resides in the fact that the decline in commodity and oil prices has tended to improve the balance for nonmanufacturing trade with developing countries.

Table 11.15 The US external balance and new investment position (billions of $ except as noted)

	1982	1983	1984	1985	1986
International investment position	136.2	88.5	4.4	−107.4	−238
Current account					
Total	−9.2	−45.6	−112.5	−124.4	−147.7
Noninterest	−28.1	−37.0	−131.3	−149.6	−170.6
(% of GNP)	−0.9	−1.1	−3.5	−3.7	−4.1
Budget deficit (% of GNP)	−4.1	−5.6	−4.9	−5.1	−4.6

Sources: US Department of Commerce; the Federal Reserve; and the IMF.

Table 11.16 US trade with developing countries ($ billion)

	All goods			Manufactures		
	Imports	Exports	Balance	Imports	Exports	Balance
1980	122.6	79.6	−43.0	29.5	55.6	26.1
1981	121.3	87.4	−33.9	35.1	61.5	26.4
1982	103.7	80.7	−23.0	37.0	55.5	18.5
1983	107.4	71.0	−54.7	45.9	45.7	−0.2
1984	125.9	72.7	−53.2	61.8	47.5	−14.3
1985	122.2	69.7	−52.5	65.5	46.0	−19.5
1986	124.8	68.3	−56.5	77.3	49.4	−27.9

Sources: GATT, Geneva; and the US Department of Commerce.

The shift in the manufacturing trade balance is, of course, not only related to the debt crisis. In fact, much of it reflects the very strong performance of Asian exporters. Even there, however, in the case of Korea, for example, the export effort is not unrelated to the debt problems of the early 1980s. But whatever has been the role of the debt problem in contributing to the US deficit, the question now is how US adjustment policies will affect the external conditions of debtor countries.

Two features of US adjustment can be highlighted as in Table 11.17. One is whether there is a hard or soft landing. The hard landing scenario envisages a collapse of the dollar caused by a loss of confidence. The dollar collapse in turn translates into a sharp upturn in US inflation and brings as a Federal Reserve response a severe tightening of monetary conditions. The result is recession and high real interest rates. The soft landing, by contrast, assumes that fiscal policy turns increasingly restrictive, and monetary policy accommodates with a decline in interest rates. The dollar falls and thus growth of output is sustained by an improvement in net exports. Growth thus is stable and inflation rises moderately. Real interest rates clearly decline.

The second dimension concerns trade policy. Here there are two possibilities: targeted restrictions on countries with large bilateral surpluses (Japan, Korea, Brazil, Mexico) or no significant change in trade policy.

Table 11.17 shows strikingly that the debt problem today remains wide open. Sustained US growth with low real interest rates *and* unimpaired market access means debt problems will become significantly smaller. Continued ability to sell in the US market, higher real commodity prices which come with dollar depreciation, and lower real interest rates all combine to create a scenario favorable for debtors. Of course, the counterpart of US external balance improvement in this case is a worsening of the net exports of Europe and Japan. But lower real interest rates have a self-correcting property in that debtor countries can reduce their noninterest surplus and yet improve their credit-worthiness. This feature means that there is not necessarily a conflict between US and debtor country objectives. When debtor countries argue for the need to reduce US deficits they presumably have this scenario in mind.

The other extreme scenario is a hard landing with trade restrictions. The consequences are obvious: recession and high real interest rates move debt service problems far beyond what debtor countries can be expected to make up for by domestic adjustments. Trade restrictions further worsen their ability to service debts. The almost certain consequence would be 1930s-style debt defaults or indefinite suspension of debt service.

Table 11.17 Consequences for debtors of US adjustment scenarios

	Soft landing	Hard landing
Trade restrictions	Moderate trouble	Debt default
No trade restrictions	Major improvement	Moratoria

Table 11.18 Interest saving from a 2.5 percentage point fall in interest rates

	$ billion	Percentage of imports
Latin America	6.0	7.8
Mexico	2.0	10.5
Venezuela	0.5	5.7
Bolivia	0.025	3.5
Chile	0.4	9.4
Argentina	0.8	15.7
Brazil	1.7	10.3
Peru	0.14	5.1

Source: United Nations Economic Commission for Latin America, Santiago, Chile.

World growth and real interest rates are central in judging the impact of alternative scenarios for debtor countries. On the side of growth, US fiscal adjustment will tend to reduce growth in the world economy. If US output growth is sustained this will mean that real depreciation sustains net exports and that accordingly foreign growth will tend to be less. It is very unlikely that Europe and Japan will provide an expansion in demand sufficient to keep world output growth constant. Thus on the growth side the expectation must be that the performance of the past few years cannot be sustained. But on the interest rate side there may be a favorable development. If the United States does adjust the budget and sustains growth by lower interest rates the dollar will depreciate and this is likely to force Europe and Japan into interest rate reductions even if that threatens monetary discipline.

The impact of interest rates on debtors' current account balances is, of course, very significant. Table 11.18 gives estimates of the impact on various Latin American countries of a 2.5 percent reduction in interest rates. It shows that the impact on individual debtor countries will depend both on their debt ratios and on the fraction of debt that is at floating rates.

The impact of interest rate changes on import availability is very significant for Mexico, Argentina, and Brazil, which are the large borrowers from commercial banks. For Latin America at large, a 2.5 percent reduction in interest rates would amount to a resource saving of nearly 8 percent of total imports. Hence the importance to debtors of the monetary policies that accompany the correction of the US deficit.

Trade barriers might not be applied uniformly across US trading partners. They might be applied only to industrial countries, specifically Japan, or only to *current account* surplus countries, rather than to countries with bilateral surpluses. For debtors the implication here is that an improvement in the debt service ability of countries like Mexico or Brazil might be paid for by extra restrictions on Korea or Taiwan. Thus developing countries as a group might experience an improvement while specific countries like Korea would bear the burden.

There is another way of looking at debtor countries and US adjustment.

Suppose that the United States in fact achieved a $100 billion reduction in the external deficit. Assume also that this had as a counterpart a $20 billion improvement in the US bilateral *trade* balance with Latin America. How can Latin America experience a $20 billion deterioration in the external balance? There are only two ways: much lower interest rates or significant extra financing. Thus any hard landing scenario without default of necessity involves a dramatic change in financing availability which is not apparent today.

The focus on the US adjustment problem throws a very different light on the links between world macroeconomics and debt problems. It suggests that the steady IMF scenario conceals that there is either good or bad news, but probably not the balanced no-news outlook implicit in Table 11.14. Of course, it is possible that US adjustment is a matter of the more distant future. In that case the IMF scenario would be more appropriate for the near term. But there would inevitably be an adjustment some time and that might be more nearly of the hard landing variety.

Is there a chance that debt problems will be solved in some other fashion by the world macroeconomy? Here one would look to a pattern of terms of trade, interest rates, and inflation of the 1970–73 variety. Since the United States is already at full employment, continuing depreciation and monetary accommodation, without fiscal contraction, will inevitably raise inflation while sustaining growth. This policy setting would ease debt problems significantly. The only question is whether the process of sliding gently into the soft landing option, with a few years' delay, can in fact be achieved. The monetary authorities would have to be sufficiently accommodating and impervious to inflation, and asset holders would have to be patient, sitting out dollar depreciation without a stampede. This does not seem to be a high-probability scenario.

11.6.3 *The commodity price problem*

The final point to raise concerns the long-term behavior of commodity prices. Both Figure 11.6 and Table 11.19 show a long-term series for the real price of commodities. Although exact comparisons across periods are impaired by the fact that these data are spliced from different series, the basic point is very striking.[5] Commodity prices in the mid-1980s have reached the lowest level in real terms since the Great Depression.

Several factors explain this low level of commodity prices. The high level of real interest rates is one and, until 1985–86, the high level of the dollar was another. But these factors are not sufficient to explain the large decline as discussed in Dornbusch (1985). Substitution toward resource-saving technologies on the demand side, and real depreciation and hence increased levels of output at given *world* real prices are often factors. Capacity expansions in many producing countries are further factors that reduce real prices. Finally, for agricultural commodities government support policies in industrial countries have played an important role.

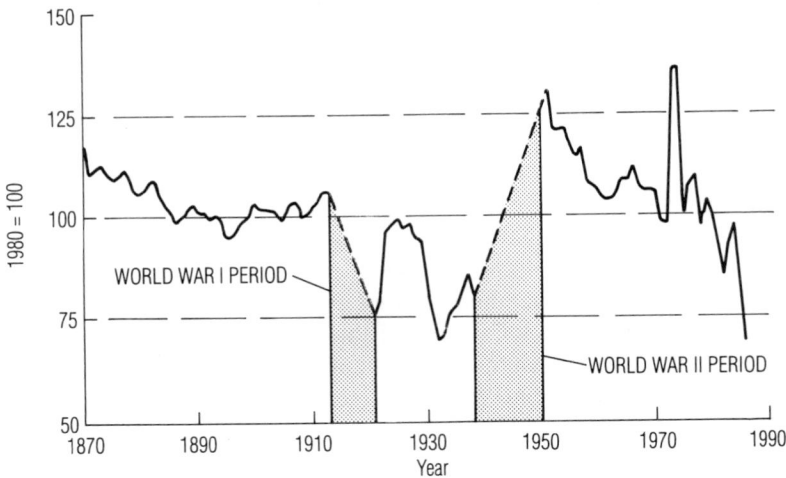

Figure 11.6 The long-term trends of real commodity prices.
(*Source*: IMF (1987).)

Table 11.19 The real price of commodities, 1950–87
(index 1980 = 100, period averages)

1950–54	124	1970–74	115	1985	85
1955–59	113	1975–79	104	1986	69
1960–64	106	1980–84	94	1987	64
1965–69	108				

Source: IMF (1987).

But this large decline in real commodity prices, which has been a decisive factor in the debt performance of several countries (for example, Argentina, Bolivia, and Peru), may well have bottomed out. Moreover, the recovery of real commodity prices may turn out to be surprisingly large and rapid. Certainly the level of real commodity prices is unlikely to return to the high of the early 1970s because structural factors mitigate so large an increase. But a resumption of inflation and much lower real interest rates will drive up inventory demand and thus bring about a significant rise, Indeed, the signs of such an increase are already quite apparent, except for food. In the one year to August 1987, the *Economist* index of all commodities increased in dollar terms by 22.1 percent, with industrial commodities rising by 46.4 percent. But that increase was not shared by food, which showed a moderate decline.

11.7 Conclusion

World macroeconomic policies and variables were until 1981–82 not the major reason for the present debt crisis. Only in 1981–82 did the sharp increase in interest rates and the decline in growth help create a crisis in the aftermath of very poor policy performance in debtor countries.

Since 1982 the world macroeconomic environment has shown an improvement. Interest rates declined in nominal and real terms, and growth has been sustained, as was expected in 1982. The only surprises were that dollar overvaluation lasted as long as it did, a smaller decline in real interest rates, and a massive decline in the real prices of commodities. The world macroeconomic environment certainly did not provide a setting in which debtor countries could grow out of their debts by export booms and improving terms of trade.

Today, five years into the adjustment process, indicators of creditworthiness show a deterioration except for the ratio of debt service to exports. And even that indicator is barely below the 1982 level. Can we expect that the world economy in the years ahead will provide a distinctly more favorable setting? The IMF outlook for the period 1988–91 shows a no-news setting: steady, moderate growth, no changes in the terms of trade, and an increase in real interest rates. In such an environment debtor countries would have to continue making massive real resource transfers to their creditors. Any improvement in their creditworthiness would have to come primarily from further domestic adjustments.

The no-news scenario conceals the wide variation of outcomes that lie ahead and depend on the nature of US adjustment. Two extreme possibilities are (1) a soft landing with significant real interest rate reductions, improving terms of trade, and sustained growth and (2) a hard landing. The soft landing would ease debt service problems in the same way as happened in 1970–73. But the hard landing, with high real interest rates and recession, possibly reinforced by protection, would certainly preclude debt service on the scale that has taken place so far. US external adjustment forces the question of how a reduction in debtor countries' noninterest balances is consistent with the lack of financing of debtors' interest payments. Without the financing there cannot be any reduction in surpluses except by moratoria or default. Thus US trade adjustment poses a major unresolved issue for the international debt problem.

Notes

1. Countries in this group are characterized by having incurred arrears in 1983 and 1984 or rescheduled their debts in the 1982–85 period.
2. On the costs of protection in a situation of credit rationing, see Dornbusch (1985).
3. See, for example, Dornbusch (1985; 1986).
4. See International Monetary Fund, *World Economic Outlook* (1986) and Dornbusch (1985).
5. See IMF (1987, pp. 90–1) for a discussion of the data.

References

Bergsten, F., W. Cline, and J. Williamson (1985) *Bank lending to developing countries: The policy alternatives.* Washington, DC: Institute for International Economics, April.

Cline, W. (1983) *International debt and stability of the world economy*. Washington, DC: Institute for International Economics, September.

Cuddington, J. (1986) *Capital flight: Estimates, issues and explanations*. Princeton Studies in International Finance No. 58 (December). Princeton, NJ: Princeton University.

Dornbusch, R. (1985) "Policy and performance links between LDC debtors and industrial countries." *Brookings Papers on Economic Activity* 2: 303–56.

Dornbusch, R. (1986) "International debt and economic instability." In *Debt, financial stability and public policy*. Kansas City, MO: Federal Reserve Bank of Kansas.

Feldstein, M. (1986) "International debt service and economic growth: Some simple analytics." NBER Working Paper No. 2076. Cambridge, MA: National Bureau of Economic Research.

Goldbrough, D., and I. Zaidi (1986) "Transmission of economic influences from industrial to developing countries." In *Staff Studies for the World Economic Outlook* (July). Washington, DC: International Monetary Fund.

International Monetary Fund (1987) *Primary commodities: Market developments and outlook*. Washington, DC: IMF, May.

Krugman, P. (1985) "International debt strategies in an uncertain world." In G. Smith and J. Cuddington, eds, *International debt and the developing countries*. Washington, DC: World Bank.

Maddison, A. (1985) *Two crises: Latin America and Asia, 1929–38 and 1973–83*. Washington, DC: Organization for Economic Co-operation and Development.

Maddison, A. ed. (1986) *Latin America: The Caribbean and the OECD*. Paris: Organization for Economic Co-operation and Development.

Marquez, J., and C. McNeilly (1986) "Can debtor countries service their debts? Income and price elasticities for exports of developing countries. " Board of Governors of the Federal Reserve, International Finance Discussion Papers No. 277. Washington, DC.

Morgan Guaranty Trust (1986) *World Financial Markets* (April).

OECD (1986) *Financing and external debt of developing countries: 1985 Survey*. Paris: Organization for Economic Co-operation and Development.

OECD (1987) *External debt statistics*. Paris: Organization for Economic Co-operation and Development.

Sachs, J. (1986) "Managing the LDC Debt Crisis." *Brookings Papers on Economic Activity* 2: 397–432.

Sachs, J. (1987) "International policy coordination: The case of the developing country debt crisis." NBER Working Paper Series No. 2287. Cambridge, MA: National Bureau of Economic Research.

Sachs, J., and W. McKibbin (1985) "Macroeconomic policies in the OECD and LDC economic adjustment." Brookings Discussion Paper in International Economics (February). Washington, DC: The Brookings Institution.

Saunders, P., and A. Dean (1986) "The international debt situation and linkages between developing countries and the OECD." *OECD Economic Studies* (Autumn), Paris.

Truman, E. (1986) "The international debt situation." International Discussion Papers No. 298. Board of Governors of the Federal Reserve (December). Washington, DC.

World Bank (1986) *A strategy for restoration of growth in middle-income countries that face debt-servicing difficulties*. Washington, DC: World Bank.

12

Reducing transfers from debtor countries

Over the past seven years a muddling-through strategy on LDC debt has helped improve bank balance sheets. Whatever the wisdom of that strategy, there is little doubt that it extracted an awesome price in debtor countries. While banks are in a much better position to face a situation of debt reduction, many debtor countries have experienced an economic and social setback if not destruction. The need for reconstruction is apparent from the dramatic deterioration in the Latin American standard of living. Figure 12.1 shows the decline and stagnation of income per head in the 1980s. But these data are favorably influenced by the Brazilian experience of moderate positive growth.

The Brady Plan for debt reduction recognizes the urgent need, political and economic, to get to work on reconstruction in Latin America. The change in strategy is late and inadequate. It imposes little structure on the debt service adjustments that are to be accomplished. In that way it may enhance the costs to banks and debtor countries of the debt impasse.

Secretary Brady has started an avalanche, impossible to reverse and, in the best of conditions, difficult to control. Under the Brady Plan banks hope to get major guarantees (at little cost) for their increasingly poor Latin loans; debtor countries see the Brady Plan as a response to their long-standing demand to write debts down to the secondary market price.

The gulf can only be bridged to both parties' satisfaction if public moneys from the IMF and World Bank are hijacked for the purpose. Without public guarantees on the required scale two possibilities emerge; either banks are forced, by regulatory requirements, to pass on to debtors relief at the expense of their stockholders, or else banks are left untouched and debtors go without much relief. In that event, no doubt, self-administered relief will become the rule.

This paper reviews the key problem of resource transfers and then evaluates alternative strategies of debt service reduction. The unifying conceptual scheme is the transfer problem in its *fiscal* and *dollar* aspects. Before we go to the transfer problem we briefly note a central fact: since 1982 the muddling-through strategy

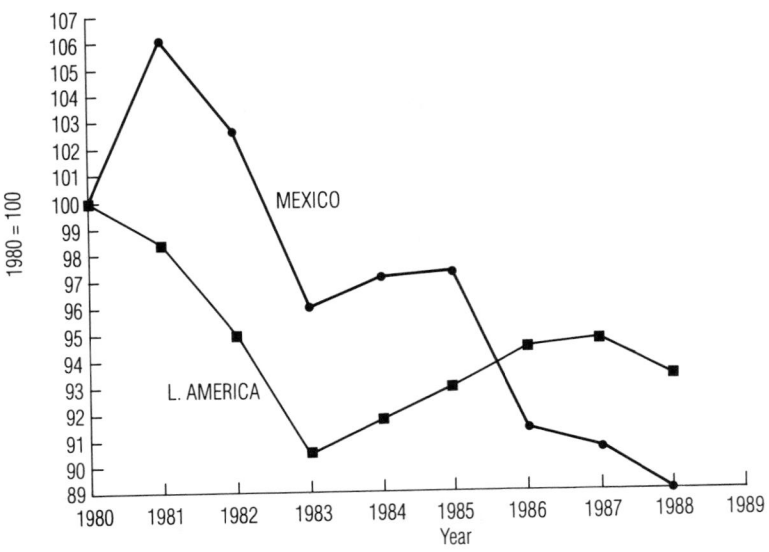

Figure 12.1 Real per-capita income.

Table 12.1 Debt burdens (external debt as a percentage of GDP)

	1980	1982	1987
Latin America	35.3	46.3	60.1
World Bank 17[a]	32.8	45.0	63.1

[a]17 highly indebted countries identified by the World Bank.
Source: World Bank, *World Debt Tables 1988–89*.

has deteriorated debt and ability for debt service (see Table 12.1). Debt ratios are *far* higher today than they were in 1982 and that point is, of course, recognized in the secondary market.

But the market also recognizes that the value of debt is impaired not only by the accrued debt overhang but also by the erosion of political will or even legitimacy of debt service.

12.1   The transfer problem and debt service fatigue[1]

Why is debt service such a problem? In one sense the answer is quite straightforward: countries that used to spend, borrowing the resources from official and private creditors (with little thought of how to service or even less repay the loans), now no longer command these resources—they are limited to spending even less than the value of domestic production. The adjustment is complicated by two facts. The first is the macroeconomics of earning foreign exchange; the second is the political economy problem of finding extra budget resources for debt service. These issues are familiar from the discussion of German reparation payments following World War I. Exactly the same issues arise in the context of the involuntary debt service now under way.

12.1.1 *The reduction in spending*

The first issue is how a country adjusts to a reduction in its spendable resources. Before the debt crisis, foreign loans supplemented domestic income, enlarging the resources that could be spent. Interest payments on loans were automatically provided in the form of new money and the principal on debts was automatically rolled over. With managing the debt so easy, and with ready access to resources beyond what was required to service the debt, spending ran high. After credit rationing began in 1982, spending had to be limited, and absorption fell below the level of output as interest now had to be paid out of current production. Interest payments now had to be earned by noninterest surpluses in the current account.

Table 12.2 shows the debt service process at work. In the post-1982 period of involuntary lending debtor countries have achieved a shift in their noninterest external balance of nearly 5 percent of GDP. This external balance improvement serves to make net transfers of interest to the creditors. It is matched by a nearly equal reduction in investment in the debtor countries.

This perverse resource transfer, of course, comes at the expense of living standards in the developing countries. But more importantly, the transfer has as a counterpart a sharp decline in investment. Interest payments thus are really financed by a mortgage on future standards of living and on the debtors' growth potential. In countries where population growth is high and income distribution is appalling such a policy may turn out to be very shortsighted.

But there remained the issue of how to distribute the cut in spending between its various components: government, consumption, and investment. As we saw above, a large part of the cut took the form of reduced investment. But there was, of course, also a decline in consumption. A fall in investment was not enough due to two special features of the adjustment process. First, cutting total demand has macroeconomic multiplier effects that translate into a reduction in output,

Table 12.2 The transfer problem in Latin America

	1970–80	1980–88
Growth	3.1	−0.8
Inflation	36.7	123.0
Investment/GDP	23.5	18.7
Transfer/GDP[a]	−2.6	3.5

[a] 1973–81 and 1982–88, respectively.
Source: IMF; and UN Economic Commission for Latin America.

income, and hence private spending. Second, at the same time as involuntary debt service started, there also occurred a deterioration in the world economy which required an extra downward adjustment in spending.

12.1.2 *The foreign exchange problem*

The second macroeconomic issue in adjusting to debt concerns the fact that the country needs to earn dollars, not pesos. In the 1970s debtors were borrowing abroad, supplementing domestic incomes with foreign resources. Since 1982 they have been forced to make large outward transfers (see Figure 12.2). These transfers require a trade surplus. The cut in spending will, of course, reduce import demand and also free exportables for sale abroad, but for two reasons that will not be enough. First, a sizable fraction of the expenditure cut will fall on domestic (nontraded) goods, not tradables. The spending cut thus creates directly unemployment rather than potential foreign exchange earnings. Even for those goods that are directly tradable it is not necessarily the case that increased supplies can be sold. Often there is the problem of obtaining market access and, if the goods are not homogeneous commodities like cotton or copper, a cut in their price is required to realize increased sales. Even then, unless demand is sufficiently responsive, total earnings may not increase.

To translate the spending cut into foreign exchange earnings, a gain in competitiveness is required. The gain in competitiveness draws resources into the tradable goods sector and in the world market makes it possible to sell the

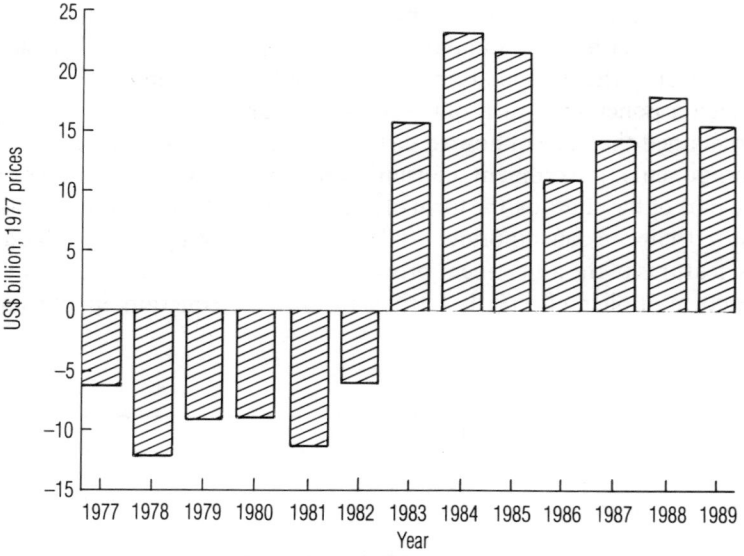

Figure 12.2 Latin America's external transfer.

increased production of tradable goods. Of course, the only way to gain competitiveness is by reducing the wage in dollars by a real depreciation. But the real wage cut also generates, at least in the short run, increased unemployment as the spendable income of workers is cut. The size of the required cut in real wages deserves further comment. It is larger, the larger the share of trade goods in income and the smaller the share of wages in GDP.

The overwhelming difficulty in the adjustment process is that external adjustment via a gain in competitiveness reduces employment. The dominant effect on employment is from the reduction in real wages and the resulting reduction in domestic demand. The positive employment response that would be expected in the tradable goods sector from the gain in competitiveness is often very weak and slow. One of the reasons for this is that expectations of a *sustained* change in competitiveness do not take hold immediately. The traded goods sector thus adopts a wait-and-see attitude, which makes real depreciation a highly precarious policy tool. The Mexican experience in this respect is particularly instructive.

A second important difficulty arises from the worldwide adjustment to forced debt service. Since most debtor countries were overspending in the early 1980s, and are now under a forced debt service regime, they all had to resort to real depreciation to enhance their competitiveness. But that means they are competitively cutting their wages relative to each other, and not only relative to those of the creditor countries. As a result an isolated country, cutting its dollar wage, say, by 50 percent, will gain much less in terms of increased dollar revenues because all the competing LDCs are doing much the same.

12.1.3 *The budget problem*

The third macroeconomic problem in the adjustment process involves the budget. Much of the external debt is public or publicly guaranteed. Of the part that was not initially, much has wound up in the public sector in the aftermath of the crises, as a result of bank failures. The government thus winds up having to service a debt which before was either in private hands or automatically serviced by new money. The problem, of course, is where to find the extra 3 or 4 percent of budget revenue that will pay these new interest costs.

There are basically four avenues: raising taxes and public sector prices; reducing government outlays; printing money; or issuing domestic debt. Raising taxes is notoriously difficult since most of the taxes are already levied in the form of social security taxes on workers. An easier solution is to raise public sector prices or to eliminate subsidies. The elimination of subsidies is particularly cheered by creditors and international agencies since it means moving closer to efficient resource allocation.[2] Of course, the imposition of extra taxes or the withdrawal of subsidies is inevitably inflationary from the price side unless the tax increase or subsidy cut is offset by a reduction in other prices or wages. Of course, from the revenue side it reduces the growth in money and hence, in combination, leads to a recession with inflationary pressure sustained by prevailing inflation.

Cutting government spending is another option. Attention here focuses on the often extreme inefficiency of the public sector. The public perceives that there must be a way to pay the bills out of increased efficiency, rather than reduced private absorption. The fact is, of course, that there is very little room for public sector improvements in the short term. Large-scale firing of redundant workers would create an overwhelming political problem. Plant closings are of the same kind, and selling inefficient, overunionized firms runs into the obvious problem that the potential buyers might need to be paid to take over the liability. Perhaps the best advice may be that public sector firms should be simply given away. The problem is that the workers might oppose even that.

The most common adjustment is a cut in or freeze of public sector wages. This has happened in most of the debtor countries, and in some cases on a very large scale. It does help the budget, but it presents its own problems. The reduction in relative wages for the public sector promotes an exodus of the wrong kind. The efficient workers leave and only those with little alternative stay in the public sector.

In many of the debtor countries the answer to forced debt service has almost inevitably been to increase government budget deficits, and to finance this by issuing debt or printing money. Money finance brings with it the problem of high and often extreme inflation. It is no accident that Argentina and Brazil experienced extraordinary inflation rates in the aftermath of the debt crisis. When deficits are financed by debt, while the imminent inflation problem may be absent, there is still the issue of excessive debt accumulation which ultimately poses the risk of an inflationary liquidation or a repudiation.

There is an interaction between the foreign exchange problem and the budget problem. The need to devalue to gain competitiveness implies that the value of debt service in home currency increases. A given payment of, say, $1 billion now amounts to more in pesos, produces a larger peso deficit and hence gives rise to the need for increased inflationary finance. Thus devaluation is a source of inflation not just directly via the increased prices of traded goods and any accompanying indexation effects. It works also indirectly by raising the required inflation tax. In the classical hyperinflations, major movements in the exchange rate were the prelude to the outbreak of uncontrolled inflation; there is some evidence that exactly the same process is at work in the debtor countries today.

The budget is also adversely affected by the problem of capital flight. To stem capital flight, provoked by the inflationary consequences of debt service or perhaps by an impending tax reform, the country will have to raise real interest rates to very high levels. These high real interest rates in turn apply to the domestic debt, causing it to grow more rapidly, and thereby raising future budget deficits and hence the prospect of instability. That in turn feeds in to more capital flight and yet higher rates. There is thus an extraordinary vicious circle surrounding the sudden need to service debt and the inability to do so through ordinary taxation.

It is worth recognizing an important tradeoff in the adjustment process. To earn foreign exchange the real wage must be cut in terms of tradable goods, thus enhancing competitiveness. But to balance the budget it is often necessary or at least recommended to cut subsidies for such items as food or transportation, and that also means a cut in real wages. There is thus competition between two targets—a cut in the dollar wage or a cut in the tortilla wage. A choice must be made because there is only so much one can cut. Because of the lags with which the trade sector adjusts, this suggests that the competitiveness adjustment should take precedence and that budget balancing should follow once the economy's resources are reallocated. Since the real depreciation by itself is already bound to produce slack, there is no risk of overheating in this sequence of adjustment.

A final point worth noting is the link between budget cutting and the extraordinary fall in Latin American investment. The reason is that in the category of government spending, the easiest cuts are in investment. Postponing investment and maintenance is much easier than firing workers. The resulting impact on aggregate investment is so large because the public sector, in the form of public sector enterprises, accounts for a large part of total investment, and because the public sector was in the forefront of adjustment. It is immediately obvious that this is a very ineffective means of adjustment, because it fails to recognize the distinction between the public sector's current and capital accounts.

12.1.4 *The special role of flight capital*

A special complication of debt service arises via private capital flight. Uncertainty about the exchange rate, or near-certainty about a forthcoming devaluation required to generate a trade surplus, will bring about an exodus of private capital. Thus, in addition to debt service, countries need resources to finance the private flight of capital. Even with stringent capital controls the net is not tight and under- or overinvoicing of trade flows provides a ready escape. But in many countries capital controls are not even feasible or advisable and hence the restraints on capital movements are very small.

Investors have an option to postpone the return of flight capital and they will wait until the front-loading of returns is sufficient to compensate for the risk of relinquishing the liquidity option of a wait-and-see position. This is the case even when interest rates are high and rewarding. Moreover, when capital does return it chooses a highly liquid form, sitting, so to speak, in the parking lot (or on the tarmac), with the engine running. There is definitely little commitment to a rapid resumption of real investment. The reason for this is residual uncertainty whether stabilization can in fact be sustained.

But how can governments reassure investors? The common answer is to bring about a "credible" stabilization. In practice, it comes down to high interest rates and a real exchange rate so competitive that expected further real depreciation is unlikely. But high interest rates are counterproductive from a point of view of growth because they lead to holding of paper assets rather than real investment. A low real exchange rate cuts the standard of living and thus reduces domestic

Table 12.3 Estimates of capital flight (cumulative without imputed interest, $US billion)

	1976–82	1983–87	1976–87 total	Per capita ($)
Argentina	22.4	6.7	29.1	924
Brazil	5.8	14.6	20.4	144
Mexico	25.3	35.3	60.6	745
Peru	n.a.	3.3	n.a.	n.a.
Philippines	4.5	1.1	5.6	98
Venezuela	20.7	19.4	40.1	2,195

Note: These estimates use the World Bank method. See Lessard and Williamson (1987).
Source: Lessard and Williamson (1987) updated by the author.

demand and profitability for all investment except in the traded goods sector.

But if real depreciation is not sufficient to bring about investment the government faces a very awkward position: income is being redistributed from labor to capital, but because the real depreciation is not sufficient, the increased profits are taken out as capital flight. Labor will obviously insist then that the policy be reversed. This uncertainty is an important feature in understanding the real relationship between real exchange rates and capital flight and the post-stabilization difficulties in developing countries.

The capital flight problem can be thought of like a bank run. If the public is concerned about the value of their assets they stage a run on the (central) bank and force depreciation. The belief that everybody else will do the same reinforces each individual investor's belief that he must move out of domestic assets because the general exodus will, inevitably, force depreciation. Hence the "run." The income distribution problems associated with the capital flight problem, whether through slow growth, high real interest rates or real wage cutting, vastly increase the debt problem.

12.2   The quality of debts

We noted above that debt ratios have been deteriorating over the muddling-through period. In this section we briefly present the deterioration of debt.

Table 12.4 shows the debt characteristics for the main Baker-15 debtors.[3] One striking fact is that US banks own only 15 percent of Latin America's total external debt. This small share reflects not only the presence of public debts in the total but also, importantly, the major participation of Japan and Europe as private creditors. Of total private claims on problem debtors, US banks hold only 18 percent.

In the banks' balance sheet LDC debts have clearly declined significantly since 1982. In that respect at least the muddling-through strategy has been successful. In 1982 the money center banks could not have withstood a significant debt write-off. Today debt reduction is clearly digestible, as Table 12.5 shows.

Table 12.4 Problem debts ($US billion, except as noted)

	Debt: Total	Private	US banks	9 banks	Price (c/$)	Debt/GDP (%)
Latin America	408.8	308.8	65.4	45.5	30.2	60.1
Argentina	59.6	47.3	8.2	6.2	17.6	73.9
Brazil	120.1	92.2	18.9	14.4	27.1	39.4
Chile	20.8	15.5	5.4	3.9	55.6	124.1
Colombia	17.2	8.3	2.2	1.4	50.5	50.2
Mexico	107.4	83.8	19.3	12.2	33.4	77.5
Venezuela	35.0	34.8	14.3	5.6	27.6	94.5
Philippines	30.2	18.2	4.2	3.0	36.5	86.5
17 WB debtors[a]	528.6	377.9	69.1	50.9	–	63.1

[a]Seventeen highly indebted countries identified by the World Bank.
Source: Federal Financial Institutions Examination Council; World Bank; and Salomon Brothers.

Table 12.5 US bank exposure in Latin America ($US billion and percentage of capital)

	1985		1988[a]	
	Exposure	%[b]	Exposure	%[b]
All banks	80.4	78.9	65.4	48.1
9 money banks	60.5	148.6	45.5	83.9

[a]September 1988.
[b]Exposure as percentage of capital.
Source: Federal Financial Institutions Examination Council.

One interesting feature of Table 12.5 is the reduction in the face value of debt that has taken place since 1985. The improvement of balance sheets has not only been achieved by raising capital and reserves. There is also a $15 billion reduction in claims achieved through various kinds of swaps and buybacks.

12.3 Debt reduction strategies

There are two central questions about debt reduction: all things considered, which is the best way to go about debt reduction and how much debt reduction is necessary. Both questions will hardly get a unanimous answer.

12.3.1 *The debt overhang*

The question of the debt overhang is perhaps hardest to address. A country's *public* debt service ability depends critically on the quality of its fiscal system. If the tax base is narrow and taxation is inefficient the scope for debt service is exceptionally limited. High external debt either means an explosion of internal debt, as countries finance interest payments abroad by borrowing at home, or means inflationary finance, reaching potentially hyperinflation, or an unjustifiable postponement of infrastructure investment in physical capital, education and health.

In the short run a debtor country can easily face up to an excessive debt because these alternate options of budget adjustment or financing provide some lee way. But, already within a few years it becomes clear that these are not realistic options. Moreover, if they are pursued too long or too vigorously they add their own difficulties via capital flight or political deterioration.

By historical and international standards the debts even of Mexico or Brazil are not record highs: British debt in the nineteenth century exceeded 200 percent of GDP and the debt ratio of Ireland or Israel today exceeds those in Latin America. But even these countries, although they have access to the world capital market, have extreme and possibly unsustainable fiscal difficulties. It is not clear what made the British nineteenth-century debt sustainable, but it is certain that any appearance of sustainability of the public debts (internal plus external) in Brazil, Mexico, or Chile, to name only three, is altogether questionable. In Mexico it is especially clear that the budget balancing has come at the price of an unsustainable roll-back of public sector investment. If growth is to resume, public sector infrastructure investment will be necessary, and that, in combination with debt service, is incompatible with budget balancing.

In the past seven years, using World Bank data, the debt–GDP ratio of highly indebted countries has increased dramatically. On the current course of the world economy a further deterioration is altogether likely.[4] Therefore *some* debt reduction is immediately appropriate. Unfortunately, there is no clearly defined threshold of unsustainability: in large measure the threshold will depend on growth rates of real income, real interest rates and expectations about the terms of trade. In an optimistic scenario for the world economy a debt ratio (again, internal plus external) of 80 percent might be sustainable. But with slow growth and high real interest rates in world markets, even that is incompatible with financial stability.

At this point there is no way of predicting which scenario will prevail. It therefore seems appropriate to make *conditional* debt reduction or, better yet, to link debt service requirements directly to the external environment and growth performance of the debtors. Specifically a scheme of debt reduction might involve a front-end removal of 50 percent of the debt combined with an interest rate on the remainder that is positively linked to the country's growth rate.

A very significant difficulty in deciding on immediate, large debt reduction arises from the fact that the debt service problem reflects not a physical inability to serve debts, but rather a combination of mismanagement, unwillingness, and political difficulty. A major fiscal reform which achieves a broad and comprehensive tax base, including specifically middle and upper income groups, is an essential counterpart of debt reduction. There is little or no excuse for the low yields from taxation in debtor countries. Debt reduction should therefore be conditioned on far-reaching fiscal reform.

A further difficulty arises in deciding how much of the debt reduction should fall on internal versus external debt. To a large extent these debt reductions are substitutable. Domestic debt reduction should certainly be contemplated as part of a major restructuring of debt and public finance.

Another point concerns external debt owed to official creditors. In the discussion on debt reduction (excepting in Africa) the attention focuses on private debt and rarely on public debt. There is very little justification to single out private creditors alone for debt reduction.

A final consideration is how to treat the sizable flight capital abroad. Under favorable conditions this clearly represents a partial, and in some countries, a major offset against debt. The difficulty is that flight capital would only return under favorable conditions and that means under conditions of major debt relief. Thus to gather command over flight capital, debt relief is necessary, but if flight capital does return less debt reduction is required. To get around this special conundrum the proposal of interest recycling deserves special attention.

In summary, there is no answer to the debt overhang problem. When the debt ratios are rapidly rising without a clear prospect of reversal there is clearly an overhang. Solutions involve two adjustments: a broader-based and more efficient taxation and public administration and a reduction in debt service. Both will contain the build-up of debt and the resulting excess debt that stems from capital flight. The distribution between the two adjustments is largely a political decision and a bargaining issue.

We next turn to the chief vehicles for debt reduction.

12.3.2 *Swaps*

Debt–equity swaps and debt–debt swaps need little comment. It is by now well established that they rarely serve the interests of the creditor. The reasons include the following four considerations:

- Conversions rarely present *additional* resources; conversions apply frequently to projects that would have taken place even without a discount. The central bank loses as a result foreign exchange that could have been used for debt reduction or other priority assignments.
- Conversions have to be financed. A country in debt difficulties typically faces far higher borrowing costs on new debt than on captive debt. As a result, the implied refinancing dramatically raises the debt service cost.
- Conversions, because they convey the right to remit earnings and principal within a few years, liquify the external debt. With a conversion a debtor loses the ability to control the outflow of foreign exchange and thus becomes more vulnerable.
- Conversions are a one-way street. If resources are committed, because of credit rationing, they are lost irretrievably.

These arguments against debt swaps have been accepted in the aftermath of a few years of bad experiences. The extravagant, unjustifiable Brazilian excesses in swapping everything that moved have no doubt been the chief piece of evidence. Other countries recognized earlier that their interests were poorly served by swaps.

The Chilean case remains the exception. The chief reason is that domestic interest rates were not far higher than in New York so that a refinancing, capturing part of the discount, could be profitable. But even in Chile the liquification of the external debt will present a major difficulty for the democratic government.

12.3.3 *Buybacks*

The development of the secondary market, just as in the 1940s, has created an active interest in debt buybacks as a means of debt reduction. In the 1940s debt repatriation was an important part of the reduction of external debt. Specifically Chile reduced its external debt in the mid-1930s by one-third, using $13 million to repurchase $88 million, thus paying on average 15 cents on the dollar.

The first major initiative on buybacks occurred in the Mexico–Morgan deal. The disappointing results of this deal arose from the fact that the cash component, in the form of a zero coupon bond, represented only a small fraction of the new instrument, leaving the chief portion in interest payments without well-established seniority. Another buyback, by Bolivia, achieved significant debt reduction. But even that operation has been questioned. The issue, hotly debated, is whether debt reduction is a good idea for a debtor country. The equation involves the alternative use of the resources committed to the buyback. It is not enough to argue that a buyback is interesting because there is a discount; there is a discount because some creditors believe that the competing uses of resources will take priority over debt service.

The case against debt buybacks has been made most forcefully by Bulow and Rogoff (1988). Their position, put simply, is this: debtor countries cannot gain when they make bad states worse by using scarce resources for debt reduction so that, as a result, good states would be even better. The only advantage of debt reduction occurs in good states. With a reduction in the face value of debt, the debtor country gains a larger share of that good state—what is left over after creditors have taken what they can up to full debt service. The more effective creditors are in collecting when countries can pay, the more interest a country has in reducing the face value of debt. But this can only occur in bad states when resources have high alternative uses. Hence the cost–benefit analysis of a buyback involves the tradeoff between good and bad states, between the discount and the extent to which creditors can enforce their claims in good states.

They argue that if in good states creditors can collect only relatively little and if conversion takes place at modest discounts, using resources with alternative uses, buybacks amount to throwing money in the wind. Put in this way, it is clear that countries and markets may have become mesmerized by the discounts and engaged in impulse buying rather than in reasoned cost–benefit analysis.

Table 12.6 Are buybacks a good idea?

		Efficiency gains:	
		Yes	No
Earmarked	Yes	Yes!	Yes
extra			
resources	No	Perhaps	No!

The Bulow–Rogoff presumption, while pointing to an important consideration, oversimplifies and possibly misses critical aspects of the issue. Table 12.6 offers a classification that brings into the discussion two important features of debt conversion and buybacks. The essential criteria are whether extra resources (strictly additional and earmarked) are made available by the rest of the world for the operation or whether a country has to use its own resources (reserves or trade surpluses). The other dimension concerns gains from a reduction in the face value of debt which here are referred to as efficiency gains. They include the beneficial effects on investment of debt reduction (and hence increased profitability of private industry via lower taxes in good states), reduced financial instability and the accompanying reduction in capital flight. A reduction in the face value of debt may or may not bring about a broad range of these benefits.

It is clear than when extra *earmarked* resources become available and can be used for debt reduction with potentially large efficiency gains a debtor should go ahead. The same remains true if the efficiency gains are negligible. But when there are no extra resources and no extra efficiency gains there is no question that countries would misallocate resources and priorities in practicing debt reduction. This leaves the only interesting case where there are no extra resources (or at least only partially) but where some efficiency gains can be expected. Here the Bulow–Rogoff cost–benefit analysis must be applied. If the efficiency gains are small (creditors cannot capture much of the extra income in a good state) then a country is better off investing than reducing the face value of its debt. This is the case Bulow–Rogoff argue holds empirically.

Others have argued that these efficiency gains may be very large because they include gains in macroeconomic stability, including sharply reduced capital flight. Of course, it is also possible that the cost of making resources available for debt buybacks is very large. This is certainly the case when, as in Brazil today, inflationary finance is used for informal debt conversions. In that case buybacks may be a source of increased rather than reduced financial instability and capital flight. Another argument which points in this direction is the fact that buybacks are a one-way street when a country is credit-constrained. Using reserves as Mexico did to retire debt seemed a good idea at the time because reserves were plentiful. But less than six months later the country is on the verge of a major devaluation because it does not have the reserves to support the exchange rate and yet does not want to face the confrontation of a stop on debt service. Bankers are pleased that they took the money then and they certainly will not give it back. Mexico would have done better to hold on to its reserves, a point many observers made already at the time. But the situation is not always as obvious as it was in Mexico's case. Unfortunately there is no simple and sturdy test of the importance of these efficiency gains and hence the argument must remain open.

Beyond the efficiency gains noted above, we must also note the implications of buybacks for creditor–debtor relations. Buybacks may be a means of conflict avoidance. It is not apparent what creditors could and would be willing to do to enforce their claims. Perhaps they could do very little and hence (morality aside) it is surprising that debtors do service at least part of their debt. But it is also possible that, particularly in the event of frivolous nonservice, creditors receive political support to inflict major damage on unwilling debtors. This uncertainty about the consequences of partial or full default is a burden on debtor economies' economic prospects. Cooperation in debt reduction schemes may be the price to pay for reduced debt service without penalty. It may simply be a "the check is in the mail" strategy which, practiced on a modest scale, avoids the necessity of keeping interest payments current on the entire debt. As long as outright nonpayment is a taboo, buybacks may be a relatively cheap rescheduling strategy. Of course, when countries pay *all* the interest, as Mexico did and Brazil expects to do, this argument does not hold.

A successful opportunity for buybacks almost seems a contradiction in terms. If debtors do have the money the discount will be small and uninteresting. If they do not have the money the discount will be large but beyond reach. But there remains an important opportunity that arises from the contamination factor: today *all* of Latin American debt trades at a discount, even that of Colombia notwithstanding the fact that this country has continuously serviced its debt in respect to interest and principal. If capital markets do not discriminate between debtors there is an opening for relatively well-performing debtors to buy out particularly ill-informed (or constrained) creditors. There is an overriding temptation for Colombia, whose debt trades at a 50 percent discount, to use its resources for buybacks rather than amortization. An even better use of the resources might be domestic investment financed by forced lending on the part of creditors.

For those debtors who face an acute liquidity shortage—for example, Mexico—the very limited resources, rather than being dissipated in buybacks, can be more effectively used in promoting domestic financial stability, imports and growth. One means of doing so is to use budget resources to service debt in local currency, allowing creditors to use them for unrestricted investment, but not for repatriation. Rather than making transfers abroad, the debtor would experience investment and growth. In a second phase, just as after World War II, there might be a cleaning-out of debts, prior to a return to the world capital market. Mexico then settled at 20 cents on the dollar and other Latin American countries, with the exception of Argentina which retired debt at par, all achieved major debt reduction. By historical standards, then, it is much too early to buy out the creditors. Ten years from now they may be eager to settle at 10 or 20 cents on the dollar. But for debtor countries holding out is also costly; the unresolved debt overhang can be a source of capital flight and macroeconomic instability. An early, even if less drastic, debt reduction can therefore be preferred.

12.3.4 *Interest reduction or buybacks?*

In the context of the Brady Plan it is useful to ask whether resources should be concentrated on reduction of principal or on interest reductions. Both contribute to a reduction of debt service, but they operate quite differently. Rolling, one year at a time, interest reductions granted in exchange for guarantees maximizes the leverage of a given pool of debt relief resources. Exit bonds paid fully are at the other extreme in that they maximize the use of scarce resources. They do so directly because debt is immediately paid off, albeit at a discount, but also because it is likely that secondary market prices will rise in the anticipation of a cash offer, as they indeed already have.[5]

A carefully designed buyback scheme should seek rolling interest reduction in preference to face value reduction. There is some scope to combine zero coupon bonds with rolling guarantees which may facilitate regulatory problems for banks. There is a strong presumption against exit bonds or major buybacks at the market price.

12.4 Interest recycling

Much of the discussion on debt reduction does not distinguish sufficiently between the two sources of debt difficulties: one is the budget problem, the other is the dollar or trade problem. It is not necessarily the case that countries experience the two problems *equally* or at all. It is perfectly conceivable that one country has a budget problem but no trade problem; the other country has a trade surplus and thus, from a foreign exchange point of view, is in a position to service debt while its fiscal situation is not sufficiently solid to entertain debt service.

When external transfer problems predominate, the problem can be addressed not only by debt service reduction but also by a fundamental restructuring of debt service in a manner which takes care of the major part of interest payments due. Actual payments in dollars would be reduced to the service of trade credit and the loans of multilateral organizations. A large share of the remaining interest payments would in part be capitalized, thus freeing resources for much needed public sector investment, and in part they would be made in local currency. Creditors who receive the local currency payments could use them for unrestricted investment in the debtor countries' economies. The only limitation on the use of funds would be that they cannot be transferred abroad. The claims to these payments could, however, be sold. Table 12.7 sets out four possible situations.

Table 12.7 Fiscal and foreign exchange transfer problems

		Severe fiscal problem	
		Yes	No
Foreign exchange problem	Yes	Debt reduction and fiscal reform	Debt reduction and recycling
	No	Debt reduction and fiscal reform	Full service?

To clarify the issue consider the cases of Brazil and Mexico in 1988. Brazil had a current account surplus of $4 billion; clearly there was no foreign exchange problem. But there was a major budget deficit, at least 4 percent GDP on official estimates but quite possibly as much as 7 percent. In Brazil's case the problem is clearly that the budget transfer, not the external transfer, was the issue. Debt reduction would help (either domestic or external!) and fiscal and public administration reform would do the same.

In Mexico's case the external balance is the problem; the budget, including real interest payments, is only in a moderate deficit, but the current account shows a deficit of more than $6 billion. In this situation interest recycling offers a possibility of avoiding extra strain from the dollar shortage.

Colombia offers another example where recycling would be useful. The budget deficit and the current account show moderate deficits. The external balance constraint is an obstacle to higher growth and higher investment. Under recycling, resources could be diverted from a trade surplus toward domestic investment. Colombia's problems are in no way extreme. In fact, the country has met debt service continuously and has been able to do so under conditions of sustained growth and moderate inflation. The difficulty, solved by recycling, is that capital markets are unwilling to provide new money simply because of Latin American contamination. Unilateral recycling, combined with some capitalization for the public sector, seems an appropriate response to this kind of market failure.

Argentina is a fourth case: here we have a large current account deficit and a large budget deficit. Nothing short of a dramatic reduction of debt service, combined with a serious public sector reform, can restore stability.

12.4.1 *Favorable features of recycling*

The advantages of interest recycling are fivefold. First, the transfer abroad of resources is suspended. Rather than running trade surpluses, debtor countries have resources freed that can be devoted to investment. Of course, serious budget action is required to ensure that in fact the resources go into investment rather than consumption. The shift of resources toward investment has two effects. It implies an expansion in capacity and thus sustains job creation. This issue is central in an economy where labor force growth rates in excess of 3 percent have created major imbalances between labor supply and demand. The expansion in capacity removes the bottlenecks which today stand in the way of growth. Growth, in turn, translates into more stable public finance via a broadened tax base.

Second, the scheme creates a more stable and prosperous business environment. With the current strategy a foreign exchange bottleneck is always around the corner and the reaction is invariably contraction of demand and exchange depreciation. This reality has led to a lack of interest in productive investment and extensive capital flight. The center of gravity has shifted to financial markets, far away from productive activity. By removing the need for immediate debt service the debtor economy can resume a more balanced position with an emphasis on long-term investment and growth. As a lever for returning capital flight there is no better way than a restoration of business confidence and an end of exchange pressure. Recycling also offers two further advantages to creditor countries: it avoids outright debt relief (or debt default) and hence avoids involvement of creditor country taxpayers on a large scale. Furthermore, by providing debtors with room for growth there is every expectation of increased exports to debtor countries and a reduction in the currently high levels of imports.

There is a third, once-and-for-all gain. In the present situation the need to maintain very depreciated real exchange rates translates into inflationary pressures and low demand in the debtors' domestic markets. The removal of external constraints allows some real appreciation and hence provides a breathing space for stabilization of inflation. Inflation stabilization is, of course, an essential quid pro quo in a restoration of normal business conditions.

Fourth, interest recycling, by removing exchange rate uncertainty, creates an essential precondition for a return of capital flight.

Fifth, creditor countries benefit from the reversal of trade surpluses; exports from developing countries will decline and imports, especially of capital goods, will rise. Thus recycling provides the financial underpinnings for solving at least a part of the US trade imbalance.

As a counterpart for acceptance of this scheme by creditors (or to make it more acceptable, in case of unilateral action) debtors would have to sustain the budget improvement and to liberalize the scope for foreign direct investment. There might be a temptation to dissipate the resources into a restoration of consumption after so many years of deprivation. But that would be unacceptable. Tough-minded fiscal measures and broad-based liberalization of investment opportunities are the quid pro quo for the suspension of resource transfers.

It is worthwhile asking how banks would deal with a recycling situation. The immediate reaction of banks to a recycling proposal is entirely negative, but the concerns are largely exaggerated and lie mostly in the accounting area. Of course, compared to a bailout by the World Bank recycling is thoroughly unattractive, but compared to default by all of Latin America recycling is strictly preferred.

Individual banks would take one of three steps. They might manage directly their receivables in local currency. This is clearly the route for banks who are now in the debt–equity swap business for their own account or banks who have sought possibilities for expanding their activities in debtor countries. Rather than funding themselves by deposit taking, they will use their own capital in the form of local currency interest payments. A second group of banks might use their local currency receivables by having them managed by major host country financial institutions—banks, money market funds or funds that invest in real assets.

A third group of banks would try and sell off their claims to avoid high transactions costs. This would typically be the case of small banks. They would sell their claims to investment funds. These funds (like the Korea Fund or the Brazil Fund that was just offered on the New York Stock Exchange) sell shares to the broad public and use the proceeds to buy assets in the debtor country. Buying claims from banks, possibly at a discount, would be a natural way of increasing the return to their shareholders.

It is instructive to go through the details of how banks would use the recycling funds to appreciate that what happens is basically a transformation of short-term, illiquid debt into long-term investment. That is an essential step in strengthening the possibilities of long-term growth in debtor countries, avoiding the recurrent bouts of rescheduling with the attendant massive capital flight.

A scheme such as this could be likened to reconstruction programs like those administered after World War I or World War II. It would extend over a decade or so. Ultimately creditors would be able to recover their principal and accumulated earnings with a guarantee of no frivolous exchange losses.

Return of flight capital would almost certainly be one of the favorable consequences of a recycling proposal. On the resource side financial stability would be enhanced, and that removes one reason for capital flight. Additionally, the sharp reduction in foreign exchange requirements for debt service clears the way for the large flow of imports required to sustain growth.

Today asset holders must wonder whether growth and debt service will be reconciled. As a result, they hang on to their dollar positions even in the presence of extraordinarily high real interest rates. Resolution of the overdeterminacy would accelerate the reflow. Paradoxically, if debt service could be recycled debtors may well have enough of a private capital inflow so that they actually can pay creditors a major part of debt service in dollars. Conversely, if creditors are then adamant, private capital will stay abroad and creditors, in the end, risk getting nothing. Just as deposit insurance stabilizes banks so does recycling stabilize the macroeconomy in a situation where there are two equilibria, one with capital moving out and the economy deteriorating, the other with capital flowing in and the economy returning to growth and financial stability.

12.5 Concluding remarks

There is a general recognition today that a resumption of growth and anything near full debt service are incompatible. Even moderate proposals, such as

Feldstein (1986), recognize that at most a portion of debt service can be transferred without prejudicing the opportunities for growth. That raises the question how the rest of debt service is to be handled. One answer is that international financial institutions must assume an increasing role.

This is indeed the banks' position as they ask for guarantees on any new money to be committed. Of course, increasing commitments by international agencies raises questions about equity: why bail out banks and Latin America rather than provide poverty relief in Africa?[6] Discussion around such issues is going in circles. In the meantime a debtor country like Mexico, having taken the first step toward growth in the form of fiscal stabilization, must move on or else face the risk of sliding back.

Notes

1. This section draws on Dornbusch (1985).
2. The fact that it is often food subsidies that are eliminated, without the proverbial neutral lump-sum tax to compensate the losers, does not seem to limit the case for the policy recommendation.
3. Not shown are various Central and South American countries, Yugoslavia, Nigeria and the Ivory Coast.
4. It is readily verified that the debt–GDP ratio evolves according to $\Delta b = (r - y)b - \sigma$, where r and y are the real interest rate and the growth rate of output and σ is the noninterest current account surplus. (It is assumed that direct investment income is offset by capital flight.) With a debt ratio of 60 percent and a real interest rate less growth of 5 percent the noninterest surplus has to be 3 percent of GDP to avoid a rising debt ratio.
5. On this point see especially Dooley (1988).
6. See Buiter and Srinavasan (1987) on this issue.

References

Buiter, W., and T. N. Srinivasan (1987) "Rewarding the Profligate and Punishing the Prudent and Poor: Some Recent Proposals for Debt Relief." *World Development* 15: 411–17.

Bulow, J. and K. Rogoff (1988) "The Debt Buy Back Boondoggle." *Brookings Papers on Economic Activity* 2.

Cardoso, E. and R. Dornbusch (1989) "Private Capital for Economic Development." In H. Chenery and T. N. Srinivasan, *Handbook of Development Economics* Vol. II. New York: North-Holland.

Corden, M. (1988) "An International Debt Facility." *IMF Staff Papers*, September.

Cumby, R. and R. Levich (1987) "Capital Flight: Definitions and Magnitudes." in D. Lessard and J. Williamson, eds, *Capital Flight and Third World Debt*. Washington, DC: Institute for International Economics.

Dooley, M. (1988) "Buy-Backs and Market Valuation." *IMF Staff Papers*, June.

Dornbusch, R. (1985) "Policy and Performance Linkages Between LDC Debtors and Industrial Countries." *Brookings Papers on Economic Activity* 2.

Dornbusch, R. (1989) Background Paper to *The Road to Economic Recovery*. New York:

Twentieth Century Fund. Mimeo, MIT.

Dornbusch, R., and F. Modigliani (1989) "Easing the Mexican Interest Burden." *Wall Street Journal*, January 3.

Feldstein, M. (1986) "International Debt Service and Economic Growth: Some Simple Analytics." NBER Working Paper No. 2076.

Froot, K. (1988) "Debt Buy-Backs." Mimeo, Massachusetts Institute of Technology.

Krugman, P. (1988) "Market Based Approaches to Debt Reduction." NBER Working Paper No. 1987.

Lessard, D. and J. Williamson, eds, (1987) *Capital Flight and Third World Debt.* Washington, DC: Institute for International Economics.

Rodriguez, C. (1988) "The Strategy of Debt Buy-Backs: A Theoretical Analysis of the Competitive Case." Mimeo, International Monetary Fund.

Williamson, J. (1988) *Voluntary Approaches to Debt Reduction.* Washington, DC: Institute for International Economics.

Part V

Country policy studies

13

Macroeconomic populism

with Sebastian Edwards

13.1   Introduction

The purpose of this study is to develop a paradigm of populist macroeconomics.[1]
Macroeconomic populism is a policy perspective on economic management that
emphasizes economic growth and income redistribution and deemphasizes the
risks of inflation and deficit finance, external constraints and the reaction of
economic agents to aggressive non-market policies.

We analyze two populist economic programs, Chile during Allende's Unidad
Popular (1970–73) and Peru under García. We show that policy experiences in
different countries and periods share common economic features, from the initial
conditions, the motivation for policies, the argument that the country's
conditions are different, to the ultimate collapse. It is clear that the Unidad
Popular of 1970–73 in Chile had political goals that were very different from the
experience in Peru. Even so, we want to emphasize that the political mobilization
strategy had strongly similar elements and that, overall, there are remarkable
similarities between the Allende experience and that of García's Peru.

The similarities in approach in Chile and Peru are particularly striking with
respect to the way policymakers viewed the objective conditions of their
economy, how they proposed that strongly expansionary policies should and
could be carried out, and how they rationalized that constraints could be dealt
with. Most impressive is the fact that in the end, foreign exchange constraints and

This is a much shortened and revised version of a paper presented at the second meeting of the
InterAmerican Seminar on Economics, IASE, Bogotá, Colombia, March 30–April 1, 1989. The
authors are indebted to conference participants, Eliana Cardoso, Vittorio Corbo, Al Fishlow, Javier
Iguiniz, Richard Eckaus, Eduardo Engel, Jose de Gregorio, Caterina Nelson, Eva Paus, Andres
Solimano, Jose Pablo Arellano, Miguel Savastano, and Andrew Zimbalist for helpful suggestions.
The research reported here is part of a project supported by the World Bank. S. Edwards gratefully
acknowledges the support of the University of California Pacific Rim Program.

253

extreme inflation forced a program of violent real wage cuts that ended in massive political instability, violence, and, in the case of Chile, even in a coup. We do not doubt the sincerity of the policymakers who embark on these programs, and we share their conviction that income distribution is unacceptably unequal. The very sincerity of these policymakers convinces us of the usefulness, and indeed the necessity, of laying out exactly how and why the programs do go wrong.

External influences (debt crises and economic blockades, among others), domestic structural policies (socialization of firms, nationalization of banks), and inconsistent fiscal and exchange rate policies bring about an unsustainable situation; inflation goes out of control, and the foreign exchange constraints force realism on policymakers. Accounts of these experiences often emphasize politics and, especially, external factors as central to the demise. External destabilization can be an important part of the unraveling of an economic program. But we emphasize the extreme vulnerability that makes destabilization possible. By and large, this potential results from unsustainable economic policies. We think that only to the extent that the mechanics of the macroeconomics of populist programs is fully understood, will these policies cease to be popular among politicians.

Before embarking on the case studies we emphasize that we do not cover the political issues which surely are equally if not more important in the historical developments in the two countries. We omit politics not because we think it is irrelevant, but because we want to highlight to the clearest extent possible the economic developments. The view we present is therefore possibly biased because it omits the political motivation, on occasions, for economic motives.

13.2 The populist paradigm

Populism has traditionally been a fuzzy concept. Political scientists have struggled to provide a meaningful and precise definition. Drake (1982), for example, emphasizes three elements of a tentative definition: populism uses "political mobilization, recurrent rhetoric and symbols designed to inspire the people," it draws on a heterogeneous coalition aimed primarily at the working class, but including and led by significant sectors from the middle and upper strata, and it "has connoted a reformist set of policies tailored to promote development without explosive class conflict." Drake (1982, p. 218) notes: "[The programs] normally respond to the problems of underdevelopment by expanding state activism to incorporate the workers in a process of accelerated industrialization through ameliorative redistributive measures."

Conniff (1982, p. 5) has argued that "populist programs frequently overlapped with those of socialism." We emphasize that the redistributive objectives are a central part of the paradigm. Whether they are motivated by a strategy of massive social reform is consequential, but is not central to our own discussion.

Populist economic programs exhibit strong similarities. In this section, we set out in paradigmatic fashion what we see as the critical common factors. In later sections we analyze these for the experiences of Chile and Peru.[2] The intellectual identification of issues is summarized under the following headings:

Initial conditions. Dissatisfaction with the country's growth performance. Most typically, though not always, the country has experienced moderate growth, stagnation or outright depression as a result of previous stabilization attempts. The experience, often—though not necessarily—under an IMF program, has reduced living standards. Serious economic inequality provides economic and political appeal for a radically different economic program. Preceding stabilizations have improved the budget and the external balance sufficiently to provide the room for, though perhaps not the wisdom of, an expansionary program.

No constraints. Policymakers explicitly reject the conservative paradigm. In their view idle productive capacity provides the leeway for expansion. International reserves and the ability to ration foreign exchange give room for expansion without the risk of running into external constraints. The risks of deficit finance are portrayed as exaggerated or altogether unfounded. It is argued that expansion is not inflationary (if there is no devaluation), because spare capacity and decreasing long-run costs contain cost pressures; in any event, there is room to squeeze profit margins by price controls.

The policy prescription. Populist programs emphasize three elements: reactivation, redistribution of income, and restructuring of the economy. The common thread here is "reactivation with redistribution." The recommended policy is to redistribute income, typically by large real wage increases that are not to be passed on into higher prices. Inflation notwithstanding, devaluation is rejected because of the inflationary impact and because it reduces living standards. The economy is to be restructured to save on foreign exchange and support higher levels of real wages and higher growth.

In populist experiments events tend to evolve in four phases or stages:

Phase I. In the first year or so, the policymakers are fully vindicated in their diagnosis and prescription: growth of output, real wages and employment are high, and the *macro*economic policies are nothing short of successful. Controls ensure that inflation is not a problem, and shortages are alleviated by imports. The rundown of inventories and the availability of imports (financed by reserve decumulation or suspension of external payments) accommodate the demand expansion with little impact on inflation.

Phase II. Bottlenecks, partly as a result of a strong expansion in demand for domestic goods, and partly because of reactions to the scarcity of foreign exchange, start to appear. Whereas inventory decumulation was an essential feature of the first phase, the low levels of inventories and inventory building are now a source of problems. Price realignments and devaluation, exchange controls, or increased protection become necessary. The government tries to stabilize, but fails to put a check on wage increases and on the growth of government expenditure. Inflation increases significantly, but wages keep up. A massive underground economy emerges. The budget deficit worsens tremendously as a result of pervasive subsidies on wage goods and foreign exchange.

Phase III. Pervasive shortages, extreme acceleration of inflation, and an obvious foreign exchange gap lead to capital flight and demonetization of the economy. The budget deficit deteriorates violently because of a steep decline in tax collection and increasing subsidy costs. The government attempts to stabilize by cutting subsidies and by undertaking a real depreciation. Real wages fall massively, and politics becomes unstable. It becomes clear that the populist policies have failed.

Phase IV. Orthodox stabilization takes over under a new government. An IMF program will be enacted; and, when everything is said and done, the real wage will have declined abruptly, to a level significantly lower than when the whole episode began! Moreover, that decline will be very persistent, because the politics and economics of the experience will have depressed investment, decapitalized the manufacturing sector, and promoted capital flight. The severity of real wage declines is due to a simple fact: capital is mobile across borders, but labor is not. Capital can flee from poor policies, labor is trapped.

After briefly analyzing the propagation mechanisms of high inflation in populist-type experiences, we turn to the episodes of Peru and Chile to sketch the policymakers' diagnosis and the actual events. We start with the Chilean case, because the facts of the entire experience can now be seen. The results suggest what to look for in the Peruvian experience.

13.3 The mechanisms of high inflation under populist macroeconomics

In this section we briefly review the relationship between key macroeconomic variables and sketch the propagation mechanisms of high inflation in populist experiments. The emphasis is put on the relationship between real wages, the real exchange rate, real interest rate, the fiscal budget and inflation. We show that policies based on wage increases and deficit expansions face severe tradeoffs. While higher wages will be achieved, inflation will erupt, competitiveness will be eroded and an external crisis will take place. We show in this section that in the short run, while international reserves last, the more severe aspects of this tradeoff can be kept under control.

The starting point is the relation between real wages, w, the real exchange rate, R, and employment. Consider a world where there are exportables, importables and nontraded goods. The consumer price index is

$$P = P_x^x P_m^m P_n^n \tag{13.1}$$

where the superscripts x and m are the share of exportables and importables in consumption. The home goods share thus is $n = 1 - x - m$. Home goods are produced using labor and importables:

$$P_n = aWZS \tag{13.2}$$

where a is the per-unit requirements of labor and imports, W is the nominal wage, Z represents the profit mark-up and S the subsidy—i.e. $S = 1/(1 + s)$, with s the percentage subsidy rate. As discussed later, the subsidy may take the form either of direct cash transfers or of negative interest rates on credit.

Exports prices are given in the world market so that the domestic price of exportables is equal to the world price P^* times the exports exchange rate e:

$$P_x = P^*e \tag{13.3}$$

On the imports side, prices are determined by the given world price, P^*, the imports exchange rate and the tariff, T:

$$P_m = \alpha\beta P^*eT \tag{13.4}$$

where α denotes the terms of trade and β, if it differs from unity, measures the differentiation of the exchange rate structure between imports and exports. Define the real exchange rate, R, as the ratio of wages to traded goods prices on a weighted basis for export and import competing industries:

$$R = (W/P_x)^{1-\sigma}(W/P_m)^\sigma = (W/eP^*)K^{-\sigma} \qquad K = \alpha\beta T \tag{13.5}$$

Equation (13.5) indicates, then, that the real exchange rate is given by the nominal wage rate measured in terms of exportables with an adjustment for the terms of trade and for exchange rate or tariff protection.

The real consumption wage, w, is given by the ratio of the money wage to the consumer price index:

$$w = W/P = \theta(R, K, ZS) \tag{13.6}$$

Equation (13.6), substituting from (13.1) to (13.5) in W/P, highlights that real wages and competitiveness are negatively related. Subsidies or reductions in profit margins play a special role since they increase real wages without a deterioration in competitiveness. Protection increases competitiveness, but it reduces real wages.

On the other hand, assume that employment, L, is demand-determined by profitability in the traded goods sector and by the derived demand for labor in the home goods sector. A fraction κ of labor income is spent on home goods, and G represents government spending on home goods. In addition, there is credit expansion, Q, which is made available to state enterprises or the private sector for spending on home goods. We then have

$$L^d = \rho(R) + \gamma\kappa(WL + P_nG + Q)/P_n \qquad \rho' > 0 \tag{13.7}$$

or

$$L = \rho(R)/(1 - \kappa/ZS) = L(R, ZS, G, K/W) \tag{13.7'}$$

According to equation (13.7′) employment is positively affected by subsidies or by a squeeze of profit margins because these raise real wages and hence demand for nontraded goods. Moreover, according to this equation, an increase in government spending and a gain in competitiveness (i.e., a decline in R) will raise the level of employment.

We further assume that there are various sources of *acceleration* of the rate of inflation:

$$\Delta \pi = \cap (L^d - L) + \lambda(w' - w) + \delta \Delta R/R - \phi \Delta S/S \qquad \text{(13.8)}$$

Implicit in this formulation is the presence of automatic indexation and hence inertia. According to equation (13.8) inflation stays constant unless one of three shocks occurs:

- corrective inflation from real depreciation or subsidy removal,
- demand inflation associated with an excess of labor demand over the level of full employment,
- social conflict shocks which arise when the target real wage, w', exceeds actual real wages.

The model is closed by the financing equations: the external balance and the budget. The external deficit depends on competitiveness and the interest differential between domestic and foreign assets adjusted for the anticipated depreciation of the exchange rate, v:

$$b = B(R, v) \qquad b_1 > 0, \quad b_2 > 0 \qquad \text{(13.9)}$$

The budget deficit, on the other hand, is assumed to depend on subsidies, on foreign exchange losses and tariff revenues, and, via tax collection, on the level of activity and hence on competitiveness:

$$d = D(S, \beta T, R) \qquad \text{(13.10a)}$$

The deficit, in turn, is financed by reserves decumulation and by money creation. Money creation depends on the budget (b), the external balance (d) and credit expansion (q), each measured relative to nominal income:

$$\dot{M} = (d + b - q)PY \qquad \text{(13.10b)}$$

To derive actual time paths of alternative policies and their impact on the path of employment, real wages and inflation the model would have to be simulated. For our purposes, however, it is already instructive in that it highlights the basic tradeoffs that are faced by a policymaker who seeks to expand the level of economic activity (i.e., reducing unemployment) via wage rate and expansionary fiscal policies. The model in fact shows that real wages can be raised either by a real appreciation (i.e., real exchange rate overvaluation) or by subsidies. But real appreciation interferes with the external constraint and subsidies are inflationary. Employment can be expanded by subsidies or by real depreciation. The former is inflationary and the latter hurts real wages. The room for policies that raise real wages *and* employment is therefore severely limited. While there is foreign exchange available the tradeoffs are not apparent, but once reserves run out the tradeoffs will suddenly, and cruelly, appear: inflation will then rapidly accelerate.

The acceleration of inflation, once it takes place, is magnified by adjustments in the financial sector.[3] Velocity rises in response to increased inflation and that implies a decline in the base for the inflation tax. But with a decline in real balances, even higher inflation rates are required to finance a given budget deficit. The increasing inflation, in turn interferes with the efficiency of revenue collection, leading to a widening of the deficit. Once inflation becomes very high the relation between inflation and the budget becomes dominant. Moreover, because of the sharp rise in velocity the deficits that can be financed at a given inflation fall radically. At this point a vicious circle takes over, and the only way out is by implementing a severe stabilization program that cuts the deficit, generates a major real depreciation and reduces real wages. As will become apparent from our analysis of the Chilean and Peruvian cases in Sections 13.4 and 13.5, this model captures some of the most important aspects of the mechanics of macroeconomic crises under populist regimes.

13.4   Economic policies in Allende's Chile

In September of 1970, Salvador Allende, the socialist candidate of the Unidad Popular (UP), was elected President of Chile. A unique political and economic experience evolved in the following three years.[4] The Unidad Popular was a political coalition of left and center-left parties dominated by the Socialist and Communist parties which sought to implement deep institutional, political and economic reforms. Its program called for a democratic "Chilean road to socialism."[5] Both communists and socialists initially recognized the multiclass nature of the Unidad Popular and considered the alliance and the politics that sustained it to be a tactical intermediate step that would help set the basis for the transition to socialism (see the discussion in Zammit 1973). Vuskovic (1973, p. 50) noted that:

> economic policy is subordinate, in its content, shape and form, to the political need for increasing the Popular Unity's support ... The urgent need to achieve rapid recovery of the economy, and to extend the benefits to the mass of the working population, cannot be undertaken in isolation from the structural changes; they are all necessarily interdependent. It is not possible to make deeper changes without broadening the Government's political support, and economic reactivation and income redistribution will provide an impulse to these fundamental changes.

13.4.1   *Initial conditions, diagnosis and short-run program*

The Unidad Popular faced a somewhat stagnated economy with a rapidly increasing rate of inflation. Between 1967 and 1970, Chile's real GDP per capita grew only at 1.2 percent—significantly below the Latin American average.

Inflation had steadily increased during the last few years of the Frei administration, reaching 35 percent in 1970. On the positive side, the balance of payments showed substantial surpluses during all but one of the Frei years and the central bank had a significant stock of international reserves of approximately US $400 million or half a year of imports.

The short-run economic objectives of the UP included:

- initiating, at a rapid speed, a whole range of structural economic transformations, including a massive nationalization program;
- raising real wages, especially for the lower classes;
- reducing inflation;
- increasing the rate of output growth;
- increasing consumption, especially among the poorer groups; and
- reducing the economy's dependence on the rest of the world.

The nationalization program was to be achieved by a combination of new legislation, requisitions, and stock purchases from small shareholders. The other goals—output and consumption growth, with rising salaries and declining inflation—were to be accomplished by an increase in aggregate demand, mainly generated by higher government expenditures, accompanied by income redistribution measures and severe administrative controls over prices.

This macroeconomic program, in the structuralist tradition, was based on a number of key assumptions. First, it was believed that there was ample excess capacity in the manufacturing sector. Second, it was thought that this low rate of capacity utilization was closely related to the existing pattern of consumption and income distribution. Third, it was assumed that there was a dualistic manufacturing sector, where firms producing "luxury" goods had excessively high capital–labor ratios. Fourth, inflation was considered to be a reflection of the economic structure, not of financial or monetary pressures. In what follows, we will analyze these key assumptions in some detail.

Significant excess capacity in the manufacturing sector was at the center of the macroeconomic program and provided the intellectual base for the belief that large fiscal deficits would not necessarily be inflationary. Américo Zorrilla, Allende's first Minister of Finance said:

> The subutilization of installed capacity is another feature of the current economic situation ... In 1969 it was possible to increase production, due to subutilization, by more than 30 percent ... [A]ccording to recent studies ... unutilized capacity has reached, in the last few years, 61 percent in the cloth industry, 50 percent in the baking industry ... 74 percent in the shoe industry, etc. [As reproduced in García (1972, p. 72).]

An important corollary of the unutilized capacity hypothesis was that firms in many sectors faced decreasing average costs so that, under proper administrative price controls, demand increases would not generate inflationary pressures.

Moreover, to the extent that many of the larger firms were indeed nationalized, as called for by the UP program, it was thought that output could be greatly increased even with price reductions. In a document prepared by the Planning Office (ODEPLAN) in 1971, it was stated that by "combining the increase in production derived from a higher use of installed capacity ... the former monopolies will be able to absorb, without problems, the required wage increases, while maintaining, *or even reducing*, prices and still generating the same surplus."

The lack of "full" utilization was, in turn, attributed to two fundamental factors: the monopolistic nature of the manufacturing industry and the structure of income distribution (Vuskovic 1970). Based on this diagnosis it was thought that if income was redistributed toward the poorer groups through wage increases, and prices were properly controlled, there would be a significant expansion of demand and output.

Regarding inflation, the UP program emphasized rigidities, bottlenecks, and the role of monopolistic pricing and played down the role of fiscal pressures and money creation.[6] Very little attention was given to the financial sector. In fact, in his memoirs, the former Allende Minister and Vice President Clodomiro Almeyda relates how, in the first meeting of the economic team after the elections, the CEPAL-oriented technocrats expressly, and convincingly it would seem, argued that monetary and financial management did not deserve too much attention.[7] Alfonso Inostroza, the president of the central bank, stated in early 1971 that the main objective of the monetary policy was to "transform it into a key instrument ... to achieve the complete mobilization of productive resources, and their allocation to those areas that the government gives priority to"—(see Inostroza 1971, p. 8).

As to Chile's external vulnerability, the UP basic program stated that, along with a reduction in import dependence, a priority of the new government would be to "execute a foreign trade policy tending to expand and diversify our exports" (Unidad Popular 1969, p. 24). This objective was to be achieved without providing any price incentives. Quite the contrary, the UP economists thought that changes in the exchange rate had very little, if any, effect on exports or imports. In fact, it was stated that an important goal of the policy was to "avoid the scandalous devaluations of [the] ... currency" (loc. cit.). Indeed, one of the first measures undertaken by the Allende administration was to eliminate the system of crawling peg that had been adopted, with great success, by the Frei administration.

The UP view of the way the economy functioned ignored many of the key principles of traditional economic theory. This was reflected not only in the greatly diminished attention given to monetary policies, but also in the complete disregard for the real exchange rate as a key variable in determining macroeconomic equilibrium. Moreover, the Unidad Popular failed to recognize that its policies would be unsustainable in the medium term and that capacity constraints were going to become an unsurmountable obstacle to rapid growth. Also, the UP technocrats greatly underestimated the role of expectations and the capacity of the public to react to severe inflationary pressures. Bitar (1986, ch. 5) portrays very clearly the government's inability to control events, and to shift the emphasis from redistribution to accumulation.

> It turned out to be very difficult to contain the forces unleashed in 1971. The sequential conception of redistribution followed by accumulation assumed that basic political and social conduct could be altered and popular expectations changed virtually instantaneously. In the next few months [early 1972] it proved impossible to apply this thinking with the facility that had been hoped for.

13.4.2 *Phase I: Rapid growth with repressed inflation*

Armed with the intellectual framework analyzed above, the UP rapidly began to implement its program in late 1970. In terms of structural reforms, two basic measures were immediately undertaken: first, the Agrarian Reform was greatly intensified, with a very large number of farms being expropriated.[8] Second, a project for a constitutional amendment aimed at nationalizing the large copper mines—until then jointly owned by large US firms and the Chilean state—was studied.[9]

In terms of macroeconomic policy, the government rapidly applied measures that were consistent with its program. Government expenditures greatly expanded and in 1971 real salaries and wages in the public sector increased by 48 percent, on average. Salaries in the private sector grew at approximately the same rate. Figure 13.1 shows the gain in real wages during this year. The short-run package was topped by a generalized scheme of price controls.

In the first two quarters of 1971, manufacturing output increased 6.2 percent and 10.6 percent compared to the same periods in the previous year. Manufacturing sales grew at even faster rates: 12 percent during the first quarter and 11 percent during the second quarter. Overall, the behavior of the economy in 1971 seemed to vindicate the UP economists: real GDP grew at 7.7 percent, average *real* wages increased by 17 percent, aggregate consumption grew at a real rate of 13.2 percent, and the rate of unemployment dipped below 4 percent. Not too surprisingly, given the behavior of real wages, there was a significant improvement in income distribution. In 1971 the labor's share of GDP reached 61.7 percent, almost 10 points higher than its 1970 level of 52.3 percent; and this happened without an acceleration of inflation. What was even more important for the UP was that the policies rapidly paid off politically. In the municipal elections of 1971, the UP parties saw their share of the vote climb from the 36 percent they had received in the 1970 presidential election to around 50 percent.[10]

All of this created a sense of euphoria in the government. The fact that the fiscal deficit had jumped from less than 3 percent of GDP in 1970 to almost 11 percent in 1971 did not worry the UP technocrats. nor did they think much on the fact that the rate of growth of the money supply had surpassed 100 percent in annual

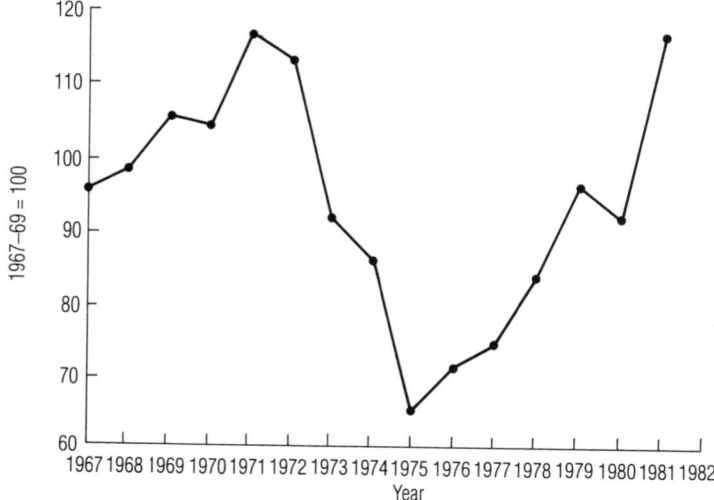

Figure 13.1 Chile: the real wage.

terms in the fourth quarter of 1971, and that the rate of growth of domestic credit to the public sector was approaching 300 percent. All of this, in fact, was part of the plan (see López 1972).

Of course, these macro policies were rapidly generating a situation of repressed inflation. The high growth rate of GDP in 1971 rested heavily on an almost 40 percent increase in the imports of intermediate goods. As a result, the stock of international reserves inherited by the Allende government was reduced by more than half in that year alone. A steep reduction of inventories was another important factor contributing to the expansion of consumption. By the end of 1971, the mounting inflationary pressures became evident (see Table 13.1). The supply problem was aggravated by a series of labor disputes in many large establishments that resulted in the takeover of those firms by their workers. In fact, this procedure became the institutionalized way in which the government seized a large number of firms.[11]

13.4.3 *Phase II: Inflation, bottlenecks and failed stabilization programs*

During 1972, the macroeconomic problems continued to mount. Table 13.1 shows that inflation reached 217 percent and the fiscal deficit surpassed 13 percent of GDP. Domestic credit to the public sector grew at almost 300 percent, and international reserves dipped below $77 million. Consumption growth dominated the expansion in demand (see Table 13.2).

The underground economy grew as more and more activities moved out of the official economy, and as a result more and more sources of tax revenues

Table 13.1 Chile: main macroeconomic indicators

	1970	1971	1972	1973
Inflation[a]	34.9	34.5	216.7	605.9
Growth	2.1	9.0	-1.2	-5.6
Real wages (1970:3 = 100)	98.4	115.1	103.5	70.3
Government revenue[b]	23.7	20.4	18.2	20.2
Government spending[b]	26.4	31.1	31.2	44.9
Budget deficit[b]	2.7	10.7	13.0	24.7
Money growth[a]	52.9	99.3	100.9	264.4
International reserves ($ million)	320	129	95	36
Trade balance ($ million)	246	73	-161	-73
Black market premium (%)	99	358	898	2349

[a] Percent, December–December.
[b] Percent GDP.
Sources: Banco Central de Chile; International Monetary Fund; Edwards (1986); Edwards and Cox-Edwards (1987); Solimano (1988).

Table 13.2 Chile: the growth rate of real GDP and demand
(percent per year)

	1970	1971	1972	1973
GDP	2.1	9.0	-1.2	-6.6
Consumption				
Private	-0.5	13.2	7.7	-6.6
Government	5.9	12.4	5.7	1.7
Investment	6.5	-2.0	-20.1	-6.0
Exports	2.1	0.8	-15.1	2.8
Imports	0.9	8.5	3.2	-5.4

Source: Banco Central de Chile, *Indicadores Económicos y Sociales 1960–1985*.

disappeared. A vicious cycle took over; repressed inflation encouraged the informal economy, resulting in reduced taxes, higher deficits, and, thus, in even higher inflation. In 1972, two stabilization programs were implemented, and both failed.

When evaluating the difficulties, the dominant view among UP economists was that the authorities had failed to impose appropriate controls in implementing the macroeconomic program (García 1972). This view guided the first, rather weak, attempt at stabilizing the economy which was launched in February 1972. No serious measures aimed at correcting the major macroeconomic causes of these problems were undertaken. It simply was not convenient to reduce government expenditures, the policy of granting salary increases that exceeded inflation was maintained, and a significant devaluation was ruled out.[12]

The most serious problem was the loss of control over wages. Unions in both nationalized and private firms demanded increasingly higher wage adjustments. The government faced a dilemma. If it refused to grant the wage adjustments, it would help the macroeconomy, but would hurt its political objectives. Under these circumstances, the government chose, every time, to uphold its revolutionary label.[13]

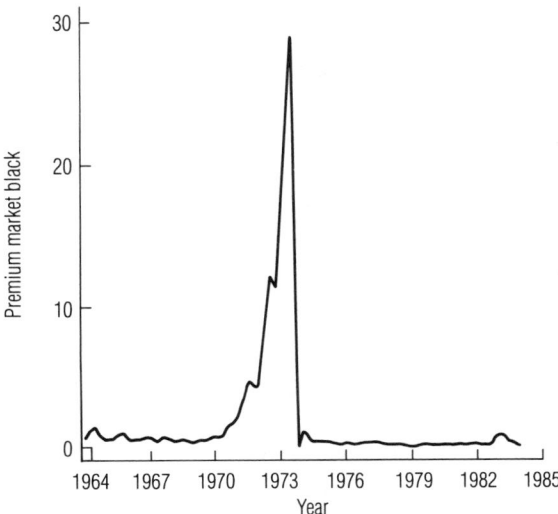

Figure 13.2 Chile: the black market for dollars.

By mid-1972, it became apparent that the February stabilization program was a failure. The underground economy was now generalized, output began to fall, open inflation reached an annual rate of 70 percent in the second quarter, foreign exchange reserves were only $82 million, and the black market rate was climbing at a very fast pace (see Figure 13.2). From a political perspective, parliamentary elections scheduled for March 1973 made the situation particularly difficult. An economic crisis would work against the UP in those elections. In August of that year, and under the political monitoring of the Communists, a new stabilization program was launched.

Unlike the previous plan, the cornerstone of the August program was a massive devaluation of the escudo. It was expected that, as a result, the ever mounting pressures on the balance of payments would subside. The program also called for two basic measures to contain the fiscal pressures. First, price increases for the nationalized firms were authorized so as to reduce the financing requirements of the newly formed nationalized sector. Second, the program called for a massive increase in production as the major way to close the gap between aggregate supply and aggregate demand. This increase in output was expected to be a response to *political* rather than economic incentives. In fact, at that time, the Communist Party's main slogan became "Let's win the battle for increased production!" The devaluation and a large number of price increases resulted in a monthly rate of inflation of 22.7 percent in August and 22.2 percent in September.

In spite of the action taken on the exchange rate front, the program failed as no change in the wage rates policy was introduced. In the second week of August, the government announced that it had reached an agreement with the national federation of workers (Central Única de Trabajadores, CUT) with respect to an across-the-board wage adjustment to be granted on October 1, except for firms subject to private bargaining. The new wage policy called for an increase in public and private sector wages by a proportion equal to the accumulated rate of inflation between January and September. In addition, the new policy called for more frequent wage adjustments (*Qué Pasa*, no. 70, Aug. 17, 1972, p. 14). In this way, by a stroke of the pen, the effects of the devaluation were fully offset.

13.4.4 *Phase III: Acceleration of inflation and chaos*

During the first quarter of 1973 Chile's economic problems reached chaotic proportions. Compared to the first quarter of 1972, inflation reached an annual rate of more than 120 percent; industrial output declined by almost 6 percent; the real exchange rate was even more overvalued, and foreign exchange held by the central bank was barely above $40 million. The black market by then covered an ever widening range of transactions in foreign exchange. The fiscal deficit continued to climb as a result of ever higher expenditures and of rapidly disappearing sources of taxation. In that year, the fiscal deficit exceeded 23 percent of GDP.

Once more the policymakers faced the options of implementing a major corrective stabilization program or of furthering the extent of controls. And once again they opted, in March 1973, for the latter. The extent of the economic crisis quickly alienated the middle classes, and the political confrontation with the opposition became increasingly severe.[14]

In concluding, we must comment on the role of domestic economic opposition and the foreign economic blockade. The strategic use of economic disruption by the opposition, foreign enterprises and foreign governments indeed played a role in the ultimate unravelling of the Allende policies. A more neutral external environment probably would have allowed the Allende experiment to continue for some time. But the uncontrolled side-effects of the consumption growth policy (shortages, inflation and related effects) sufficiently weakened the ability to govern.[15] As a result, destabilization by domestic opposition forces and foreign companies and governments could be effective. We advance this view as a hypothesis.

On September 11, 1973, the Allende presidency came to a sudden and shocking end. When the military took over, the country was politically divided and the economy was in shambles. Inflation was galloping, relative price distortions—stemming mainly from massive price controls—were generalized; black market activities were rampant; real wages had fallen drastically; the economic prospects of the middle class had been greatly damaged; the external sector was facing a serious crisis; production and investment were falling steeply; and the government finances were completely out of hand. This was the beginning of Phase IV, where frightful real wage cutting (see Figure 13.1 above) took over.

13.5 Growth with redistribution in García's Peru

When García assumed the Peruvian presidency in August 1985, he captured the world's imagination: a dynamic, charismatic leader taking charge of a country desperately in need of social and economic progress. The fact that he adopted a confrontational attitude on external debt did not hurt his image, either in Latin America or in progressive circles in Europe and the United States. On the domestic front, he had an unambiguous message: growth and redistribution. That policy lasted two years before running aground in a catastrophic manner.

In early 1988, García's populist government staged a dramatic turnaround on the policies that had driven the country to bankruptcy: budget cutting, real wage cutting and massive exchange depreciation were the predictable aftermath of three years of reckless mismanagement. But that was not the end of the story, hyperinflation was to follow and the political consequences of economic destruction and pauperization are still to come. Real wage cutting and yet worse poverty, in the Peruvian context, may well be the opening phase for massive and perhaps violent confrontations.[16] In the rest of this section we analyze in some detail the recent experience with populist policies in Peru. The analysis shows a remarkable similarity between this case and the Chilean episode.

13.5.1 *From Belaunde to García*

In the 1950s and 1960s Peru experienced significant growth of real per-capita income and moderate rates of inflation.[17] Table 13.3 shows that the problems of declining per-capita income and high inflation date from the second half of the 1970s.

In the past 25 years, three major stop–go phases can be discerned. The first was the Belaunde expansion which crashed in 1967–68. The second phase ran until 1974. During this period the extremely favorable world environment permitted a massive expansion, with an average growth rate of per-capita income of 3.7 percent per year (see Figure 13.3).

The second Belaunde administration (1980–85) had to cope with extraordinarily adverse conditions. Belaunde inherited an economy with deep social problems: per-capita income had declined since 1974 and, the external balance improvement of the late 1970s notwithstanding, the interventionism of the military government had created pervasive distortions. The possibility of advancing the economy was drastically limited as a result of a combination of shocks: the world recession of 1980–82, terms-of-trade deterioration, the explosion in world interest rates and

Table 13.3 Peru: growth and inflation (percent per year)

	1950–60	1960–70	1970–75	1975–80	1980–85
Growth per capita	2.8	2.6	1.6	−1.0	−4.2
Inflation	8.0	9.3	12.6	50.0	102.1

Source: Kuczynski (1977); Central Bank; and Ministry of Finance.

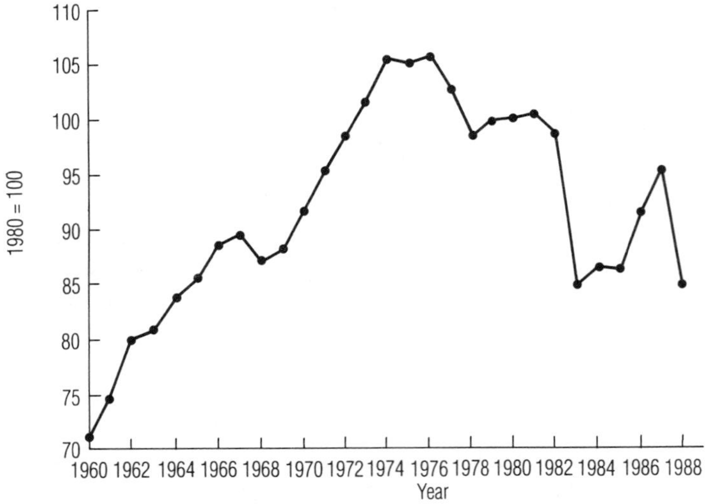

Figure 13.3 Peru's real per-capita income.

the resulting rise in debt service obligations, external credit rationing, and natural disasters. These shocks combined to choke off any room for expansion. In 1982–83, under an IMF program, real GDP per capita declined by 16 percent and inflation nearly doubled to 112 percent.

This disastrous economic performance of the Belaunde government led to a total rout in the elections and thus brought García into power in 1985 with 45.8 percent of the votes.[18] The election which swept García into office in a landslide victory carried one clear message: growth first! (see Ortiz de Zevallos 1989). This message, regardless of its feasibility, conditioned the economic policies of the García administration from the very beginning and is now taking the country to the brink.

13.5.2 *Diagnosis and policies: The heterodox program*

In July 1985, the last month of the Belaunde administration, inflation reached an annual 250 percent. Unemployment was pervasive, idle capacity abounded, and real wages had been reduced in an effort to cope with the external crisis. Against this background, García's government developed a populist project of expansion, entitled "Growth with Redistribution", which emphasized economic recovery combined with disinflation.

Three points are central to an understanding of why economic policy took the form it did. The first is the impressively unequal distribution of income. Figure 13.4 shows the income distribution in Peru with a diagram widely used by the authorities. The striking fact is that 1 percent of the population receives nearly half the national income (see Glewwe 1988).

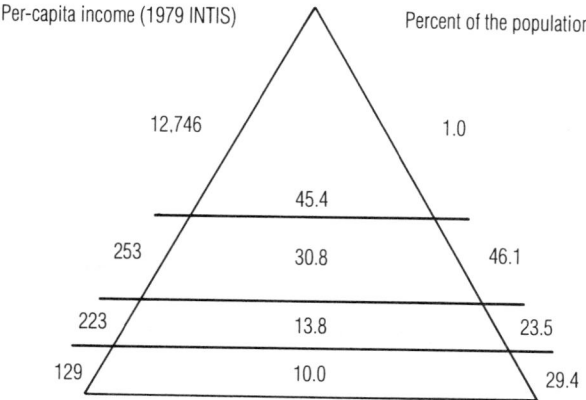

Per-capita income (1979 INTIS)   Percent of the population

12,746   1.0

45.4

253   30.8   46.1

223   13.8   23.5

129   10.0   29.4

Figure 13.4 Peruvian income distribution.

The second is that policymakers were impressed with the large gap between actual and perceived potential output. In Carbonetto *et al.* (1987, p. 41), it is estimated that actual output was only 66 percent of potential output in 1984, leaving a 34 percent gap to be made up by the judicious choice of policy.

The third consideration is that Peruvian economists, in company with economists throughout Latin America, were unimpressed with the effectiveness of IMF programs. It should be remembered that at this time Israel and Argentina made their heterodox stabilization efforts, as did Brazil shortly afterwards. The orthodox approach to stabilization had been discredited by the strong recessionary effects and the absence of any success stories. The alternative, heterodoxy, had all the appeal of offering an end to inflation without the attendant costs of unemployment.[19]

Against this background, the general theme of economic policy was summarized in the *Plan Nacional de Desarrollo 1986–90* (p. 63) from which we quote extensively.

The new economic policy seeks to pass from an economy of conflict and speculation to one of production and consensus. In this economy it is possible to make compatible stability, growth, distribution and development in a context of national planning which finds concrete expression in dialogue and social and economic concertation.

Planning of economic development will be full, decentralized and participatory and concertation will center on the effort to make compatible the generation of savings and productive investment with attention paid to the undelayable priority of attending to social needs. We need to reconcile economic efficiency with social equity in a productive dynamics which is fundamentally sustained by domestic resources.

Specific premises and prescriptions in the national development strategy can be paraphrased as follows (*Plan Nacional de Desarrollo 1986–90*, pp. 63–5):

- The necessity to redistribute income as a means for sustained growth and the possibility to bring together with the redistribution process the necessary capacity to save and invest.
- Salaries and profitability: The generalized and open-ended restraint on wages reduces profitability because it reduces workers' purchasing power, bringing about recessive effects that reduce demand and thus the benefits of a dynamic economy.
- The fiscal deficit: The fiscal deficit is not necessarily inflationary. It only is so if domestic demand exceeds potential output. With substantial idle capacity there is a need for a certain deficit.
- Money creation: Must increase demand, thus allowing an increase in real liquidity since the opposite would slow growth.
- Interest rates: Increased real interest rates do not raise savings, since the latter depend fundamentally on income, but they discourage productive investment.

The specific targets of the economic program are set out in Table 13.4. The new economic policy was based on four measures (Carbonetto *et al.* 1987, p. 15) which in many ways resemble the Allende policies which we discussed above:

- Rapid expansion of effective demand via real wage increases.
- Financial deregulation to give firms relief and contain cost pressures by reducing financial costs of enterprises, effective interest rates, indirect taxes and other elements of costs.
- Reestablishment of selective exchange rates and abandonment of the devaluation policy.
- The external accounts were to be kept in balance by the growth in exports, import substitution and limitations on debt service to be compatible with acceptable growth. Of course, many of the foreign exchange and growth policies on which any success of the plan might have depended never saw the light of day. This is particularly the case for foreign exchange savings strategies.

Table 13.4 The 1986–90 Peruvian economic development plan

	1985	1986	1987	1988	1989	1990
Growth						
GDP	1.4	6.5	6.2	6.1	6.3	6.2
Consumption	0.1	8.5	6.3	5.7	5.0	5.2
Exports	3.5	−13.6	4.8	5.8	5.9	5.9
Imports	−24.6	5.0	13.7	11.9	5.6	7.4
Investment	−12.3	12.0	14.4	11.8	11.6	10.7
Budget deficit[a]	0.6	2.3	2.3	2.1	1.8	1.6

[a] Percent of GDP.
Source: Presidencia de la República (1986).

Table 13.5 Peruvian macroeconomic indicators

	1985	1986	1987	1988
Inflation[a]	158	63	115	1722
Growth	2.5	9.5	6.9	−8.4
Real wage[b]	111	126	137	105
Trade balance ($)	1173	−67	−463	−84
Government revenues[c]	42.7	32.1	25.9	23.5

[a] December–December.
[b] Index July 1985 = 100.
[c] Percent of GDP.
Source: World Bank; Ministry of Finance; National Institute of Planning.

Figure 13.5 Peru: the real wage.

13.5.3 *Phase I: The first two years*

The immediate priority for the García administration was to introduce a "heterodox" program of stabilization: inflation reduction via an incomes policy combined with a massive reactivation of the economy.

In the short term, the heterodox program was immensely successful. Inflation declined sharply (as shown in Table 13.5), employment increased, and the real wage was pushed up substantially (as shown in Figure 13.5). In the last quarter of 1987, the real wage stood 52 percent above the level of 1985. Growth, too, had been very substantial. In 1986, the economy grew by 9.5 percent; and in 1987, by another 6.9 percent.

It is important to recognize just how successful the heterodox approach is.

Given enough foreign exchange and a depressed economy, expansion of *domestic* demand can work. In fact, the success is broadly shared because the recovery of demand can raise firms' profitability by raising capacity utilization. That was indeed the case in Peru. A year after the program started García was celebrated by the business class for the success of his recovery strategy. Private investment increased by 24 per cent in 1986 and another 18.6 percent in 1987.[20]

By early 1987, the program was at the peak of its success: real GDP had grown cumulatively more than 20 percent since the third quarter of 1985, while inflation had been reduced from 188 percent to only 75 percent. Despite the startling success, the strain was starting to appear in rising cost pressures and a growing loss of foreign exchange. However, as in the case of Allende's Chile, these strains were obvious to economists, but were far from alarming to policymakers or the public.

13.5.4 *Phase II: Inflation and collapse*

The turning point came in July 1987, in the form of a political conflict that erupted as a result of a proposal to nationalize the banking system. On July 27, 1987, President García declared (see Presidencia de la República 1987b, p. 1):

> In Peru, today, the financial system is the most powerful instrument of concentration of economic power and thus of political influence; it is the major obstacle to the democratization of production and the accumulation of the surplus.

At the time the right, with public appearances of Vargas Llosa, dramatized the shift in government policies toward socialism. This juncture also represented the end of the recovery policy and the turning point toward inflation and foreign exchange crises. Although the constraints tightened only gradually and bottlenecks emerged only in few places during the remainder of 1987, it is fair to say that July–August of that year represented a crucial period, after which the continuation of expansionary policies could no longer be defended.

Populist programs such as that practiced in Peru fail when the economy runs out of foreign exchange and when the controls that support the initial redistribution and expansion have to be dismantled. By late 1987, growth was petering out and inflation, brought about by external constraints, bottlenecks and the adjustment of severe price distortions, exploded.

To understand what went wrong it helps to return to the basic philosophy of the program. This is fully documented in *El Perú Heteródoxo: Un Modelo Económico*, a 500-page book published in mid-1987 by the economic architects of the program (see Carbonetto *et al.* 1987). The most striking revelation of this book is the extraordinary extent to which policymakers in the García administration, as had the Allende policymakers before them, diverged from accepted economics. Thus we learn (pp. 75–6) that

> An examination of the Peruvian record reveals that periods of moderate inflation are associated with expansionary fiscal policies. And periods of major inflation are

associated with fiscal restraint. Thus, the record shows exactly the opposite of what is predicted by a theory which explains inflation by fiscal deficits.

And, to dispel any doubts (p. 82):

> If it were necessary to summarize in two words the economic strategy adopted by the government starting in August 1985 they are *control* (meaning control of prices and costs and recognizing that this could be done only temporarily for the first twelve months) and *spend*, transferring resources to the poorest so that they increase consumption and create a demand for increased output, thus "justifying" that idle capacity be put to use.
>
> It is necessary to spend, even at the cost of a fiscal deficit, because if this deficit transfers public resources to increase consumption of the poorest they demand more goods and this will bring about a reduction in unit costs. Thus the deficit is not inflationary, on the contrary! This constitutes without doubt the basic premise on which the economic team acted and the major departure from the earlier strategy that had emphasized adjustment from the demand side.

Peru learned in 1987–88 that there indeed are serious tradeoffs in policy: continued rapid growth and massive real wage increases are incompatible with moderate inflation.[21] In 1986 inflation was only 63 percent, far below the level at which the program started. But the experience of high growth with moderate inflation, after a while, became an artifact of the controls and subsidies on public sector prices and on foreign exchange. Subsidies and controls were used to avoid price increases in politically sensitive areas. In 1987–88, most petroleum products sold at one-third their July 1985 price. Electricity prices, the price of rice, and bus fares had declined by more than a third, as had the real price of foreign exchange (see Table 13.6).

13.5.5 *Phase III: The hyperinflation*

When adjustments in the controlled prices had to be made, inflation accelerated rapidly.[22] Naturally, the massive increase in the budget deficit also contributed to the acceleration of inflation. The deficit, in turn, greatly increased as a consequence of a massive policy of subsidies, and as a result of the extraordinary decline in real tax collection (see Table 13.7). In 1975–86, tax collection had

Table 13.6 Peru: real levels of controlled prices (July 1985 = 100)

	Dec. 1986	Dec. 1987	Dec. 1988
Average[a]	75	59	58
Rice	73	61	47
Light, electricity	49	40	16
Telephone	84	87	32
Gas	58	33	25

[a] Weighted by expenditure shares.
Source: Apoyo.

Table 13.7 Peru: public sector financing requirement (percent of GDP)

	1985	1986	1987	1988[a]
Overall public sector deficit	4.4	6.7	9.9	6.1
Budget deficit	2.4	4.9	6.5	5.3
Central Bank losses	1.9	1.8	2.8	0.8
Credit to development banks	0.8	1.4	1.9	0.8
Public sector financing requirement	5.1	8.1	11.2	6.9
Domestic financing	1.2	5.7	9.8	6.9

[a]Estimate.
Source: World Bank; Central Bank; and Ministry of Finance.

averaged above 12 percent of GDP, and in 1985, it rose to 13.2 percent. However, by 1988, and as a result of a sharp decline in compliance, tax collection had fallen to only 7.5 percent of GDP. Additionally, the central bank's policy of multiple exchange rates contributed in an important way to the deficit. This policy alone resulted in losses amounting to 2 percent of GNP from buying foreign exchange at a high price from exporters and selling it at a low or subsidized price to importers.

The large budget deficit not only contributed to inflation, but also affected the allocation of credit and hence investment. While foreign exchange reserves lasted, the government could sell foreign exchange rather than borrow in the home market or print money. However, with reserves precariously low, there was no room left for further foreign exchange sales to finance the deficit (see Figure 13.6).[23] The declining reserves forced a more consistent exchange rate policy which immediately raised the inflation rate. Thus external financing of the budget

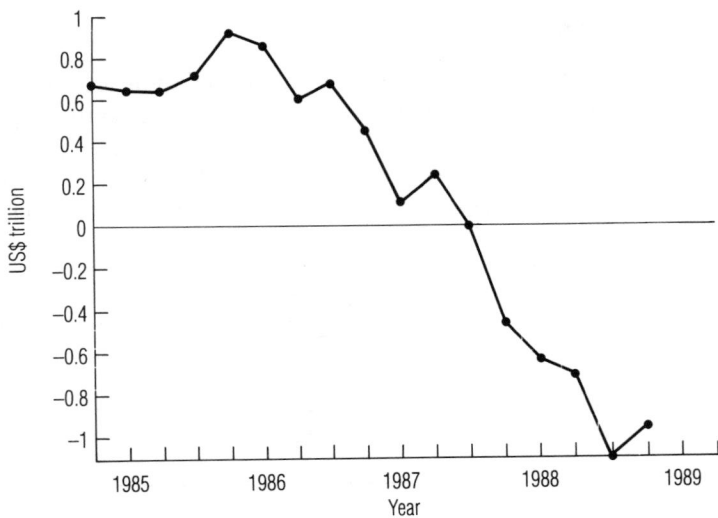

Figure 13.6 Peru: net foreign reserves.

deficit ultimately had an inflationary cost, even though it may have been delayed by a year or two.

As has traditionally been the case in populist experiences, the government also resorted to the banking system to help finance the deficit. High reserve ratios for banks or direct financing requirements effectively achieved this. The counterpart of this policy was a 30 percent decline in real bank credit to the private sector in three years.

Since September 1987, the World Bank and Peruvian authorities had been discussing stabilization. But the political impetus for major policy changes was missing. The only impetus for change came from the external balance side where a crisis had been building up quite visibly. The trade surplus of above $1 billion in 1985 had become a deficit by 1987. Reserves declined by over $1 billion to the point where net reserves were negative at the beginning of 1988. The response to the looming foreign exchange crisis was a major devaluation in late 1987, which in the short run resulted in a small real depreciation. This helped stem capital flight and the widening trade deficit for some time. However, as in Allende's Chile, shortly after this corrective step, generalized and massive wage increases were granted. In a vicious cycle, then, accelerating wage and price increases eroded the initial gain in competitiveness. The renewed appreciation of the real exchange rate for imports since the end of 1987, and the resulting exchange losses of the central bank, signal the government's inability to force a real depreciation.

13.5.6 *Phase IV: What next?*

Economic mismanagement need not be shortlived. If the politics is supportive and external destabilization is not a factor, such a regime can last another year or even more. At the time of writing (1989) there seem to be few avenues open to Peru. One possibility is that García makes time by radicalizing his own position and policies in the direction of socialism and increasing government intervention. A massive program of nationalizations and control, of the type Allende pursued in his last year, would give the government more than a few months of breathing space, except if it were overthrown.

But while there is apparent stability, the extreme reduction in living standards and the growing number of strikes do suggest that surviving to the elections in April 1990 will not be easy.[24] The very depth of the economic collapse in late 1988 caused so sharp a fall in imports that the external constraint, for a while, was lessened. The real exchange rate in the informal market actually declined to pre-1987 levels. But the collapse of real wages and activity was devastating. In fact, official estimates placed the decline in per-capita real income, between 1987 and April 1989, at 25 percent (see Table 13.8). Just how far the disintegration of the economy has gone is apparent from a survey in January 1989 reported by *Apoyo*, an economic consulting service in Peru. Middle- and upper-income respondents predominantly indicated that they would buy dollars given extra income. Of the lower-income groups, more than half reported that they would spend the extra income on food.

Table 13.8 Peru: real wages and real per-capita GDP, 1985–1989 (index July 1985 = 100)

	Real wages			
	National average	Minimum wage	Government	Per-capita GDP[b]
1985	111	120	113	100
1986	126	124	118	107
1987	137	131	136	112
1988	105	118	101	110
1989[a]	56	64	43	81[c]

[a] July 1989.
[b] Index, 1985 = 100.
[c] April 1989.
Source: Ministry of Economics, Peru.

13.6 Concluding remark

It is clear that the two instances of populism discussed here led to disastrous consequences for those who were meant to be the beneficiaries. The central question, then, is whether populist policies are downright unsustainable, or whether there is a variant which, properly executed, can in fact succeed. We leave to further research the elaboration of the thesis that expansionary policies—somewhat similar in spirit to populist policies—can succeed provided they stay far clear of foreign exchange constraints, emphasize reactivation only for a brief initial period and then shift to growth policies. Most important for success, expansionary policies need to be aware of capacity constraints and have to rely for their financing on an extremely orthodox fiscal policy and rigorous tax administration. Within those restrictions it would appear that there is room left for achieving redistributive objectives in an effective way.[25]

When looking forward into the next few years, one cannot avoid wondering whether economic systems have "memory," and whether the mistakes of past populist regimes have been learned. This question is particularly relevant for the Chilean case where in March 1990 a new government—in all likelihood of center-left persuasion—will face urgent and immediate pressures to improve the social conditions of the poor. Needless to say, it is not possible to answer this question today. However, both the writings of the economic team of the likely new Chilean government, as well as the economic program of the *Concertación*, do suggest that some of the more important lessons regarding the design of economic policy have indeed been absorbed. Only the passing of time will allow us to verify this conjecture.

Notes

1. See also Sachs (1989), where the same issue is pursued.
2. In a larger project we expect to look at a significant number of experiences in Latin America to get a sharper picture of the phases and ultimate breakdown of programs.
3. See Dornbusch and de Pablo (1988) on the inflation dynamics.
4. See Oppenheim (1989) for a recent review of the literature on this experience.
5. See Stallings (1978) and de Vlyder (1974) for a discussion of politics and economics in Chile.
6. Of course, this was consistent with the structuralist view on inflation. See Sunkel (1960) and Baer and Kersternetzky (1964).
7. See, for example, the 1971 CIAP Report reproduced in *Panorama Económico*, no. 260, Feb.–Mar. 1971, p. 36.
8. The agrarian reform law passed by Congress during the Frei administration provided the necessary tool. See Alaluf *et al.* (1972).
9. On June 11, 1971, Congress unanimously approved the constitutional reform that nationalized large copper mines. See Geller and Estevez (1972), and Ffrench-Davis and Tironi (1974). The reforms of the banking system and large manufacturing firms were somewhat more difficult, because the government lacked the institutional channels for implementing the nationalization program. Initially, this obstacle was overcome by purchasing blocks of shares—especially bank shares—at very high prices. These acquisitions were complemented by a process of requisition based on an old, and until then forgotten, decree law promulgated during the short-lived Socialist Republic of 1932.
10. The strong showing in early municipal or Congressional elections was not uncommon in Chile. In fact, the Frei government had a similar experience in 1965.
11. See Dornbusch and Edwards (1989) for a more detailed discussion of the nationalization process. See also Alaluf *et al.* (1972).
12. In 1971 a small devaluation was followed by the creation of four different exchange rates.
13. Moreover, a number of economists argued that higher real wages could be sustained as long as the government was able, via increased controls, to extract additional "surplus" from the private sector. See Bitar (1979).
14. Of course, it must be remembered that, in the midst of this polarization, the support commanded by Allende actually grew: whereas in 1970 the UP received the votes of 30 percent of the electorate, in the municipal elections of 1971 it reached 50 percent and even in 1973 its share still stood at 44 percent.
15. Rosenstein-Rodan (in Orrego Vicuna 1975, pp. 219–20) notes of the Allende policies, oriented toward consumption: "This part of Allende's policies was more Populism than Socialism. Even Fidel Castro is supposed to have observed 'Marxist socialism is a revolution of production—this is a revolution of consumption'."
16. More so than in any other country of Latin America, economic performance is central to maintaining the very precarious social peace in Peru. At issue is not only the possible confrontation between left and right. Far more dangerous is the widening conflict opened by the Maoist *Shining Path* guerrillas. The outcome is wide open because of the divisions between rich and poor, the city and the sierras, white and indios.
17. See Thorp (1987), Thorp and Bertram (1978), and Kuczynski (1977) for history and extensive references.
18. See Wise (1988) and Ortiz de Zevallos (1989) for a review of politics.
19. See Dornbusch (1982, 1988a), Bresser Pereira and Nakano (1987), and Bruno *et al.* (1988).

20. See Centro de Economía Aplicada (1988) and especially Iguiniz (1988) for an evaluation of the first three years of the program.
21. This, of course, is exactly what we point out in our model in Section 13.2.
22. See Dornbusch and Edwards (1989) for further details on this issue.
23. The net reserves included on the liability side $800 million of arrears to the IMF. The gold position of the central bank had been revalued at various points and amounted to $659 billion in December 1988.
24. By April 1989 the decline in economic activity and the restrictions of imports had become so massive that an actual reserve recovery had taken place. The reserve gains were sufficient to feed a rumor of another reactivation program.
25. See Dornbusch and Edwards (1989) for a detailed discussion on three alternative future scenarios for Peru. See Edwards (1989) for a discussion on the inability of the Peruvian advisers to learn from the Chilean experience.

References

Alaluf, D. *et al.* (1972) *La economía chilena en 1971.* Santiago: Instituto de Economía de la Universidad de Chile.

Almeyda, C. (1987) *Reencuentro con mia vida* Santiago: Ediciones del Ornitorrinco.

Baer, W., and I. Kersternetzky (1964) *Inflation and Growth in Latin America.* New Haven, CT: Yale University Press.

Bitar, S. (1979) *Transición, socialismo y democracia.* Mexico City: Siglo XXI.

Bitar, S. (1986) *Chile. Experiment in Democracy.* Philadelphia, PA: Institute for the Study of Human Issues.

Boorstein, E. (1988) *Allende's Chile.* New York: International Publishers.

Bresser Pereira, L. C., and Y. Nakano (1987) *Inertial Inflation.* Boulder, CO: Westview Press.

Bruno, M., G. di Tella, R. Dornbusch, and S. Fischer (1988) *Inflation stabilization. The experience of Israel, Argentina, Brazil, Bolivia and Mexico.* Cambridge, MA: MIT Press.

Carbonetto, D., *et al.* (1987) *El Perú Heteródoxo: Un Modelo Económico.* Lima: Instituto Nacional de Planificación.

Centro de Economía Aplicada (1988) *Evaluación de dos años y medio de gobierno, Julio 1985–Diciembre 1987.* Lima: CEA.

Conniff, M. (1982) *Latin American Populism in Comparative Perspective.* Albuquerque: University of New Mexico Press.

de Vlyder, S. (1974) *Allende's Chile.* Cambridge: Cambridge University Press.

Dornbusch, R. (1982) "Stabilization policies in developing countries: What have we learned?" *World Development* 10(9) (Reprinted in *Dollars, Debts and Deficits.* Cambridge, MA: MIT Press, 1987.)

Dornbusch, R. (1988a) "Inflation stabilization: The role of incomes policy and of monetization." In *Exchange Rates and Inflation.* Cambridge, MA: MIT Press.

Dornbusch, R. (1988b) "Peru on the brink." *Challenge* 30 (Sept/Oct): 31–7.

Dornbusch, R., and J. C. de Pablo (1988) *Deuda externa e inestabilidad macroeconómica en Argentina.* Buenos Aires: Editorial SudAmericana.

Dornbusch, R., and S. Edwards (1989) *Macroeconomic Populism in Latin America.* Working paper No. 2986. Cambridge, MA: NBER.

Drake, P. (1982) "Conclusion: Requiem for populism?" In M. L. Conniff, ed., *Latin American Populism in Comparative Perspective.* Albuquerque: University of New Mexico Press.

Edwards, S. (1986) "Stabilization with liberalization: An evaluation of ten years of Chile's experience with free market policies, 1973–1983." In A. Choksi and D. Papageorgiou, eds, *Economic Liberalization in Developing Countries.* Oxford: Basil Blackwell.

Edwards, S. (1989) "The debt crisis and economic adjustment in Latin America." *Latin American Research Review* 3. 172–86.

Edwards, S., and A. Cox-Edwards (1987) *Monetarism and Liberalization. The Chilean Experiment.* Cambridge, MA: Ballinger.

Falcoff, M. (1989) *Modern Chile 1970–1989.* New Brunswick, NJ: Transaction Publishers.

Ffrench-Davis, R., and E. Tironi, eds. (1974) *El cobre en el desarrollo económico nacional.* Santiago: Ediciones Nueva Universidad.

Foxley, A. (1981) "Stabilization policies and their effects on employment and income distribution." In W. Cline and S. Weintraub, eds, *Economic stabilization in developing countries.* Washington, DC: Brookings Institution.

Foxley, A. (1983) *Latin American experiments in neoconservative economics.* Los Angeles: University of California Press.

Foxley, A., and O. Munoz (1974) "Income redistribution, economic growth and social structure: The case of Chile." *Oxford Bulletin of Economics and Statistics* 36(1).

García, Norberto (1972) "Algunos aspectos de la política de corto plazo en 1971." In D. Alaluf *et al.*, eds, *La economía chilena en 1971.* Santiago: Instituto de Economía de la Universidad de Chile.

Geller, L., and J. Estevez (1972) "La nacionalización del cobre." In D. Alaluf *et al.*, eds, *La economía chilena en 1971.* Santiago: Instituto de Economía de la Universidad de Chile.

Glewwe, P. (1988) "The distribution of welfare in Peru 1985–1986." Mimeo, World Bank.

Herrera, C. *et al.* (1987) *Reactivación y Política Económica Heteródoxa 1985–1986.* Lima: Fundación Friedrich Ebert.

Iguiniz, J. (1988) "Evaluación crítica de la política económica bajo García: Balance a los tres años de gobierno." Mimeo, Fondo de Región Andina, Lima.

Inostroza, A. (1971) "El programa monetario y la política de comercio exterior de la Unidad Popular." *Panorama Económico.* March.

Kuczynski, P.-P. (1977) *Peruvian Democracy under Economic Pressure.* Princeton, NJ: Princeton University Press.

López, J. (1972) "La economía política de la Unidad Popular: Una evaluación de su primer año de gobierno." In D. Alaluf *et al.*, eds, *La economía chilena en 1971.* Santiago: Instituto de Economía de la Universidad de Chile.

Martner, G., ed. (1971) *El pensamiento económico del gobierno de Allende.* Santiago: Editorial Universitaria.

Ministerio de Economía (1987) *Programa trienal 1988–1990.* Lima: Ministerio de Economía.

Nove, A. (1976) "The political economy of the Allende regime." In P. O'Brien, ed., *Allende's Chile.* New York: Praeger.

Novoa, E. (1971) "Vías legales para avanzer al socialismo." *Revista Mensaje* 167.

ODEPLAN (1971) "Objetivos del Plan 1971." In G. Martner, ed, *El pensamiento económico del gobierno de Allende.* Santiago: Editorial Universitaria.

Oppenheim, L. (1989) "The Chilean road to socialism revisited." *Latin American Research Review* 24(1): 155–83.

Orrego Vicuna, F. ed. (1975) *Chile: The Balanced View.* Santiago: Institute of International Affairs, University of Chile.

Ortiz de Zevallos, F. (1989) *The Peruvian Puzzle.* New York: Twentieth Century Fund.

Pazos, F. (1972) *Chronic Inflation in Latin America.* New York: Praeger.

Presidencia de la República (1986) *Plan Nacional de Desarrollo 1986–1990.* Lima: Instituto Nacional de Planificación.

Presidencia de la República (1987a) *Plan Nacional de Desarrollo 1988.* Lima: Instituto Nacional de Planificación.

Presidencia de la República (1987b) *Porque la Estatización del Sistema Financiero Peruano.* Lima: Instituto Nacional de Planificación.

Presidencia de la República (1987c) *Diagnóstico y Programación 1987*. Lima: Instituto Nacional de Planificación.

Ramos, J. (1980) "The economics of hyperstagflation." *Journal of Development Economics* 7: 467–88.

Ramos, J. (1986) *Neoconservative Economics in the Southern Cone of Latin America, 1973–1983*. Baltimore, MD: Johns Hopkins University Press.

Rosenstein-Rodan, P. (1974) "Why Allende failed." *Challenge*, 17 (May–June): 7–13.

Sachs, J. (1989) *Social Conflict and Populist Policies in Latin America*. Working paper No. 2897. Cambridge, MA: NBER.

Seers, D. (1964) "Inflation and growth: The heart of the controversy." In W. Baer and I. Kerstenetzky, eds, *Inflation and Growth in Latin America*. New Haven, CT: Yale University Press.

Solimano, A. (1988) *Política de Remuneraciones en Chile: Experiencia Pasada, Instrumentos y Opciones a Futuro*. Colección Estudios CIEPLAN, No. 25. Santiago: CIEPLAN.

Stallings, B. (1978) *Class Conflict and Economic Development in Chile, 1958–73*. Stanford, CA: Stanford University Press.

Stallings, B. (1988) "Self-destruction of an auspicious initiative: Peruvian debt policy under Alan García." Mimeo, University of Wisconsin, Madison.

Sunkel, O. (1960) "Inflation in Chile: An unorthodox approach." *International Economic Papers* 10: 107–31.

Thorp, R. (1978) "Trends and cycles in the Peruvian economy." In P. Bardhan *et al.*, eds, *International Trade, Investment, Macro Policies and History*. Amsterdam: North Holland.

Thorp, R., and G. Bertram (1978) *Peru 1890–1977*. New York: Columbia University Press.

Unidad Popular (1969) *Programa Básico de Gobierno*. Santiago: Editorial Universitaria.

Vuskovic, Pedro (1970) "Distribución del ingreso y opciones de desarrollo." *Cuadernos de la Realidad Nacional*, Sept.

Vuskovic, Pedro (1973) "The economic policy of the Popular Unity government." In J. A. Zammit, ed., *The Chilean Road to Socialism*. Austin: University of Texas Press.

Wise, C. (1988) "Peru in the 1980s: Political responses to the debt crisis." Mimeo, Columbia University, New York.

World Bank (1985) *Peru. Country Economic Memorandum*. Washington, DC: World Bank.

World Bank (1988) *Peru: Policies to Stop Hyperinflation and Initiate Economic Recovery*. Washington, DC: World Bank.

Yanez, J. (1978) "Una corrección del indice de precios al consumidor durante el periodo 1971–73." In F. Contreras, ed., *Comentarios Sobre la Situación Económica*. Santiago: Instituto de Economía de la Universidad de Chile.

Zammit, J. A., ed. (1973) *The Chilean Road to Socialism*. Austin: University of Texas Press.

14

Brazilian debt crises:
Past and present
with Eliana A. Cardoso

> Deficits innumerable, annual, perennial, everlasting and ever increasing deficits!
> In these three syllables is comprehended all the mystery of Brazilian finance, the
> head and front of its offending.
>
> Wileman (1896)

Brazilian debt problems have troubled world capital markets for more than 150 years. A major lesson from that history is the extraordinary repetition of events. The same themes, even the very same language, reemerge every time a sudden halt to lending brings about illiquidity, funding loans, moratoria, and then, soon, renewed lending.

Sometimes the precipitating events are domestic, as in the nineteenth century. At other times, as in the 1930s or the 1980s, a sudden deterioration of the world economy makes a previously accumulated debt overly large and burdensome. The exact details differ, but the broad outlines are always the same. Our interest is to highlight these common features, but we also emphasize how access to the world capital market has served as an essential element in a development strategy. That access was important in the nineteenth century, and it was essential again in the 1970s. This discussion raises the question of where development finance will come from, now that bank lending has dried up.

Our discussion is in five parts. Sections 14.1 through 14.3 report on Brazilian debt history: we start with a discussion of the late nineteenth century, then cover the interwar experience, and, finally, the run up to the 1980s debt crisis. Section 14.4 asks what went wrong with the muddling-through strategy initiated in 1982. The paper concludes with the issue of how to reconcile growth with debt service and offers a proposal.

We thank Peter Lindert for helpful comments. Tim Vogelsang provided valuable research assistance.

14.1 Lessons from the past

Before studying the Brazilian debt crises, it is useful to reflect on two questions: What is the source of debt crises? How are debt crises ultimately resolved?

We start with a conceptual framework. Equation (14.1) shows the financing of external interest payments by three alternative sources: a noninterest current account surplus (NICA); new debt issues, the proceeds of which pay the interest (and amortization) on existing debt; and other net capital inflows, specifically direct foreign investment.

$$\begin{matrix} \text{Interest} \\ \text{payments} \end{matrix} = \text{NICA} + \begin{matrix} \text{Net increase} \\ \text{in debt} \end{matrix} + \begin{matrix} \text{Other net capital} \\ \text{inflows} \end{matrix} \qquad \textbf{(14.1)}$$

A debt crisis can arise for one of four reasons, which often emerge in combination. First, domestic fiscal and/or political disorder translates into trade deficits or a reduction in the noninterest current account surplus.

Second, world economic shocks to a country's terms of trade deteriorate export earnings or increase import costs, or shocks to a country's markets reduce export revenue.

Third, nondebt capital inflows that are used to finance interest payments and trade deficits suddenly dry up.

Fourth, rolling of debt (principal and interest) is disrupted by a loss of confidence on the part of the world capital market. Taussig (1928) and Kindleberger (1984), in particular, have emphasized the cutoff of external loans as the precipitating factor in major debt crises.

It is apparent that these disturbances tend to come together: when a country's terms of trade deteriorate, investment opportunities are much less attractive, and hence investment capital from abroad dries up. Knowledge of a financial problem ensures that competitive bond holders will be leery of buying new debt issued to tide the country over the difficulty.

The inevitable outcome, as Brazil's financial history amply demonstrates, is a funding crisis and an interruption of debt service. In terms of equation (14.1) this is equivalent to "involuntary interest capitalization."

Next, how do debt problems go away? Domestic adjustment programs almost invariably are an essential part of restoring confidence on the part of creditors. But a favorable turn of the world economy (whether through war or improved terms of trade) is equally critical. There is no precedent in Brazilian history for one of these factors alone being enough.

Third, reduction of the debt burden by an adjustment of terms is often part of a return to the capital market. This was clearly the case in the 1942 debt consolidation.

With this background we have all the ingredients to study the debt crises of the 1890s, 1930s, and 1980s.

14.1.1 *An overview of the 1890s*

Brazil went into debt in her very infancy. The history of the Brazilian Empire is one of budget deficits financed by external and domestic borrowing. Minister Ouro Preto's report on the budget situation at the time of the proclamation of the Republic shows that taxes and other revenues during the time of the Empire covered only 30 percent of total expenditures. The rest was financed by debt which the Brazilian Republic later inherited.

When the Brazilian Republic was declared in 1889, the external public debt already amounted to £33 million. Ten years later, with an external public debt of almost £50 million, the first debt crisis was brought about by falling coffee prices.

Rippy (1977) notes that in the 60 years following Brazilian independence from Portugal in 1824, British investors preferred Brazil as a field of investment to any other Latin American country because Brazil was politically more stable. By 1890, however, the British already had a larger stake in Argentina.

More than half of the British investment in Brazil was in government bonds. Although some of the Brazilian states failed to meet their obligations, the Brazilian national government had an excellent record. Capital invested in Brazilian bonds brought good returns: the average annual nominal yield seldom fell below 4 percent until after 1931.

Direct investment was insignificant before 1840 but then grew particularly fast in 1840–75, and immediately before World War I. Using the *South American Journal* as a source, Rippy (1977) observes that British investments in Brazil were less diversified than in Argentina. They were concentrated in railway enterprises, with public utility investment next in size. The average nominal yield of the British capital invested in Brazilian railways remained above 5 percent per annum, except for a few years during the depression of 1890s.

Table 14.1 shows the stock of foreign capital in Brazil between 1885 and 1913.[1] Until 1900 almost all capital inflows were of British origin, but by 1905 the stock of direct investment from the USA and European countries was already 40 percent of the total. Nevertheless, British capital continued to represent more than 80 percent of the stock of public debt until 1913.

Capital inflows came in waves that were in large measure dictated by the

Table 14.1 Stock of foreign capital in Brazil, 1885–1913 (£ millions)

	Direct investment	Public debt	Total
1885	24.4	23.2	47.6
1895	40.6	39.0	79.6
1905	75.1	88.3	163.4
1913[a]	255.9	151.7	407.6

Source: Stone (1977, Table 6) and Abreu (1985, Table 1). There is a discrepancy between the two sources concerning British loans in 1895. Stone's numbers, which are reported in our table, exceed Abreu's by almost £20 million.

Table 14.2 The balance of payments in Brazil, 1890–1913 (£ millions, accumulated end-of-period flows)

	1890–99	1900–1904	1905–1909	1910–1913
Current account	−39.1	35.4	14.0	−48.4
Trade balance	28.8	70.3	83.7	38.7
Freight and insurance	32.5	18.0	26.5	30.0
Remittances and travels	8.7	4.9	7.2	8.1
Interest and amortization	26.7	12.0	36.0	49.0
Capital inflows	30.0	12.0	76.3	135.9

Source: Goldsmith (1986, Table III-9).

supply of savings in the United Kingdom. Net transfers of resources from abroad were positive in the 1890s, negative between 1900 and 1909, and positive again in the years preceding World War I. Table 14.2 shows estimates of the balance of payments between 1890 and 1913.

Three kinds of disturbance dominated the experience of the 1890–1913 period:

1. Sharp movements in the world price of coffee and the evolution of the rubber trade.
2. Domestic financial instability that expressed itself in budget deficits and money creation.
3. Movements in the availability of external credit which at times dampened the extent of domestic inflationary finance but also acted as an independent source of disturbance to the economy.

Figure 14.1 highlights the behavior of the money stock and the exchange rate.

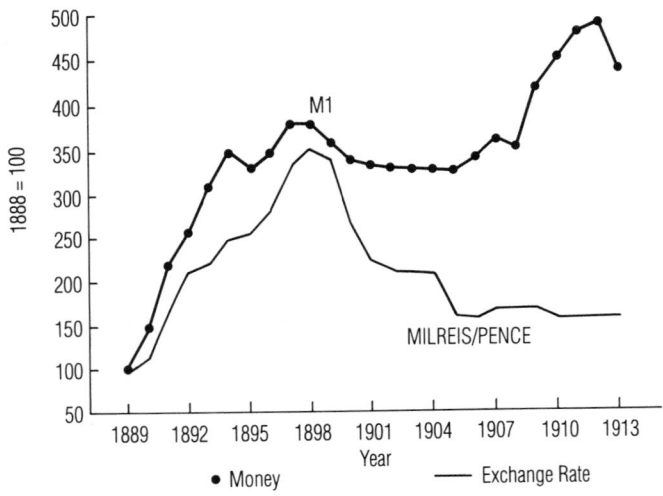

Figure 14.1 Money and exchange rate.
(*Source*: Instituto Brasileiro de Geografia e Estatística.)

Table 14.3 Inflation and price of coffee in Brazil, 1891–1913

Period	Inflation (average %)	Price of coffee in London (1888 = 100)		
		High[a]	Average	Low[b]
1891–94	24	130	112	98
1896–1900	2	92	61	47
1901–1905	−5	63	55	47
1906–1913	2	122	82	58

[a]The highest yearly index during the period.
[b]The lowest yearly index in the period.
Source: IBGE, *Series Estatísticas Retrospectivas*; and Goldsmith (1986).

Three broad periods can be distinguished. The first one, starting in the 1880s, was marked by extreme domestic instability and inflation. The years of the *Encilhamento* were characterized by very high inflation, which was more than 30 percent per year in 1891 and 1892. With reinforcement by a dramatic fall of coffee prices in 1896–1900 to less than half of 1891–94 prices, exchange depreciation was massive. This period lasts to 1898.

Contrary to common belief, the Baring crisis and external credit rationing were not decisive factors in the Brazilian experience of the 1890s. Fishlow (1988) observes that external loans continued to be contracted during 1893 and again in 1895–97. Transfers of resources from abroad were positive until the eve of the 1898 Funding Loan. The threat of Brazilian default in 1898 was brought about by continually falling coffee prices. Table 14.3 shows the price of coffee between 1891 and 1913.

In the second phase, between 1898 and 1905, a funding loan and a shift from money to debt finance introduced deflation. The currency appreciated and was then stabilized in 1905. The crisis of the second half of the 1890s culminated with the 1898 Funding Loan, whose conditionality terms were as harsh as those imposed by an IMF agreement. By 1903 the price of coffee had fallen to 36 percent of its level ten years before. Deflation and depression lasted until 1905.

In the third phase, from 1906 to 1912, world trade prices were exceptionally favorable—coffee prices doubled between 1906 and 1912. This was a period of prosperity. The recovery of coffee prices, the rubber boom, and capital inflows in the form of portfolio as well as direct investment helped sustain growth. This period came to an end when coffee prices collapsed in 1913–14. Once again, in 1914, a new funding loan was required.

Next, we look at each of these phases in more detail.

14.1.2 *From the Encilhamento to the crisis*

In the late 1880s the money supply expanded rapidly in response to demands for increased credit. Pressure for monetary expansion came from the abolition of slavery in 1888. More money was needed to sustain a new wage-based labor market, as well as to permit cheap credit, compensating landowners for the capital losses from the emancipation. The argument that the existing stock of paper currency was too small for Brazil, owing to the great size of the country, the limited use of cheques, and the general habit among small traders of keeping large sums of money on hand instead of depositing them in banks, was advanced. Supporters of the gold standard protested: how was the required volume of currency to be determined?

After the proclamation of the Republic, the expansionist doctrine was supported by the Finance Minister Rui Barbosa, and the supply of money almost doubled in 1890. A series of decrees authorized additions to the volume of inconvertible paper money. London disapproved:

> Of the issue of new financial decrees by the Brazilian Government there is no end, scarcely a week passing without their number being added to.[2]

> some of the States are said to be in difficulties, but as the *Rio News* points out "they are always in trouble and at this very moment spending money as though they had inexhaustible resources" ... Capitalists on this side of the world, we should think, hesitate very considerably before lending the Finance Minister of Brazil ten millions sterling to assist him and his Government in the kind of "rake's progress", upon which they appear to be so anxious to enter.[3]

Brazil was said to be following the example of Argentina, where events leading up to the Baring crisis are described by Hyndman (1892) as follows:

> The history of the loans to the Argentine Republic, now that it has become history, is surprising, indeed. A country which had a national debt of £10,000,000 in 1875, contrived to raise it to £70,000,000 in 1889 ... All the money markets were competing with one another for a share of these good things. London, Paris, Brussels, Berlin, each was ready to outbid the other for the privilege of taking up ventures and floating loans which, at any other time, would have been regarded as very doubtful security, when the nature of the country, the character of the population, and the instability of its political institutions were carefully considered ...

In Brazil, the government financial policy resulted in a proliferation of new banks, at the same time as new companies were started in every branch of commercial and industrial enterprise. Their shares were sold at constantly increasing prices as soon as they were issued. As had just happened in Argentina, "railways, docks, tramways, waterworks, public buildings, mansions, all were being carried on in hot haste." A boom took off. *The Economist* commented:

> As capital cannot be attracted, the printing presses are to be set to work, and new issues of inconvertible paper currency poured out. In that way temporary relief may be afforded, and fresh fuel will be heaped upon the fire of speculation. But what the ultimate result of this policy must be, we see in the case of Argentina, and it is time that all who have a stake in Brazil should be called upon to take note of the direction in which she is drifting.[4]

The comparisons with Argentina finally aroused the protest of a correspondent from Rio de Janeiro:

Permit me to say that a comparison of the finances of Brazil with those of the Argentine Republic is as absurd as to compare the resources natural and otherwise and the trade of the two countries. The Brazilians are a different race of people, and the administration of public affairs has always been a reasonably honest one. The credit of this country has always been maintained at a high level. There is, doubtless, speculation by officials in Brazil, but there has never been such dishonesty as in the Argentine Republic, where an honest official of high or low degree was, and is now, the exception to the general rule ... The prosperity of Argentina during the past 15 years, so much vaunted, has been almost wholly fictitious. Since 1882, more than £120 million of foreign capital has been poured into that country—a great part of which has been stolen by corrupt officials, and as much more planted in public works that will never be remunerative.[5]

But *The Economist* was convinced of the correctness of its prediction and went further in its comparisons with Argentina:

Those interested in the stability of Brazilian finance are beginning to fear, and not without some cause, that the same policy of currency inflation that has brought the Argentine Republic to grief is being pursued by the Brazilian Government.[6]

Economic and political instability were, in fact, on the rise. At the end of 1891, the Marshall da Fonseca dissolved the Congress and proclaimed martial law throughout the country. For some time it had been known that considerable tension between the executive government and the Chambers existed, principally on matters of financial policy. The policy of the government was to increase the already largely inflated stock of paper currency by further issues. But the Congress demanded that the flood of inconvertible currency should cease and that a check should be put upon the action of the Banco da República, which was indulging in excesses somewhat similar to those of Argentine banks. The dispute ended in rupture, and for a short while, the promoters of the expansionary policy held the field.

A Committee of the Chamber, appointed to inquire into the affairs of the Banco da República, concluded that excessive issue of paper money had promoted stock exchange gambling, which had withdrawn capital from legitimate enterprises and led to a serious depreciation of the currency. The Banco da República had played a prominent part in promoting this speculation, and the committee recommended that it should be required to reduce different accounts and to limit the issue of notes. The minister of finance was opposed. He believed that if a halt were put to money creation, a crisis would ensue. Moreover, he believed that there was no need to hold gold against the notes and that the credit of the state was sufficient to guarantee conversion of the notes. Nevertheless, the Congress, by a majority of 100 to 12, passed the second reading of a bill restricting the issues of paper money.

The company mania subsided, and the first burst of wild speculation passed. For many bubble companies, the day of reckoning had come. Shares that once sold at a high premium now could not find buyers at less than half the paid-up capital. Banks ceased to pay interest on deposits. The process of liquidation was under way. *The Economist* commented:

Although the finances of Brazil have fallen into serious disorder they have not yet lapsed into anything like the deplorable condition of those of Argentina and Uruguay. Besides, ... on her recent outburst of extravagant speculation, it is with her own and not with borrowed money that Brazil has been dealing.[7]

As Figure 14.1 shows, the milreis underwent rapid devaluation. Again the comparisons with Argentina are inevitable. Whether the peso depreciated because of the overissue of banknotes in Argentina or because of the sudden halt in new foreign lending is still debated in the literature. A monetarist position tends to attribute the depreciation to the new bank laws passed in Argentina in 1887, but Williams (1920) claims that cutoff of the capital flow produced the depreciation.[8] Similar questions arose in the case of Brazil. Fishlow (1988) argues that capital inflows did not affect the behavior of the Brazilian exchange rate in the 1890s, and Cardoso and Fishlow (1983) show that the monetary expansion was not enough to explain the behavior of the exchange rate, which was clearly influenced by the price of coffee.

External confidence was shaken not only by the expansionary policies but also by the political instability that led to the resignation of the Marshall da Fonseca. Rebellion and military repression came in 1893 and 1894. Despite mounting internal and external problems and the negative effects of the Baring crisis on evaluation of Latin American creditworthiness, Brazil did not default and continued to have limited access to foreign loans. *The Economist* reproduced an extract from *Rio News* in connection with the Brazilian loan issued by the Rothschilds in 1893:

the general scheme is for the government to guarantee these loans in return for the use of the proceeds not required by the borrowing companies. For instance, a railway company borrows enough for completion of an extension which may require several years to construct, and the treasury undertakes to guarantee the loan or the privilege of having the use of the money until required. Should it be inconvenient for the treasury to advance the funds required at any time, means will of course be found to delay the construction. These companies, therefore are to be used for obtaining loans for the treasury, which loans are not to figure in the public indebtedness of the country. ... Employing round numbers, the loan yielded £3 million. This, at the current rate of exchange should have yielded the company $57.84 million, but we are informed that the treasury had taken the loan at 20d, or at a cost of $36.15 million, the company thus losing the important sum of $21.69 million. .... We cannot believe that these gentlemen (the directors of the company) are such blind and hopeless fools as this operation implies, consequently the treasury must have given something more than the bare 20 pence announced by the Press.[9]

Fishlow (1988) points out that the government continued to meet its foreign obligations, despite increasing debt service owing to exchange depreciation. Government debt service more than doubled between 1892 and 1894, amounting to more than 100 percent of the trade surplus. External resources were required to help meet interest payments and amortization. In 1895 a new Brazilian loan was offered for public subscription. The loan was for £6 million and was to bear 5 percent interest, the issue price being 85 percent. *The Economist* commented on the terms of the loan:

> It is clear from this that the financial position of the country has become utterly unsound, and that if strenuous and successful efforts be not made to economize in every possible direction, Brazil will follow some of its neighbours into the ranks of the insolvent.[10]

The milreis continued its decline until 1898, and matters went from bad to worse. The hope that financial affairs in Brazil would improve with the advent to power of the new president, Campos Salles, soon gave place to the question of whether national bankruptcy could be avoided. The exchange rate had collapsed, adding very heavily to the domestic cost of providing for service of the foreign debt. No wonder, then, that Brazilian bonds fell (Figure 14.2). *The Economist* predicted ruin:

> The recent mails to hand from Brazil show that default in the service of the foreign debt is regarded locally as only a question of time. The differences in opinion refer only to the causes of the present situation and the method in which the crisis is to be met.[11]

One current of opinion ascribed the impending default almost solely to the fall in coffee prices, and called upon European financiers to come forward and save

Figure 14.2 Monthly prices of Brazilian bonds, 1890–1914 (price in pounds sterling, issued 1888, 4.5 percent).
(*Source*: *Commercial and Financial Chronicle*, various issues.)

the credit of the country. It pointed out the disasters likely to follow a default in the debt service and the railway guarantees and believed that European financing would not be so blind to its own interest as to allow it to take place.

The Economist argued the opposing view, reproducing an extract from *Rio News*:

> Years ago it was pointed out that the policy which the public men of Brazil were pursuing would certainly lead to bankruptcy. They have known that large deficits were being realized every year, and that their extravagance would certainly increase them. But they live in a fool's paradise and would not see the fatal termination of such a policy. .... If we are not mistaken, we shall soon be hearing that it is the duty of foreign banking houses to help us out of our difficulties by loaning us more money. Such a claim would be worse than absurd. Brazil has no one to blame for her financial troubles but her own public men.[12]

As it became evident that the financial position of the Brazilian government was desperate, the rearrangement of the debt took the form of a funding loan. The plan provided for funding of the interest on external debt and the internal gold loan of 1879 for a period of three years, and also for certain accounts payable annually for railway guarantees. During the period of moratorium, holders of the bonds and guarantees would receive 5 percent bonds in lieu of the stipulated amounts in gold. As part of the funding arrangement, the government was to deposit with three foreign banks in Rio de Janeiro the equivalent of these bonds in paper money, at the exchange rate of 18d per milreis. The paper money was either to be destroyed or, if and when the exchange rate was favorable, used to buy foreign exchange at 18d to the milreis to be remitted to London. The theory was that the excess of paper money was one of the causes of the fall in the exchange rate. Reducing the outstanding paper currency would cause the exchange rate to appreciate. If the appreciation went far enough to admit the purchase of exchange at 18d, it would be possible to accumulate a gold fund that would then be available when the payment of interest in cash was to be resumed three years later.

Some time later, *Rio News* commented:

> Whilst, it is indisputable that by a series of well considered measures Government is gradually introducing order into financial chaos and improving its finances, yet the economical situation is not better, but, in truth, more desperate than ever, and scarcely likely to improve for some time to come, until, in fact, coffee ceases to fall, and the rise that must come some day recommences.[13]

Joaquim Murtinho, the Brazilian Minister of Finance, interpreted the crisis as a result of excess money creation.[14] He attributed the economic crisis to the decrease of the value of Brazil's most important product, coffee. The decline of coffee prices in turn was attributed to overproduction which was explained by the enormous issuance of paper money that excited the fever of speculation. Thus, according to Murtinho, the inflation of the currency constituted the root cause from which all the economic ills of Brazil had sprung. His main conclusion was that the progressive increase of the volume of paper money was the determining factor in the simultaneous depreciation of its value and of the fall of foreign exchange. Even *The Economist* found Murtinho's position exaggerated:

> He is thus a very stalwart of the quantitative theory of money, a theory which, in our opinion, he presses to an undue extreme. ... It would be interesting to know what the finance houses here who negotiated those loans have to say with regard to Dr. Murtinho's assertion that they knew their proceeds were to be entirely devoted to paying the interest on previous issues. If they had that knowledge they must have been aware that a collapse was inevitable, and that consequently investors who responded to the appeals made to them were certain to suffer loss. But, however that may be, the long catalogue of financial abuses given by Dr. Murtinho shows that infinitely greater reforms than a mere tinkering reduction of the paper currency are needed to put the finances of the country in the way to rehabilitation.[15]

The widely shared view was that Brazilian problems were rooted in large government deficits. Wileman (1896, p. 17), a classic source on this period, notes:

> Deficits innumerable, annual, perennial, everlasting and ever increasing deficits!
> In these three syllables is comprehended all the mystery of Brazilian finance, the head and front of its offending.
> It is truism that without deficits there would be no national debt and no inconvertible government issue, because debt, deficits and inconvertible paper money are all, in a sense, synonymous.

And as long as cuts in the deficits were not imposed, just burning paper money was not seen as a solution:

> Whence the Brazilian Government were obtaining the money with which to withdraw notes from circulation, in accordance with the provisions of the funding Loan, has been somewhat of a mystery, as there is no surplus of revenue available for the purpose, but on the contrary a chronic deficit. ... The government has been only substituting one form of paper debt for another, and as the new debt bears interest, whereas the old did not, the financial position, instead of being bettered, is being made worse.[16]

Despite criticism from abroad as well as unpopularity and rebellion at home, Murtinho's tight monetary policy, combined with large improvements in the trade balance (in part due to the beginning rubber boom), stabilized the exchange rate after 1903. The cost was economic recession. But soon afterward, rising coffee prices and a favorable balance of payments would attract a new surge of foreign investment and renewed loans. Prosperity returned in the second half of the 1900s and would last for the next half decade.

By 1911 the public debt had increased to £145 million; the second debt crisis, as well as the second funding loan, was imminent. Finance Minister Rivadavia Correa noted:

> In finance the essential fact is that debts are paid with funds obtained from new loans. This has been the rule for us for already many years. What is new is that this time the loan is made by the same people to whom we owe the overdue interest.[17]

14.2 The 1930s crisis

Brazil did not miss out on the 1920s. The first American issue was sold in 1921. Prior to World War I, Brazil had raised her foreign loans in London. Sixty percent of the external obligations outstanding in 1930 was still denominated in sterling. By then, the external public debt had risen to £250 million (more than 1 billion US dollars) and it was time for yet another debt crisis, a moratorium, and shortly afterward, the third funding loan. But in the next few years regular debt service could not be maintained even with a restructuring. As a result of the depression, service was suspended in 1931–32. Application of part of the reduced funds available for debt service to the market purchase of bonds, depreciated by the default, became common.

Table 14.4 shows Brazilian public debt and debt service in the interwar period. The dramatic increase in the debt service ratio (counting only public debt and not including important private debt and income from direct investment) explains the liquidity problem.

In barely 40 years the bond holders were forced to accept three voluntary abatements of their contractual claims, marked by the fundings of 1898, 1914, and 1931. In February 1934, a "readjustment plan" named after Finance Minister Osvaldo Aranha was put into effect. It effected a unilateral scaling down of payments. In previous difficulties a funding load had provided the extra resources to satisfy existing creditors partially. This was the first time that debt service terms were unilaterally reduced, and some payments suspended.

Starting in November 1937, there was a complete suspension of debt remittances. Brazil's dictator Getulio Vargas explained:

> We stopped the service of the external debt, moved by circumstances beyond our control. This does not mean the rejection of earlier commitments. All we need is time to resolve difficulties that we did not create and to readjust our economy, transforming potential wealth in resources that will permit us to repay, without sacrifices, our creditors. Gone are the days when our obligations were written abroad, at the discretion of banks and intermediaries.[18]

Table 14.4 Brazilian trade and debt in the interwar period ($ millions)

	External debt[a]	Debt service[a]	Debt service ratio[b]
1926	1053.0	60.3	13.1
1927	1012.4	62.3	14.5
1928	1108.3	69.2	14.6
1929	1125.6	76.3	16.7
1930	1204.1	74.7	24.0
1931	1037.7	68.4	28.3
1932	1112.5	73.0	40.4
1933	953.1	78.5	35.0

[a] Public debt only.
[b] Ratio of public debt service to merchandise exports.
Sources: Werhahn (1937); and *Estatísticas Históricas do Brasil* (1987).

Not until 1940, with the help of World War II, was partial debt service resumed, under a modified version of the previous schedule. This involved a further cut in the original rates of payment.

In late 1943 Brazil implemented a unilateral exchange offer to consolidate debt service in a manner that is highly suggestive of possibilities today. The American press reacted with sympathy, as shown in an article in *Barron's*: "In retrospect, we find that Brazil always paid on its foreign obligations when it was able to do so."[19]

Not everybody, however, would agree with such a statement. A notable exception appeared in *The Economist*:

> The whole story [of the Brazilian reschedulings] confirms the belief, expressed here more than once, that Brazil's intention has throughout been to escape from her obligations as lightly as possible and that she was enabled to do so by persistent disagreement between the representatives of America and Britain, and by the inability or unwillingness of the British authorities to play any effective part in securing reasonable terms.[20]

The 1943 plan consolidated the entire Brazilian debt, stretched the maturities by 40 to 60 years, and adjusted down both principal and interest. Creditors were offered a choice between two plans: *plan A* involved no reduction of principal, but interest rates would be reduced from more than 6.5 percent to 3.375 percent (and less) with a provision for a sinking fund. Debt service (interest plus sinking fund) amounted to between 2.9 and 5.1 percent of principal per year. According to *plan B*, for every $1000 of original bonds, bond holders would receive a cash payment of between $75 and $175, a new bond with a face value of $800 (or $500 in some cases), and a coupon rate reduced to 3.75 percent. The bonds had no fixed maturity but were entitled to a sinking fund. Interest plus sinking fund amounted to a combined debt service rate of 6.4 percent. In addition, the Brazilian government guaranteed the service of state and municipal bonds assenting to plan B, should the individual debtor fail to make the required remittances.

Dollar issues constituted only about one-third of the foreign indebtedness of Brazil. The bulk of the obligations consisted of sterling loans, and the amount of service funds allotted to British creditors was based on the 65.8 percent of total debt held by them.

Once again, *Barron's* and *The Economist* disagreed as to which of the plans offered better terms. *The Economist* believed that plan A, retaining the nominal capital intact, was the better option to take in the case of bonds with a low market value.[21] *Barron's* stated that much more favorable treatment was available under plan B, which could be accepted only through the last day of 1944. It also explained the reason that plan A was offered at all considering that plan B was far superior. Since the creditors were given one unfavorable and one favorable choice with a time limit, the number of assents was probably higher than it would have been otherwise. And Brazil, no doubt, would find it worthwhile to offer better terms for its external creditors if the external debt could be cut from $837.7 million to $521.5 million, assuming 100 percent acceptance of plan B.[22]

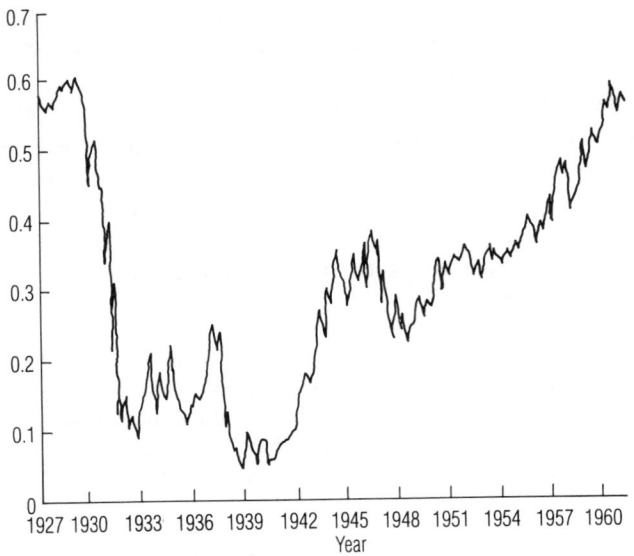

Figure 14.3 Monthly prices of Brazilian bonds, 1927–60 (relative to price of US long-term bond).
(*Source*: *Commercial and Financial Chronicle*, and Federal Reserve Board.)

By early 1946, 78 percent of the bond holders had assented to the exchange offer. Plan A had been chosen by 22 percent of the bond holders, and 56 percent had opted for plan B. Figure 14.3 shows the monthly maximum price in New York of a Brazilian bond[23] with original terms of 6.5 percent interest and a 1957 maturity date. After 1943 the price refers to the same bond, now stamped for plan A, interest adjusted to 3.375 percent and the maturity stretched to 1979. (Throughout, the price is expressed relative to the price of a 30-year US government bond with a 6.5 percent coupon.) The interesting point here is that after the 1943 downward adjustment in terms, with repudiation threats removed, the bond actually *increased* in value. Table 14.5 brings out this point further by showing the annual high and low quotations on the bond.

The increase in the bond price reflects a combination of three factors. First, the fact of a settlement eliminated the fear of more significant debt reduction or even near-repudiation. By comparison, in 1944 Mexico settled at 10 cents on the

Table 14.5 The bond price in New York ($ per $100 face value)

	1939	1940	1941	1942	1943	1944	1945	1946
Low	10.4	11.3	11.5	16.9	23.0	39.0	51.9	43.3
High	19.8	18.9	18.3	20.3	33.8	50.5	63.5	68.0

Source: *Commercial and Financial Chronicle*.

dollar, without payment for 30 years of interest arrears! Second, the wartime improvement in Brazil's external balance created objective conditions for debt service. Third, the already likely prospect of European depreciation would reduce the value of external debt denominated in francs or sterling for a country that had developed significant trade relations with the United States. Each of these three factors is reflected in the strengthening of the market for Brazilian bonds.

From a rock bottom in 1940, prices increased over the next ten years more than sevenfold, yielding a compound rate of return (interest plus capital gains) of 125 percent per year! As a result Brazilian loans are seen as unusually attractive. This analysis, however, leaves out the financial consequences for widows and orphans who sold out at the bottom.

14.3 The 1982 debt crisis

Brazil's debt problems did not end in 1943. New debt difficulties emerged in the early 1960s and again in the 1980s.

14.3.1 *From the 1940s to the 1970s*

Figures 14.4 and 14.5 show the real debt per capita and the debt–export ratio[24] between 1929 and 1986. The relatively low and decreasing levels of external debt recorded in the first postwar quinquennium are a legacy of the prewar experience. The 1943 plan helped reduce the size of the debt from its peak level of more than $1 billion in the early 1930s to some $600 million in 1946. In addition, a strong postwar recovery in Brazil's export prices postponed the need to explore new sources of external credit.

In the early 1950s, however, the country experienced huge trade deficits, which resulted primarily from the relaxation of import controls to permit stockpiling of materials during the Korean War. Those imports were initially financed by commercial arrears which were, in the following year, refinanced by short- and medium-term loans. By 1953 the external debt had doubled to more than $1 billion. Figure 14.6 shows the trade balance (as a fraction of GDP) for the 1913–64 period. It is apparent that the postwar deficits form an entirely new pattern.

By now, recourse to the world capital market and foreign resources in order to finance an ambitious industrialization drive had become necessary. Total capital inflows, both direct investment and loans, increased sharply after 1955, especially with suppliers' credits. At the end of 1961, a time of political unrest, the external debt stood at double its 1955 level, and the country was ready for yet one more external crisis. As the economic situation deteriorated, capital inflows virtually ceased. The World Bank, previously an important source of official resources for Brazil, did not authorize a single loan between 1960 and 1964.

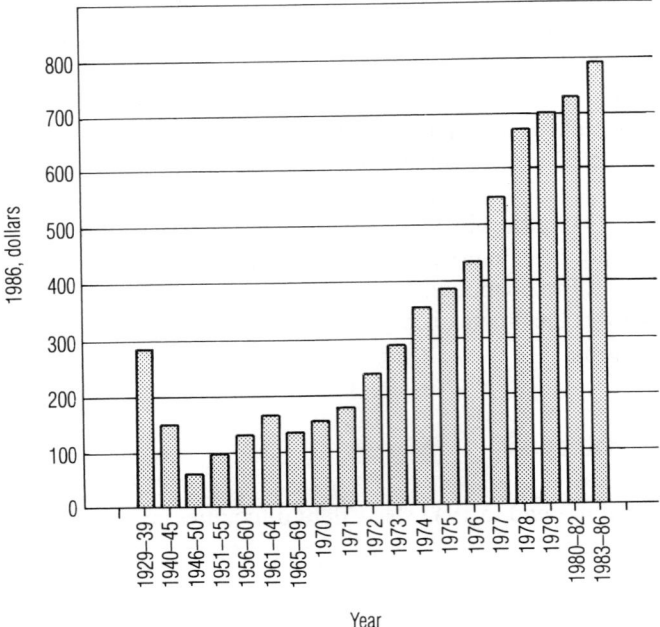

Figure 14.4 Brazil's real debt per capita, 1929–86.

Debt rescheduling and new credits[25] became available after the military coup in 1964. Thereafter the government consciously embarked on a policy of tapping private capital markets to underwrite rapid expansion.

Two main features distinguish the postwar evolution of Brazil's balance of payments on the current account. First, this balance was almost continually unfavorable. Between 1950 and 1986 there was a surplus in only eight years. Second, the deficit on the current account, which was relatively small until 1969, increased sharply after 1970.

14.3.2 The origins of the 1982 crisis

The existence of a large deficit on the current account up to 1983 was regarded as normal, because developing countries are importers of capital. The deficits rose sharply after 1970 and created one of the preconditions for renewed debt problems.

But the existence of debt is not enough for financial troubles. Always and invariably, world economic deterioration needs to come about to complete the picture of too much debt service and too little foreign exchange. We next look at how world economic developments helped bring about the 1982 crisis.

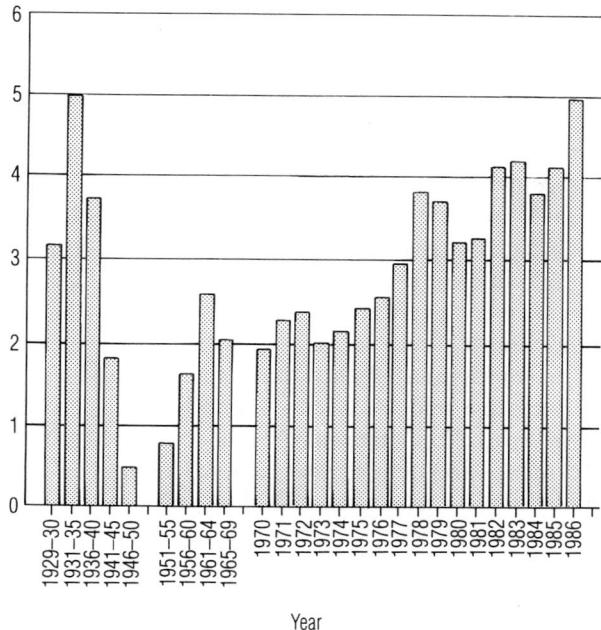

Figure 14.5 Brazil's debt–export ratio, 1929–86.

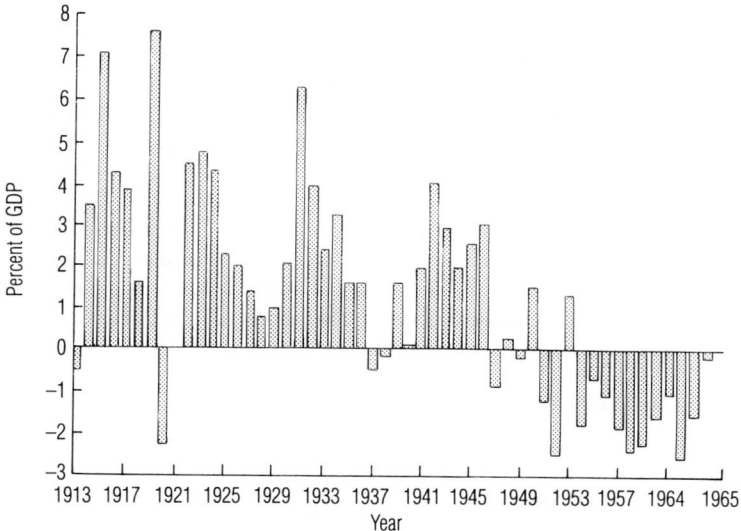

Figure 14.6 Brazil's trade surplus, 1913–65.
(*Source*: Goldsmith (1986).)

When the debt crisis erupted in Mexico in the summer of 1982, and in all of Latin America shortly after, three common sources of the debt problems could be easily identified.

First, the world economy was very badly off: economic activity was more depressed than at any time since the Great Depression. Interest rates were at their highest levels in decades. Real commodity prices were sharply depressed, and the dollar was overly strong. Recovery of the world economy was certain. As a result there was an expectation of cyclically rising manufactures exports, rising real commodity prices, declining real interest rates, and even of an early fall of the dollar. This favorable perspective for the world economy suggested that the burdens of debt service would almost surely vanish.

Second, debtor countries had mismanaged their economies beyond belief; overvalued exchange rates, pervasive budget deficits, unproductive spending, and capital flight had absorbed scarce foreign exchange resources and stood in the way of better trade performance and debt service ability. The possibility of using resources more efficiently implied, of course, that debt service would not necessarily be at the cost of reduced standards of living.

Third, a return to voluntary lending could only be envisaged if debtor countries made the best efforts to cooperate with the system, adjusting and servicing debts to the fullest extent possible. Debtor countries agreed to do their utmost to promote a return of voluntary lending, so as to be in a position to call on foreign saving for development finance. There was no doubt that foreign lenders would resume lending, once creditworthiness (defined objectively in terms of debt ratios) was restored.

These three problems applied quite uniformly to all Latin debtors, even though the proportions in which each was responsible for the troubles of the region or for each individual country differed. Not surprisingly, observers disagreed on the weight assigned to each of these considerations. Characteristically, US officials saw the mess in the debtor countries as the cause of the debt crisis:[26]

> the debt crisis just did not happen in 1982 or was not the result of the increase in the oil price shock of 1979–80 or the rise in the dollar exchange rate. The cause of the debt crisis had its domestic origins in the economic policies of the debtor countries and so what we are seeing and what we will continue to see is a change in these policies—budget deficits, excessive government spending, government interference in the markets, price controls, and so on.

Latin American observers, by contrast, gave far too little weight to their own dramatic mismanagement and the resulting debt accumulation. World macro-economic developments, shown in Table 14.6, are seen by them as the outstanding source of problems.

14.3.3 *The Brazilian case*

Brazil's case is interesting in that it does not meet the image of capital flight, overvaluation, or massive inefficiency in the public sector.[27] Increased interest

Table 14.6 World macroeconomic indicators

	Real commodity prices (1980 = 100)[a]	LIBOR (%)	Inflation (%)[b]	World activity (%)[c]
1960–69	115	5.2	1.0	6.2
1970–79	115	8.0	11.4	3.4
1980	100	14.4	13.0	0.0
1981	96	16.5	−4.1	−7.0
1982	89	13.1	−3.5	−3.3
1983	98	9.6	−3.3	3.3
1984	101	10.8	−2.5	6.5
1985	88	8.3	−0.4	3.0
1986	72	6.9	13.7	1.0
1987	63	6.8	12.8	2.2

[a] Measured in terms of manufactures export prices of industrial countries.
[b] Rate of increase of industrial countries' unit export values.
[c] Industrial production.
Source: IMF; and Economic Commission for Latin America.

Table 14.7 Contribution of external shocks to debt accumulation, 1978–82 ($ billions)

	Oil (1)	Export volume (2)	Interest rates (3)	Total debt shock	Net debt outstanding
1978					36.2
1979	1.8		0.3	2.1	46.4
1980	5.7	0.6	1.1	7.4	57.7
1981	7.1	1.4	2.5	11.0	68.0
1982	6.1	2.4	5.9	14.4	83.5

Note: The calculations are based on the 1978 oil price and 1978 real interest rates (in terms of the US deflator), and export performance is based on deviations from an export regression.
Source: Cardoso and Fishlow (1989b, Table 3.1).

rates and sharply augmented debt burdens are the most immediate cause of the foreign exchange shortage. If not for the Mexican crisis, rolling over of debts and some domestic restraint and cleaning up might well have made the problems disappear into the background.

Table 14.7 shows the impact of external shocks on the Brazilian external debt. The data reported draw on a counterfactual analysis developed in detail in Cardoso and Fishlow (1989b) to determine by how much the external debt increased compared to what it would have in the absence of external shocks. Between 1978 and 1982 the *actual* current account shifted by $13 billion toward a deficit. The counterfactual analysis demonstrates that the current account deterioration and the resulting increase in indebtedness can be explained for the most part, by the impact of the slowdown in exports, the increased real interest rate, and higher real oil prices. These calculations do not even include the impact of reduced real commodity export prices or the interest on the extra debt that was due to the shocks.[28]

The table shows that between 1978 and 1982 a cumulative sum of $35 billion—three-quarters of the total net debt accumulation—can be accounted for by the adverse external environment. The fact that external shocks can explain so much of the debt accumulation does not, of course, imply that there was no Brazilian policy mistake involved.

The policy mistake is well explained by Finance Minister Delfim Neto's memorable phrase: "Debts are not paid, debts are rolled." Nevertheless, relatively permanent shocks need adjustment, not financing. The Brazilian policy mistake, if any, was failure to adjust to external shocks. But then in 1982 everybody was busily explaining how the world economic shock was transitory.

14.4 What went wrong with muddling through?

The muddling-through strategy initiated by the Federal Reserve, the Treasury, and the IMF in 1982 was predicated on the assumption that a return to creditworthiness (via adjustment and a more favorable world economy) would come fast, visibly, and without extreme costs for either borrowers or lenders. This view was shared by some observers. Cline (1984), who was foremost in setting out a framework and forecasts, saw Brazil, in particular, as one of the countries with a favorable outlook in its ability to return to creditworthiness. Table 14.8 shows forecasts for Brazil laid out by Cline (1984) in 1983. The baseline scenario assumed the following 1983 to 1986 averages: a growth rate of industrial countries of 2.6 percent, $30 a barrel of oil, LIBOR (London Interbank Offer Rate) at 9 percent, and a cumulative 10 percent dollar depreciation.[29]

Although the current account deficit was approximately what had been predicted, the debt accumulation and increase in the debt–export ratio turned out to be far larger than the forecast. The difference in the debt accumulation arose from the fact that Brazil experienced large capital outflows (in part connected with debt–equity swaps), whereas the Cline scenario anticipated substantial inflows. More recently, capital flight has become an additional source of capital outflows. The serious discrepancy between the actual debt–export ratio and Cline's forecast was due to the fact that Cline assumed a doubling of the value

Table 14.8 Cline's 1983 forecasts for Brazil and actual outcome ($ billions, except as noted)

	Current account[a]	Noninterest current account	Interest[a]	Debt increase[b]	Debt/exports[c]
Cline's forecast	−3.4	5.8	9.2	4.1	2.0
Actual	−3.0	8.0	10.8	27.3	4.2

[a]Annual average 1983–86. [b]Cumulative increase in total debt, in billions of US dollars 1982–86.
[c]Ratio of net debt to exports.
Source: Cline (1984, Table 3.3); IMF; and Banco Central.

of merchandise exports, whereas even in 1986 the export level was only 10 percent above that of 1982.

Developments of the past five years proceeded in a very different direction from the 1982–83 expectations. It is clear that a return to voluntary lending to Brazil is not on schedule. Even though in 1986, a return to the capital market seemed possible, at least in the rhetoric of the creditors, the chances today are once again quite remote. The 1987 moratorium and domestic disarray, including more than 600 percent inflation, were enough to disabuse any lender of the notion that the debt strategy was on course.

Today the muddling-through strategy, even with Baker Plan enhancements, is widely considered to be a failure. The problem was not with growth in industrialized countries. The 1982 IMF economic outlook in the base scenario, to use a specific benchmark, anticipated a growth rate of 2.2 percent on average for the period 1984–86, whereas the actual growth rate was 3.1 percent. However, there were four factors that clearly diverged from the 1982 scenario.[30]

First, real interest rates were expected to decline much further than they did. The outlook was for real interest rates to average only 2 percent in 1984–86 (using the US GNP deflator to measure inflation). In fact, real rates averaged 5.4 percent, and even in 1987 they still uncomfortably exceeded the early expectations. Given the sensitivity of major debtors to an increase in interest rates, this represents a major deterioration in the outlook. (This is compounded by the fact that Brazil's spreads did not actually decline, unlike those of other major debtor countries.) The chief reason for high interest rates was the US budget deficit.

Second, real commodity prices were expected to recover from what was thought to be a cyclical low. However, they kept on falling, even from their 1982 levels. By early 1987 the real price of non-oil commodities was at its lowest level since the 1930s. It had become increasingly clear that much of the decline was not cyclical but was rather an irreversible decline in real commodity prices due to capacity expansion and commodity-saving innovation and substitution on the demand side. For agricultural goods, in particular, immense productivity growth and increasing self-sufficiency of many traditional importers, as well as price support policies in industrial countries, had led to worldwide oversupply.

Third, there was the unexpected (but historically well-known) "transfer problem." This is the catchall phrase that describes problems that result from the attempt to transfer resources representing a significant share of GDP from debtors to their creditors.[31] There are three aspects of the transfer problem that deserve emphasis. First, the effort in the budget to service debts (including interest) rather than to roll them strains budgetary resources and leads to inflationary money creation. If domestic debt is issued to acquire the resources for external debt service, then the domestic debt accumulation foreshadows debt and deficit problems that are merely postponed. Second, the effort to transfer resources abroad requires an improvement in competitiveness that is itself inflationary.[32] It is more inflationary, the stickier are real wages. Moreover, these two factors interact: the need to depreciate the real exchange rate in order to transfer resources abroad raises the real cost of debt service measured in terms of the domestic tax base.

The third aspect of the transfer problem concerns the manner in which the transfer is financed on the resource side: the required trade surplus may come out of reduced consumption (public or private) or out of reduced investment. When investment declines, as has been the case in Latin America, there is concern about sustainable growth. The notion that the transfer could be financed by asset sales, thus apparently avoiding any crowding out, is an illusion, as Simonsen (1985; 1986) has forcefully pointed out.

Finally, cartel fatigue is now pervasive. The precarious cohesion of the creditor cartel is increasingly being tested as reschedulings are becoming open-ended and the mirage of an early return to normal fades away. Differences between large and small banks and, now, even between large and medium-sized banks are becoming starker. Differences between European banks, those in Japan and the major US banks are also apparent. Congress increasingly takes the view that the current handling of the debt problem is not in the public interest. Staffs of the multinationals, though perhaps not their management, admit openly to the implausibility of muddling through. Every new rescheduling is said to be the last that could possibly be done, but the next one is already on the calendar.

While the previous four factors have undoubtedly worked to the detriment of a steady, smooth disappearance of the debt problem, there has been at least one favorable factor, namely, oil prices. Oil prices, in Brazil's case, provided important offsetting good news. From a level of $34 in 1982, world oil prices declined to an average of only $25 in 1983–86. By 1987 the price was a mere $18. The favorable oil price helps explain how, in 1985, the entire Brazilian interest bill could be paid out of trade surpluses.

More recently, since 1987, sharply increasing commodity prices further contributed to alleviating the debt service problem, at least with regard to the external transfer problem. But despite sharply rising commodity prices in world markets, in early 1988 prices of those commodities of interest to Brazil had not yet returned to their 1983 levels.

14.5 The current situation

The situation today is captured well by the large discount for Brazilian debts in the secondary market (Table 14.9). Brazil has emerged from the moratorium of

Table 14.9 The discount in the secondary market for Brazilian debt (in US dollars)

7/85	7/86	1/87	7/87	9/87	6/88
$0.75	$0.73	$0.74	$0.57	$0.39	$0.51

Source: Salomon Brothers.

1986, but the attempt to regularize relations with her creditors has no counterpart in domestic macroeconomic improvements. Hence the chances of uninterrupted external debt service must be viewed as slim. With inflation running in mid-1988 far above 500 percent and with public debt growing in real terms, rolled from day to day, the debt problem cannot be said to be on the road to improvement—hence the discount on external debt in the secondary market.

Much of the problem with external debt today reflects the disastrous state of domestic macroeconomics and an unwillingness to pay. The objective ability to service debt, in the long run, is much less in question than the willingness of the government to perpetuate the political and economic mistake of continuing the muddling-through strategy.

Debt service raises three issues, among others. The first is the net resource flow abroad. Figure 14.7 shows that since 1982, Brazil has been transferring resources abroad at an average rate of more than 2 percent of GDP. In the absence of increased saving, this transfer must come at the expense of domestic investment. Second, the inability to correct the budget implies that much of the external debt service is now financed either by inflationary money creation or by increases in domestic public debt. The real value of the domestic public debt is 60 percent higher today than in 1982. Thus a domestic public debt problem arises as a byproduct of the attempt to contain the growth of external indebtedness.

Third, the transfer of resources abroad requires a real exchange rate that has depreciated far more than would be the case with a balanced noninterest account

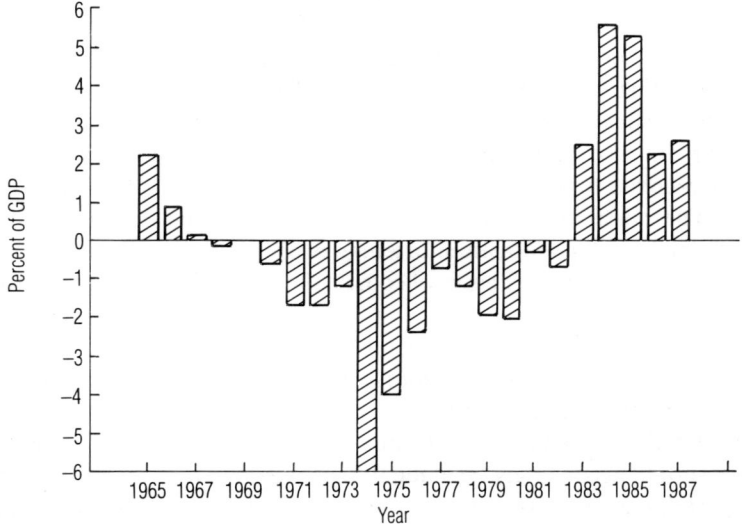

Figure 14.7 Brazil's transfer of resources, 1970–87.
(*Source*: Banco Central, *Brazil Economic Program*, June 1988, p. 53.)

Table 14.10 Macroeconomic indicators for Brazil, 1970–87 (annual average percentage)

Period	Real growth per capita	Inflation rate (IGP-FGV)	Investment/GDP	Resource transfer abroad/GDP
1970–75	7.4	23	22.8	−2.54
1976–80	4.5	57	22.5	−1.87
1981–85	−0.7	173	18.5	2.5
1986	5.3	65	20.5	2.3
1987[a]	0.4	416		2.6

[a] Estimates.
Source: Banco Central.

or even a deficit. As a result there are adverse effects both on the standard of living and on the budget. In the budget the real depreciation will tend to raise the value of external debt service in terms of the tax base and hence create an even worse public finance problem.

The transfer problem highlights the domestic costs of bringing about, in the budget and external balance, a premature transfer of real resources toward the creditors. The costs take the form of depressed living standards, hyperinflation, sharply reduced investment, and hence the prospect of reduced long-term growth opportunities. The insistence on cash collection of the past five years has aggravated these transfer problems dramatically. Even in Brazil, where foreign resources had on balance been wisely invested at least until the late 1970s, the costs were significant, as is apparent from Table 14.10 which shows the deterioration in macroeconomic performance in the 1980s.

Per-capita income is barely above the 1980 level (of course, that performance is far better than elsewhere in Latin America), investment has declined, and inflation is proceeding at unprecedented rates. Domestic mismanagement accounts for much of this poor performance, but there is little question that the external environment also played a role. In particular, the policy of allowing domestic debt to increase to service external debt has evolved into a now massive fiscal problem. The possibility of a default on *domestic* public debt is widely recognized and is reflected in a drastic shortening of the average maturity of the domestic debt to only a few days. This is, of course, the setting in which a funding crisis can emerge.

There is little doubt that domestic policy mistakes account for a large part of the current difficulties. This does not, of course, imply that external debt service can or should go on unchanged, with all adjustments falling exclusively on the home economy. Creditors stand to gain from an improved Brazilian macroeconomy, and they should accordingly be made to participate in the reconstruction effort. The major adjustment must come in domestic public finance, but creditors should contribute by financing domestic investment in the critical transition period. We now sketch the key features of such a proposal.

14.6 A debt proposal

Are there ways in which the long-term interests of debtors and creditors can be reconciled? The answer is yes! A scheme that recycles a large part of the interest payments in the country does away with the need for trade surpluses and the resulting crowding out of investment. This would thus make it possible to have investment and growth and yet provide creditors with debt service, albeit in investments that cannot be repatriated for the time being.

Practically, this could be achieved by adopting the following procedure. A trade surplus of perhaps 1 percent of GDP would be used to service a minor part of the debt, mostly trade credit and debts to governments and multilateral agencies. A minor portion of these resources might also be used, in the form of auctions to buy up the claims of small foreign creditor banks who are willing to accept deep discounts.

The major part of the debt would be paid in investment certificates (Baker certificates)—cruzados that are in part automatically loaned to the government to finance public sector investment and in part can be used to finance loans or acquisition of assets in Brazil. The only restriction on the disposal of Baker certificates or the investments they generate would be that they could not be transferred out of Brazil. In combination with a serious fiscal reform, this shift in debt servicing would restore normal growth and investment and thus provide maximum assurance of an ultimate transfer of resources to the creditors.

This scheme basically gives Brazil some years to restore a normal macroeconomy before resuming resource transfers abroad. It emphasizes that debt service is ultimately best guaranteed by investment and growth.

Appendix 14A

Table 14A.1 External debt

Period	Total debt (billions of current dollars)	Real debt per capita (in 1986 $)[e]	Debt/income (index 1970 = 100)[f]
1929–39	1.190[a]	287	582.3
1940–45	0.855[a]	153	255.8
1946–50	0.600[b]	60	81.9
1951–55	1.227[c]	96	107.4
1956–60	2.201[c]	131	123.5
1961–64	3.545[c]	168	133.5
1965–69	3.755[c]	138	103.1
1970	5.295[c]	156	100.0
1971	6.622[c]	179	105.9
1972	9.521[c]	239	129.4
1973	12.572[c]	291	141.3
1974	17.166[c]	355	162.2
1975	21.171[c]	389	173.1
1976	25.985[d]	438	181.9

Table 14A.1 (*cont*).

Period	Total debt (billions of current dollars)	Real debt per capita (in 1986 $)[e]	Debt/income (index 1970 = 100)[f]
1977	35.737[d]	551	224.2
1978	48.111[d]	675	268.4
1979	56.104[d]	706	268.2
1980	64.648[d]	712	254.0
1981	75.511[d]	742	280.7
1982	83.265[d]	751	288.6
1983	91.632[d]	779	314.8
1984	102.039[d]	815	319.3
1985	105.126[d]	795	294.9
1986	110.572[d]	798	280.6

Sources: [a]Abreu (1978, Table 1) figures converted into dollars.
[b]Donnelly (1973).
[c]Banco Central do Brasil, long- and medium-term debt.
[d]Banco Central do Brasil, long-, medium- and short-term debt.
[e]Nominal debt deflated by US implicit price deflator for GNP, *National Income and Product Accounts of the US*, US Departement of Commerce. Brazilian population before 1950 from Villela e Suzigan, *Politica de Governa e Crescimento da Economia Brasileira 1899–1945*. IPEA/INPES, Rio de Janeiro, 1973. After 1950, IMF, *International Financial Statistics*.
[f]Obtained by dividing the index of the real debt per capita by the index of the real GDP per capita.

Table 14A.2 Brazilian debt and deficits

	1982	1983	1984	1985	1986
PSBR[a]	15.8	19.9	23.3	27.5	10.8
Operational deficit[b]	6.6	3.0	2.7	4.3	3.7
Total debt/GDP	28.8	45.0	47.7	49.2	46.9
Resource transfer abroad[c]	−0.6	2.4	5.6	5.1	2.5
Share of external debt in total debt	55.5	64.1	60.4	59.3	59.11

[a]Public sector borrowing requirement, percent of GDP.
[b]Percent of GDP.
[c]Nonfactor current account, percent of GDP.
Source: Banco Central do Brasil, *Brazil Economic Program*, Vol. 17, June 1988.

Table 14A.3 Brazil: structure of the external debt, 1987

	$ billions	%
Total	110.4	100.0
Official institutions	28.3	25.6
Internation organizations	13.7	12.4
Governments	14.6	13.2
Private lenders	82.1	74.4
Banks	75.0	68.0
US banks	(22.2)	(20.1)
Other	7.1	6.4

Source: Banco Central.

Notes

1. Rippy (1977), Edelstein (1982), Feis (1965), Stone (1977), Avramovic (1964), and Wileman (1896) discuss capital flows to Brazil during the nineteenth century.
2. *The Economist*, November 29, 1890.
3. *The Economist*, October 4, 1890.
4. *The Economist*, January 10, 1891.
5. Letter from Mr Gibson to *The Economist*, December 13, 1890.
6. *The Economist*, January 10, 1891.
7. *The Economist*, October 24, 1891.
8. See Williams (1920), Kindleberger (1985), Fishlow (1988).
9. *The Economist*, May 27, 1893.
10. *The Economist*, July 20, 1895.
11. *The Economist*, April 23, 1898.
12. *The Economist*, April 23, 1898.
13. Reproduced in *The Economist*, August 26, 1899.
14. See the *Brazilian Review*, October 3, 1899.
15. *The Economist*, October 29, 1899.
16. *The Economist*, October 7, 1899.
17. Quoted in Campos (1946); our translation.
18. Quoted in Boucas (1950); our translation.
19. *Barron's* National Business and Financial Weekly, April 20, 1942, p. 18.
20. *The Economist*, December 18, 1943, p. 817, "Squeezing the Lender." In the following issue, December 25, pp. 833–4, *The Economist* further criticizes the Brazilian settlement and states:

    > the British authorities were unwilling or unable to put any pressure on the Brazilian government in favour of a less inequitable settlement. And it is an open secret in the city that the reason for the authorities' reluctance was the fact that Washington would not permit it. ... To put the question quite bluntly, the British holder of Brazilian obligations has been made to sacrifice to Pan-Americanism. ... There are higher things at stake than Brazilian bonds. Least of any journal in the country would *The Economist* object to anything that smooths the path of British–American cooperation, even if it involves some sacrifice. If this is Washington's idea of a fair bargain, there is nothing to be done but to acquiesce.

21. *The Economist*, December 23, 1944, p. 852.
22. *Barron's*, January 31, 1944, p. 8.
23. Weekly prices of Brazilian Bonds are found in *The Commercial and Financial Chronicle*.
24. Sources are given in Appendix 14.A.
25. Bitterman (1973) provides a description of the 1961 and 1963–64 consolidations.
26. Statement by Ciro DeFalco, US Treasury, before a conference cosponsored by the Joint Economic Committee and the Congressional Research Service, *Dealing with the Debt Problem of Latin America*, p. 76.
27. See Dornbusch (1985a; 1985b), Simonsen (1986), and Cardoso and Fishlow (1987).
28. For an alternative calculation, broadly consistent with the estimates reported here, see Dornbusch (1985a). It is shown there that in the period 1978–82 a \$34.9 billion increase in debt, compared to the counterfactual scenario, can be attributed to higher oil prices and increased interest rates. This number is virtually identical to the estimate in the text, although it was arrived at in a very different fashion.

29. The actual 1983–86 averages are 3.5 percent growth, $24.50 a barrel of oil, LIBOR at 9 percent and 8 percent cumulative dollar depreciation.
30. See IMF, *World Economic Outlook*, April 1982, for the initial scenario.
31. See Fraga (1986), Dornbusch (1985a, 1989), and Webb (1988) for a discussion of the transfer problem in relation to debt service and for comparisons between the experience of Weimar Germany and Brazil.
32. We are, of course, abstracting from the possibility of achieving a gain in competitiveness by an absolute fall in wages and prices by deflation. In the context of inflation rates between 50 and 200 percent, a reversion to nineteenth-century adjustment modes seems unlikely.

References

Abreu, M. de Paiva (1978) "Brazilian Public Foreign Debt Policy, 1931–1943," *Brazilian Economic Studies* 4. Rio de Janeiro: IPEA.

Abreu, M. de Paiva (1985) "A divide pública externa do Brasil, 1824–1931," *Estudos Econômicos* 15(2): 167–89.

Avramovic, Dragoslav (1964) *Economic Growth and External Debt*. Baltimore, MD: Johns Hopkins University Press.

Bittermann, Henry (1973) *The Refunding of International Debt*. Durham, NC: Duke University Press.

Boucas, Valentim (1950) *Historia da divida externa*. Rio de Janeiro.

Calogeras, J. Pandia (1910) *La Politique monétaire du Brésil*. Rio de Janeiro: Imprimeria Nationale.

Campos, Claudionor de Souza (1946) *Divida Externa*. Rio de Janeiro.

Cardoso, E., and Fishlow, A. (1983) "Exchange Rates in Nineteenth Century Brazil: An Econometric Model." *Journal of Development Studies* 19(2): 170–8.

Cardoso, E., and Fishlow, A. (1989a) "Lessons of the 1890s for the 1980s: Comments." In G. Calvo, R. Findlay, P. Kouri and J. Braga de Macedo (eds), *Debt, Stabilization and Development*. Cambridge, MA: Basil Blackwell.

Cardoso, E., and Fishlow, A. (1989b) "Macroeconomics of Brazilian External Debt." In J. Sachs, ed, *Developing Country Debt and Economic Performance*, Vol. 2 NBER Project Report. Chicago: University of Chicago Press. pp. 269–92.

Castro Carreira. Liberato (1889) *Historia financeira e orcamentaria do imperio do Brasil desde a sua Fundação*. Rio de Janeiro: Imprensa Nacional.

Cline, W. (1984) *International Debt*. Cambridge, MA: MIT Press.

Donnelly, J. T. (1973) "External Financing and Short-Term Consequences of External Debt Servicing for Brazilian Economic Development, 1947–1968." *Journal of Developing Areas* (April): 411–30.

Dornbusch, R. (1985a) "External Debt, Budget Deficits and Disequilibrium Exchange Rates." In G. Smith and J. Cuddington, eds, *International Debt and Developing Countries*. Washington, DC: World Bank.

Dornbusch, R. (1985b) "Policy and Performance Linkages between LDC Debtors and Industrial Nations." *Brookings Papers on Economic Activity* 2.

Dornbusch, R. (1987) "Stopping Hyperinflation: Lessons from the Experience of Germany in the 1920s." In R. Dornbusch, S. Fischer and J. Bosson, eds, *Macroeconomics and Finance: Essays in Honor of Franco Modigliani*. Cambridge, MA: MIT Press.

Dornbusch, R. (1989) "Background Paper." In *The Road to Recovery*. Taskforce reprint of the Twentieth Century Fund, New York.

Edelstein, Michael (1982) *Overseas Investment in the Age of High Imperialism*. New York: Columbia University Press.

Feis, Herbert (1965) *Europe The World's Banker, 1870–1914*. New York: Norton.

Feldstein, M. (1986) "International Debt Service and Economic Growth: Some Simple Analytics." NBER Working Paper No. 2076.

Feldstein, M. (1987) "Latin America's Debt." *The Economist*, June 27.

Fishlow, A. (1988) "Lessons of the 1890s for the 1980s." In R. Findlay, ed., *Debt Stabilization and Development*. Oxford: Basil Blackwell.

Fraga, A. (1986) *German Reparations and Brazilian Debt: A Comparative Study*. Princeton Studies in International Finance, International Finance Section, Princeton University.

Goldsmith, Raymond (1986) *Desenvolvimento financeiro sob um seculo de inflação*. São Paulo: Harper and Row do Brazil.

Hyndman H. M. (1892) *Commercial Crises of the Nineteenth Century*. Reprinted by Augusts M. Kelley, New York, 1967.

Instituto Brasileiro de Geografia e Estatística (1986) *Estatísticas Históricas do Brasil*. Rio de Janeiro: IBGE.

Kindleberger, Charles (1984) "The 1929 World Depression in Latin America from Outside." In R. Thorpe, ed., *Latin America in the 1930s*. London: Macmillan.

Kindleberger, Charles (1985) "Historical Perspective on Today's Third-World Debt Problem" and "International Propagation of Financial Crises." In *Keynesianism vs Monetarism*. London: George Allen & Unwin, pp. 190–211 and 226–39.

Maddison, A. (1985) *Two Crises: Latin America and Asia 1929–38 and 1973–83*. Paris: OECD.

Marques Moreira, M. (1986) *The Brazilian Quandary*. New York: Twentieth Century Fund.

Ministério da Fazenda, República do Brasil (1987) "The Financing of Economic Development in the Period 1987–1991." Brasilia, March 31.

Nogueira Batista, P. (1983) *Milo e realidade da divida externa brasileira*. Rio de Janeiro: Paz e Terra.

Pelaez, Carlos Manuel, and Wilson Suzigan (1976) *Historia monetaria do Brasil*. Rio de Janeiro: IPEA/INPES.

Rippy, J. Fred (1977) *British Investment in Latin America, 1822–1949*. New York: Arno Press.

Simonsen, M. (1985) "The Developing Country Debt Problem." In G. Smith and J. Cuddington, eds, *International Debt and the Developing Countries*. Washington, DC: World Bank.

Simonsen, M. (1986) "Brazil." In R. Dornbusch and L. Helmers, eds, *The Open Economy: Tools for Policy Makers in Developing Countries*. Washington, DC: World Bank.

Stone, Irving (1977) "British Direct and Portfolio Investment in Latin America before 1914." *Journal of Economic History* 37(3): 690–722.

Taussig, F. W (1928) *International Trade*. New York: Macmillan.

Webb, S. (1988) "Comparing Latin American Debt Today with German Reparations after World War I." US Department of State, Planning and Economic Analysis Staff. PASA Working Paper No. 5, February.

Werhahn, P. (1937) *Kapitalexport und Schuldentransfer im Konjunkturverlauf*. Jena: Verlag Gustav Fischer.

Wileman, J. P. (1896) *Brazilian Exchange: The Study of an Inconvertible Currency*. Buenos Aires: Galli Bros. Reprinted in 1969, New York: Greenwood Press.

Williams, John H. (1920) *Argentine International Trade under Inconvertible Paper Money, 1880–1890*. Cambridge, MA: Harvard University Press.

15

Brazilian debt and economic reconstruction

> "In retrospect, we find that Brazil always paid on its foreign obligations when it was able to do so".
>
> *Barron's*, April 1942

In the past five years Brazilian macroeconomic policy has been deplorable: hyperinflation, a worsening of income distribution and significant capital flight are only some of the highly visible signs of deterioration. Yet, rightly or wrongly, Brazilian optimism remains unbroken. The perception is widespread that it takes little to move the economy back to growth and investment, resuming one of the outstanding performances in world economic history. This is all the more striking since the current stabilization makes up in vigor what it lacks in sense, fulfilling altogether President Collor's prediction that his policies would "leave the Right speechless and the Left perplexed."

The stabilization effort, from the freeze of financial assets and the suspension of subsidies to tax collection and enforcement, from industrial policy to import liberalization, has touched raw nerves in Brazil's economy. It remains to be seen whether the program increasingly gains a foothold and achieves a transition toward market-oriented policies or whether Brazil reverts increasingly to a command economy. At this stage there is little question that President Collor will succeed; the question is at what. He is by far the strongest political personality Brazil has seen in decades, with a powerful base in popular support. He is determined to transform Brazil and there is no question that he will shape events in the next decade; it is not certain today that all this implies a shift toward financial stability and sustainable growth. President Collor's enthusiasm for a market economy and for turning Brazil into a First World country is less apparent today than during the campaign; his political base supports more nearly economic populism and regimentation than free enterprise. The business community so far has been victimized by the program and has not been given a voice in the management of stabilization and reform. Thus there is genuine uncertainty as to the course of Brazil's economy.

External debt is not a central problem of the Brazilian economy; it is a headache, but not a decisive affliction. The chief reason is that Brazil is large, inward-looking and substantially impervious to world opinion or sanctions by the creditors. There is no link whatsoever between capital flight and the success or failure of debt politics, quite unlike in Mexico. If anything, the strong nationalism of the Brazilian business community contrasts sharply with the insecurity in Mexico. In Brazil, a tough stand on debt is popular not only with the left but also with the São Paulo business community. As a consequence, reaching a debt agreement is neither a precondition nor even a particularly favorable event in the context of domestic stabilization. Even the threat of a suspension of trade credit, so effective in other countries, has left Brazil largely unimpressed. There is simply no lobby to support debt service, neither industrialists nor financiers, neither exporters nor the man in the street. And this has always been so in the history of Brazil's external debt.

Against this background poor debt policies can happen easily; debt can become even more of a political issue, it can become a vehicle for corruption (as it did in the Sarney period), or it can simply be neglected for lack of interest and priority. It is unlikely that at this time policymakers are totally dominant and the talent is spread very thin. Debt can wait.

The main objective of Brazil is to reconstruct and move ahead so that by the year 2010 the country can claim the status of an OECD member. In the past decade Brazil receded from the threshold of that status while competitors like Korea have pushed ahead, at least on the economic front. That gap can be made up, but it requires a substantial reconstruction. Debt issues are part of that reconstruction, though of course only in a minor way.

15.1 Priorities

The 1980s were a lost decade, far more so than suggested by the zero growth of per-capita output. Brazil has caught fire, the economic horizon has shrunk to a week or less, social and economic stability continues to weaken, even only two months into stabilization. But, unlike Argentina or Peru, Brazil has the means to support an outstanding economic performance. These possibilities of reconstruction and ultimate progress are the motive for support of a dramatic adjustment effort to put financial stability in place so that economic activity can return to normal.

Although Brazil did not suffer a decline in real income per capita in the 1980s, unlike virtually all other Latin American countries, stagnation is not an enviable performance compared to that of Asian competitors (see Figure 15.1). Moreover, per-capita income is a poor measure of the institutional deterioration and the setback in investment in human capital, technology and world competitiveness.

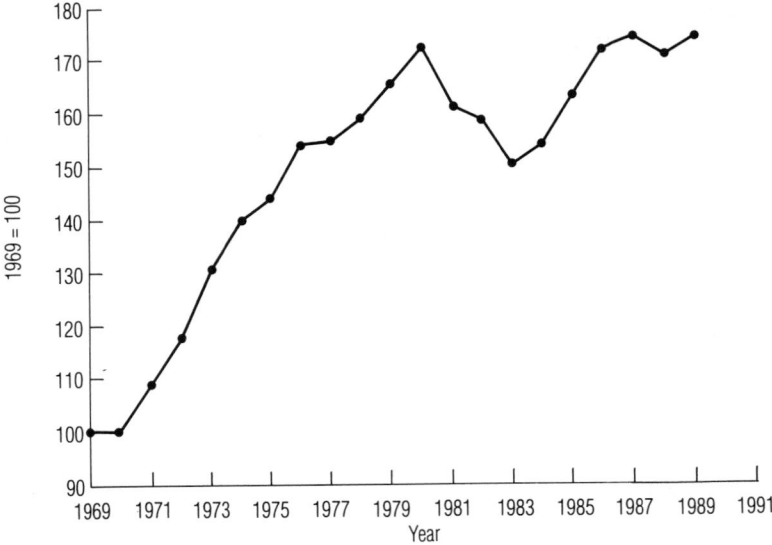

Figure 15.1 Brazil: per-capita real GDP.

Table 15.1 Long-term trends (average annual growth)

	1950–59	1960–69	1970–79	1980–89
Real per-capita GDP	3.3	2.7	6.0	0.0
Inflation	18.8	45.2	31.1	258
NICA[a]			−2.3	2.3[b]

[a] Noninterest current account percent of GDP.
[b] 1980–88.

Until that task of reconstruction is accomplished the horizon of the productive sector is no longer than the maturity of the domestic debt, and that is a week at most. The economic reconstruction program must target three objectives:

- an immediate and lasting end to inflation and instability;
- economic and institutional reconstruction;
- creating an economic environment that shifts Brazil over the next two decades into the group of advanced countries.

The current task is to put an end to inflation, adopt policies that promote reconstruction and develop the institutions that induce strong long-term economic development. The immediate priority continues to be the control of inflation. Fiscal austerity is at the center of the program and provides the guarantee for ultimate success. Incomes policy has lost its appeal; after the poor experience with heterodoxy, in an overreaction, deindexation and recession are now the tool for disinflation. Although inflation is no longer at extreme levels, substantial uncertainty continues. It is essential to push further budget balancing while at the same time avoid a growing overvaluation of the exchange rate and a sharp, possibly cumulative decline in economic activity.

Zero inflation is desirable, but 20 percent inflation per year, or even 50 percent, can be accepted. The lesson of past experience is to abandon sharp disinflation (and overvaluation) before they become a political and economic problem. Mexico, which now has inflation of 15–20 percent per year, offers a good example. An even better example is Chile, where inflation has been 20 percent in the past five years without in any way detracting from the impression of an "economic miracle."

After stabilization, the next step is institutional reform: deregulation that allows the formation of companies without tedious and cumbersome approval procedures. The need to absorb labor released by the government and the financial industry makes this an important priority. The deregulation includes the unlimited access of foreign direct investment subject to Brazilian law.

The success at disinflation and fiscal stabilization should be cemented, once it has been demonstrated, by the creation of an independent central bank and the removal of exchange control for commercial transactions.

The legal system needs to be reinforced to make contracts more enforceable and therefore provide fuller room for economic activity and roll back illegality and the underground economy.

Reform of the banking system is also important. Restoration of financial stability invariably involves excess capacity in the banking system. Reform is therefore appropriate and should, conveniently, include the Banco do Brasil.

Once the fire is put out and institutions are created or rebuilt to support economic activity without inefficient or arbitrary government intervention, two more steps remain in the development strategy.

First, the government must engage in a major effort at fostering education. The lesson from Asia is that education provides social mobility and hence social justice. It is also the most powerful ingredient for a country to absorb the available knowledge worldwide, thus facilitating the catching-up process. Brazil cannot become an advanced country without a fundamental reassessment of its approach to education.

Second, infrastructure investment has been neglected in the 1980s: the government must undertake these investments. A cost–benefit approach must avoid waste, a sensible tax system must facilitate the financing, but the work must be done. The overall level of investment brings with it growth in productivity. Capital accumulation is not the only source of economic development, but countries that have invested at high rates show the most decisive economic modernization and advance.

Critical attention to income distribution is essential if political radicalization and the resulting economic deterioration are to be avoided. Brazil's income

Table 15.2 Comparative per-capita growth and investment (percent per year)

	1970–79 Inv./GDP	Growth	1980–88 Inv./GDP	Growth
Brazil	26.8	5.2	21.0	0.2
Korea	27.6	7.7	29.4	6.2

Table 15.3 Income distribution (percentage of income)

Households	1980	1988
Bottom 20%	2.9	2.2
Top 10%	46.8	49.5

distribution is one of the worst in the world (Table 15.3). High inflation and disinflation based on real wage cutting have made things much worse. In the past year real wages declined by 20 percent! Sustained growth may create an atmosphere where a rising tide raises all ships, but without growth political instability becomes extremely likely, and political instability, of course, has very adverse effects on economic performance.

15.2 External debt

Much of the problem with the external debt today reflects the disastrous state of domestic macroeconomics and an unwillingness to pay. The objective ability to service debts, in the long run, is much less in question than the willingness of the government to perpetuate the political and economic mistake of continuing the muddling-through strategy.

In Brazil's case debt service is largely a question of willingness, not of ability to pay. The external debt can be paid as the economy is rebuilt, and it should. But external debt service should not become an obstacle to reconstruction. Nothing short of time and performance can bring about this improvement. In this respect history will repeat itself and creditors cannot expect faster results than in the 1930s and 1940s (see Figure 15.2). Before turning to specific debt strategies, we review here the economic and political context on which Brazil's debt strategy is

Table 15.4 Brazilian external debt, 1988 (US$ billion)

	1985	1988
Total external	104.6	114.6
Long-term debt:	90.7	101.4
Official creditors	15.4	24.6
Commercial banks	67.3	67.6

Source: World Bank.

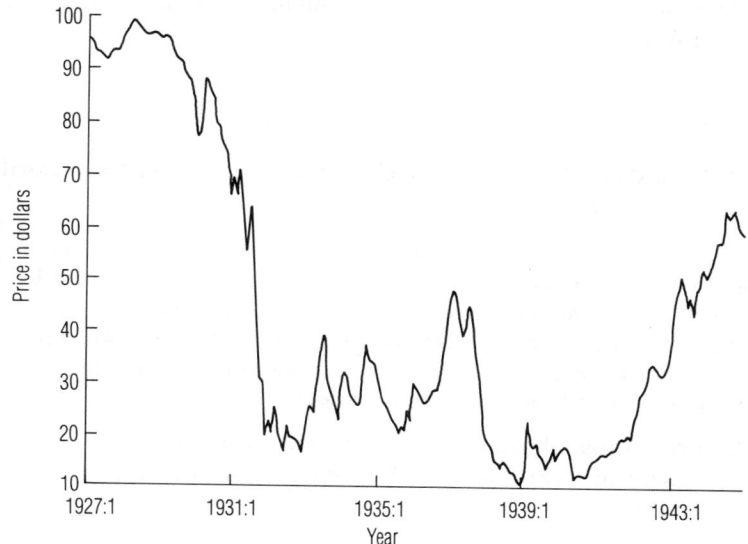

Figure 15.2 Brazilian bond prices, 1927–44 (6.5 percent issued 1926, due 1957).

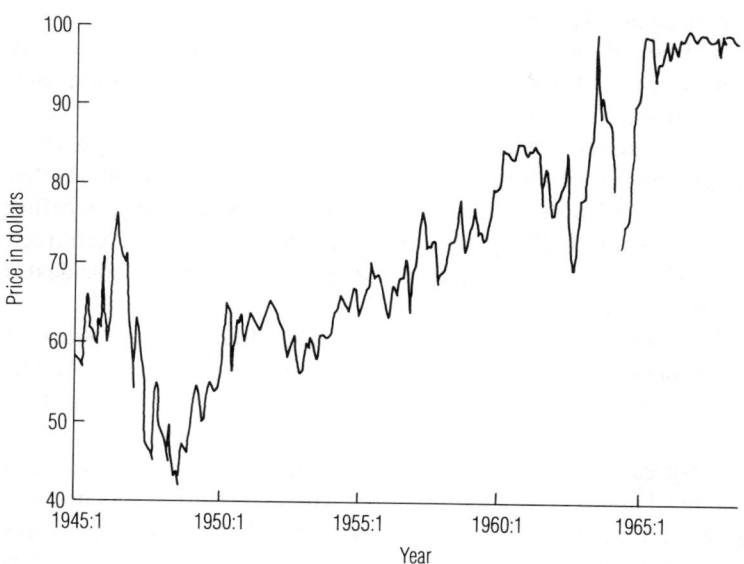

Figure 15.3 Brazilian bond prices, 1945–68 (3.375 percent due 1979).

formulated. The point of this discussion is to highlight that Brazil is in a very different situation from Mexico.

15.2.1 *Attitudes*

Brazil's attitude toward debt today is not much different from the view expressed by Getulio Vargas in 1937:

> We stopped the service of the external debt, moved by circumstances beyond our control. This does not mean the rejection of earlier commitments. All we need is time to resolve difficulties that we did not create and to readjust our economy, transforming potential wealth in resources that will permit us to repay, without sacrifices, our creditors. Gone are the days when our obligations were written abroad, at the discretion of banks and intermediaries.[1]

Some of the features of that Brazilian attitude toward debt, and the Brazilian perception of external constraints, are worth spelling out in the impressionistic way in which they are felt:

- Brazil is an inward-looking, nationalistic country. Brazilians are unimpressed with what happens in New York (and certainly Washington). Their frame of reference is domestic and they have no feeling of vulnerability in the way that Mexico so conspicuously has.
- Brazil has a basic decency about paying debts, but there is no deep commitment to exact timetables; there is certainly a recognition that domestic priorities must be attended to first.
- Brazilians do not understand much about the debt issue; this applies to ministers and to the man in the street. There is an increasing question whether the money is "in fact" owed, whether it has already been repaid, whether sums due are the result of US policies rather than Brazilian use of resources. In sum, the legitimacy of the debt, *in toto*, is questioned. Making some deal is therefore indispensable.
- The lessons from the moratorium are not clear; many doubt that it in fact cost Brazil much. Sanctions against Brazil are altogether implausible. Brazil holds in her hands too many of the assets of the major corporations of industrial countries.
- There is widespread perception that in 1988–89 commercial banks and Brazilian financial market participants got by with an extraordinary amount of debt liquidation, at great social costs. Financing of debt conversions was responsible for a significant portion of money creation in 1988–89 and thus for the hyperinflation.
- Brazil cannot count on as much foreign political support as Mexico. In the opinion of the outside world, mismanagement has been far more significant and the country's resources stand up much better to debt servicing. Given the little external support that can be expected, Brazil is better served by

structuring a solution that meets her own needs. If such a solution offers the prospect that ultimately the debt is paid then creditors, too, should be satisfied.

- There is no way of providing assurance or guarantee of future debt service. Therefore the country is best served by a solution that is economically and politically viable while having the property that it ultimately leads to full debt service.

- Where Mexico had to undo a legacy of inefficiency and poor management, under the strain of reduced oil prices and active capital flight, Brazil had used the debt wisely for investment, had not experienced capital flight and had fallen into severe mismanagement only quite recently. Better policies could therefore go much further in servicing debt without undue strain at home. However, Brazil should not rush payments and should not accept that her creditors impose a premature *effective* debt liquidation.

- Unlike in the case of Mexico, a good debt settlement has little effect; it certainly could not be relied on to mobilize a massive reflow of flight capital which in turn could serve as a pillar for stabilization and debt service. In fact, a debt agreement would have only minor impact on domestic financial stability. Unlike in Mexico, it would certainly not lower the rate at which the government can borrow in the domestic capital market.

- Getting ahead in the world economy involves primarily the ability to attract *direct* foreign investment and technology and to be able to penetrate foreign markets. Neither has much, if anything, to do with debt service. In fact, the more severe the burden of debt service a country undertakes, the more reduced is prosperity and the less is the attraction for foreign investors to come in. Severe commitments to service debt prejudice the liquidity of foreign investment.

- Commercial bank creditors have lost much of the legitimacy for priority treatment; their active involvement in mobilizing capital flight has given them a bad name. World public opinion (though not the governments of industrial countries) favors radical debt reduction.

- The history of Brazilian debt shows that foreign money is irresistibly attracted to the country; sooner or later it will come back. Debt policy can do little to speed up this process. In the meantime emphasis on foreign direct investment, and a credible policy in this respect, have a more serious payoff than a major debt settlement that undertakes important front-end debt service.

- External debt service was an important part of the fiscal problems of the past five years. If fiscal consolidation is now the rule, a parallel treatment of domestic and foreign debt is only fair.

- External debt is never amortized, except by mistake. Finance Minister Rivadavia Correa noted this already in 1911:

In finance the essential fact is that debts are paid with funds obtained from new loans. This has been the rule for us already many years. What is new is that this time the loan is made by the same people to whom we owe the overdue interest.[2]

Delfim Neto reemphasized the point when he remarked: "debt is rolled, not paid."

- Debt problems are not new; in the past 100 years Brazil has experienced four or five crises. Sooner or later credit reopens. For example, following the suspension of interest payments in the 1930s, in 1943 Brazil implemented a unilateral exchange offer to consolidate debt service in a manner that is highly suggestive of possibilities today.

  The 1943 plan consolidated the entire Brazilian debt, stretched the maturities by 40 to 60 years, and adjusted down both principal and interest. Creditors were offered a choice between two plans. Plan A involved no reduction of principal, but interest rates were reduced from more than 6.5 percent to 3.375 percent (and less) with a provision for a sinking fund. Debt service (interest plus sinking fund) amounted to between 2.9 and 5.1 percent. According to Plan B, for every $1000 of original bonds, bond holders would receive a cash payment of between $75 and $175, a new bond with a face value of $800 (or $500 in some cases), and a coupon reduced to 3.75 percent. The bonds had no fixed maturity but were entitled to a sinking fund. Interest plus sinking fund amounted to a combined debt service rate of 6.4 percent.

- The country must recognize and exploit two facts: commercial bank credit at LIBOR plus 13/16 is the cheapest credit Brazil can get today, either at home or abroad. It is therefore a mistake to pay off prematurely these cheap loans. Moreover, the secondary market offers substantial discounts (see Table 15.5) and any debt arrangement should exploit this direction for more effective amortization.

- The external balance supports *some* debt service; Brazil does have trade surpluses (see Table 15.6). But it would be a mistake to use all the slack that is available for servicing debt rather than for the purpose of a more dramatic reconstruction. Investment has lagged in the past years and trade liberalization

Table 15.5 The discount in the secondary market for Brazilian debt (cents per dollar, offer price)

7/85	7/86	7/87	7/88	7/89	7/90
75	73	57	52	30	24

Source: Salomon Brothers.

Table 15.6 Current account ($US billion)

	1986	1987	1988	1989
Current account	−5.3	−1.4	4.9	1.4
NICA	4.0	7.4	14.7	11.2
Interest	−9.3	−8.8	−9.8	−9.8
Trade balance	8.3	11.1	19.1	16.1

Source: *Conjuntura*, March 1990.

Table 15.7 Gross tax burden (percentage of GDP)

1970	1975	1980	1985	1988
26.0	25.2	24.7	22.0	19.8

will cost foreign exchange. Therefore any debt arrangement should mostly rely on the passage of time: high growth rates of income (in dollars) reducing the debt–income ratio, rather than rapid amortization.

- Fiscal reform, a solution to domestic debt and vigorous privatization will ultimately move the budget to a more sustainable situation and thus contribute to financial stability.

Much of the problem of the past few years is the complete collapse of a good tax system; unlike in Argentina, for example, where taxation has always been awful, Brazil did have in place a well-functioning, productive tax structure. It only needs to be rebuilt with accompanying improvements on the side of public spending, subsidy elimination and pervasive privatization.

Even though one can be optimistic about the possibilities of budget improvement one must not overlook the serious need for social capital formation. There is a repressed need for investment in the public sector that is only partially met by the proceeds from privatization or by shifting public sector companies to the private sector. Government investment requires resources and one obvious and cost-effective way to obtain these is by lengthening the low-cost foreign debt.

In summary, there is ample room to rephrase and sharpen these impressionist statements, but the basic point is that they do capture the political and economic situation of Brazil correctly. Brazil is very different from Mexico: Brady-style deals promise less and are less justified, rapid debt service cannot be imposed and should not be accepted. The appropriate solution is a debt settlement that stretches the debt far out while at the same time offering a plausible scheme of liquidation over time. Debt redemption can only be contemplated in the sense that the debt–income ratio falls off significantly over time.

Table 15.8 Brazilian real gross investment (percentage of GDP, 1980 prices)

1980	22.9	1985	16.7
1981	21.0	1986	19.0
1982	19.5	1987	18.1
1983	16.9	1988	17.3
1984	16.1	1989	17.9

Source: R. Bonelli and E. Landau, *Brazil in the 1980s: Facts and Figures*. Rio de Janeiro INPES/IPEA, 1990.

15.2.2 *Alternatives*

There are a number of alternative approaches worth considering: swaps; unorthodox debt settlement; a moratorium; and the Brady Plan. None of them offers the potential of the preferred mechanism already sketched above.

Swaps

Debt–equity swaps and debt–debt swaps need little comment. It is by now well established that they rarely serve the interests of the debtor. The reasons include the following four considerations:

- Conversions rarely present *additional* resources; conversions apply frequently to projects that would have taken place even without a discount. The central bank loses as a result foreign exchange that could have been used for debt reduction or other priority assignments.
- Conversions have to be financed. A country in debt difficulties typically faces far higher borrowing costs on new debt than on captive debt. As a result, the implied refinancing dramatically raises the debt service cost.
- Conversions, because they convey the right to remit earnings and principal within a few years, liquify the external debt. With a conversion a debtor loses the ability to control the outflow of foreign exchange and thus becomes more vulnerable.
- Conversions are a one-way street. If resources are committed, because of credit rationing, they are lost irretrievably.

These arguments against debt swaps have been accepted in the aftermath of a few years of bad experiences. The extravagant, unjustifiable Brazilian excesses of 1988–89 in swapping everything that moved have no doubt been the chief piece of evidence.

The Chilean case remains the possible exception. The chief reason is that domestic interest rates were not far higher than in New York so that a refinancing, capturing part of the discount, could be profitable. But even in Chile the liquification of the external debt will present a major difficulty for the democratic government. In fact, in 1993–95 there will be major pressure on the balance of payments from the possibility of repatriation of funds under the conversions programs of the Pinochet government. This makes the point that conversion programs in fact liquify the external debt.

Debt–equity swaps are primarily a balance sheet operation, not a net resource transfer. One might argue that the government could target deals to make them less a transaction in existing assets and instead directed toward new, extra investment. Thus debt–equity swaps will finance investment, but they finance it at the budget cost of a subsidy investment that would have taken place anyway.

Balance sheet tricks are not a substitute for gaining extra real resources for investment. Improved government budgets in the debtor countries, increased

Table 15.9 External deposits of Brazil ($ billion)

1985	1986	1987	1988
9.8	12.0	11.3	14.4

Source: IMF.

private saving, increased efficiency in their public sector, and net resource transfers from abroad are the only way for investment and growth to return. Of course, Brazil (and other debtors) should open all doors to foreign direct investment—the sooner and wider, the better. But there is no justification for subsidizing such investment.

Unorthodox mechanisms

Brazilian citizens hold assets abroad. In part these represent legal holdings, but in large measure they are the result of capital flight in violation of tax laws. The exact size of these assets is unknown, but data for bank accounts give some idea (see Table 15.9).

A politically attractive option is to pass domestic Brazilian legislation that allows foreign creditors to claim these assets as an offset against their claims. The chief problem is that there is not enough to go around—bank claims exceed recorded deposits by nearly $50 billion. Such a solution, therefore, would be more spectacular than effective.

Moratorium

An indefinite suspension of interest payments is likewise ineffective. A country cannot really run away from its debt, it can only choose when to face up to it.

A moratorium is a needlessly messy solution; it hurts creditors whose rating in the world capital market deteriorates and who as a result are less able to make concessions. At the same time, it does not offer lasting relief. On the contrary, it leads to an accumulation of interest and ill will. As a medium-term strategy it therefore does not pay. Of course, as a negotiation device it is plausible. But even in that context, because it reduces the ability of creditors to offer a good settlement, debtors must recognize that they may be cutting into their own flesh.

Brady Plan

In the aftermath of the US Treasury initiative it seems plausible to put a Brady Plan solution high on the list. Brazil would develop in the context of an IMF and World Bank program a list of debt reduction options—interest reduction, principal reduction and new money commitments. Support from the multilateral agencies and possibly some industrial countries might offer enhancements that sweeten the haircuts.

The political argument for a Brady Plan solution is strong: any country that proposes to service its debt without any recourse to debt reduction schemes would seem to be letting banks off too easily, failing to take advantage of the Treasury invitation to shed some of the burden. Yet, it seems implausible to expect that Brazil would really emerge with a particularly good deal. The country is too well placed to service its debt and the argument for important external support and debt reduction is not overwhelming.

Going the Brady route in the end might turn out to be politically frustrating, with too little control of events and a messy moratorium as an expression of the ultimate failure of that strategy. Brazil is too large to accept playing Washington's games, accepting tutelage and the Treasury definition of what is or is not an acceptable arrangement. The country therefore should define its own debt settlement outside the parameters of the Brady Plan.

15.2.3 *A good debt strategy*

We identify here five ingredients for a good debt strategy:

1. It should be simple.
2. Over time the debt should become less and less of a problem until it literally disappears.
3. The debt settlement does not interfere with financial reconstruction, leaving room in the budget and in the external balance.
4. The burden that is assumed can in fact be carried so that full compliance, year after year, ultimately builds up a record that enhances creditworthiness and the value of the claims.
5. Creditors who are willing to wait should be paid the full amount they are owed.

A plan

A specific proposal ensures that the entire debt is paid ultimately and that creditors who want early retirement can exercise the option. A straightforward, effective scheme works as follows:

- The external debt is restructured as a long-term instrument with automatic capitalization at LIBOR plus 13/16.
- Every month the government devotes $250 million to repurchase debt from anyone who tenders in the auction.

The proposal ensures that banks will suffer less and less from a very depressed secondary market price reflecting the random uncertainties of Brazilian policy so much critiqued by the international community, and so expensive to the country and without many offsetting benefits. At the same time the amortization schedule does not put unreasonable cash flow pressure on the capital market, the exchange market or on the country's reconstruction. Over time, as Brazil performs and debt is retired through redemption at auction and through growth, secondary market prices will come to reflect increasingly Brazil's ability and willingness to pay.

This proposal satisfies the above criteria. First, it is radically simple. An effective proposal needs to imply a falling debt–income ratio over time. The retirement at auction with a specified payment ensures significant principal reduction while the discounts last. These principal reductions make room for interest capitalization without the risk of a rising debt–income ratio. As a result, creditors who hold out and do not surrender their claims at auction can in fact participate in a rising secondary market price and cumulative full payment of their claim.

The attraction of the arrangement is that it is entirely voluntary: anyone who wants to receive in full can hold out for 20 years, anyone who wants to leave can do so, at a loss, and thus enhance the credibility of the debt settlement for those who remain. A decade or two later the country can look back and assert that it fully honored its debt!

Two questions must be asked. First, can the country in fact plausibly commit annual debt service of $3.0 billion to be spent on repurchases? Here the trade statistics (see Figure 15.4) leave absolutely no question. The trade balance is strong and easily supports the expenditure. In fact, one can go further to argue that in good years there should be extra allocations for repurchase so that creditors can share in the strong performance of the Brazilian economy.

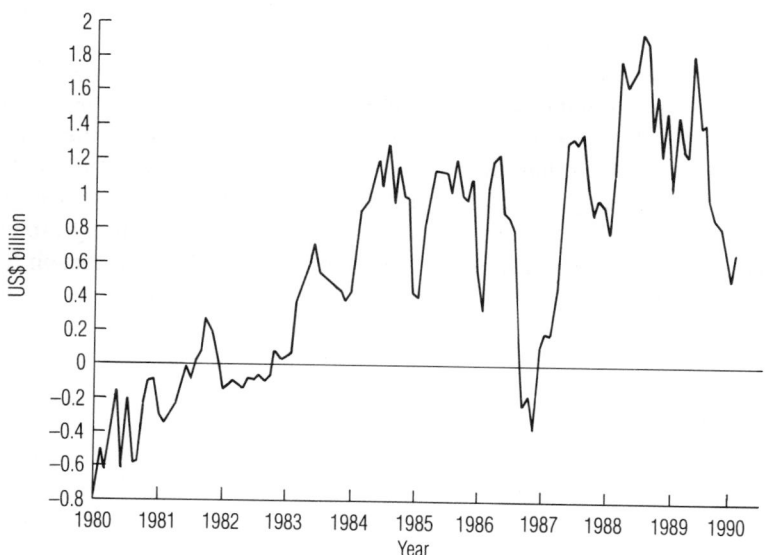

Figure 15.4 Brazil's trade surplus, 1980–90.

The second question concerns the creditors: what will the banks say? It is not clear whether banks like the arrangement; but it is clear that banks do not really know what is good for them, at least not in the herd of 500.

Brazil can and ultimately will pay; accordingly creditors should be eager to collaborate in a plan that ultimately pays their loans (in which case they would, of course, not want their money back), that is politically acceptable in Brazil and therefore forestalls other schemes that have punitive connotations, and that makes a maximum contribution to Brazilian economic and financial reconstruction. This latter feature is the only real basis on which debt service can ultimately be expected.

Banks have a poor record in debt negotiations, having too eagerly accepted debt reduction. In Brazil's case, looking beyond the immediate troubles of the Collor Plan, writeoffs are totally unwarranted. Brazil and her creditors can agree on a plan of capitalization and regular redemption at auction which, once it has become a monthly routine, will soon be reflected in an improving secondary market valuation.

Rhetoric

While Brazil can afford basically to disregard the interests of her creditors, it is not clear that this is the best strategy. In an optimistic scenario the Brazilian economy will stabilize over the next year, feeding the latent optimism and leading to a resumption of growth. On such a trajectory, Brazil will want to have a good working relationship with the world capital market. Specifically, there is little merit in a gratuitous confrontation with the creditors.

Creditors will be in a better position to accommodate Brazil's favorite debt service plan if they are not handicapped by unnecessary regulatory conflicts and by noisy debt rhetoric that worsens the creditors' rating in the financial markets. Whatever is done, it should be handled professionally in a manner that makes the outcome look as promising for a commitment to long-term debt service as possible. That advice, of course, applies on both sides of the bargaining table; when banks threaten debtors with a trade credit embargo there is little reason to expect that the debtor will not respond with an equal noise level.

Notes

1. Quoted by Valentim Boucas, *Historia da Divida Externa*, Rio de Janeiro (1950).
2. *See* Claudionor de Souza Campos, *Divida Externa*, Rio de Janeiro (1946).

16

Mexico:
Stabilization, debt, and growth

16.1 Introduction

Mexican history in the past decades has been shaped by proximity to the US—Porfirio Díaz said "Mexico is so close to the United States and so far from God." Very significant inequality in income distribution, vast oil wealth, and, so far, surprising political stability are other important characteristics. A large external debt and unfavorable terms of trade have, for the time being, put an end to growth and aggravated financial instability far beyond anything Mexico has experienced in the post-war period.

The Mexican economy today is at a crossroads. A major stabilization is under way. With prudent management and some luck on external factors, notably oil, there is a good chance of a return to growth and stability. But Mexican history is checkered and policy mistakes abound. After six years of crisis and adjustment the room for mistakes has become very small. The extent of economic stress in the Mexican economy, and the considerable lack of confidence of the Mexican public, is brought out by a public opinion poll reported in the *New York Times* (November 6, 1986). Inflation was singled out as problem number one by 53 percent of the respondents, and (as shown in Figure 16.1) inflation then was only half the rate of late 1987! An astounding 54 percent of the respondents felt that Mexico would never emerge from the economic crisis, and another 30 percent thought it would take more than ten years. The stabilization program under way has started reversing these expectations and offers a genuine prospect of renewed financial stability.

This paper discusses two topics that are now at the center of Mexican

I am indebted to Eliana Cardoso, Jorge Hierro, Alejandro Reynoso, Sergio Sanchez and Luis Tellez for many helpful conversations. My discussants, John Black and Richard Eckaus, made helpful suggestions. Tim Vogelsang provided most valuable research assistance.

325

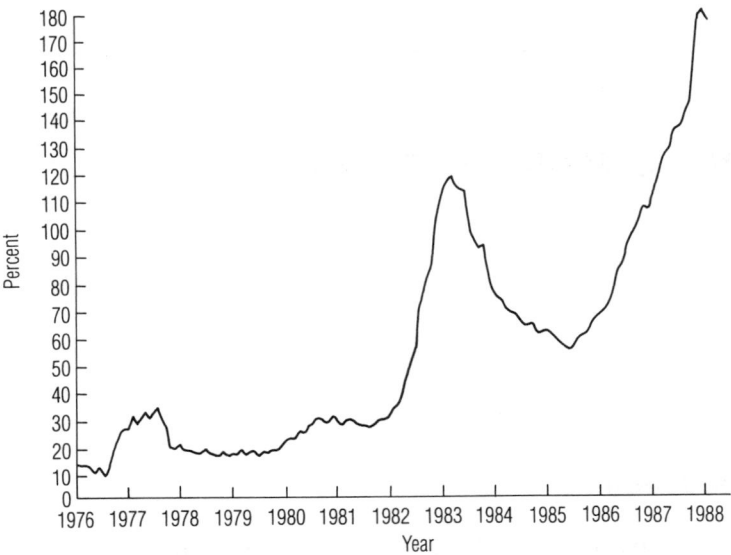

Figure 16.1 The inflation rate (percentage last 12 months).
(*Source: International Financial Statistics.*)

macroeconomic policy debate: the scope for and ways of reducing inflation, and the question of growth in the absence of external resources including the problem of capital flight. Inflation is discussed in the context of the new programs, known from the experiences of Peru, Argentina, Brazil and Israel, that combine incomes policy with monetary and fiscal policy. We emphasize the extent to which the fiscal correction which has already been implemented places Mexico in a favorable situation, quite unlike the case of other Latin American countries. The chances for success of inflation stabilization depend critically on the budget. The strong budget improvement of the past few years provides the most difficult component for incomes policy-based stabilization. With the budget under firm control, the stabilization program that is being implemented under the title *"pacto de solidaridad"* thus stands a serious chance of success.

The discussion of debt and growth brings up the question of resource requirements for growth. With large net outward resource transfers, as has been the rule in the past years, there are very strong limitations to growth. This raises the question of a policy toward external debt. Recycling of interest payments is proposed as a means for the country to have the resources for growth without actual debt relief. Recycling would also suspend the problem of capital flight which today takes on bank-run-like features.

Figure 16.2 shows the history of the Mexican real exchange rate, measured as the ratio of Mexican to US consumer prices in a common currency. Because of high capital mobility and a pervasive consciousness of financial fragility, capital

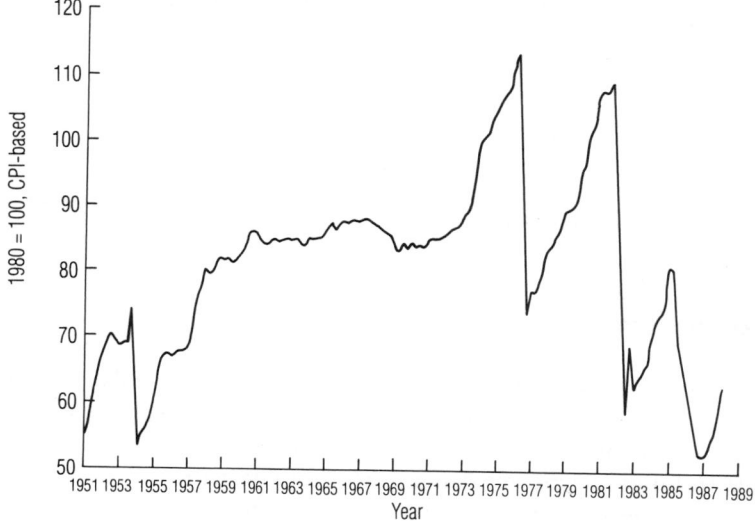

Figure 16.2 The Mexican–US real exchange rate.
(*Source: International Financial Statistics.*)

flight has made policy more difficult in Mexico. The high mobility of capital leaves basically no option but to accept that asset holders have easy access to the world capital market, so that exchange rate management must carefully avoid overvaluation. Given the large (short-run) scope for using exchange rates to promote disinflation and enhance standards of living, however, political instincts often deal in the opposite direction. The interaction of budget correction, inflation stabilization and solutions to the debt problem represents the chief vehicle through which a return of flight capital can be achieved. The return of flight capital is unlikely to be the panacea that solves Mexico's problems, but it can be an important part of the solution.

A historical and international perspective is useful to remind us that Mexico has a tradition of low inflation and high per-capita growth. On both counts the past six years have been disastrous. The contrast between the historical record and the recent experience helps explain the emphasis on inflation fighting in the current stabilization and the urgent need to return to growth. Political stability will be more than precarious if there is no success on both counts soon. In fact, however, there is room for optimism. Mexico may well be the Latin American country with the brightest prospects in the next decade.

Section 16.2 presents a broad overview on the evolution of the Mexican economy and looks at some history, followed by a review of the sources of the 1982 crisis, and a study of the Mexican macroeconomic experience since 1982. The remaining sections focus on inflation stabilization, the problem of moving from stabilization to growth, and the question of how to reconcile growth and debt service.

Table 16.1 Comparative levels of real per-capita income (index: United States = 100)

	1955	1972	1980	1985
Mexico	24	28	32	28
Argentina	30	41	40	30
Brazil	15	20	27	23
Korea	12	17	25	31
Spain	31	50	52	48
United States	100	100	100	100

Source: Summers and Heston (1984) and update.

16.2 An overview

Mexico is an upper-middle-income developing country and a member of the group of newly industrialized countries (NICs). In terms of real per-capita income Mexico ranks above Brazil and below Korea or Spain. The comparison shown in Table 16.1 uses real income data adjusted for international purchasing power comparisons. On that basis Mexico has less than one-third of the US standard of living. The 30 percent growth in the relative standard of living, between 1955 and 1980, has since shrunk back as a result of the poor growth performance of the 1980s.

16.2.1 *Macroeconomic performance*

The macroeconomic performance of the past few decades is shown in Table 16.2.[1] Until the early 1970s Mexico was a low-inflation country. In fact, the exchange rate relative to the US dollar was kept fixed, with unrestricted convertibility, for the entire period from 1954 to 1976. Since then inflation has increased sharply to nearly 200 percent in 1986–87 (Figure 16.1). That is far less than in Brazil or Argentina. But for Mexico, given both US proximity and a very low inflation experience in the postwar period, inflation became the number one problem, even dominating the stark decline in the standard of living.

Per-capita growth in Mexico in the period 1900 to 1940 averaged only 0.7

Table 16.2 Long-run performance of the Mexican economy (average annual percentage change, except as noted)

	Per-capita Growth	Inflation	Transfer abroad[a]	Real wage[b]
1940–54	3.0	10	n.a.	0
1955–72	3.3	5	−0.7	3.7
1973–81	2.6	22	−1.3	3.1
1982–87	−2.6	91	6.9	−8.3

Notes: [a] % of GDP.
[b] Purchasing power of wages.
Source: *Estadísticas Históricas*.

Table 16.3 Macroeconomic performance during the past four *sexennios* (percentages per year)

Period	President	Growth per capita	Inflation
1965–70	Díaz Ordaz	3.4	3.6
1971–76	Echeverría	2.7	14.1
1977–82	López Portillo	3.1	30.5
1983–88	de la Madrid	−2.5[a]	90.0[a]

Note: [a] 1983–87.

Source: Cardoso and Levy (1987), updated by the author.

percent. In fact, in 1940 real per-capita income was at the same level as it had been in 1910! But in the next four decades, between 1940 and 1980, per-capita income growth averaged an impressive 3.1 percent, just slightly below that of Brazil. It is worth noting that this high per-capita income growth occurred even though population growth over the four decades averaged as much as 3.2 percent per year.

An alternative view of the macroeconomic record organizes data in the *sexennia* corresponding to the six-year presidential term. This is done in Table 16.3 for the last four presidencies. The comparison brings out just how poorly the current administration stands up by comparison with previous presidencies, although this is largely the mortgage left by the López Portillo overborrowing and overvaluation and the oil crisis of 1986.

Until the 1982 debt crisis, Mexico drew regularly on foreign resources to supplement domestic saving and finance growth.[2] Resource transfers from the rest of the world (net imports in the GNP accounts) averaged nearly 1 percent of GDP in the period 1955–81. This is far less than it was in Korea, for example, where the corresponding number averaged 8 percent. But even so it represents a steady external supplement to growth finance. Mexico's earlier experience is reviewed in Section 16.2.2.

Income distribution is among the worst in the world, matched by few countries other than Brazil. In the late 1970s, the latest period for which data are available, the lowest 20 percent of households had a share of 2.9%, and the top 20 percent received 40.6%. The top 5 percent of households received 25% of all incomes (see World Bank, *World Development Report*, 1987 and *Estadísticas*). Since the 1970s income distribution has certainly worsened. The adverse effect on income distribution of the large decline in real wages since 1980, shown in Table 16.2, has been aggravated by the poor performance of employment growth. In 1987 employment levels in manufacturing were 14 percent below those of 1981, the previous peak year, and total formal employment was stagnant. Since employment growth is the main channel through which income distribution is improved, as Chenery (1974) has shown, there is little doubt that distribution has worsened over the 1980s. The deterioration of income distribution presents a significant threat to political stability and limits the range of options for stabilization and growth.

Table 16.4 Indicators of the size of the public sector

	Value added (% of GDP)	Share in total investment (%)
1965–69	11.7	37.5
1970–75	14.5	33.6
1975–79	19.4	41.9
1980–84	26.3	44.0
1985–86	23.9	36.3

Source: Adapted from Gil Díaz (1987a).

An important feature of Mexican development in the past 20 years has been the growing share of the public sector in economic activity. In part this is a reflection of the increased importance of oil. More importantly, it reflects a massive expansion of the government sector in a large number of economic activities (see Table 16.4). The fact that the period 1980–84 corresponds to the maximum public sector participation is an important hint to the contribution of an overexpanding public sector in creating the debt crisis.

16.2.2 *Debt history*

Mexico as a debtor has a checkered history. Between 1910 and 1920 Mexican debt went into default and the price of Mexican bonds fell from 95 cents on the dollar to only 30 cents. An International Committee of Bankers (ICB) was formed in the early 1920s to attempt a renegotiation, but the various debt service plans never came to work. By 1930 Mexican debt was trading at 10 cents on the dollar, declining to as little as 1.4 cents in 1932. In 1942–46 the entire Mexican obligations—bond issues and their arrears of 30 years, railroad bonds, claims of the oil nationalization—were renegotiated. Dollar bonds, for example, were reduced to 20 cents on the dollar. The New York Council of Foreign Bold Holders protested the settlement, recommending against acceptance:

> The plan of service offered under this agreement, involving as it does, a reduction of principal, cancellation of a very large part of the back interest, payment of the current interest at an exceedingly low rate … involves principles which the Council has not admitted in its dealings with foreign governments. (Foreign Bond Holders' Protective Council, *Annual Report* 1961, p. 110.)

But even so, most bond holders assented without much delay. By 1954 the ICB was dissolved and by July 1960 the remaining bonds outstanding, $35 million, were called for redemption. Marconi (1967), reviewing Mexican external resources, concludes that in the 1950s external long-term capital inflows averaged $100 million per year, rising to $300 million in 1963 and rapidly increasing from there. US bank claims on Mexico were $400 million in 1958 and had risen to $1 billion by 1964. External debt service increased between 1957 and 1964 from $100 billion to $450 billion.

It is interesting to observe that the 1960 cleaning up of the bonded external debt was, in fact, the prelude to reentry into the international bond market. At the same time as the bonds were called for redemption a first $100 million loan by an insurance company was reported.

> Mexico is closing a checkered page in financial history, a story of default and rebirth that goes back to the misty era of international promise that preceded World War I ... The turn of the century investors had vision but were off in their timing ... How were they to know that the bonds they bought would stop paying interest and remain in bad standing for a quarter of a century? Nor did they sense, when the bonds were restored to good standing during World War II, that within another 15 years Mexico would be borrowing $100,000,000 from Prudential Life Insurance Company and would thereby be the envy of all of Latin America. The 46 years between the defaulting of the external bonds in 1914 and the granting of the Prudential loan will go down as marking the financial coming-of-age of the Latin republic ...
> With most of the old bonds sucked out of the market by the redemption call last week, most of this lingering public evidence of Mexico's long struggle to live down the old debt default has been wiped out for good. (*New York Times*, July 3, 1960.)

Soon public bond issues followed. In July 1963 a syndicate led by First Boston underwrote a public bond issue of $40 million, with maturities between 3 and 15 years:

> An old friend is returning to the public bond markets here this week after an absence of 53 years. ... Mexico's return to the public bond market here is considered a milestone in that country's recent financial history, far more important than the borrowing. In fact, Mexico has been a steady customer for United States and international banking institutions since the end of World War II. (*New York Times*, July 14, 1963.)

In April and July 1964 two further bond issues of $25 and $35 million, due in 1979, were marketed by First Boston and Kuhn Loeb. Mexico was safely back in the world capital market. (See Foreign Bond Holders' Protective Council *Annual Report* 1962–64, pp. 101–4.)

In the 1950–80 period Mexico steadily received external resource transfers (Figure 16.3) but the external deficits remained very small—an average of 1 percent of GDP—and were in part financed by direct foreign investment in Mexico. As a result there was no significant build-up of debt. Table 16.5 highlights the relative importance of direct investment, which was high until the early 1970s but declined in the following decade as debt finance increased sharply.

As shown in Figure 16.4, in the early 1970s, the external debt ratio was less than 20 percent of GDP. Despite a small bulge in 1976–77, associated with the macroeconomic instability and depreciation of that period, by 1980 the debt ratio was still below 30 percent. The large run-up in debts is concentrated in the period 1980–82. From December 1970 to December 1982 the Mexican external debt increased from $40 billion to $91 billion! The subsequent path of the debt–income ratio is determined by the combined effect of the noninterest current account

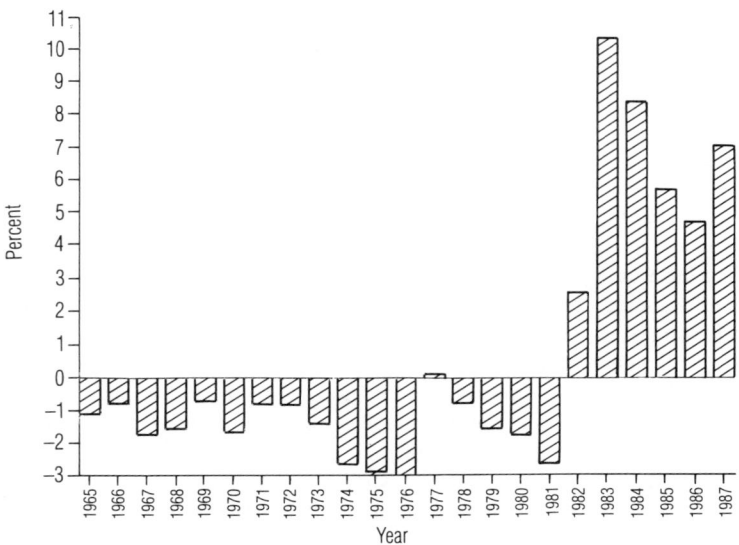

Figure 16.3 External transfers (noninterest current account, percent of GDP). (*Source*: Banco de México, *Indicadores Económicos*.)

Table 16.5 External obligations (US$ billion)

	Direct foreign investment stock	External debt
1973	3.1	10.0
1983	13.6	89.4

Source: Goldsbrough (1984); Rubio and Gil Díaz (1987).

(always in surplus after 1982), interest burdens, and the effect of real depreciation on the dollar value of Mexican GDP. We look at these factors in more detail below.[3]

By August 1982 Mexico had borrowed so much that vulnerability to domestic and external shocks forced the country into a moratorium. It is interesting to ask whether markets anticipated the crisis. One answer is provided by the price of a long-term Mexican bond traded in New York and shown in Figure 16.5 (an 8.125% coupon bond with a maturity of 1997). To separate the effect of long-term interest rate variations from the market evaluation of the riskiness of Mexican debt, we express in Figure 16.5 the bond price relative to the market price of a hypothetical risk-free 8.125% coupon bond with the same 1997 maturity. Accordingly the fluctuations shown in Figure 16.5 represent exclusively the perception of risk associated with Mexican debt. Figure 16.5 shows that, following the troubles in the mid-1970s, bond prices recovered to near par. There were some setbacks in 1980 and 1981, but basically the debt crisis came as a great surprise to bond holders (see Edwards 1986, for an analysis of bond yields in the

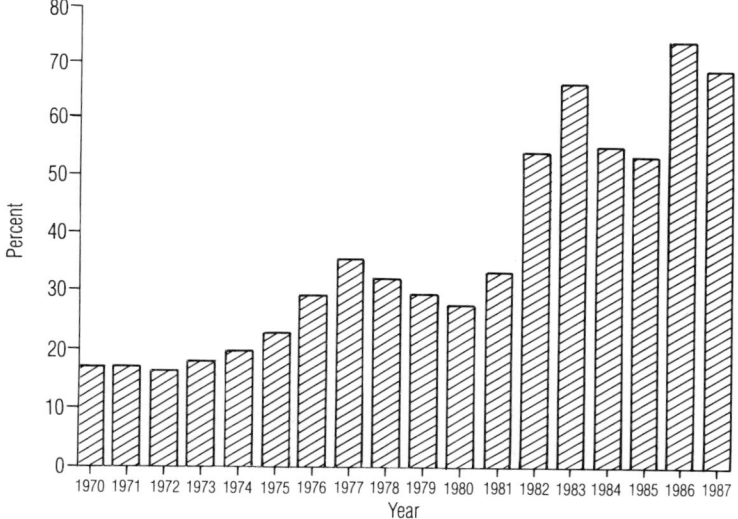

Figure 16.4 The external debt (percent of GDP).
(*Source*: Banco de México and Gil Díaz (1987a).)

Figure 16.5 The Mexican bond price in New York (percentage of risk-free US bond price).
(*Source*: *Wall Street Journal*; and Data Resources Inc.)

1982 crisis). This is seen from the sharp fall in the relative price in 1982 to only 50 percent of the value of a risk-free bond of the same coupon and maturity.

Bank lending came to an end in the first half of 1982. The last loan floated was a jumbo loan of $2.5 billion in May–June, with only 75 of 650 banks subscribing despite the attractive terms (see Zedillo 1985, p. 316). With no new credits available to roll over the maturing principal and fund the interest payments, Mexico was illiquid. The old bankers' adage was borne out again: "It is not speed that kills, it is the sudden stop!"

16.2.3   *The 1982 crisis*

The sources of the Mexican debt crisis in 1982 have been reported in a number of studies (Zedillo 1985; Solis and Zedillo 1985; Kraft 1984; Bailey and Cohen 1987). What were the factors chiefly responsible for the crisis? First, 1982 was the last year of the *sexennio*, an election time which traditionally is an occasion for macroeconomic recklessness, just as 1976 had been. Second, fiscal policy turned very expansionary. In only three years, the primary budget deficit increased from 3 percent to 8 percent of GDP, despite a major increase in the real price of oil which directly benefited budget receipts. As Zedillo (1985, p. 310) notes: "To the international bankers' comfort, Mexico became the 'champion of absorption'— not only of its own oil revenues, but of others as well." Third, between 1979 and 1981 the real exchange rate appreciated by almost 25 percent. Fourth, in 1982, real interest rates on one-month deposits averaged -20 percent as shown in Figure 16.6. Adjusting for exchange depreciation, the losses on domestic assets were even larger.

The negative interest rates on domestic deposits, and the overvaluation, combined to create a massive incentive for dollarization and flight of capital abroad.[4] As shown in Figure 16.7, a first wave of dollarization occurred following the 1976 depreciation. Another build-up can be seen in 1981–82 when the share of Mexdollar deposits in total deposits increased from less than 20 percent to more than 40 percent. Dollarization was only part of the flight from money. The general phenomenon of flight from the peso has given rise to an entire literature on "peso problems" and "speculative attacks" on unsustainable exchange rate regimes (Lizondo 1983; Krugman 1979; Flood and Garber 1984; and Blanco and Garber 1986). Capital flight reached at least $17 billion in 1981–82. Figure 16.8 shows official estimates of capital flight. As there is a considerable divergence between these estimates and those of Morgan Guaranty,[5] three different estimates of the rates of capital flight in the 1974–84 period are reported in Table 16.6.

Finally, the fifth contributing factor was the sharp increase in world interest rates as the USA shifted to tight monetary policy. Between 1978 and 1981 the three-month LIBOR rate increased from 8.8 percent to 16.8 percent. By itself this increase in interest rates, if financed by new loans, would have raised the debt burden by 8 percent per year.

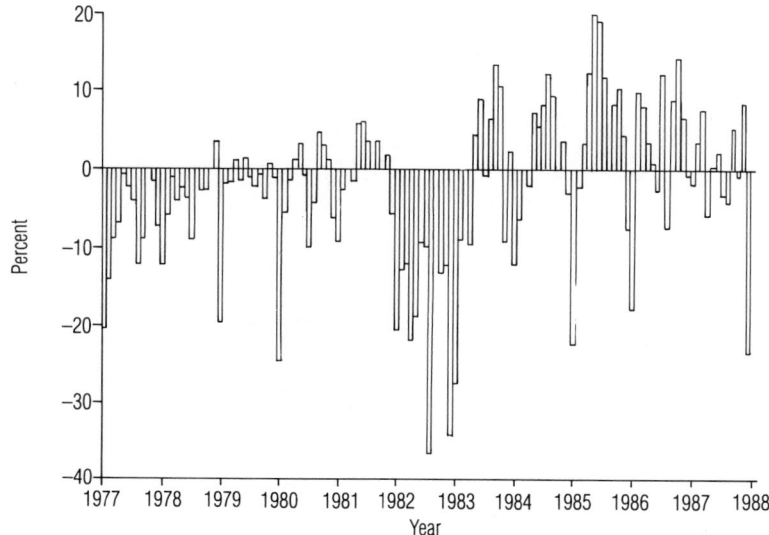

Figure 16.6 Real interest rates, one-month deposits (percent per year). (*Source*: Data Resources Inc.)

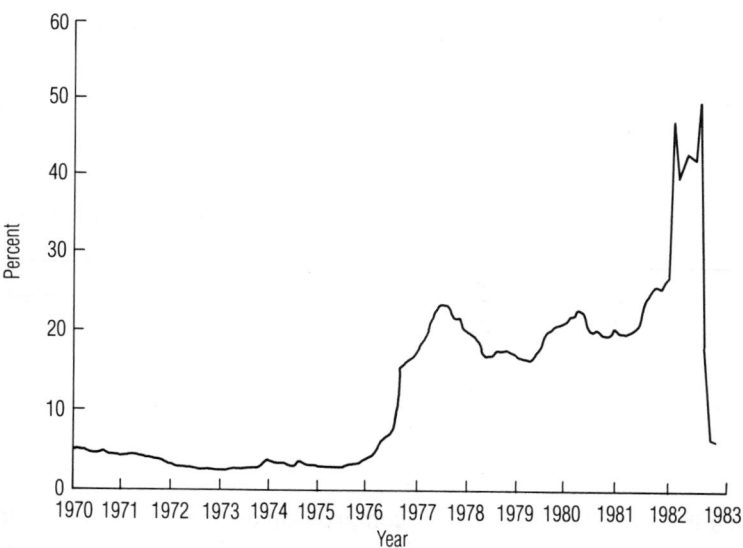

Figure 16.7 Coefficient of dollarization (dollar deposits as percentage of all deposits). (*Source*: Zedillo (1987), updated by the author.)

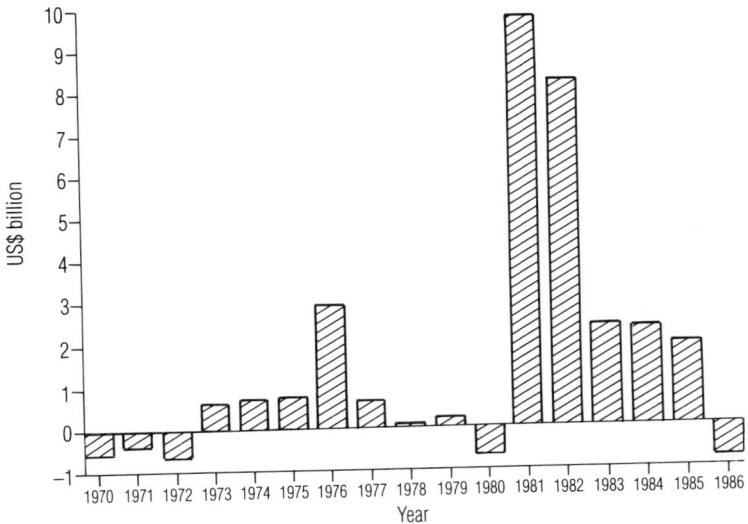

Figure 16.8 Capital flight (US$ billion).
(*Source*: Zedillo (1987), updated by the author.)

Table 16.6 Estimates of capital flight (US$ billion)

	1976–79	1980–82	1983–84
Morgan Guaranty	13.1	22.5	17.7
Cuddington	5.9	23.4	6.9
Zedillo	3.9	17.3	4.6

Source: Lessard and Williamson (1987).

Table 16.7 Sources of increase in the external debt; 1979–81 (percentage of total debt increases)

	1979	1980	1981
External shocks	33.1	28.7	16.2
Interest rate	25.9	27.2	17.8
Internal shocks	66.9	71.3	83.8
Capital flows	49.7	44.3	55.7

Source: Solis and Zedillo 1985, Table 10.6.

Solis and Zedillo (1985) have offered a decomposition of the increase in debt in 1979–81 (see Table 16.7). They conclude that most of the debt increase was the result of domestic policy shocks. Among these, "other capital flows," plainly capital flight, are the most significant factor. The attribution of two-thirds and more of the debt increase to internal shocks leaves no doubt that the 1982 crisis was "made in Mexico." By contrast, much of the adjustment difficulty of the period following 1982 resulted from a very unfavorable external environment and the intensive vulnerability imposed by a large debt.

16.2.4 *The experience since 1982*

The adjustments which the Mexican economy has undergone since the 1982 crisis have taken up the entire *sexennio* of the de la Madrid administration. For the major part policies have been directed at two targets: budget consolidation as a precondition for inflation stabilization, and an improved ability to service the external debt. These targets have been achieved, but at a severe cost in terms of reduced standards of living and poor employment performance. Attainment of these goals was rendered much more difficult by the sharp decline in real oil prices which started in 1983, but was particularly dramatic in 1986–87 when the real oil price had declined 65 percent below the 1980 peak. The growth of employment in the formal sector, which had averaged 4 percent in the 1970s, fell off to only 0.2 percent in 1982–86. At the same time the labor force grew at an estimated 3.6 percent p.a. The World Bank (1987) estimates that by 1986 20 percent of the labor force was absorbed by the informal sector or employed in the USA.

Budget consolidation

Budget cutting was fierce. The primary deficit was cut from 7 percent of GDP in 1982 and brought to a surplus of 5 percent in 1987. By comparison with the budget experience of industrialized countries, this represents an incredible achievement. A cynic might argue that budget cutting to such a degree is possible only when the initial fat matches the task. There may be some truth in this, but it must also be remembered that the oil decline by itself reduced revenues and hence worsened the budget. Table 16.8 shows that, comparing 1982 and 1986, the share of oil revenues in GDP was unchanged despite their massive absolute decline. The reason is that the large real depreciation raised the value of oil receipts in terms of domestic goods.[6]

Budget adjustment involved important changes in the composition of outlays. Interest outlays increased by 8 percent of GDP, but total outlays declined by 1.5

Table 16.8 The composition of the budget (percentage of GDP)

	Revenues		Outlays	
	Total	Oil	Total	Interest
1982	30.1	11.5	45.5	8.3
1984	33.0	15.5	39.8	12.0
1986	30.4	11.4	44.0	16.4
1987[a]	30.0	11.8	44.0	19.4

Note: [a] preliminary.
Source: *Hacienda Finances Públicas*, 1977–86 and *Estadísticas de Finances Públicas*, March 1988.

Table 16.9 The external balance (US$ billion)

	Receipts			Outlays	
	Current account	Total	Oil	Total	Factor payments
1982	−6.2	26.2	16.4	32.7	12.5
1984	4.2	30.1	16.4	27.3	10.1
1986	−1.7	24.2	6.3	25.8	9.5
1987	—	30.5	8.6	26.6	9.4

Source: Banco de México, *Informe Anual*, various issues.

percent: the noninterest component of outlays was cut by an astounding 9.6 percent of GDP. A significant part of these spending cuts took the form of reduced investment.

External debt service

The real exchange rate and real wages were the principal means through which the government achieved external competitiveness. The current account and its composition are shown in Table 16.9. Since 1982 interest payments have declined, notwithstanding the increase in the external debt. The major reason is the sharp decline in LIBOR rates from 13.3 percent in 1982 to 6.9 percent in 1986. Another reason is the grace period on the payment of private sector external debt under the FICORCA regime. The decline in oil prices implied a $10 billion loss in export revenues. Despite that loss, the external deficit declined, and by 1987 a surplus emerged due to the reduction in net factor payments abroad (mostly interest) and the contraction of import spending. Increased export revenue contributed somewhat to absorbing the shock.

The counterpart of the very large real depreciation (nearly 40 percent by June 1987), shown in Figure 16.9, is a sharp decline in the real wage. The real wage is shown in Figure 16.10. From a plateau in 1975–82, the manufacturing real wage has declined by almost 35 percent. The decline in the real minimum wage, shown in Figure 16.11, amounted to almost 45 percent. This decline in the standard of living is an inevitable counterpart of the deterioration in Mexico's external condition. The large external debt, and the deterioration in the terms of trade (including changes in real interest rates) imply that the pre-1982 standard of living cannot be sustained today. Table 16.10 shows that the terms of trade deterioration, even excluding oil, has been significant.

In terms of per-capita growth the *sexennio* of President de la Madrid was, of course, extremely expensive. Per-capita income declined between 1982 and 1988 by 13–15 percent. Thus, although there was significant growth on the manufacturing exports side, the net effect of the fiscal and real exchange rate measures was a sharp contraction. Real wage cutting, rather than translating rapidly and pervasively into employment creation, especially in exports and import substitution, brought about a recession. This dominant impact of real wage cutting, and

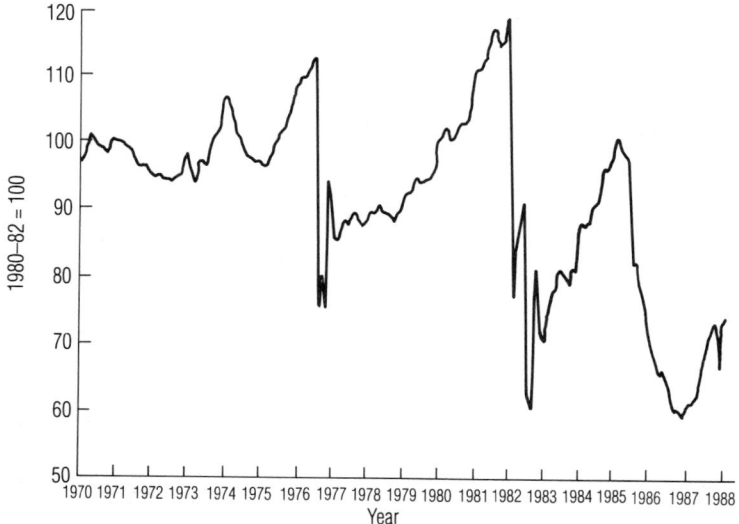

Figure 16.9 The real exchange rate.
(*Source*: Morgan Guaranty, *World Financial Markets.*)

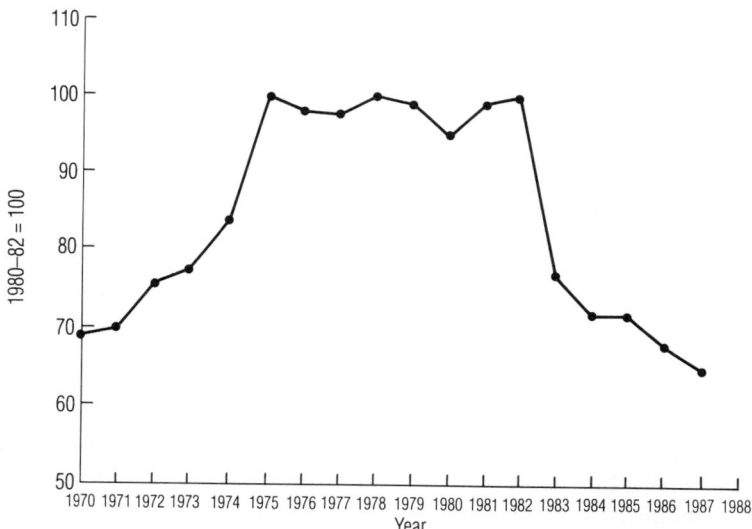

Figure 16.10 The real manufacturing wage.
(*Source*: Banco de México, *Indicadores Económicos.*)

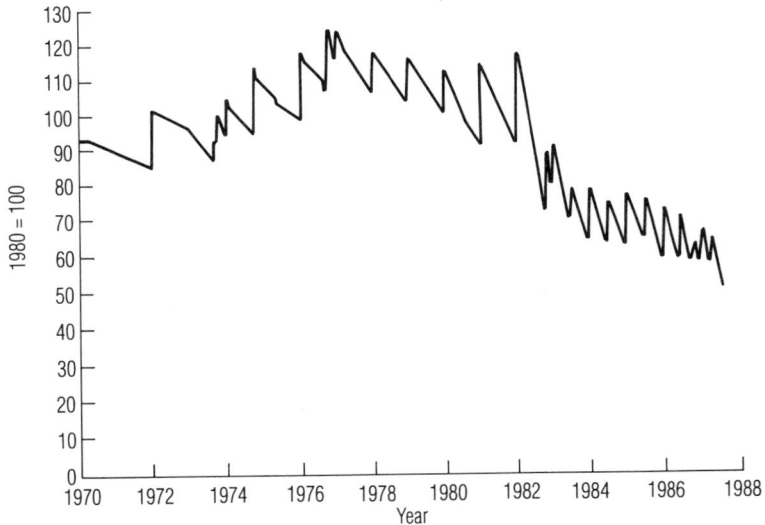

Figure 16.11 The real minimum wage.
(*Source*: Banco de México, *Indicadores Económicos*.)

Table 16.10 The terms of trade (index: 1980–84 = 100)

	Total	Nonoil	Adjusted for interest rates
1970–74	94	115	110
1975–80	97	126	115
1980–84	100	100	100
1985	83	85	72
1986	60	81	56
1987	66	—	68

Note: The terms of trade adjustment for interest rate changes assumes as a benchmark the average real interest rate of 1950–86. See *Informe*, p. 107.
Source: Rubio and Gil Díaz (1987); and Banco de México, *Informe Anual*, 1986 and 1987.

budget cutting, on real domestic demand and output was, of course, to be expected. Díaz Alejandro (1964), Krugman and Taylor (1981), as well as Serven (1986), all have made the point that the stimulating effects on output and employment of depreciation, especially in the context of semi-industrialized countries, are a slow and precarious process.

As shown by Figure 16.9, the last years of the Echeverría and López Portillo administrations—in 1976 and 1982, respectively—were marked by sharp real depreciations as the inevitable outcome of excessive demand and overvaluation. Not surprisingly, attention now focuses on 1988, the last year of the de la Madrid administration. Will the stabilization program now under way succeed?

Restrictive fiscal and monetary policies are pushing the economy into recession and the exchange rate policy, which is being used to help stop inflation, has already led to real appreciation of more than 15 percent since early 1987. A shift toward overly expansionary policies or a new run on the currency could upset the policies and lead to yet another instance where the last year of a presidency is synonymous with chaos. As we shall see below, there is room for confidence, but a healthy dose of skepticism is also appropriate.

16.3 Inflation stabilization

Stopping high inflation involves two issues. One is to set monetary and fiscal policies on a course consistent with low inflation. Monetary and fiscal austerity are the *sine qua non* of a successful inflation stabilization. Countries with a moderate inflation experience may be in a position to allow temporary departures from conservative policies without immediate, large inflation risks. But countries which have undergone a major inflation shock are especially vulnerable and hence do not have much leeway for departing from strict orthodoxy. The openness of the economy and the risk of capital flight, with the accompanying destabilizing effect of currency depreciation, further enhance the requirement for orthodoxy. Modern literature emphasizes buzzwords like commitment, reputation, credibility, signals. They all have a germ of truth. The basic message is that the deficit needs to be at least balanced and money growth, beyond limited remonetization, cannot afford to run at high rates, certainly not to finance budget deficits.

The other, equally essential, condition for disinflation is an incomes policy that helps coordinate the end of inflation among the decentralized wage and price setters, including the government itself. The coordination issue is essential for two reasons. First, wages and prices are set for a given period in an unsynchronized manner. Hence a sudden end of inflation involves difficult adjustments in relative prices for various agents who find themselves in different positions in the adjustment cycle. Second, even if there were perfect synchronization in the timing of all wage and price setting, there remains an issue of coordination: each agent has to guess what every other agent will be doing. The government can play a major role in coordinating this shift to low inflation by an incomes policy. Such an incomes policy is a transition regime, it cannot be a permanent corset or a substitute for financial policies consistent with low inflation.

Beyond helping with the coordination issue the incomes policy provides temporary protection for price stability. With incomes policy a valuable breathing spell is instituted in which price stability can be established without recession. The resulting strong political support for the program and the policymaker yields a platform from which to make the inevitable adjustments in the budget, which are the ultimate pillars of stabilization, and to create the confidence for a resumption of private investment which must be the engine of post-stabilization growth. But mistaking the breathing spell for success, and failure to use the political support at its height for the difficult task of fiscal correction, will mean that the program must soon slip. And when it does slip, it often does so irrecoverably, as the experiences in Brazil and Argentina demonstrate. The stabilization experience in other countries is particularly relevant for Mexico because it demonstrates that incomes policy is not enough. Only in Israel and Bolivia did the program succeed and in those cases fiscal policy provided the essential help (in Bolivia's case the essential move was to stop external debt service; in Israel US aid supported the initial budget correction).

Mexican inflation stabilization has been under way since December 1987. In the framework of a social pact the government has undertaken to reduce inflation by the end of 1988 to less than 30 percent or, more precisely, less than 2 percent per month. The program has been successful in its initial stages. Inflation declined from 15.4 percent in January 1988 to only 3.1 percent in April 1988 and 2 percent estimated for May 1988. The main mechanism for this inflation reduction has been a coordinated program of reduced exchange rate depreciation, reduced inflation of public sector prices and agreements for a significant part of private sector prices. A freeze on the exchange rate, wages, public sector prices and a range of private prices is the cornerstone of the program.

16.3.1 *Inertial inflation and coordination*[7]

That aggregate demand discipline is a necessary condition for sustained price stability has long been known by economists and by well-advised policymakers. Yet it may not be sufficient to stop inflation, or at least it may fail to work under conditions of tolerable unemployment. This is demonstrated by the failure of a number of IMF-supported programs that ignored the problem posed by inflationary inertia.

Inertial inflation

The major part of a high inflation is essentially inertia. Inertial inflation means that inflation today is approximately equal to what it was yesterday (with possible effects from the economy's cyclical position and supply shocks). It is not only "too much money chasing too few goods" (cyclical effects), nor only oil or agricultural price increases, nor real depreciation (supply shocks), but also the sheer fact that inflation yesterday means inflation today. The reason for this inertia is primarily explicit or implicit indexation interacting with staggered wage setting. This may take the form of a legally imposed wage rule, according to which wage adjustments today are based on the inflation over the past year or the past six months. More informal wage bargaining may lead to the same result. The same mechanism also works via expectations. In setting their prices firms will have to estimate their own cost increases and the price increases of competing firms. The best guess is that, cyclical and supply shock factors aside, inflation today will be approximately what it was yesterday. Figure 16.11, which shows the real minimum wage, illustrates this process for Mexico. The spikes correspond to the restoration of purchasing power when compensation is given for past inflation. Between readjustment periods the real wage is eroded. It is typical of the high inflation process that, as external shocks feed into the process, the adjustment periods shorten and inflation accelerates.

Because everybody believes that inflation will in fact be approximately what it was yesterday, the public acts on these expectations and will therefore set prices accordingly. Firms will give wage concessions matching these inflation expectations (it is much easier to give wage increases in line with expected inflation than go through the risk of a strike). If everybody acts in this manner, then in fact the expected inflation turns out to be the actual inflation; and if yesterday's inflation is the benchmark, then today's inflation will come out to be much the same as it was in the past. Cyclical factors and supply shocks, including the need for real depreciation to cope with the debt crisis, are the chief reasons why inflation has exploded in many countries. The inertial part of inflation, other things being equal, would tend to make for rather stable inflation, at some particular level. But the extra elements can cause inflation to move, and often to move sharply. The cyclical factor is quite obvious in that it is simply demand inflation or cooling down of inflation due to slack in activity and employment. Yet it is worthwhile to recognize an asymmetry. There is no upper limit for firms' price increases in response to excess demand, but in reverse the argument does not apply. Stopping inflation of 150 percent by slack is very difficult. Even as restrictive policy cuts nominal spending, firms are forced in the labor market to make wage concessions

Table 16.11 Recent high inflation experiences (annual and quarterly averages of monthly inflation rates)

	Argentina	Bolivia	Brazil	Mexico	Peru	Israel
1980	6.0	3.3	5.0	2.0	4.0	7.2
1981	6.2	2.2	6.2	2.0	4.7	6.6
1982	8.5	7.4	6.0	3.9	4.7	6.8
1983	13.2	11.5	7.6	6.0	6.4	7.8
1984	18.0	24.4	9.5	4.3	6.4	13.8
1985:1	24.1	92.4	12.0	5.1	10.5	10.3
1985:2	28.4	42.0	8.2	2.7	11.6	13.7
1985:3	3.6	63.1	11.5	3.9	8.2	11.5
1985:4	2.5	6.0	12.3	5.1	2.8	2.1
1986:1	3.1	13.7	10.1	6.0	4.9	0.6
1986:2	4.4	2.9	0.8	5.7	3.7	2.2
1986:3	7.6	1.6	0.8	6.3	4.0	1.0
1986:4	5.4	0.3	3.5	6.8	4.0	2.2
1987:1	7.4	1.6	14.1	7.3	5.8	1.5
1987:2	5.2	0.6	24.6	7.8	5.7	1.3
1987:3	11.9	0.5	5.1	7.6	7.0	1.0
1987:4	11.1	—	15.0	10.0	8.0	1.5
1988:1	11.0	—	20.0	9.5	15.4	1.8

Source: International Financial Statistics.

based on past inflation. Their cost increases thus might be of the order of 150 percent and it is quite inconceivable that simply by reducing profit margins they would be able to reduce inflation significantly. In the same way a cut in wage settlements below the prevailing rate of inflation will not make much of a difference to high inflation. Giving wage increases of 120 percent instead of 150 percent would mean a very large cut in the real wage but only a very minor reduction in inflation. Governments in high inflation countries have therefore little hope but to try and stem further inflation deterioration. They naturally turn to incomes policy as a politically acceptable means of stopping inflation. Incomes policy is a means of breaking the inertial forces, thus shifting the economy instantly from a high inflation state to a low one.

Coordination

One issue in stopping inflation is the coordination of price and wage decisions. To introduce disinflation someone must start offering cuts either in profit margins or in real wages. The initial disinflation can then be passed along through indexation into a gradual path of further disinflation. Realistically, there will be no volunteers for such an approach. Everybody wants to see the fact of zero inflation before they themselves will set their own price or wage increases at zero. But if everybody adopts a "wait-and-see" attitude then, of course, inflation will continue. An attempt to restrict demand would translate almost entirely into reduced employment and practically not at all into lower inflation. The dismal performance of the economy and the lack of success at inflation fighting would make any such campaign shortlived. The scenario thus described shows that coordination becomes essential to achieve good results. A system of temporary control of wages, prices and the exchange rate is the coordinating device to reduce inflation.

It might be argued that if the government does undertake to produce the right kind of monetary and fiscal policy, then the public cannot escape the conclusion that, in fact, inflation has been left dead in its tracks. Unable to escape that conclusion, everybody will act on it and hence inflation will be dead. But there are two separate and crucial slips in this argument. One concerns the government's inability credibly to precommit to future policies. The other, which is more novel, concerns the problem of coordination in a world of price setters.

No government can commit itself definitely, credibly and beyond doubt to what it (or its successor) might do tomorrow. The institutional setting for such a precommitment does not exist (one thinks of constitutional amendments, the gold standard and what not). Because the government cannot lock away its policies beyond doubt, the public always recognizes that there is some possibility that policy will not stick to a noninflationary stance. Specifically, if agents do not quite believe that policy will stick, then they all will behave somewhat defensively, charging some wage and price increases which then force the government to suspend the policy. The expectation that this is indeed the policy persuades agents to disbelieve the possibility of an instant end to inflation. These ideas assign the government a double task: to ensure credibility of the aggregate demand policy consistent with disinflation and to coordinate the expectations and actions of individual wage and price setters. Of course, the chances of hitting instantly a zero-inflation, low-unemployment, zero-shortage equilibrium via an incomes policy are remote. Wage-price controls will almost inevitably lead to some shortages unless there is a generalized recession that cuts demand. The central question is what is worse in terms of social welfare: product shortages that may eventually be overcome by imports, or a generalized shortage of jobs.

Risks of misalignment

The costs of an incomes policy will depend significantly on how well the instruments are managed and aligned. The risk is that when inflation has disappeared it has been replaced by a new problem such as exchange rate overvaluation or pervasive bankruptcies. The various instruments of an incomes policy (exchange rates, wages, public and private sector prices and the nominal money stock) must be carefully matched. Failure to align these policy instruments can easily lead to dramatically poor performance. The clearest example of a poorly aligned policy might be the Chilean stabilization of the late 1970s. The budget had been moved to balance and, indeed, to a surplus. Money was under tight control and inflation was gradually declining, although very slowly. To speed up disinflation, the government opted to stop the exchange rate depreciation that had previously been used to avoid a loss of competitiveness in the face of continuing inflation. But the government failed to recognize that wage indexation, geared to the past inflation, implied cost increases for firms without providing offsetting relief on prices. The exchange rate soon became grossly overvalued, leading ultimately to the worst kind of speculation and financial instability. The need for a matching of instruments applies also to the money stock. As we will discuss below, successful disinflation requires determined (though careful and limited) monetization of the economy.

Because of information externalities, the coordinating role for an incomes policy arises when macroeconomic noise and uncertainty are large relative to the microeconomic uncertainties in each individual market. This explains why, in a second stage of a stabilization program, removing wage–price controls gradually, at successive sectoral steps, will result in less uncertainty and lower subsequent inflation than removing controls in one shot. The one-shot approach would simply bring back the uncertainty of each individual agent as to what every other agent will do. As a result, at the stage of liberalization there would be defensively large price increases which might well wreck the inflation stabilization. Achieving consistency in the defreezing stage is thus an important and difficult task.

16.3.2 *The budget and inflation*

In this section we look at the fiscal preconditions for successful disinflation. Two points are made. First, the measured budget deficit is a poor indicator of the state of the budget when inflation suddenly ceases. Because of the inflation component of domestic debt service, it tends to overstate the relevant deficit. Second, we ask what is a reasonable fiscal position with which to enter a disinflation program. The common perception is that inflation is caused by budget deficits. We draw attention here to the fact that budget deficits are high because of inflation. This unusual direction is important in assessing public finance in inflationary episodes and developing a judgment about the fiscal policy changes required in implementing stabilization.

The first reason why inflation increases deficits is the Olivera–Tanzi effect. Inflation, combined with lags in tax collection, implies that the real value of tax collection arriving in the hands of the government is lower the higher the rate of inflation. If last year's income taxes were to be paid only this year with 100 percent inflation and without indexation of tax liabilities, the government would find itself with only half of the real value of taxes it would receive without inflation, without lags or with exact indexation. The second interaction between inflation and the deficit stems from the inflation component of debt service. Part of government outlays will be the service of the internal and external debt. Interest rates will reflect expected inflation and depreciation. This link between inflation and nominal debt service has led to the recognition that two different measures of the deficit must be distinguished: the actual deficit and the inflation-adjusted or operational deficit (see Appendix 16.A for a discussion of budget measures).

In 1987, the actual Mexican deficit was 15.8 percent of GDP while the operational budget showed a surplus of 1.2 percent of GDP. The former calculates the deficit taking full nominal interest payments as the measure of debt service, while the latter only includes real interest payments and excludes the inflationary component of interest (the inflationary erosion of the principal). The importance of inflation adjustments in the budget is apparent in Table 16.12. The

Table 16.12 The budget and the public debt (percentage of GDP)

	PSBR[a]	Primary[b] deficit	Operational[c] deficit	Public debt domestic	external
1980	7.9	3.2	4.2	—	18.4
1981	14.8	8.4	8.8	15.3	22.3
1982	17.6	7.6	5.2	19.1	36.6
1983	9.0	−4.4	1.9	18.6	44.4
1984	8.7	−4.9	0.6	17.7	38.2
1985	10.0	−3.6	1.1	17.6	38.3
1986	16.0	−2.2	1.8	19.8	53.2
1987	15.8	−4.9	−1.2	17.1	—

[a] Public sector borrowing requirement.
[b] Noninterest budget.
[c] Adjusted for the inflationary erosion of public debt denominated in pesos.
Source: Gil Díaz (1987a; 1987b), Rubio and Gil Díaz (1987), Banco de México, *Informe Anual*, 1986, 1987; and calculations by the author.

Table 16.13 Operational budget deficits (percentage of GDP)

	1984	1985	1986	1987
Argentina	10.8	7.0	4.3	6.8
Brazil	1.6	4.3	3.6	5.5
Israel	18.4	−1.0[a]	−4.5[a]	0.0
Mexico	0.6	1.1	1.8	−1.2
Peru	6.3	2.4	4.8	6.3

[a] Including US aid.
Source: Various central banks.

operational or inflation-adjusted budget is now in balance and the primary budget shows a substantial surplus. In this sense the famous IMF dictum, "a deficit is a deficit is a deficit!" is a poor starting point for analyzing the fiscal fundamentals required for a successful stabilization. In other words, when the operational deficit is balanced the government no longer requires inflationary finance to pay its way. That situation exists in Mexico today.

But supposing that we accept the operational budget as a measure of the state of public finance, how much of a surplus is required to promise a successful disinflation? There is no firm answer to that question. Much depends on public confidence and understanding. The comparison of different stabilization experiences in the past few years provides some guidance. Table 16.13 shows the operational deficits of four countries that have used incomes policy programs. Israel succeeded, while Argentina, Brazil and Peru failed dramatically. Not surprisingly, these were the countries with large deficits. But note that already in 1987 the Mexican budget showed a surplus of the same magnitude as that of Israel at the time of stabilization. For 1988, budget plans call for a further fiscal tightening, and the first quarter certainly showed these plans to be effective. On a comparative basis we therefore conclude that the budget stance is definitely not a detriment to stabilization. There might be a temptation to go much further with fiscal austerity just to be entirely certain that stabilization succeeds, but there are clearly tradeoffs. Too much austerity, beyond the current surplus, would risk a deep slump in economic activity which carries its own risks. If stabilization is not followed by a resumption of growth, then the sustainability of the budget cuts soon comes into question. Thus, excessive zeal on the budget carries its own serious risks.

16.3.3 *Real interest rates during stabilization*

Inflation stabilization, in high inflation experiences, is often accompanied by an explicit monetary reform. The traditional way to signal new rules of the game is to announce the independence of the central bank and an end to automatic financing of the budget by the printing press. However, it is important here to read the fine print. In the 1920s the stabilizations did, indeed, involve institutional changes and limitations on the access of the government to the printing press, but that did not in fact imply an end to money creation for two reasons. One was that in some cases the transition was characterized by a large, once-and-for-all issue of money. In Germany in 1923 the ceiling was set at 500 percent of the existing money stock (Sargent 1986; Dornbusch 1987). Beyond this once-and-for-all fiduciary issue there was also the possibility of the money stock increasing in the course of domestic private credit expansion or the monetization of reserve inflows. The experience from the classical stabilizations was one of extremely large increases in nominal money—several hundred percent—consistent with price stabilization. The explanation for this large, noninflationary money creation is quite obvious. During the high inflation period the cost of holding noninterest-bearing money becomes extremely high. As a result, real money balances decline, or the velocity of circulation increases. This is the famous "flight from money." The financial system accommodates the flight from money by creating highly liquid interest-bearing or indexed liabilities—the "overnights" which practically serve as money.

In the course of stabilization the reverse occurs. The disappearance of inflation raises the demand for M1 or real transactions balances. It is necessary to increase the nominal money supply through one means or another to avoid extravagantly high nominal and real interest rates. A noninflationary expansion in the money stock is needed to meet the additional demand for money, the well-known reliquification of velocity problem. M1 can expand to replace other financial assets without risk of renewed inflation. The problem is to fine-tune this expansion and to identify which aggregates must expand. Failure to expand M1, or too gradual an increase, means that the economy will slide into a recession because of a liquidity crunch. But too rapid or too large an expansion leads to a loss of credibility and reigniting of inflation.[8]

In the Mexican stabilization now under way the issue of high real interest rates is certainly relevant. Table 16.14 shows the short-term interest rate and the biweekly inflation data for the period since December 1987. The table shows that real interest rates in April exceeded 30 percent per year. It might be argued that these realized real rates do not match with expected real rates, that the expectation of a breakdown of the program is reflected in high nominal rates; the

Table 16.14 The recent Mexican experience: interest and inflation rates (percentage per year)

	Inflation	1 month rate	3 month rate
January 1988	464	158	156
February	160	154	154
March	82	97	80
April	44	63	54
May	25	51	45
June[a]	—	40	32

[a] Second week.
Source: Banco de México.

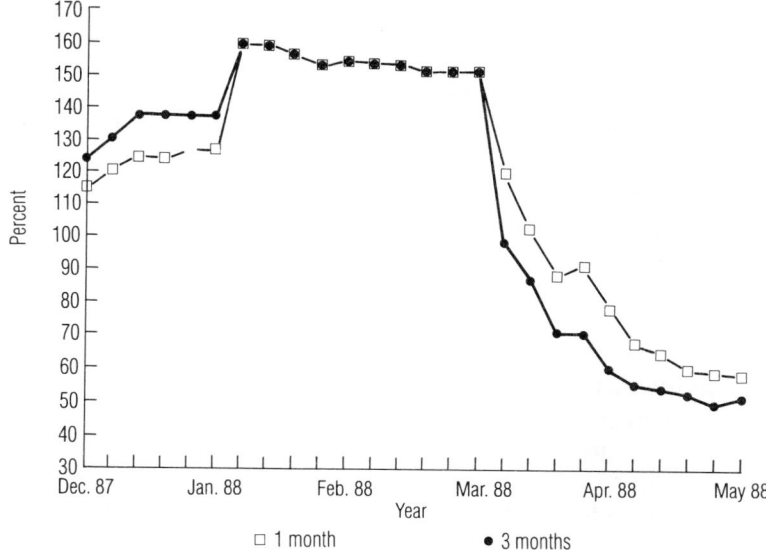

Figure 16.12 Treasury bill rates (percentage per year).
(*Source*: Banco de México.)

actual success then turns realized real rates unexpectedly positive and large. This view is contradicted by the evidence on the term structure of interest rates shown in Figure 16.12. The downward-sloping term structure seems to rule out a serious confidence problem and to offer the ground for a fairly robust rejection of the expectations interpretation of high realized real rates.

The challenge today, part of an incomes policy, is to bring down real interest rates fast enough to avoid a recession without, however, risking capital flight. Indeed, high real interest rates drive small and medium-sized indebted firms into bankruptcy, and deteriorate the budget position because of the significant domestic debt. Bringing down interest rates requires a more rapid rate of domestic money expansion. This can be done directly by monetizing reserve inflows that come from the repatriation of flight capital. But there is some extra room for domestic credit creation. Of course, the behavior of reserves is the key signal to know how rapidly monetary expansion can afford to proceed. In concluding, we note one point that is often omitted: reducing inflation is not the whole game. The challenge is to do so in a way that translates soon into a growth program.

16.3.4 *The transition*

The bad news about stabilization is that the first step, stopping inflation, is the easy part. The greater difficulty is to move from there to sustainable growth. The difficulty arises because while the government can help coordinate disinflation and set with its fiscal austerity the basic financial framework for growth, it cannot make the growth. The private sector must take over and move ahead with investment, production and employment. At this stage of the stabilization process, the difficulty is that austerity is good for financial confidence, but it does not do much for business confidence. Inevitably the monetary and fiscal austerity cools down domestic demand and accordingly, except where backlog is large, there is little incentive to invest. In fact, the high real interest rates favor postponing investment. Typically firms may be prepared to invest—the fundamentals are now right— but they will wait for the "right time." However, if everybody waits for the right time no investment in fact is happening. As a result the economy is bound to fall into a slump—what in the German experience was called the "stabilization crisis." The budget cannot help get out of that situation, nor can a cheap money policy.

The risk of a major slump has two important implications. One is that the government should not be overambitious in eradicating inflation "once and for all." An overambitious plan on inflation—0 percent per month, not 2 or 3 percent—will require too long and make too deep a recession, thus aggravating the difficulty of a spontaneous recovery.[9] Second, as we shall argue below, there are important links between the debt strategy and growth. A policy of recycling interest payments would definitely be a major investment incentive.

16.4 External debt and growth

Mexico is one of the 17 Baker problem debtors. With Brazil she is the leading debtor and, as in the case of Brazil, the debt trades at less than 50 cents on the dollar. Improvements in the Mexican economy notwithstanding, as recently as 1985 the discount was only 20 percent. Table 16.15 shows a comparison and reports the composition of creditors.

16.4.1 *The debt problem*

The problem of debt is that the burden of debt service, in the budget and in the external balance, is a source of inflation, overly low standards of living and much too low investment. The financial instability which comes from strained budgets, high and rising inflation and frequent depreciation has proved a powerful incentive to capital flight. Attempts to stem capital flight by high interest rates have brought about bankruptcy and budget problems. Sharply undervalued exchange rates, which might stem capital flight, in turn risk promoting political instability as a result of the very low real wages which this policy would imply. A major acceleration of inflation has been apparent not only in Mexico but throughout the debtor economies in the last few years. Inflation rates have increased because the attempt to gain competitiveness through depreciation could not effectively be stopped from affecting domestic wages and prices. In many cases debt service was financed by outright money creation. High, rising

Table 16.15 Seventeen highly indebted countries

Country	Debt[a] Total	Banks All	USA[b]	Total per capita	Per-capita consumption growth, 1980–87 (annual average)	Price[c] cents/$
Argentina	49.4	42.4	8.5	1592	−1.2	28
Bolivia	4.6	1.2	0.1	407	−5.2	11
Brazil	114.5	84.2	21.9	702	1.1	46
Chile	20.5	17.1	6.4	1666	−2.2	59
Colombia	15.1	7.5	2.0	517	0.2	65
Costa Rica	4.5	2.3	0.4	354	−1.4	15
Ecuador	9.0	6.3	n.a.	928	−2.2	34
Ivory Coast	9.1	5.5	0.4	892	−4.3	32
Jamaica	3.8	6.6	0.2	1583	−1.4	33
Mexico	105.0	90.5	24.0	1313	−2.7	48
Morocco	27.0	5.5	0.8	1205	0.8	50
Nigeria	27.0	14.9	0.9	274	−6.5	29
Peru	16.7	8.9	1.2	827	−0.2	5
Philippines	29.0	17.6	5.0	527	−1.0	51
Uruguay	3.9	3.0	0.9	1267	−2.4	59
Venezuela	33.9	33.7	16.4	1904	−4.6	46
Yugoslavia	21.8	15.2	2.0	936	−0.5	49

[a] Debt data are in billions of US dollars except per-capita debt which is in dollars.
[b] US bank exposure as of June 1987.
[c] Secondary market valuation in cents per dollar, bid price March 1988.
Source: World Bank; IMF; and Goldman Sachs.

and uncertain inflation has provided a very unfavorable climate for private markets. Financial considerations, not productive investment, are in the forefront and capital flight has become pervasive.

To a large extent the attempt to find resources for debt service has come at the expense of investment. Investment has been depressed in debtor countries because governments have found it easier to cut investment budgets rather than raise taxes or reduce spending programs. The lack of growth, or outright contraction, and the disturbed financial conditions, have also depressed private investment, as shown in Table 16.16.

In Mexico, unlike many other debtor countries, the collapse of investment has not been extreme. Moreover, over 1975–84, unproductive investment may have

Table 16.16 Gross investment (percentage of GDP)

	Total	Public	Private
1970–74	19.2	6.5	12.8
1975–79	21.3	8.9	12.4
1980–84	21.5	9.5	12.0
1985	16.9	6.0	10.9
1986	15.5	5.2	10.3
1987	15.3	5.1	10.2

Source: Banco de México and, for 1985–87, *Hacienda México: Economic and Financial Statistics*, November 1987.

Table 16.17 Real fixed investment (index: 1970 = 100)

	Total	Construction	Machinery and equipment
1970–74	114	112	116
1975–79	159	156	163
1980–84	202	202	203
1985	174	187	156
1986	153	170	131

Source: Gil Díaz (1987b).

been excessive. While both observations are correct, a countervailing argument is that with a labor force growth of more than 3.5 percent, failure to expand capital at a rapid rate implies a growing, acute imbalance between actual capacity and the level of capacity needed to sustain high levels of employment. Low public sector investment builds up dangerous bottlenecks which stand in the way of an ultimate resumption of growth. Table 16.17 shows an index of the real level of investment spending in Mexico. The dramatic decline to the levels of a decade ago is alarming. An index of population, for comparison, increased from 100 in 1970 to 157 in 1986. Investment per capita, outside construction (which was strongly supported by the earthquake) thus declined sharply. Per head of the labor force the decline was even sharper (with a labor force growth averaging 3.5 percent, the labor force index would have risen from 100 in 1970 to 173 in 1986).

16.4.2 Debt and growth

Suppose Mexico were to succeed in the current inflation stabilization and could then embark on a program of growth. It is certainly not extreme to envisage a plan of 3.5 percent growth, just above the rate of labor force growth. The question is whether a 3.5 percent growth path is consistent with continued, full external debt service. If not, one must ask what should give: debt service or growth. Table 16.18 shows the external balance and the debt ratios in the 1980s. The question is

Table 16.18 External debt and the current account (percentage of GDP)

	Current account		External debt	
	total	noninterest	total	public sector
1970–74	−2.7	−1.4	17.7	12.0
1975–79	−3.6	−1.6	30.1	22.1
1980	−4.3	−1.8	27.7	18.4
1981	−5.8	−2.7	33.5	22.3
1982	−3.7	2.6	54.4	36.6
1983	3.8	10.3	66.6	44.4
1984	2.5	8.4	55.4	38.2
1985	0.7	5.7	53.8	38.3
1986	−1.0	4.7	74.3	53.2

Source: Banco de México, *Indicadores Económicos*.

whether there is enough of a noninterest surplus in a growth scenario to provide for debt service.

To provide the simplest possible answer to this question, we abstract from the many bottleneck issues (Selowsky and van der Tak 1986). The difference between the amount of capital required for growth and domestic saving defines the required external resources. The calculation allows us to see whether the debt–income ratio would be rising or falling under the specified program.

The evolution of the debt–income ratio can be decomposed as follows:[10]

$$
\begin{array}{l}
\text{Chance in the} \\
\text{debt–income ratio}
\end{array}
=
\begin{bmatrix}
\text{debt–income} \\
\text{ratio}
\end{bmatrix}
\times
\begin{bmatrix}
\text{real} & & \text{real} \\
\text{interest} & - & \text{growth} \\
\text{rate} & & \text{rate}
\end{bmatrix}
$$

$$
+
\begin{bmatrix}
\text{required} & & \text{consumption–} \\
\text{investment–} & + & \text{income} & -1 \\
\text{income ratio} & & \text{ratio}
\end{bmatrix}
$$

As a benchmark, assume that the consumption–income ratio remains constant at 77 percent, which occurs when per-capita consumption is constant and when GDP grows at the same rate as the population, i.e. 3.5 percent. For a GDP growth rate of 3.5 percent p.a., the target investment–income ratio is set at 20 percent. This would occur if capital depreciation represents 11.25 percent of GDP while each increase in GDP requires, very optimistically, 2.5 times its value of net new capital. Thus the growth path leaves a noninterest surplus of 3 percent of GDP. The first term in the decomposition includes debt service as well as investment income on direct foreign investment. Thus, assuming a debt ratio of 80 percent and an excess of interest rates (inflation-adjusted) over growth of about 2 percent, the first term comes to 1.6 percent. Accordingly the noninterest surplus in this calculation is more than sufficient to stabilize the debt–income ratio.

The calculation might appear comforting: growth can be achieved without risk on the debt side. But that would disregard a number of very strong assumptions that have gone into the scenario. First, the single most important assumption is that per-capita consumption stays constant. If political stability requires growth of per-capita consumption, an increase of just 2 or 3 percentage points will immediately upset the debt service calculations. Second, the calculations maintain a constant debt–income ratio. That is not consistent with creditors' views. They want to see a reduction in absolute exposure, not an increase at the rate of 3.5 percent per year. Third, the calculation is very optimistic in its assessment of investment productivity and depreciation requirements. A more conservative view is that the general capital shortage that has accumulated, and the obsolescence of capital, require an investment spur.

There are also two optimistic modifications. The first one is that a successful inflation stabilization could draw in flight capital and foreign direct investment. This would obviate the need for commercial banks to finance the interest bill. The second modification is that the ongoing privatization and trade liberalization raise investment efficiency, and productivity more generally. This allows the economy to achieve growth without as high an investment requirement as was posited above.

It is difficult to know where exactly the balance of considerations lies. The enhanced productivity that comes with privatization is certainly a factor and so is the inflow of nondebt finance. But these tend to take time and the return to growth assumes urgency after yet another year of declining per-capita income. The major consideration would seem to be the path of per-capita consumption. Fiscal policy can do much to control that, but there is very little question that political stability will require growing per-capita income levels. Consequently, the debt problem is not under control. Even if lenders agreed to a policy of a constant debt–income ratio, meaning substantial extra loans, this would not be enough to support an adequate growth path. It is, therefore, important to ask how growth and debt service can be reconciled. We review here two possible directions: market-related mechanisms such as debt–equity swaps or buybacks as one means, and interest recycling as the other.

16.4.3 *Market-related mechanisms*

Over the past few years an active secondary market for developing country debt has emerged. In this market, debts trade at significant discounts. These discounts suggest a variety of ways in which investors and/or debtor countries could take advantage of this market for debt reduction and profit opportunities. Two possibilities in particular are noted: debt-equity swaps and buybacks.

Debt–equity swaps

In a debt–equity swap a commercial bank sells debt to a private investor who presents the claim to the debtor government for payment in local currency, the proceeds to be used for investment. How successful debt–equity swaps are for debtor countries depends on a variety of features. At one extreme, debt–equity swaps may merely replace investment that would have occurred anyway, leaving the authorities without any significant share in the discount while requiring the financing of the local currency payment via money creation or expensive domestic debt finance. The large investment by Nissan in Mexico is typically given as an example of an operation that had already been planned and was about to be implemented when debt–equity swaps emerged and were used as a financial vehicle for the operation. At the other extreme, the discount may be the leverage that provides foreign investment with the required return, while the authorities share in the discount to an extent that the swap reduces effective interest payments.

There is some illusion about the balance of payments effects of debt–equity programs. Since they give rise to future profit remittances, some way down the road, the balance of payments effect is a reduced outflow of interest payments but an increased outflow of profit remittances. There is no presumption that the net effect should be favorable. Moreover, it appears now that in Brazil, for example, debt–equity swaps have become basically a borrowing operation where "side letters" arrange for external interest payments dressed up as profit remittances. A major shift in this direction may well deteriorate the regulatory climate for bona fide investment. Mexican policymakers are aware of the potential difficulties. They have started judging debt–equity swaps more accurately in terms of the costs and benefits. That has dampened some of the early enthusiasm, but it may also have cleared the road for them to become a more productive, albeit smaller, part of long-term debt solutions.

Buybacks

In the 1930s and 1940s defaulted debt of Latin America traded at large discounts and much of it was ultimately "repatriated" through buybacks by the debtor governments. At the time, debt holders' protective councils severely protested this practice. They argued that resources not used for interest payments could not be applied to buy back bonds at deep discounts, when these discounts reflect primarily an unwillingness to pay. Today the *pari passu* clause in commercial bank debt contracts proscribes buybacks, but the idea that debtor countries could achieve important debt reduction through this route is widely accepted. Several countries have in fact used the secondary market to buy back private debts. In the case of Mexico this has occurred on a significant scale. So far, apparently, public debts have not been returned on any scale.

The scope for buybacks is intrinsically limited: to be able to buy back on a large scale, the debtor needs resources which, if they were available and used, would mean that the claim should not trade at a large discount. Only when information is very imperfect, creditors are very impatient, or because regulatory and tax considerations create asymmetries, can we expect a situation where debtors can retire debt advantageously. But even then the amounts will tend to be minor. The only reason at all for buybacks is if commercial banks feel, rightly or wrongly, that one piece of Latin American debt is as bad as another, whatever the debtor country. In that event, because of the contamination effect, there is room for the relatively better-placed countries to take advantage of the across-the-board discount for a refinancing operation. (See Portes 1987, on the history and possibilities of buybacks.) In principle, buybacks might help repatriate private capital flight or reduce debt service. Allowing residents to participate in the external purchase of debts to be converted by the central bank into domestic interest-bearing liabilities is a means of capturing the external discount and splitting it between residents and the central bank. This has, in fact been done with success in Chile. But once again, this will be particularly attractive only when interest rates in the debtor country are not far in excess of rates on external debt and if foreign exchange availability is plentiful. Such a combination would be rare. Accordingly, the scope for market-related debt reduction schemes, while potentially present, is in fact limited. This was amply demonstrated by the very limited success of the recent Mexico–Morgan attempt.

16.4.4 *Recycling of interest payments*

Today Mexico is paying all the interest that is owed abroad. The decline in investment and the depressed economic conditions make this possible. However, a resumption of growth and of public sector investment would very quickly worsen the external balance.

A fundamental restructuring of debt service, which addresses the major part of interest payments due, is the best solution. Actual payments in dollars would be reduced to serve trade credit and the loans of multilateral organizations. A large share of the remaining interest payments would in part be capitalized, thus freeing resources for much needed public sector investment, and in part they would be made in local currency. Creditors who receive the local currency payments could use them for unrestricted investment in Mexico. The only limitation on the use of funds would be that they could not be transferred abroad. The claims to these payments could, however, be sold. Basically this scheme amounts to a debt–equity swap applied to interest payments rather than to the principal. It amounts to a recycling of interest payments to finance reconstruction and development.

Advantages

It will help to see the mechanics of a recycling scheme by focusing on the national income accounting identities relating investment on one side and the resource availability for investment on the other side. The government sector is included in saving and investment.

$$\text{Investment} = \text{Saving} + \text{Noninterest current account deficit} \qquad (16.1)$$

Today the budget correction has raised the national saving rate and reduced the rate of investment because of reduced public sector investment spending. As a counterpart of higher saving and reduced investment there is a large external surplus which finances the payment of interest and even debt retirement. Recycling would not reduce the national saving rate—the government would maintain fiscal austerity, thus freeing resources for investment. But now the external surplus would be replaced by an increase in the rate of investment. The reduction of the surplus would arise because firms would divert sales from exports to the home market and imports of investment goods would sharply rise.

The advantages of the interest recycling are threefold. First, the transfer of resources abroad is suspended. Rather than running trade surpluses, resources are freed for investment. Of course, serious budget action is required to ensure that in fact the resources go into investment rather than consumption. The shift of resources toward investment has two effects. First, it implies an expansion in capacity and thus sustains job creation. This issue is central in an economy where fast labor force growth has created major imbalances between labor supply and demand. The expansion in capacity removes the bottlenecks which today stand in the way of growth. Growth in turn translates into more stable public finance via a broadened tax base. The second advantage of the scheme is to create a more stable and prosperous business environment. With the current strategy, a foreign exchange bottleneck is always around the corner and the reaction is invariably contraction of demand and exchange depreciation. This reality has led to a lack of interest in productive investment and extensive capital flight. The center of gravity has shifted to financial markets, far away from productive activity. By removing the need for immediate debt service the debtor economy can resume a more balanced position with an emphasis on long-term investment and growth. As a lever for returning capital flight there is no better way than a restoration of business confidence and an end of exchange pressure. Recycling also offers two further advantages to creditor countries: it avoids outright debt relief (or debt default) and hence avoids taxpayer involvement on a large scale. Furthermore, by providing debtors with room for growth there is every expectation of increased exports to debtor countries and a reduction in the currently high levels of imports. There is a third, once-and-for-all gain. In the present situation the need to maintain very depreciated real exchange rates translates into inflationary pressures and low demand in the debtors' domestic markets. The removal of external constraints allows some real appreciation and hence provides a breathing space for stabilization of inflation. Inflation stabilization is, of course, an essential quid pro quo in a restoration of normal business conditions.

For creditor countries the reversal of trade surpluses has immediate interest; it means that exports from developing countries will decline and imports, especially of capital goods, will rise. Thus, recycling provides the financial underpinnings for solving at least a part of world trade imbalances. As a counterpart for acceptance of this scheme by creditors (or to make it more acceptable, in case of unilateral action) Mexico would have to sustain the budget improvement and to liberalize foreign direct investment. There might be a temptation to dissipate the resources into a restoration of consumption after so many years of deprivation, but that would be unacceptable. Tough-minded fiscal measures, and broad-based liberalization of investment opportunities are the quid pro quo for the suspension of resource transfers.

It is worthwhile asking how banks would deal with recycling. The immediate reaction of banks is entirely negative, but their concerns are largely exaggerated and lie mostly in the accounting area. Of course, compared to a bailout by the World Bank, recycling is thoroughly unattractive, but compared to default by all of Latin America, recycling is strictly preferred. Individual banks would take one of three steps. They might manage their receivables directly in local currency. This is clearly the route for banks which are now in the debt–equity swap business for their own account or banks which have sought possibilities for expanding their activities in debtor countries. Rather than funding themselves through deposits, they will use their own capital in the form of local currency interest payments. A second group of banks might use their local currency receivables by having them managed by major host country financial institutions—banks, money market funds or funds that invest in real assets. A third group of banks would try and sell off their claims to avoid high transactions costs. This would typically be the case for small banks. They would sell their claims to investment funds. These funds (like the Korea Fund or the Brazil Fund that was just offered on the New York Stock Exchange) sell shares to the broad public and use the proceeds to buy assets in the debtor country. Buying claims from banks, possibly at a discount, would be a natural way of increasing the return to their shareholders.

It is instructive to go through the details of how banks would use the recycling funds to appreciate that what happens is basically a transformation of short-term, illiquid debt into long-term investment. That is an essential step in strengthening the possibilities of long-term growth in debtor countries, avoiding recurrent bouts of rescheduling with the attendant, massive capital flight. A scheme such as this could be likened to reconstruction programs like those administered after World War I or World War II. It would extend over a decade or so. Ultimately creditors would be able to recover their principal and accumulated earnings with a guarantee of no frivolous exchange losses.

Capital flight and bank runs

Return of flight capital would almost certainly be one of the favorable consequences of a recycling proposal. On the resource side, financial stability would be enhanced, which removes one reason for capital flight. Additionally, the sharp reduction in foreign exchange requirements for debt service clears the way for the large flow of imports required to sustain growth. The capital flight problem can be thought of like a bank run. If the public is concerned about the value of their assets they stage a run on the (central) bank and force depreciation. The belief that everybody else will do the same reinforces each individual investor's belief that he must move out of domestic assets because the general exodus will, inevitably, force depreciation. Hence the "run." But if the external balance constraint is suspended, via recycling, then there is no concern with exchange depreciation. On the contrary, the bank is safe and flight capital will return.

Today asset holders must wonder whether growth and debt service will be reconciled. As a result they hang on to their dollar positions even in the presence of extraordinarily high real interest rates. Paradoxically, if debt service can be recycled, Mexico may well have enough of a private capital inflow so that it actually can pay creditors a major part of debt service in dollars. Conversely, if creditors are adamant, private capital will stay abroad and creditors, in the end, risk getting nothing. Just as deposit insurance stabilizes banks, so does recycling stabilize the macroeconomy in a situation where there are two equilibria, one with capital moving out and the economy deteriorating, the other with capital flowing in and the economy returning to growth and financial stability.

The chief mode of operation of the recycling proposal is not to reduce the present value of obligations. The interest of debtors and creditors alike is to return the economy to a situation where growth and financial stability make debt service plausible. To do so there needs to be a temporary suspension of the external drain. But because private capital cannot be controlled effectively, there needs to be suspension of convertibility for the organized creditors. Diamond and Dybvig (1983, p. 418) have described funding crises for firms in terms that can easily be adapted to the problems of the Mexican economy faced by capital flight:

> Suppose one lender expects all other lenders to refuse to roll over their loan to the firm. Then, it may be his best response to refuse to roll over his loans even if the firm would be solvent if all loans were rolled over. Such liquidity crises are similar to bank runs. The protection from creditors provided by the bankruptcy laws serves a function similar to the suspension of convertibility (in a banking crisis). The firm which is viable but illiquid is guaranteed survival.

Suspension of convertibility for creditors could be done by a moratorium on interest payments or by paying interest into frozen accounts. These schemes inevitably are far more detrimental to creditors, and hence less acceptable, than recycling would be after even a brief period. If, as expected, it leads after a few years to a significant reflow of capital the means will be there to open the bank and allow withdrawals on a more stable basis.

16.4.5 *Risks for creditors*

There is a general recognition today that a resumption of growth and anything near full debt service are incompatible. Even moderate proposals, such as Feldstein (1986), recognize that at most a portion of debt service can be transferred without prejudicing the opportunities for growth. That raises the question how the rest of debt service is to be handled. One answer is that international financial institutions must assume an increasing role. This is, indeed, the banks' position as they ask for guarantees on any new money to be committed. Of course, increasing commitments by international agencies raises questions about equity: why bail out banks and Latin America rather than provide poverty relief in Africa? (See Buiter and Srinivasan, 1987.) Discussion is going in circles. In the meantime a debtor country like Mexico, having taken the first step toward growth in the form of fiscal stabilization, must move on or else face the risk of sliding back.

Mexican officials have always insisted that Mexico does not want confrontation on the debt. This position has once more been expressed by the Mexican debt negotiator, Jose Angel Gurria (1988) in his presentation to the official party's committee on international issues. But this time the official message went further: over the course of the next *sexennio*, Mexico must grow at 5–6 percent per annum to avoid further increases in unemployment. The financing of this growth path requires a significant increase in domestic saving and, as a complementary condition, the elimination of external transfers. Over the next few months, Gurria noted, every step would be undertaken to explore market-based, voluntary debt alternatives. If they should fail the international community must offer a solution or else face unilateral action.

No action is expected until a change in the US administration, in January 1989. The US Treasury's policy, stuck on a treadmill of pretense and make-believe, is likely to stall any fundamental change in policy during the election. But with a new administration a serious discussion of debt is unavoidable. At the time it is well to remember the conclusions of the report sponsored by the Royal Institute of International Affairs (1937):

> Maintenance of debt service upon the foreign capital invested in a country is affected by a number of factors. In the first place, creditors' receipts will be dependent not merely upon the ability but also the willingness of debtors to pay. Many countries have discontinued service payments on their debts even when their financial position was sufficiently sound to enable such payments to be made. Usually, defaults have taken place when the possibility of obtaining fresh supplies of capital seemed remote, and when appearances suggested that there was little to be gained—except in prestige from the fulfilment of obligations.

Appendix 16A: The budget and budget concepts

This appendix presents in Table 16A.1 data for the Mexican budget and offers a brief account of definitions and concepts used in the text. The purpose is to demonstrate that the operational deficit is the appropriate measure in judging the consistency of fiscal policy with only moderate inflation.

Buiter (1985) provides a definitive account of alternative budget measures (see, too, the presentation by Tanzi, Blejer, and Teijeiro 1987). We start with a review of the actual budget deficit, denoted by AD, its components and its financing. The budget deficit is financed in one of three ways: sale of securities to the banking

Table 16A.1 The budget deficit measures and financing (percentage of GDP)

	Total[a]	Primary	Operational[b]	Financing[c] Domestic	External
1965–69	1.8	—	1.3	2.4	1.2
1970–74	5.1	—	2.7	3.0	2.1
1975–79	8.1	2.5	4.4	3.9	4.0
1980–84	12.2	2.0	4.1	9.8	2.6
1985	10.0	−4.5	1.1	9.9	1.1
1986	16.0	−2.2	1.8	16.6	0.8
1987	15.8	−4.9	−1.2	11.6	1.4

[a] Financial deficit or public sector borrowing requirement.
[b] The operational deficit adjusts only for the inflationary erosion of public debt denominated in pesos.
[c] Financing of the financial deficit.
[d] 1977–79.
Source: Gil Díaz (1987b); and Banco de México, *Informe Anual*, 1986 and 1987.

system (i.e. money financing); sale of securities to the public or abroad; asset sales to the public or abroad.

Let $L = B + eB^* + H$ denote government liabilities, with B domestic liabilities, B^* foreign liabilities in foreign currency, e the exchange rate, and H standing for monetary liabilities, i.e. high-powered money. The price level is denoted by P. Then:

$$DL/P = \text{Budget deficit} = AD \tag{16A.1}$$

On the outlay side of the budget a distinction is made of three separate items: the noninterest deficit, NID; inflation-adjusted interest payments on domestic debt plus the value (unadjusted) of external interest payments, $rB + i^*eB^*$; and the inflationary component of domestic interest payment, pB.

$$AD = NID + rB + i^*eB^* + pB \tag{16A.2}$$

where AD is the actual budget deficit, NID the noninterest budget deficit, p the rate of inflation, r the home real interest rate (i.e. nominal rate less inflation), and i^* the foreign interest rate.

Inflation-adjusted budgeting can best be understood in terms of the economic definition of the budget. The economic definition of the budget, referred to here as the economic budget deficit, is the increase in the real value of total net government liabilities. We denote the economic deficit by ED and distinguish it from the actual deficit or public sector borrowing requirement.

$$D(L/P) = \text{Change in the real value of government liabilities} = ED \tag{16A.3}$$

An increase in the real value of liabilities is interpreted as a deficit, a reduction as a surplus. This economic deficit can be related to the actual deficit. From the definition of (L/P) we have:

$$D(L/P) = DL/P - p(L/P) \tag{16A.4}$$

Accordingly the economic deficit is equal to the actual deficit less the inflationary erosion of government liabilities.

$$ED = AD - \text{Inflationary erosion of all government liabilities}$$

$$= AD - pH - pB - (p - d)eB^* \tag{16A.5}$$

where d denotes the rate of exchange depreciation. The basic point then is that measured deficits overstate the economic deficit because of the inflationary erosion of government liabilities. Now we can decompose the budget deficit as in equation (16A.1) to obtain:

$$ED = NID + rB + (i^* + d - p)eB^* - pH \tag{16A.6}$$

Assuming that the real exchange rate is constant, the term $d - p$ will cancel and we are left with the economic deficit as the sum of the noninterest deficit plus real interest payments on all debt less the inflationary erosion of the government's monetary liabilities.

Two central budget concepts can be explained in terms of this equation. The primary deficit is the noninterest deficit, NID. The operational deficit is the

Table 16B.2 Key macroeconomic data (percentage of GDP, unless otherwise mentioned)

Year	Growth (% p.a.)	Investment	Private saving	Budget deficit	Current account		Real exchange rate[b]	Real wage	Inflation (% p.a.)
					Total	NICA[a]			
1970	6.9	18.1	18.9	1.4	1.9	1.7	100	79	5.2
1971	4.1	18.8	18.0	0.8	1.1	0.8	99	87	5.2
1972	8.4	19.4	20.4	3.0	0.6	0.8	95	92	5.0
1973	8.4	20.6	21.5	4.0	1.0	1.4	99	90	12.0
1974	6.1	20.9	22.0	3.8	2.7	2.7	101	90	23.7
1975	5.6	21.6	21.4	4.9	3.3	2.9	101	93	15.1
1976	4.2	20.9	21.0	4.7	2.1	2.9	100	100	15.7
1977	3.4	18.8	22.2	5.4	-0.2	-0.1	89	102	28.9
1978	8.2	20.0	22.3	5.5	0.8	0.8	90	100	17.5
1979	9.1	22.0	22.4	6.3	2.4	1.6	94	99	18.2
1980	8.3	23.4	22.8	6.8	4.5	1.8	103	96	26.3
1981	7.9	24.9	23.1	13.6	5.1	2.7	115	99	27.9
1982	-0.5	21.0	25.6	16.2	-0.1	-2.6	83	100	63.0
1983	-5.2	16.0	22.9	8.5	-5.8	-10.3	79	77	101.8
1984	3.6	16.3	23.2	7.3	-5.6	-8.4	82	72	65.4
1985	2.7	16.9	23.8	8.3	-4.3	-5.7	91	73	57.7
1986	-3.8	15.5	n.a.	15.2	-1.0	-4.7	65	106	106.0
1987[c]	1.1	15.3	n.a.	15.8	3.1	—	67	—	140.0

[a] NICA = noninterest current account deficit.
[b] Index: 1980–82 = 100.
[c] Estimates.

Source: Banco de México, *Indicadores Económicos*, and Morgan Guaranty.

primary deficit plus real interest payments, $NID + rB + (i^*d - p)eB^*$. Neither of these two concepts measures the economic deficit; nor, however, does the actual deficit.

When inflation abruptly ends, different budget concepts are strongly affected. The actual budget deficit will decline because the inflationary component of interest vanishes. On the other hand, the inflationary erosion of real balances ceases and hence the economic budget deficit will increase unless there is an offsetting reduction in real interest payments or a reduction in the primary deficit. This increase in the economic deficit simply reflects the fact that the inflation tax pH is being abandoned when inflation ceases. Using Mexican 1987 data, the operational budget shows a surplus of 1.2 percent and inflationary erosion of real balances amounted to 3.6 percent of GDP. Thus, in 1987 there was an economic surplus of 4.7 percent of GDP. If inflation were to cease the economic surplus would shrink to the size of the operational surplus. This makes the case for using the operational budget as a measure of the economic deficit when there is no inflation.

Notes

1. For an impressive collection of historical statistics see Instituto Nacional de Estadística, Geografía e Informática, *Estadísticas Históricas de México*, Mexico, 1986.
2. For Mexican debt history of the nineteenth and twentieth centuries, see Turlington (1930), Tellez (1986) and Vogelsang (1987) in addition to the London and New York foreign bond holders' protective association publications.
3. At the end of 1982 private external debt was $18 billion. The government provided an exchange risk guarantee and peso financing for those firms which restructured their debts long-term (beyond eight years for principal, with a four-year grace period).
4. Dollarization refers to the holding of dollar-denominated deposits in Mexican banks, the so-called Mexdollars. The term also denotes more broadly the flight from local currency to dollars held in the form of either US currency or deposits in US banks. As an indication of the size of Mexican deposits in the US, more than 20 percent of bank deposits in El Paso (Texas) are owned by Mexicans. On dollarization, see especially Ortiz (1983), Ramírez-Rojas (1985) and Reynoso (1988).
5. See Lessard and Williamson (1987), Zedillo (1987), Deppler and Williamson (1987), Morgan Guaranty (1986a; 1986b), Khan and Ul Haque (1985) and Cuddington (1987), for discussion of conceptual issues and estimates for Mexico.
6. A real depreciation raises income from oil (at given production level) but also increases foreign debt service (for a given level of debt outstanding). Consequently, the budgetary effect of a real depreciation is proportional to the difference between the share of oil income in GDP and the share of debt service. In 1982 that difference amounted to about 8 percent of GDP. In 1984, following depreciation, it had risen to nearly 10 percent.
7. This section draws on Dornbusch and Simonsen (1987).
8. There is evidence of a ratchet effect; during high inflation the real money demand schedule shifts to the left and that shift is not subsequently reversed. Thus, an inflation history permanently damages the financial system.
9. As one US senator observed in the context of ending the war in Vietnam, successful policy is to "announce victory and get out."

10. If B is the external debt (in real pesos), Y real GDP and y the GDP growth rate, $\Delta b = \Delta B / Y - by$ where $b = B/Y$, the debt–income ratio. The increase in the debt, ΔB, is given by interest payments, $i*B$, plus the noninterest current account deficit. The latter is equal to the investment requirement determined by target growth, consumption and the level of output: $\Delta B = i*B + (I + C - Y)$ so that $\Delta b = (i* - y)b + (I/Y + C/Y - 1)$.

References

Bailey, N., and R. Cohen (1987) *The Mexican Time Bomb*. New York: Twentieth Century Fund.

Blanco, H., and P. Garber (1986) "Recurrent Devaluation and Speculative Attacks on the Mexican Peso." *Journal of Political Economy*.

Buiter, W. (1985) "A Guide to Public Sector Debt and Deficits." *Economic Policy*.

Buiter, W., and T. N. Srinivasan (1987) "Rewarding the Profligate and Punishing the Prudent and Poor: Some Recent Proposals for Debt Relief." *World Development*.

Cardoso, E., and S. Levy (1987) "Mexico". In R. Dornbusch and L. Helmers, eds, *The Open Economy*. Oxford: Oxford University Press.

Chenery, H. (1974) *Redistribution with Growth*. Oxford: Oxford University Press.

Cohen, D. (1985) "How to evaluate the solvency of an indebted nation." *Economic Policy*.

Cuddington, J. (1987) "Macroeconomic Determinants of Capital Flight: An Econometric Investigation". In D. Lessard and J. Williamson, eds, *Capital Flight and Third World Debt*. Washington, DC: Institute for International Economics.

Deppler, M. and M. Williamson (1987) "Capital Flight: Concepts, Measurement and Issues." IMF Staff Studies for the World Economic Outlook. Washington, DC: International Monetary Fund.

Diamond, D. and P. Dybvig (1983) "Bank Runs, Deposit Insurance and Liquidity." *Journal of Political Economy*. 91: 401–19.

Díaz Alejandro, C. (1964) *Exchange Devaluation in a Semi-Industrialized Country*. Cambridge, MA: MIT Press.

Dornbusch, R. (1986) "Special Exchange Rates for Capital Account Transactions." *World Bank Economic Review*, 1: 3–34.

Dornbusch, R. (1987) "Lessons from the German Inflation Experience of the 1920s." In R. Dornbusch, S. Fischer, and J. Bossens, eds, *Macroeconomics and Finance*. Cambridge, MA: MIT Press.

Dornbusch, R. and M. Simonsen (1987) *Inflation Stabilization with Incomes Policy Support*. New York: Group of Thirty.

Edwards, S. (1986) "The Pricing of Bonds and Bank Loans in International Markets." *European Economic Review*. 30: 565–90.

Eichengreen, B., and R. Portes (1988) "Settling defaults in the era of bond finance." CEPR Discussion Paper, No. 272.

Feldstein, M. (1986) "International Debt Service and Economic Growth: Some Simple Analytics." NBER Working Paper No. 2076.

Flood, R., and P. Garber (1984) "Collapsing Exchange Rate Regimes: Some Linear Examples." *Journal of International Economics*. 17: 1–13.

Gil Díaz, F. (1984) "Mexico's Path from Stability to Inflation." In A. Harberger, ed, *World Economic Growth*. San Francisco: Institute for Contemporary Studies.

Gil Díaz, F. (1985) *"Changing Strategies" in Mexico and the United States: Studies in Economic Interaction*. Boulder, CO: Westview Press.

Gil Díaz, F. (1987a) "Mexico's Experience with Foreign Aid." Mimeo, Banco de México.

Gil Díaz, F. (1987b) "Inflation and Inflation Stabilization: Lessons from Mexico." In M. Bruno, Guido di Tella, Rudiger Dornbusch and Stanley Fischer, eds, *Stopping High Inflation*. Cambridge, MA: MIT Press.

Gil Díaz, F. (1988) "Mexico's Debt Burden." Mimeo, Banco de México.

Gil Díaz, F., and R. Ramos Tercero (1988) "Lessons from Mexico." In M. Bruno *et al.*, eds, *Inflation Stabilization*. Cambridge, MA: MIT Press.

Goldsbrough, D. (1984) *Foreign Private Investment in Developing Countries*. Washington, DC: International Monetary Fund.

Gurria, J. A. (1988) "Política de Deuda y Financiamento Externo." Mimeo, Ministry of Finance, Mexico.

Khan, M. and N. Ul Haque (1985) "Foreign Borrowing and Capital Flight." *IMF Staff Papers*, 32: 606–28.

Kraft, J. (1984) *The Mexican Rescue*. New York: Group of Thirty.

Krugman, P. (1979) "A Model of Balance of Payments Crises." *Journal of Money, Credit and Banking*, 11: 311–25.

Krugman, P., and L. Taylor (1981) "The Contractionary Effect of Devaluation." *Journal of International Economics*, 11: 445–56.

Lessard, D., and J. Williamson (1987) *Capital Flight and Third World Debt*. Washington, DC: Institute for International Economics.

Lizondo, S. (1983) "Foreign Exchange Futures Prices under Fixed Exchange Rates." *Journal of International Economics*, 13: 69–84.

Marconi, Y. (1967) "Mexico's Economic and Financial Record." Board of Governors of the Federal Reserve Staff Economic Studies.

Morgan Guaranty (1986a) *World Financial Markets*, March.

Morgan Guaranty (1986b) *World Financial Markets*, September.

Ortiz, G. (1983) "Dollarization in Mexico: Causes and Consequences." In P. Aspe, R. Dornbusch and M. Obstfeld, eds, *Financial Policies and the World Capital Market. The Case of Latin America*. Chicago: University of Chicago Press.

Portes, R. (1987) "Debt and the Market." Mimeo, CEPR.

Ramírez-Rojas, C. (1985) "Currency Substitution in Argentina, Mexico and Uruguay." *IMF Staff Papers*, 33: 629–67.

Reynoso, A. (1988) "Capital Flight: The Case of Missing Markets." Mimeo, MIT.

Royal Institute of International Affairs (1937) *The Problem of International Investment*. London: Oxford University Press.

Rubio, L., and F. Gil Díaz (1987) *A Mexican Response*. New York: Twentieth Century Fund.

Sargent, T. (1986) *Rational Expectations and Inflation*. New York: Harper and Row.

Selowsky, M., and H. van der Tak (1986) "The Debt Problem and Growth." *World Development*, 14: 1107–24.

Serven, L. (1986) "The Effects of Devaluation." Unpublished Ph.D. dissertation, Massachusetts Institute of Technology.

Solis, L., and E. Zedillo (1985) "The Foreign Debt of Mexico." In G. Smith and J. Cuddington, eds, *International Debt and the Developing Countries*. Washington, DC: World Bank.

Summers, R., and A. Heston (1984) "Improved International Comparisons of Real Product and its Composition." *Review of Income and Wealth*, 30: 207–62.

Tanzi, V., M. Blejer and M. Teijeiro (1987) "Inflation and the Measurement of Fiscal Deficits." *IMF Staff Papers*, 34: 711–38.

Tellez, L. (1986) "Essays of an Open Economy: The Case of Mexico." Unpublished dissertation, Massachusetts Institute of Technology, Cambridge, MA.

Turlington, E. (1930) *Mexico and Her Foreign Creditors*. New York: Columbia University Press.

Vogelsang, T. (1987) "Determinants of Mexican Bond Prices for the Period 1919–1931." Mimeo, Massachusetts Institute of Technology.

World Bank (1987) *Mexico after the Oil Boom*, Washington, DC.

Zedillo, E. (1985) "The Mexican External Debt: The Last Decade." In M. Wionczek, ed., *Politics and Economics of the External Debt Crisis*. Boulder, CO: Westview Press.

Zedillo, E. (1987) "Case Studies: Mexico." In D. Lessard and J. Williamson, eds, *Capital Flight and Third World Debt*. Washington, DC: Institute for International Economics.

17

Mexico:
How to recover stability and growth

After the collapse of the European Monetary System—the currency crises of September 1992 were nothing less— the enthusiasm for monetary integration in North America must be dampened. This is all the more the case in that Mexico's situation is not unlike that of Italy or Britain. Mexico is defending a patently overvalued exchange rate by high interest rates and an apparently unyielding commitment to avoid depreciation. Just as in the case of peripheral EMS members, moving forward toward tighter commitments and less central bank independence is tempting because it would seem to give credibility relief in a situation where high interest rates are straining growth and financial stability.

A monetary arrangement cannot do miracles. History is not a seamless web; events such as the US Congressional vote on NAFTA or the Mexican presidential election in 1994 will become the focal points for speculative attacks. How, then, can crisis be avoided? The recommendation here is to accept higher inflation rather than keep living on the verge of a speculative attack.

The paper briefly reviews Mexican exchange rate history. It proceeds from there to the current predicament. The concluding section reviews immediate policy alternatives.

17.1   History

Financial instability in Mexico dates back to the mid-1970s, in the aftermath of the oil price increases. In the period from 1955 to 1975 the exchange rate was fixed and the currency was freely convertible; public finance was sound, money was managed conservatively, and inflation remained moderate.

The interlude of stability ended with the oil bonanza. Inflation jumped rapidly from 5 to 12 and then 25 percent. In 1975–76 the first devaluation in two decades disrupted financial stability. Inflation, which had been less than 5 percent for two decades went double-digit and never came back to this day (see Table 17.1).

Table 17.1 Mexican macro history

Period	Inflation	Growth	Current account[a]
1965–69	3.5	6.8	−2.2
1970–74	10.2	6.8	−2.8
1975–79	19.0	6.1	−3.6
1980–84	53.7	2.7	−2.1
1985–89	77.3	1.0	−0.4

[a]Percentage of GDP.

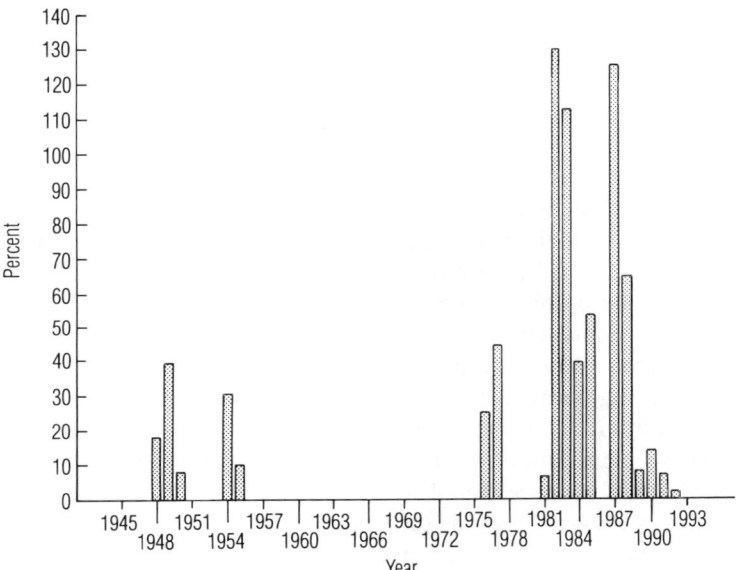

Figure 17.1 Peso depreciation (percent per year relative to US$).

Even though inflation performance deteriorated, the period of high oil prices meant continuing strong growth. External borrowing which had already become significant in the early 1970s was kept up and in fact increased. Inflation increased, currency overvaluation became larger, capital flight started and then everything collapsed. By 1982, Mexico was unable to roll its debts and went into moratorium followed by concerted lending.[1]

The rest of the decade, with continuing debt problems aggravated by high world interest rates and domestic financial instability, meant low growth and massive real depreciation. Populism had its play for a brief while in 1982, including exchange control and bank nationalization. But then the pendulum swung massively in the other direction. For the past six to eight years conservative reform has been under way.[2] The current account deficit declined,

Table 17.2 Mexico: current economic indicators

	1988	1989	1990	1991	1992[c]	1993[c]
Growth	1.7	3.3	4.4	3.6	2.7	3.0
Inflation	114.2	20.0	26.7	18.8	11.2	7.0
Budget[a]	−3.6	−1.7	1.8	2.7	2.9	2.1
Current account[b]	−2.4	−3.9	−7.1	−13.3	−20.0	
Import growth	36.7	21.3	18.8	16.6	12.3	9.1
Export growth	5.8	2.5	3.5	5.1	2.2	4.6

[a]Operational budget as % of GDP, excluding debt reduction and privatization.
[b]$US billion.
[c]Government forecast.
Source: Banco de México.

much lower oil prices notwithstanding, the budget was balanced, and inflation was brought down from a peak level of 160 percent reached in 1987. The adjustment took a heavy toll:

- real wages declined by at least 30 percent;
- per-capita real GDP fell by 15 percent;
- investment declined to only 17.6 percent on average in the period 1985–91.

But in 1990 the first payoff on reform and stabilization was apparent. Growth increased substantially (even in per-capita terms it became positive), inflation declined, and foreign capital rushed in. But almost at the same time an exchange rate overvaluation started developing.

17.2 The problem

The current problem of the Mexican economy is the overvalued exchange rate. There are two immediate symptoms of the overvaluation. One is the large increase of Mexican wholesale prices (in dollars) relative to those in the United States. This is shown in Figure 17.2. We return to this figure, but already note now the clear election-year collapse pattern.

The other symptom is the large deterioration of the trade balance and the current account. The trade balance (Figure 17.3) showed a surplus in the early 1980s, but by now comes to a deficit of close to $20 billion at an annual rate. The current account, as a percentage of GDP reaches now 5–6 percent, the same size as just prior to the debt crisis.

There are four separate reasons for the large trade deterioration. The first is trade liberalization: Mexico was a closed economy to all intents and purposes. And if it was not quite that, the payments crisis of the early 1980s did the rest. Quotas abounded and tariff rates were as high as 100 percent. Import permits were a routine requirement.

Over the past six years trade has been liberalized on a unilateral basis. Table

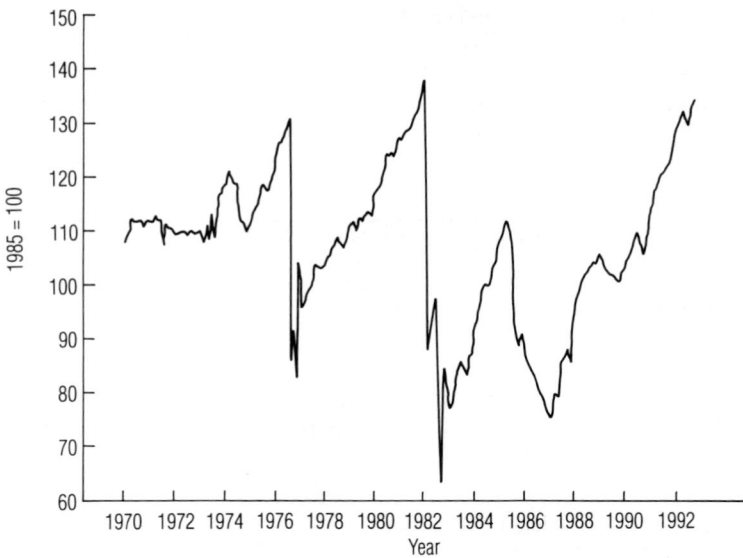

Figure 17.2 Mexico–USA: relative wholesale prices.

Figure 17.3 Mexico: trade balance.

Table 17.3 Import increase (US$ billion)

	1986	1991
Imports	12.4	38.2
Consumer goods	0.8	5.6
Intermediates	8.6	24.1
Capital goods	3.0	8.5

Source: Banco de México.

Table 17.4 Mexican trade restrictions (percent)

	1985	1989
Import license coverage	92.2	22.3
Reference price coverage	18.7	0
Maximum tariff	100.0	20.0
Average tariff	23.5	12.5

Source: USITC.

17.4 shows in one way the extent of liberalization. But a more tangible way is, of course, to look at the massive deterioration of the trade balance. Note from Table 17.2 that strong import growth, not negative export performance, is the basis for trade deterioration.

If trade problems are to be avoided, trade liberalization should be accompanied by real depreciation. The opening on the side of imports proceeds at a far more rapid pace than any beneficial effects on the export side. True, better intermediate goods, for example, may help make exports more competitive and better machinery may put some industries in a position to produce at quality levels appropriate for demanding outside markets. But these adjustment are far more time-consuming than the immediate response on the import side. Moreover, with financial constraints and poor growth, importing is a far easier way of pursuing a modernization strategy than to try and replicate foreign goods for the home market.

In sum, trade liberalization creates a presumption that real depreciation is appropriate; if it does not happen there is overvaluation.

The second reason for the large trade deterioration is lower oil prices: except for a brief upward flurry during the Gulf War, oil prices in dollars are far below the levels of the early 1980s. As a result, Mexican oil export revenues in 1991 were only half those of 1984.

The third reason is stronger growth: the increase in demand naturally spills over into increased imports. This effect is more important in that low levels of capacity in Mexico, because of many years of low investment, reduce the ability of firms to meet increased demand.

Higher demand growth also translates into imports because of higher investment to expand capacity and increasing levels of intermediate goods imports.

The fourth reason is overvaluation: real appreciation must certainly also account for some of the trade deterioration. As Figure 17.2 shows, Mexican wholesale prices in dollars relative to those in the United States have increased since their bottom in 1986 by 50 percent. For the moment we focus merely on the increase without passing judgment on how much is *over*valuation. The mere fact of an increase ought to worsen the trade balance.

Before moving to policy responses, we present briefly a stylized model of exchange rate-based stabilization and the resulting risk of overvaluation.

17.3 Explaining overvaluation

There are two competing interpretations for the real appreciation. One direction is decidedly classical—new or old. In this rendition an *autonomous* capital inflow translates into an increase in absorption. With an increase in demand relative to available output, the prices of nontraded goods rise relative to tradables, as does the full employment wage. The capital flow itself would be explained by renewed access to world capital markets and the resulting relaxation of credit constraints in the home economy. The link from capital inflows to spending can be based on the cost of capital arguments or on an expansion of credit and reduced credit rationing.

The end of the episode, in this appreciation, comes from the sudden withdrawal of capital. The resulting cut in spending and financing forces a sharp real depreciation. A major inflation or a sharp fall in output would not be part of this story and hence puts in question this interpretation.

The alternative hypothesis focuses on cost-based pricing, exchange rate setting and wage setting. The simplest model is an accelerationist Phillips curve where inflation increases when wage increases and depreciation outpace the prevailing rate of inflation. A simple model helps formulate the problem of real currency appreciation.[3] Let P, W, and E be the log level of prices, wages and the exchange rate, and lower-case letters stand for their rates of change, with π the rate of inflation. The unemployment rate (or the GDP gap) is represented by y.

$$\dot{\pi} = (1 - \alpha)(w - \pi) + \alpha(e - \pi) \tag{17.1}$$

$$w = \pi - \sigma y \tag{17.2}$$

$$y = \theta(i^* + e + \Delta - \pi) - \lambda(E - P) + f \tag{17.3}$$

$$CA = \mu(E - P) + v(i^* + \Delta + e - \pi) + \rho f \tag{17.4}$$

where i^* and i are foreign and home interest rates and Δ denotes the political risk premium. Fiscal restraint is denoted by f, and the current account surplus is denoted by CA.

Equation (17.1) represents a standard accelerations pricing equation: inflation has inertia.[4] Deceleration is only possible if wage inflation or the rate of currency

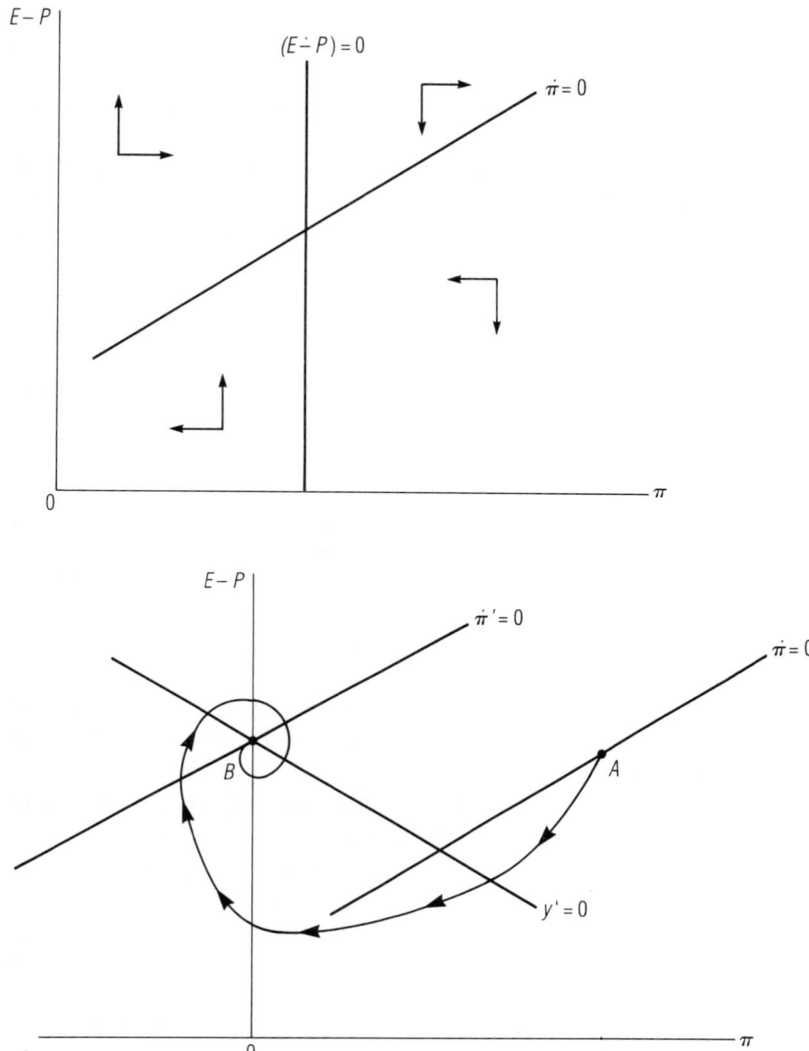

Figure 17.4

depreciation can be brought down below the prevailing rate of inflation. Equation (17.2) describes wage inflation. The rate of increase of wages, because of explicit or implicit indexation, is equal to the rate of inflation but with an adjustment for cyclical conditions. In equation (17.3) the unemployment rate is determined by real interest rates and by the level of competitiveness.

Figure 17.4 shows the phase diagram of this model, using equation (17.3) and the combination of equations (17.1) and (17.2):

$$\dot{\pi} = \gamma(e - \pi) + (1 - \alpha)\lambda(E - P) - (1 - \alpha)\theta(i^* + \Delta)$$
$$\gamma = [\alpha - (1 - \alpha)\theta] \tag{17.5}$$

The diagram is drawn for a given rate of depreciation e_0 and it is assumed that the term γ is positive.

Consider now a program of disinflation. Starting in a steady state at point A, the government reduces the rate of depreciation to zero and sustains the now fixed exchange rate. The new long-run equilibrium is at point B where inflation has come down to zero.

The immediate impact of the rate fixing is to cut nominal interest rates and hence the real interest rate so that demand increases. Higher demand and the elimination of depreciation next lead to real *appreciation*. The instant rise in the level of demand, output and employment gradually wears off. Ultimately the loss in competitiveness returns the economy to normal levels of output and then creates a recession. The economy will return to full equilibrium, with reduced inflation, only after *de*flation has restored the initial level of competitiveness. Protracted unemployment is the rule. Moreover, in the early phases of the adjustment program the current account turns toward deficit.

The model is oversimplified in a number of respects. First, there are no lags in the adjustment of demand and the current account to changes in the real exchange rate. In addition, the adjustment to real exchange rate changes assumes an immediate dominance of substitution effects, contrary to the Díaz Alejandro hypothesis. Second, the monetary mechanism operates entirely through interest rates and there is no special role for credit or confidence. Third, wealth effects and asset processes play no role.

Even though these aspects of the adjustment process are absent, the highly stylized model captures the patterns of the adjustment process. It highlights, in particular, that on the way to full disinflation high unemployment and large deficits constitute major confidence blocks to the continuation of the program. And if confidence does break down, so does the financing of external imbalances. Interest rates will soar, output will fall faster and ultimately the program is abandoned.

The discussion of Mexico's program would not be complete without an important emphasis on incomes policy. The inflation reduction from triple-digit levels was achieved substantially by a program of containing wage increases. Reflecting the *pacto*, the wage formula might be written as in equation (17.2a) below, where institutional real wage compression takes the role of unemployment in reducing current wage settlements *below* the prevailing rate of inflation.[5] Given such a wage policy, exchange rate policy also makes a contribution by cutting depreciation below the prevailing rate of inflation.

$$w = \gamma\pi - \sigma y \qquad 0 < \gamma < 1 \tag{17.2a}$$

The success of the incomes policy might be measured by the disinflation. On that measure, it has unquestionably been successful; but that is not enough. The extra test is whether the real exchange rate has remained competitive, and here

Mexico has probably failed. But before declaring failure, it is appropriate to investigate some arguments that justify substantial real appreciation.

17.4 Counter-arguments

There are basically two arguments in support of the view that Mexico's real exchange rate, all appearances notwithstanding, is not really overvalued. The first argument compares Mexico in 1986 and 1992. In 1986 Mexico was on the ropes; access to the world capital market had been cut off, inflation was extreme, reforms had barely begun and capital flight remained a serious issue. In this precarious economy that was basically under siege, the real exchange rate just had to be rock-bottom low.

Consider next 1992: reforms on an extraordinary scale have moved Mexico to the forefront of high performance in policy around the world; world capital markets are therefore allowing Mexico to borrow with ratings upgraded steadily; capital is flowing in at rates that are almost troublesome. The stock market in dollars increased by 400 percent over the 1988–91 period. This is an economy where there is a reform bonus to be collected, and that means real appreciation. In fact, the argument can be made that it is the inflow of capital that is the driving force of inflation and real appreciation.[6] The argument is entirely correct for the case of Mexico, just as it was correct in Spain. The only question is how much of a real appreciation is warranted.

Here another argument comes into play, again drawing on the analogy with Spain. The forthcoming ratification of NAFTA creates incentives for US capital and capital from other industrialized countries to be invested in Mexico. The financing of external imbalances is thus at best a short-term problem—from here to spring or, at worst, fall of 1993 when NAFTA is completed. Once direct investment flows come on stream there is medium-term financing which bridges the gap between modernization that is under way and the ultimate payoff in a strong export base. The argument is rounded off by highlighting that a significant portion of the trade imbalance reflects investment goods so that at best there is a mismatch between the hot money funding and the cool investments.

One further argument in support of the status quo runs this way: there is now a budget surplus in Mexico. A country with a budget surplus cannot have financial instability. The external deficits are private, the government is managing public finance very conservatively—this is not Italy!

There is no question that normalization must yield *some* bonus in terms of real appreciation. The central question is when it should be collected. The risk of the current strategy is that it is collected as a prepayment, before reforms fully carry their benefits and while trade deficits are large by historical standards and growing. The risk of the present strategy is that Mexico could be caught with large deficits and no financing, being forced into abrupt and massive real depreciation or the reintroduction of severe trade controls. Relying on the farsightedness of foreign investors seems a precarious strategy.

In summary, the exchange rate is overvalued *and* on current policy will become more overvalued over the next year. The current pace of the crawl—about 4 percent per year—falls far short of the inflation rate which, although declining, is still running at about 10 percent. It is not implausible that inflation convergence will occur only after another 5 percent loss in competitiveness. Moreover, there is no automatic mechanism in place to revert the loss in competitiveness. That, of course, implies extra vulnerability, and is reminiscent of Chile in the late 1970s. To draw attention to the parallel we spend a moment reviewing the Chilean experience.

17.5 The Chilean experience, 1979–82

An immediate example of the problem at hand is Chile in the 1970s. Chile then was much in the same position as Mexico today: the budget had been balanced, trade had been liberalized, reform was pervasive. But inflation remained as a significant irritant. To bring down inflation, an exchange-rate-oriented stabilization was designed; massive real appreciation ensued. At first the appreciation was justified by the improved prospects of a reforming and modernizing economy. Next they were explained by real appreciation under the pressure of capital inflows. The declining rate of loss of competitiveness was offered as the promise of an ultimate recovery of competitiveness. Then, finally, external events—the debt crisis—pulled the rug from under the currency. Of course, the implication is not that everything would otherwise have gone well. Rather it is that the country's vulnerability had become such that any major event would be enough to trigger the collapse.

The Chilean events are clear-cut. Major reforms, including balancing the budget, had put Chile on a path of stability. Inflation was the remaining blemish. With a heavy dose of the law of one price, it was easy to imagine that a vicious circle of inflation and depreciation was at work. If depreciation could be stopped, via a number of channels from expectations to competition, inflation would come down rapidly. Following on that logic, the peso was fixed in 1979 and kept at 39 pesos to the dollar until 1982.

Table 17.5 shows clearly the success of the strategy: inflation did fall and by 1982 had indeed become moderate and even not far out of line with the then high world inflation. But in the transition, inflation in dollars exceeded world inflation all the time and as a result a major real appreciation ensued.

Of course, in the initial stages the strategy commanded great popularity. Real wages were rising steeply, which fueled demand and growth. Over time, though, the combined effects of trade opening and real appreciation created a widening trade deficit, a slowdown in demand growth and rising unemployment. The end of the episode was the dramatic collapse of the bubble in 1982.

Needless to say, Chile learned a lesson from the 1978–82 adventure. Subsequent exchange rate policy was exemplary and supported strong recovery and growth even if it did help achieve a dramatic disinflation.

Table 17.5 Chile's adventure: 1979–82

	1979	1980	1981	1982
Inflation				
CPI	33	35	20	10
WPI	49	40	9	7
Wages	47	46	29	11
Depreciation	18	5	0	31
Trade balance[a]	−0.4	−0.8	−2.7	0.1
Growth	8.3	7.8	5.5	−14.1

[a]$US billion.
Source: IMF.

17.6 Possible policy responses

In this section we explore several strategies for dealing with the overvaluation problem and moving to a stable financial system.

The first is: sit tight, don't blink, do nothing. This option recognizes that doing anything different from what is done is politically difficult and therefore not acceptable. In this perspective, the problem is minimized by appealing to the fact that unit labor costs in the maquila industry are already increasing at no more than the US pace, that CPI-based real exchange rate comparisons are inappropriate because many subsidy removals that affect consumers do not affect competitiveness. The perspective also highlights the imminent favorable effects of a NAFTA conclusion—specifically, major capital inflows in the form of direct investment.

The basic posture is to start from the end, the premise that nothing *can* be done, and proceed from there to rationalize that nothing *need* be done, really. The position is *locally* stable since the public deeply believes that the government would hate to do anything. Therefore, until a major focal point occurs, the situation can evolve as it has over the past year without the risk of a run.

There is a powerful line of argument that seeks to underpin the do-nothing strategy by institutional mechanisms: specifically, the creation of an independent central bank. Italy's example shows that the shift to a far more independent central bank held off the crisis for a while because real interest rates were raised to the sky, but it did not prevent the run.

The second strategy is: hold on, make a recession. This position does recognize that there is a problem and that something has to be done. But because inflation is accepted as the overriding priority, the only strategy left is to slow down the economy forcefully by a tighter fiscal stance and by tight money. Growth has already come down to only about 2 percent, and 1993 will have that and not much more. That rate, of course, lies even below the rate of labor force growth and thus is far, far away from a growth sufficient to avoid rising unemployment. If the Okun's law estimate in the USA is a 2.5 percent growth so as to keep unemployment constant, the equivalent number in Mexico is 4 percent or even higher.

The problem with this strategy is that it aborts the very implementation of modernization and reform. Investment will not pick up, political popularity of reform will fade and by the time the election comes, there is no assurance that all is well. The calculation that there will be a substantial cushion for a sharp growth spurt in 1994 may turn out to be wrong. In fact, the strategy may well run into conflict, with increasing uncertainty about the sustainability of the parity; increasing real interest rates even beyond current levels (see Figure 17.5) will then create far more of a crunch than is now expected. Ultimately the strategy may fail, just as it did in the United Kingdom.

The third strategy is a last maxi-devaluation. For many observers outside Mexico (excluding this author), devaluation UK-style is the obvious answer. Devalue the peso by, say, 20 percent, declare that this is the very last time, and enjoy prosperity for ever more. To enhance credibility, accompany the devaluation by a major fortification of the monetary institutions: an independent central bank, a constitutionally fixed parity, etc.

The trouble with this strategy is that it will wreak havoc in financial markets and in the labor market. In financial markets it has come to be expected that the government will not devalue—if there are problems, the pace of the crawl picks up, but no discrete parity changes. Reversal of this established mode would take the financial market back to the mid-1980s and it might prejudice the newly gained access to world capital markets.

In the labor market, a devaluation would cause conflict. Labor has cooperated

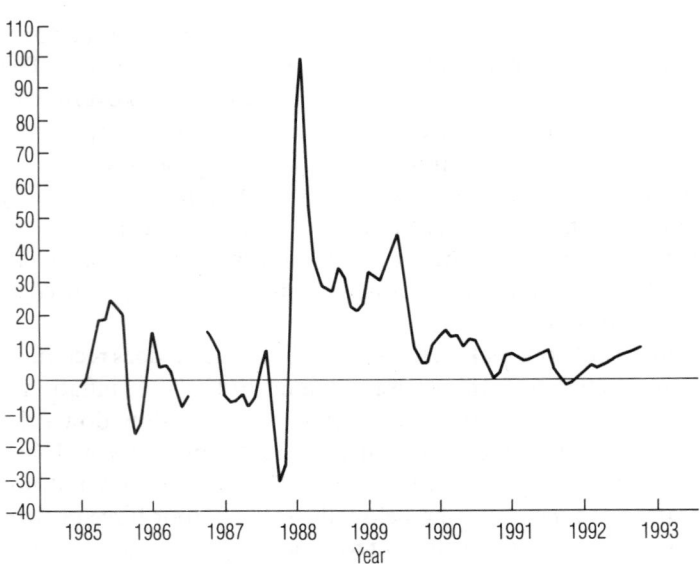

Figure 17.5 Mexico: real interest rate on CETES (WPI adjusted, annual rates).

in a number of *pactos* and by now there is clearly *pacto*-fatigue. A devaluation would be a confrontational breach of arrangements that might well lead to political mobilization and from there to increasing uncertainty about the course of capital flight and about inflation.

The fourth strategy is to increase the pace of the crawl. This strategy is condemned as being out-and-out inflationary. The most adamant opposition assets that the *real* exchange rate cannot be changed by a faster crawl—inflation will simply pick up and that is that. Of course, one cannot defend that view and at the same time applaud the recent shift of the crawl from 2 to 4 percent per year.

The strategy of a faster crawl would accept an increase of inflation to 15–18 percent as the price for gaining competitiveness and the price for avoiding a recurrence of the exchange rate and social crises of the past election years. The pace of the crawl would be stepped up immediately to 22 percent per year, declining slowly toward 17 percent over 18 months. With current inflation near 10 percent, the real exchange rate would start depreciating. Of course, inflation would gradually rise—more so the less success there is in containing wage adjustments. Over 18 months the depreciation and inflation rates would converge somewhere around 17 percent. That, unfortunately, represents a high level of inflation, but it is far better than a collapse of the exchange rate, also followed by inflation but quite possibly also by a loss of control.

It helps to return to Chile's case. Over the past decade Chile's inflation has averaged 13 percent and nobody seems to notice. The reason is Chile's economic miracle—an average growth rate of 22 percent per year. Chile has the right priorities, reform, and growth. Fighting inflation to the bitter end always means the bitter end of the policy, not the end of inflation. The notion that prosperity can emerge in an economy that is under siege, as Mexico's is, defies all good economic theory. Inflation is a very serious problem and the authorities are right to have taken it down to less than 20 percent.

The art of inflation fighting is to know when to stop. A wise US senator, when asked for counsel advice on what to do about the unending Vietnam war, advised: declare victory and get out. Mexico's authorities should reassess their priorities and shift to a model where growth comes first, but inflation is firmly contained at a 20 percent barrier. That is possible, as Chile's example of the past decade shows quite convincingly.

17.7 And then?

The suggestion that Mexico should crawl faster, recover competitiveness and accept inflation in the upper teens is profoundly unsatisfying for those who look to monetary arrangements as a key ingredient in economic success. Would it not be a good idea to join a North American monetary union and abolish the peso altogether? Would inflation not be gone with a stroke of the pen and interest rate premiums down to nothing?

Mexican insistence on its national identity and independence, more even than Canada's, makes a dollarization implausible (unlike in Argentina), at least in the near term. Running macroeconomics with a view to a distant fixed rate, should disinflation succeed, is immensely costly. It has just failed in Europe— France is still in the ring, the peripheral countries have already been carried off stage. Hard money talk has had a decade; it is time for pragmatism to take over again. Pragmatism does not mean acceptance of any inflation; it simply means that growth also counts. Disregard for growth ultimately means the hard money strategy will fail.

Notes

1. See Cardoso and Levy (1988) and Dornbusch (1988).
2. See Aspe (1992), Ortiz (1991), Ize and Ortiz (1987), Gil Díaz and Ramos Tercero (1988), and Loser and Kalter (1992).
3. See also Dornbusch (1979), Rodriguez (1982), Dornbusch and de Pablo (1990) and Edwards (1989).
4. On the disinflation problem, see Calvo (1983), Chadha, Masson and Meredith (1992), Dornbusch and Fischer (1993), Edwards and Montiel (1989), and Vegh (1992).
5. With productivity growth there is room for some growth in real wages even with a disinflation strategy. But the need for fiscal balancing by removing subsidies to consumers works in the other direction.
6. See Hanson (1992). Mathieson and Rojas-Suarez (1992), and Calvo, Leiderman, and Reinhart (1992) on the opening of capital accounts in connection with real appreciation. Here the return to voluntary lending is equivalent to a capital account opening.

References

Agenor, P., J. Bhandari, and R. Flood (1992) "Speculative Attack Models of Balance of Payments Crises." *IMF Staff Papers*, June.

Aspe, P. (1992) *Stabilization and Reform. The Mexican Way.* Cambridge, MA: MIT Press.

Banco de México, S.A. *The Mexican Economy* (annual), various issues.

Bufman, G., and L. Leiderman (1992) "Israel's Stabilization: Some Important Policy Lessons." Mimeo, Tel Aviv University.

Calvo, G. (1983) "Staggered Contracts and Exchange Rate Policy." In J. Frenkel, ed., *Exchange Rates and International Macroeconomics.* Chicago: University of Chicago Press.

Calvo, G., L. Leiderman, and C. Reinhart (1992) "Capital Inflows and Real Exchange Rate Appreciation in Latin America: The Role of External Factors." Mimeo, International Monetary Fund.

Cardoso, E., and S. Levy (1987) "Mexico." In R. Dornbusch and L. Helmers, eds, *The Open Economy: Tools for Policymakers in Developing Countries.* Oxford: Oxford University Press.

Chadha, B., P. Masson, and G. Meredith (1992) "Models of Inflation and the Costs of Disinflation." *IMF Staff Papers*, June.

Dornbusch, R. (1979) *Open Economy Macroeconomics.* New York: Basic Books.

Dornbusch, R. (1988) "Mexico: Stabilization, Debt and Growth." *Economic Policy*, 7:

233–81. (See also Chapter 16, this volume.)

Dornbusch, R., and J. C. de Pablo (1990) "Debt and Macroeconomic Instability in Argentina." In J. Sachs, ed., *Developing Country Debt and Economic Performance*. Chicago: University of Chicago Press. (See also Chapter 18, this volume.)

Dornbusch, R. and S. Fischer (1993) "Moderate Inflation." *World Bank Economic Review* 7: 1–44.

Dornbusch, R., F. Sturzenegger and H. Wolf (1990) "Extreme Inflation: Stabilization and Dynamics." *Brookings Papers on Economic Activity* 2: 1–84.

Edwards, S. (1989) *Real Exchange Rates, Devaluation, and Adjustment*. Cambridge, MA: MIT Press.

Edwards, S., and P. Montiel (1989) "Devaluation Crises and the Macroeconomic Consequences of Postponed Adjustment in Developing Countries." *IMF Staff Papers*, December.

Hanson, J. (1992) "Opening the Capital Account." World Bank, Working Paper WPS 901.

Gil Díaz, F., and R. Ramos Tercero (1988) "Lessons from Mexico." In M. Bruno *et al.*, eds, *Inflation Stabilization*. Cambridge, MA: MIT Press.

Ize, A., and G. Ortiz (1987) "Fiscal Rigidities, Public Debt, and Capital Flight." *IMF Staff Papers*, June.

Khor, H., and L. Rojas-Suarez (1991) "Interest Rates in Mexico." *IMF Staff Papers*, December.

Loser, C., and E. Kalter (1992) *Mexico: The Strategy to Achieve Sustained Economic Growth*. IMF Occasional Paper No. 99.

Mathieson, D., and L. Rojas-Suarez (1992) "Liberalization of the Capital Account." Mimeo WP/92/46, IMF.

McLeod, D., and J. Welch (1991) "North American Free Trade and the Peso." Mimeo, Fordham University.

Ortiz, G. (1991) "Mexico Beyond the Debt Crisis: Toward Sustainable Growth With Price Stability." In M. Bruno *et al.*, eds, *Lessons of Economic Stabilization and Its Aftermath*. Cambridge, MA: MIT Press.

Rodriguez, C. A. (1982) "The Argentine Stabilization Plan of Dec 20." *World Development*, 10: 801–11.

Taussig, F. (1928) *International Trade*. New York: Macmillan.

Vegh, C. (1992) "Stopping High Inflation." *IMF Staff Papers* 39(3): 626–95.

18

Debt and macroeconomic instability in Argentina

with Juan Carlos de Pablo

18.1 Introduction

In 1985, after 40 years of financial instability, Argentina reached once again near-hyperinflation conditions. Budget deficits were the immediate cause, but the deeper roots must be seen in ill-fated policy experiments of the 1970s. The destructive pendulum between populists and market-oriented reformists has meant that much of the national wealth is held abroad, taxes are paid by only a few, and the general atmosphere is one of skepticism about everything Argentine. Mallon and Sourrouille (1975, p. 11) have drawn attention to this steady conflict when they write:

> Decision makers in Argentina have quite consistently attempted to adopt policy positions that seemed designed to tear society apart rather than to forge new coalitions. . . . Major policy disagreements in modern Argentine history have their main roots in the conflict between two divergent streams of thought: liberalism of the British Manchester School variety and what can be called national populism. . . . In general, the liberals have stood for the virtues of a society open to international opportunities and influences, whereas the national populists have emphasized indigenous, autonomous development.

This paper investigates the interaction between domestic macroeconomic instability and external constraints. We study these relationships by focusing on the past decade in which four very different periods can be distinguished:

1. The Martínez de Hoz period of the second half of the 1970s when external debts were accumulated in the context of an incompatible mix of policies: persistent deficits, a strongly overvalued currency, and liberalization of capital flows.
2. The period running from the end of the 1970s to the hyperinflation. In this period debt and foreign exchange problems, war and domestic politics are the reasons for an inflation explosion.

3. The Austral stabilization plan.
4. The post-Austral quest for a resumption of growth.

18.2 A long-run perspective

Although we only focus on the past ten years, we place our analysis in a long-run context. This is appropriate since debt problems and financial crises are at least 100 years old in Argentina. One hundred years ago Argentina's inability to service foreign debt nearly brought down the City of London in the famous Baring panic of 1890; the Tornquist monetary reform dates back to 1899.

It is important to view developments in this long-term perspective because it highlights how Argentina has lost its position in the world economy steadily during this century.[1] Carlos Díaz Alejandro (1970, p. 1) reminds us of this decline:

> It is common nowadays to lump the Argentine economy in the same category with the economies of other Latin American nations. Some opinion even puts it among such less developed nations as India and Nigeria. Yet most economists writing during the first three decades of this century would have placed Argentina among the most advanced countries—with Western Europe, the United States, Canada, and Australia. To have called Argentina "underdeveloped" in the sense that word has today would have been considered laughable.

If in 1900 Argentina had a US standard of living, then the decline has been long and deep. Summers and Heston (1984) estimate that in 1950 Argentina had only 41 percent of the US standard of living (against 80 percent in Australia and Canada). By 1985 the standard of living had slipped to only 30 percent of the US level. Figure 18.1 shows the level of per-capita real income in Argentina over the past 45 years.

There is a striking difference between the steady expansion of the thirty years to 1975 and the stagnation and decline that have occurred since then. The contrast could not be stronger: from 1945 to 1975 per-capita income grew at an annual rate of 1.7 percent. From 1975 to 1985 it fell at an annual rate of 1.7 percent.

The other dimension in which Argentine performance has shown a dramatic deterioration is inflation and fiscal stability. Of course, there have been frequent precedents of massive inflation and depreciation. But the experience of the past decade, with two near-hyperinflations, stands out. In 1899 *Banker's Magazine* already reported of South Americans and their currency:[2]

> [They] are always in trouble about their currency. Either it is too good for home use, or, as frequently happens, it is too bad for foreign exchange. Generally, they have too much of it, but their own idea is that they never have enough ... the Argentines alter their currency almost as frequently as they change presidents. ... No people in the world take a keener interest in currency experiments than the Argentines.

The experience with the destruction of the financial system in the past 15 years has certainly reinforced that keen interest and expertise. Figure 18.2 shows the

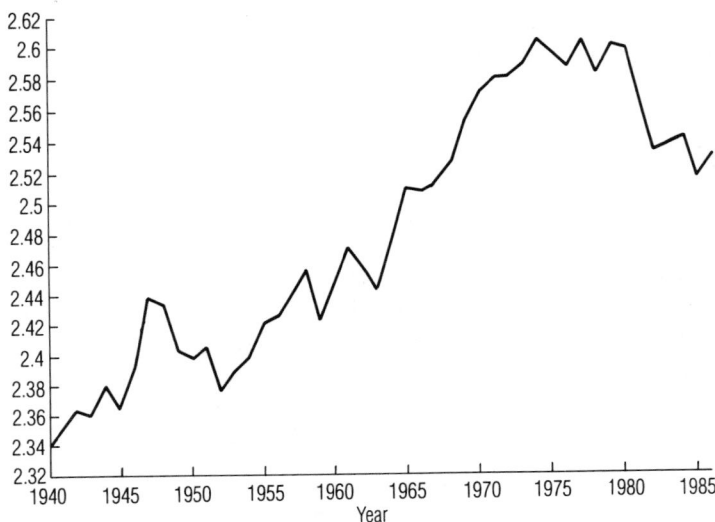

Figure 18.1 Real per-capita GDP (logarithm).

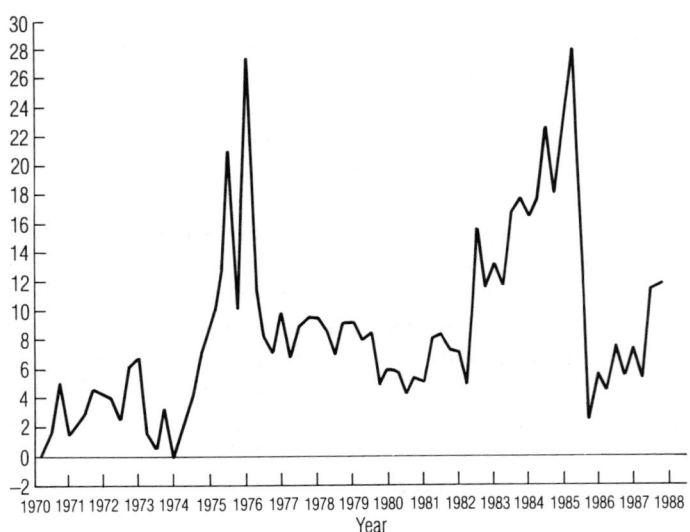

Figure 18.2 Inflation rate of the CPI (quarterly average of monthly rates).

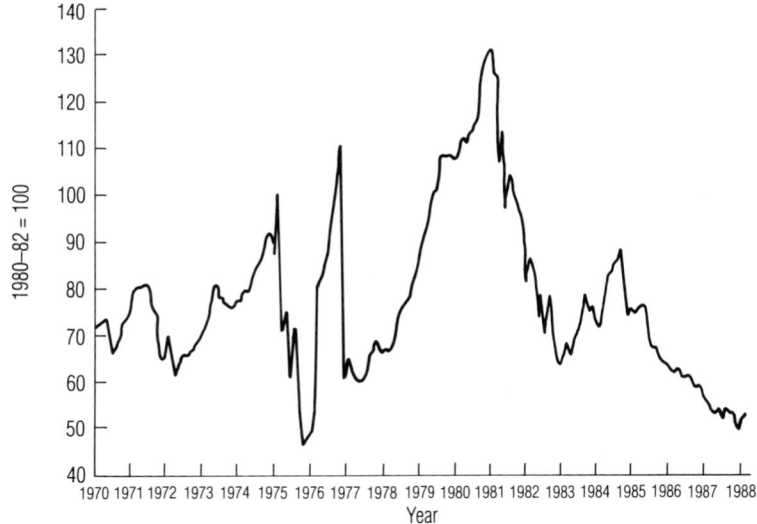

Figure 18.3 Real exchange rate.

monthly rate of inflation since 1970. In interpreting the graph one should bear in mind that a monthly rate of inflation of 6 percent corresponds to 100 percent per year, and 22 percent per month yields an annual rate of 1,000 percent. Inflation passed 2,000 percent both in the Perónist period of 1975–76 and again in the pre-Austral period of early 1985. At no time in the past ten years did it fall below 100 percent for any length of time.

The third broad feature that we want to draw attention to concerns the real exchange rate. This is a key price in any economy and even more so in Argentina. Figure 18.3 shows the real exchange rate measured as the ratio of Argentine manufactured prices relative to those of her trading partners.[3]

The extraordinary variations in Argentina's external competitiveness are tied closely to the macroeconomic policy mistakes, capital flight induced by these mistakes, and the present debt crisis. The outstanding episode, clearly apparent in Figure 18.3, is the real appreciation of 1979–81. For the period 1970–78 the real exchange rate averaged 73; it increased to 108 over the next three years before declining back to an average of 75 in the 1982–86 period. By March 1987 it had fallen to almost a third of the peak value during the period of most extreme overvaluation. The swings in the real exchange rate capture best the seesaw nature of Argentine policies. In some periods unimaginable damage is done to the productive and financial structure and then a period of repair follows where austerity and real depreciation restore the case for yet another political, fiscal, or foreign exchange adventure.

Table 18.1 shows the debt accumulation over the past 15 years. There is

Table 18.1 Argentina's external debt

	1975	1978	1979	1982	1985
Total external debt[a]	7.9	12.5	19.0	43.6	48.3
Public[a]	4.0	8.4	10.0	28.6	40.0
Reserves[a]	0.6	5.8	10.1	3.0	6.0
Net debt/exports[b]	260	110	120	540	520
Debt/GDP[b]	18.6	23.9	30.2	60.3	64.5
Interest payments/GDP[b]	0.7	1.4	1.4	2.4	5.7

[a] US$ billion.
[b] Percent.
Source: World Bank; BCRA; and Morgan Guaranty Trust.

considerable uncertainty about the size of the external debt prior to the late 1970s and available estimates from various official sources vary widely. Estimates of the BCRA (Banco Central de la República Argentina) show that the debt varied between $2.5 and $3 billion in the 1960s, starting at about the same level as it ended. But from 1970 on, external debt steadily increases both for the private and for the public sector. Between 1970 and 1977 the external debt rises by $6 billion and in the next four years by more than $30 billion.

With this broad overview of the past decade we now turn to a review of the principal episodes. We use these episodes to describe and explain the relevance to the debt problem, or the role of the external debt in creating domestic macroeconomic difficulties. A brief chronology of dates and important facts helps place the events in context.

18.2.1 *The Martínez de Hoz period (March 1976 to March 1981)*

When de Hoz assumed power as finance minister of the military government, consumer prices in the previous month had increased at an annual rate of 5,000 percent and output had declined sharply. The black market premium for foreign exchange exceeded 200 percent.[4] The new program was to stabilize the macroeconomy, as a first priority, and then to renovate industry and financial markets. Macroeconomic stabilization was under way quite rapidly so that inflation soon fell to less than 150 percent.

A financial reform was implemented in June 1977 that aimed to liberalize capital markets and link Argentina more effectively with the world capital market. Already in late 1976 foreign exchange transactions were completely liberalized *on capital* account and this was done so effectively that for the next four years the black market premium was zero. Figure 18.4 shows the black market premium and brings out the striking interlude of free capital mobility between the Perónist period and the aftermath of the collapse of Martínez de Hoz's policies.

Inflation failed to decline further once it had come to the 150 percent range. To make further inroads, policymakers opted for what Fernández (1985) has called

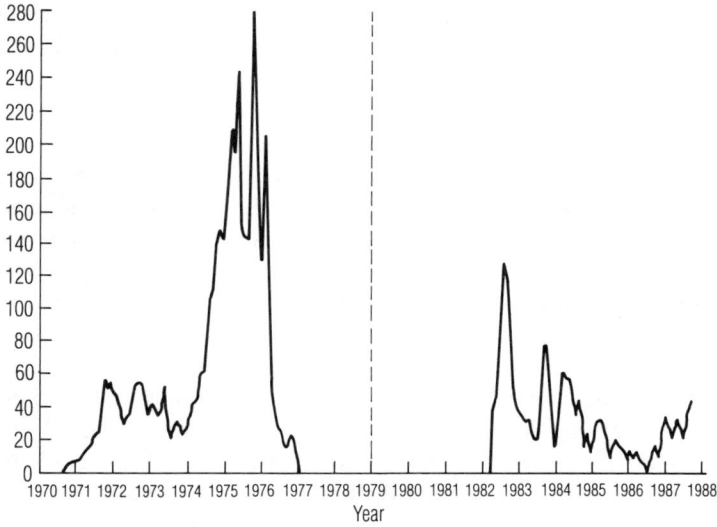

Figure 18.4 Exchange rate gap, parallel/official (australs per US$).

an "expectations management approach." Beginning in 1979 they pre-fixed the rate of exchange depreciation with a *tablita*, announcing ahead of time gradually declining rates of deprecation. These announcement were repeated on a rolling (though shortening) basis so as to create an environment where economic agents could discern a government commitment to disinflation embodied in the timetable for declining rates of exchange depreciation.

This policy was expected to reduce inflation through three separate channels. First, reduced rates of depreciation would directly reduce the rate of import price inflation. Second, reduced depreciation would enforce a discipline on domestic price setters. Third, in an environment where inflation to a large extent depended on expectations, the rule or precommitment introduced a fixed point around which expectations could rally. Needless to say, the intellectual underpinnings of such a program relied on the belief that the "law of one price" would be strongly operative.

Inflation responded to this policy and gradually fell throughout 1980 to reach a bottom well below 100 percent. But gradually, during 1978–80, the *real* exchange rate appreciated because inflation consistently outpaced the rate of depreciation. We saw in Figure 18.3 that the cumulative overvaluation reached 50 or even 60 percent. But while the overvaluation ultimately led to capital flight and collapse of the financial system, the early stages were quite the opposite. The high interest rates—relative to world rates and the preannounced rate of depreciation—gave rise to an (almost) risk-free speculation in favor of Argentine assets. As a result, private sector borrowing abroad increased to take advantage of the relatively low foreign interest rates and a massive capital inflow developed. This is shown in Table 18.1 in the large increase in central bank reserves between 1978 and 1979 and the matching increase in private external borrowing.

The trade and employment effects of the overvaluation were slow to come. Díaz Alejandro (1964) has shown that the real income effects of a real depreciation tend to be dominant in the early stages, before substitution effects take over. For the real appreciation of 1977–80 the reverse applied: the increase in real income created an expansion in demand and thus seemed to validate the Martínez de Hoz approach by creating inflation reduction with rising real income. This factor was reinforced by the fact that trade protection, even with liberalization measures, kept the economy relatively closed, which dampened the disinflation effects of the *tablita* but also the effects in the real sector.

By 1979–80 the overvaluation had become so extreme that financial markets increasingly took the view that depreciation would have to come sometime. Even though the government asserted that the policy would be continued, and could be financed, speculation increasingly went in the direction of dollar purchases. The regime of unrestricted capital mobility introduced in late 1976 facilitated this capital flight to the maximum. Hence in 1980–81, the central bank and public sector enterprises were forced to borrow massively abroad to obtain the foreign exchange which was then sold in support of the exchange rate policy. Private speculators in turn bought the dollars and applied them abroad. With the round trip complete, commercial banks in New York, Zurich, and Tokyo had lent to the government the resources to finance capital flight which returned to the same banks as deposits. Of course, capital flight was not limited to dollar deposits. Investments in financial markets were important, as was real estate abroad.

A variety of estimates is available on the accumulation of external assets by Argentines during this period. These estimates are typically formed as residuals from debt and balance-of-payments data. They are obtained by deducting from the recorded increase in gross external debt the current account and recorded capital flows in the form of direct investment and changes in reserves. Dornbusch (1985), for example, calculates that capital flight in 1978–82 amounted to $23.4 billion. In a review of various estimates, the IMF (Watson *et al.* 1986, p. 142) reports capital flight amounting cumulatively to about $15 billion in 1979–81. Rodríguez (1983) estimates that between 1979 and 1982 the external assets of Argentineans increased from $10 billion to $34 billion. The estimates would have to be revised upward to the extent that underinvoicing of exports and overinvoicing of imports was a significant channel of capital flight in this period.

Both the fact of and the motivation for the wave of capital flight in the late 1970s are very clear. Unlike in other debtor countries—for example, Brazil or Chile—mismanagement of the exchange rate combined with an opening of the capital account are the almost exclusive explanations for the massive debt accumulation. One must understand the particular background to appreciate that in Argentina's case the government has an external debt, but the private sector has external assets of at least half the size. Moreover, that process was carried further over the next few years as the government increasingly took over all external debt in the course of sustaining failing financial institutions. In 1980 about half of the debt was owed by the public sector, and in 1985 that share had increased to 82 percent.

18.2.2 *From Martínez de Hoz to Alfonsín (March 1981 to December 1983)*

The end of the military government did not come early. The Martínez de Hoz overvaluation had sown the seeds of financial destruction, but the actual unraveling came only over the next four years. The world economy contributed to the difficulties of the debt crisis: sharply declining commodity prices and much higher interest rates brought with them difficulties in servicing the external debt.

But domestic events certainly were the dominant factor. First came the undoing of the overvaluation. This started with the change of presidents: the incoming president, months before taking office, declined to comment on his exchange rate policy. This served as an obvious indication to anyone that devaluation was ahead and hence capital flight became massive. Central bank reserves declined by more than $5 billion and public external debt increased sharply. Finally Martínez de Hoz was forced by his successor, not yet in office, to bring his own expectations management and credibility approach to an end by devaluing the currency.

Over the next three years exchange depreciation and inflation became endemic, rising from less than 100 percent to 600 percent at the time Alfonsín took office. Changes in public finance and financial markets were particularly important in this period. Exchange control was instituted once again, and the black market premium reemerged (see Figure 18.4). The central bank, in an effort to ensure continuing trade flows, started exchange rate guarantee programs only to find that it could never sustain the guaranteed exchange rates. As a result of losing a string of bets in the foreign exchange market, the budget deteriorated dramatically. The deterioration was reinforced by financial failures that turned up in the public sector, by the burden of external interest payments, and by deteriorating terms of trade. The conflict in the South Pacific added to the loss in confidence and devastation of public finance.

The economics of this period of deterioration can be expressed in terms of a simple model of deficit finance and of financial markets. Suppose the budget deficit represents a fraction, g, of national income, and let velocity of high-powered money be an increasing function of the rate of inflation. Then it can be shown that the rate of inflation, p, will be an increasing (and steeply rising) function of the deficit, but it will also depend on financial institutions.

$$p = (ag - y)/(1 - bg) \qquad (18.1)$$

The higher the level of noninflationary velocity, a, and the more responsive velocity is to inflation as measured by the parameter b, the more dramatic the inflation impact of budget deficits.

This framework helps to identify the interaction of deficits, external debt service, real depreciation, and financial markets in generating the inflation explosion of 1981–84. Increasing burdens of debt service, because of higher interest rates and real depreciation, increased the budget deficit ratio, g, and hence raised money creation and inflation. The institutional response of financial markets to higher inflation aggravated this impact by a flight from money. The reduction in money holdings was facilitated by an increasing range of interest-bearing substitutes. As these came increasingly into play, velocity sharply increased (a and b in equation (18.1) increased) and that meant the inflation rate associated with a given deficit ratio also escalated.

The 1981–84 period thus represents an unraveling of the artificial stability of the late 1970s. Several events, each in itself extraordinary, combined to make the crisis large: the initial overvaluation had been extreme; the financial sector had been allowed to become overexposed in speculation; private capital flight had been massive; and finally the world economy turned unfavorable just at the wrong time. Each of these factors deteriorated the budget and hence reinforced inflation.

18.2.3 *Alfonsín (January 1984–)*

These difficulties carried over to the beginning of the Alfonsín administration. Large real wage increased in 1983–84 created problems for the budget and for the external balance. Inflation rapidly escalated and negotiations with creditors and the IMF did not bring a solution.

The inflation issue soon became the single most pressing problem. In early 1985 annualized monthly rates of inflation rose toward 1,500 percent and beyond. The possibility of a hyperinflation was entirely realistic since the inflation process itself eroded the real value of tax collection as well as the financial system, so that ever more money needed to be created to finance an ever widening deficit. Because IMF programs seemed unable to cope with the inflation problem on a timetable and in a fashion that was politically acceptable, and because the sheer pace of disintegration was so rapid, the government considered extreme measures. The monetary reform known as the Austral Plan was just that, an all-out attempt to stop hyperinflation.

The details of the June 1985 Plan of Economic Reform, which is now called the Austral Plan, were as follows:

- a real depreciation and a sharp increase in real public sector prices. An export and import tax, a forced saving scheme, and accelerated tax collection;
- a wage–price–exchange rate freeze;
- a new money, the Austral, and a promise not to create money to finance the budget;
- a conversion scale for existing contracts that would adjust them so as to keep real burdens unchanged in the face of the unanticipated reduction in inflation;
- an IMF agreement and a rescheduling agreement with the creditors.

Table 18.2 Response to the Austral plan (percentage of the sample responding positively)

	1984 Dec.	May	1985 Aug.	Dec.	1986 Apr.
Austral plan			74	68	52
Economic management	19	10	40	35	19
Government in general	46	35	57	52	36
President Alfonsín	72	64	74	71	61

Source: La Nación.

The stabilization immediately reduced inflation to levels of only 1–2 percent per month. The decline in inflation and the fiscal measures brought about a rapid and major shift in the budget. High real interest rates and the budget improvement created an atmosphere of at least temporary stabilization. The black market premium vanished. For a country that had been on the verge of hyperinflation the stabilization created an immense relief, but it also left considerable skepticism as to the possibility of stopping inflation by edict. The skepticism extended in particular to the government's ability to achieve sufficient budget control to reduce permanently the need for inflationary money creation.

But even if skepticism persisted, the stabilization proved to be an important political move and as such a stepping stone for a more fundamental stabilization. A public opinion survey presents an assessment over time of the public response to policy and management. The data are reported in Table 18.2.

This was not the first time Argentina had used wage–price controls to stop inflation. Indeed, in 1975–76 this was tried, and the experience ended in an outburst of repressed inflation. The Austral Plan has in fact not brought price stability. Inflation today is back to the 100–200 percent rate. But the important achievement is that inflation was brought down from more than 2,000 percent and that this was accomplished without a decline in economic activity, rise in unemployment, or reduction in the purchasing power of wages.

Today there is little risk that in the near term the stabilization will collapse. That confidence makes it possible and fruitful for the government to concentrate on the two key issues: how to achieve further budget improvement so as to bring inflation down to less than 20 percent; and how to restore investment and growth. External debt and debt service have a bearing on each of these questions.

18.3 Investment, debt, and the budget

The budget influences inflation as well as investment and growth because it influences the distribution of resources in the economy. If the government commands a large share of the resources, less is left for the private sector. The government may use these resources to service the external debt by means of noninterest external surpluses; it can use the resources to support consumption; or it can make them available for investment. The possible choices of budget

Table 18.3 Budget (percentage of GDP, budget basis)

	Expenditure	Revenues	Budget deficit
1980	43.9	36.4	7.5
1981	49.1	35.8	13.3
1982	48.2	33.1	15.1
1983	51.6	34.8	16.8
1984	46.2	33.4	12.8
1985	47.4	41.5	5.9
1986	43.4	39.8	3.6

Source: BCRA.

strategy then are to service the debt, sustain consumption, or use resources for growth. Table 18.3 shows the budget of the consolidated government.

Two points must be distinguished when looking at the budget impact on the economy. One is the *way* in which the government finances its outlays, i.e. by regular taxes, by borrowing, or by the inflation tax. The second, possibly related, is how the tax system determines the allocation of resources among sectors. To illustrate, the government can replace the inflation tax with outright taxes and there will be little effect in the aggregate except that inflation will decline. But if the inflation tax declines without an offsetting increase in outright taxes then an offsetting reduction in absorption needs to occur: either the government cuts its spending or it reduces its debt service.

For the country at large there is a tradeoff between consumption, investment, and net resource transfers abroad. These points can be brought out by looking at the GDP identity:

$$\text{Output} = \text{Net resource transfer abroad}$$

$$+ \text{Investment} + \text{Consumption} \qquad \textbf{(18.2)}$$

where consumption denotes private and public sector consumption, and investment, likewise, includes the private and public sectors. With a given amount of resources or output available (because the economy is fully employed already) the budget and the external debt strategy now determine inflation and growth.

To show the range of options we can look at two particular scenarios. One possibility is to keep budget adjustments to a minimum, not to interfere with consumption and yet foster growth via increased investment. That strategy requires, as equation (18.2) shows, that resource transfers abroad can no longer occur or must even be reversed. In a second scenario the government seeks both investment and continued, partial debt service. In that case the resource shortage calls for crowding out of consumption by outright taxation or by the inflation tax.

Over the past few years crowding out of investment, not consumption, has been the rule. By maintaining relatively tight money and a strongly competitive exchange rate the government has crowded out private investment, with

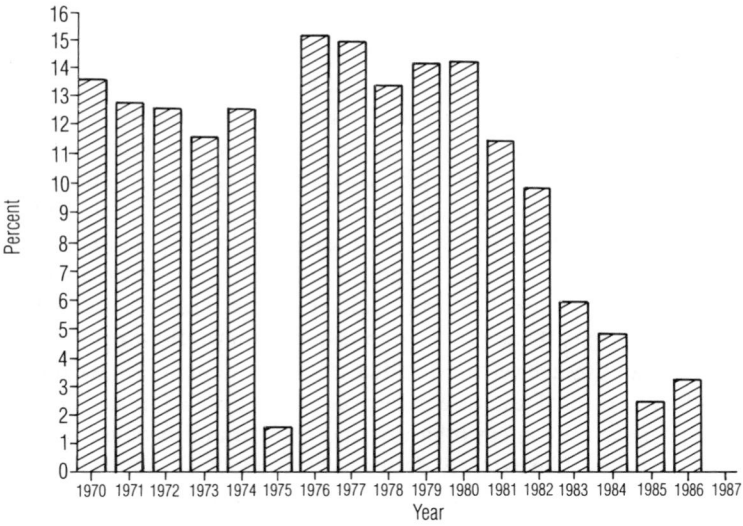

Figure 18.5 Private investment (percentage of GDP).

consumption and transfers abroad absorbing the available resources. The adverse effect of positive and often high real interest rates on investment is all the more punishing in that uncertainty about future budget trends, debt service, and hence interest rates, makes it unwise to repatriate capital or risk borrowing.

Figure 18.5 shows the extraordinarily low rate of investment (as a percentage of GNP) in Argentina. Net investment in fact is zero or negative. With productive capacity not expanding, or even shrinking, there is no source of growth in the standard of living. Hence the question is whether the current policy mix can be sustained much longer without doing irreparable damage to the productive system and thus to the long-run viability of the economy. The flourishing of the underground economy is certainly a warning signal of a very undesirable trend.

IMF programs for Argentina, in the absence of an official change in the debt strategy, anticipate that the current account deficit gradually declines as a ratio of GDP and ultimately turns toward surplus. The 1986 program, for example, anticipated that by 1990 Argentina's current account would reach a modest surplus of 0.2 percent of GDP. That means, of course, net resources transfers in the full amount of interest liabilities and no "new money" except for principal. This strategy, if it is to be consistent with even moderate growth of the economy's supply side, requires a major shift in the budget to contain consumption. That can take the form of a much higher inflation tax or a much higher outright form of taxation.

Latin American leaders advocate a different scenario. They claim that net resource flows need to be reversed and that the noninterest surpluses can come down. Resources need to be transferred inward again, they argue, so that they can supplement scarce domestic saving in financing domestic investment. Such a reversal of resource flows encounters the problem of creditworthiness. If now debtor countries like Argentina experience difficulties in servicing the debt, it is plausible that yet more debt should be added. Feldstein (1987) has made the case that some countries, in particular Brazil, can both borrow and grow without risking the build-up of an unsustainable debt. It is difficult to see that possibility in Argentina, except in the context of a major restructuring of the public sector.

But if increased reliance is placed on external resources by reducing net transfers abroad, the question must be asked how the extra space thus gained should be used. Once again a fiscal reform could translate these resources into growth of productive capacity. Using them for consumption would simply reduce creditworthiness and thus presage yet another financial crisis sometime in the future.

Argentina thus faces a critical juncture in respect to fiscal policy. Fiscal choices today are critical because they affect inflation and growth and because there is little room left for mistakes. The external debt service is a key variable because it presently absorbs resources that could be available for growth. But resource savings due to reduced external debt service (assuming there is no debt forgiveness) can only be used productively if fiscal reform translates them into sharply higher investment and growth. The critical decisions to make that possible have as yet not been reached. Moreover, if capital markets are unwilling to lend on a major scale then most of the growth must be financed by reduced consumption. Thus the policy mistakes of the 1970s directly translate into a growth crisis for the 1980s.

The present effort to stabilize the budget and hence bring about growth and financial stability goes in its implications much beyond the economic sphere. Political and institutional instability in Argentina resembles that of the Weimar Republic and Central Europe in the 1920s or the Fifth Republic in France. The political instability in turn influences economics because it stands in the way of continuity and farsightedness in economic policies. If, as has been the case in Argentina, the average tenure of a central bank president is less than a year, this is certainly not conducive to a long view. The attempt at reconstruction under way today is thus of extraordinary significance. This also implies that increased flexibility of external constraints associated with debt service assumes particular importance.

Appendix 18A

Table 18A.1 Key macroeconomic variables

	GDP[a] growth	Inflation[a] (CPD)	Budget[b] deficit/GDP	Noninterest[b] current account/GDP	Real[c] exchange rate	Terms[c] of trade
1970	5.4	21.7	2.0	0.3	56.7	106.6
1971	3.7	39.1	4.6	−0.6	49.7	116.4
1972	1.9	64.1	6.1	0.2	52.9	125.7
1973	3.5	43.8	8.6	1.5	58.6	134.6

Table 18A.1 (*cont.*)

	GDP[a] growth	Inflation[a] (CPD)	Budget[b] deficit/GDP	Noninterest[b] current account/GDP	Real[c] exchange rate	Terms[c] of trade
1974	5.7	40.2	8.5	1.3	71.2	117.8
1975	−0.4	335.1	15.6	−2.2	36.9	111.5
1976	−0.5	347.5	10.6	2.9	46.4	95.8
1977	6.4	160.4	5.0	3.9	50.7	92.7
1978	−3.4	169.8	6.7	4.9	64.7	83.5
1979	6.7	139.7	6.7	−0.1	83.4	88.4
1980	0.7	87.6	8.6	−6.1	100.0	100.0
1981	−6.2	131.3	18.0	−2.7	69.5	113.8
1982	−4.6	209.7	18.9	3.3	48.9	98.5
1983	2.8	433.7	17.8	3.9	58.8	94.1
1984	2.6	688.0	13.8	4.2	58.4	101.7
1985	−4.5	385.0	5.1	6.2	48.9	88.4
1986	5.7	81.9	4.7	1.9	45.2	78.4

[a] Percent per year.
[b] Percent of GDP.
[c] Index 1980 = 100.

Table 18A.2 The external sector

	Current account US$ million	% of GDP	Interest[a] payments	Noninterest[a] current account	Terms[b] of trade	Debt[c] /GDP	Real[b] exchange rate
1970	−159.0	−0.8	−222.5	63.6	106.6	16.7	56.7
1971	−389.0	−1.8	−255.9	−132.8	116.4	18.2	49.7
1972	−223.0	−1.0	−273.0	50.0	125.7	21.8	52.9
1973	721.0	2.7	−317.0	1,038.0	134.6	20.0	58.6
1974	127.0	0.4	−298.0	425.0	117.8	20.4	71.2
1975	−1,284.0	−3.5	−460.0	−824.0	111.5	18.6	36.9
1976	665.0	1.7	−465.0	1,130.0	95.8	18.6	46.4
1977	1,290.0	3.0	−370.0	1,660.0	92.7	19.2	50.7
1978	1,833.0	4.0	−405.0	2,238.0	83.5	23.9	64.7
1979	−537.0	−1.0	−493.0	−44.0	88.4	30.2	83.4
1980	−4,767.0	−7.6	−947.0	−3,824.0	100.0	37.3	100.0
1981	−4,714.0	−7.4	−2,965.0	−1,749.0	113.8	48.1	69.5
1982	−2,357.0	−3.8	−4,403.0	2,046.0	98.5	60.3	48.9
1983	−2,461.0	−3.8	−4,983.0	2,522.0	94.1	59.5	58.8
1984	−2,391.0	−3.5	−5,273.0	2,888.0	101.7	60.5	58.4
1985	−953.0	−1.5	−4,879.0	3,926.0	88.4	64.3	48.9
1986	2,645.0	−4.0	−3,934.0	1,289.0	78.4	—	45.2

[a] US$ million.
[b] Index 1980 = 100.
[c] Percent of GDP.

Table 18A.3 Key relative prices[a] (indices 1980 = 100)

	Agriculture/ nonagriculture (wpi)	Real public sector prices	Real wages	Terms of trade	Real exchange rate	Relative price of land
1970	119.05	106.30	—	106.6	56.69	190.16
1971	132.14	100.13	263.25	116.4	49.69	216.39
1972	152.38	97.64	216.16	125.7	52.92	308.20

Table 18A.3 (*cont.*)

	Agriculture/nonagriculture (wpi)	Real public sector prices	Real wages	Terms of trade	Real exchange rate	Relative price of land
1973	141.67	107.61	267.77	134.6	58.62	249.18
1974	123.81	151.71	264.36	117.8	71.15	337.70
1975	97.62	158.53	217.64	111.5	36.92	319.67
1976	104.76	131.63	124.01	95.8	46.46	478.69
1977	111.90	130.05	83.01	92.7	50.69	393.44
1978	109.52	133.60	79.59	83.5	64.69	124.59
1979	110.71	104.59	70.73	88.4	83.38	93.44
1980	100.00	100.00	100.00	100.0	100.00	100.00
1981	90.48	115.88	106.46	113.8	69.54	63.93
1982	103.57	111.29	139.89	98.5	48.92	103.28
1983	107.14	131.50	152.54	94.1	58.77	159.92
1984	101.19	147.24	142.94	101.7	58.38	145.90
1985	85.71	159.97	110.34	88.4	48.92	—
1986	109.52	147.77	110.06	78.4	45.15	—

^aDeflated by GDP deflator.

Table 18A.4 Inflation and the financial sector

	Inflation	Budget deficit/GDP	Base/GDP	M1/GDP	M2/GDP	M3/GDP	M4/GDP
1970	21.7	2.03	0.12	0.15	0.25	0.25	0.25
1971	39.1	4.58	0.10	0.13	0.22	0.23	0.23
1972	64.1	6.10	0.09	0.11	0.19	0.21	0.21
1973	43.8	8.60	0.13	0.11	0.20	0.22	0.22
1974	40.2	8.52	0.14	0.14	0.25	0.27	0.28
1975	335.1	15.59	0.16	0.09	0.14	0.16	0.17
1976	347.5	10.56	0.14	0.07	0.11	0.12	0.16
1977	160.4	5.04	0.16	0.06	0.14	0.15	0.16
1978	169.8	6.67	0.14	0.06	0.18	0.18	0.20
1979	139.7	6.65	0.09	0.06	0.19	0.19	0.21
1980	87.6	8.56	0.08	0.07	0.21	0.21	0.23
1981	131.3	17.97	0.09	0.05	0.20	0.20	0.22
1982	209.7	18.78	0.29	0.05	0.17	0.16	0.19
1983	433.7	17.76	0.29	0.04	0.13	0.14	0.14
1984	688.0	13.79	0.20	0.04	0.11	0.12	0.12
1985	385.0	5.10	0.12	0.05	0.11	0.11	0.13
1986	81.9	4.70	0.09	0.05	0.14	0.16	0.18

Table 18A.5 The budget and interest payments (percentage of GDP)

	Budget deficit	Interest on foreign debt	Interest on domestic debt	Operational deficit
1961	3.79	0.02	0.06	3.71
1962	6.80	0.04	0.05	6.71
1963	6.59	0.02	0.07	6.50
1964	5.60	0.03	0.09	5.48
1965	2.87	0.03	0.05	2.79
1966	3.65	0.03	0.05	3.57
1967	1.83	0.03	0.03	1.77
1968	1.72	0.03	0.04	1.65

Table 18A.5 (*cont.*)

	Budget deficit	Interest on foreign debt	Interest on domestic debt	Operational deficit
1969	1.28	0.03	0.03	1.22
1970	2.03	0.15	0.26	1.62
1971	4.58	0.21	0.27	4.10
1972	6.10	0.31	0.25	5.54
1973	8.60	0.18	0.36	8.06
1974	8.52	0.18	0.61	7.73
1975	15.59	0.16	0.53	14.90
1976	10.56	0.15	1.33	9.08
1977	5.04	0.14	1.00	3.90
1978	6.67	0.17	1.76	4.74
1979	6.65	0.10	1.93	4.62
1980	8.56	0.30	1.55	6.71
1981	17.97	3.47	2.75	11.75
1982	18.78	4.36	3.87	10.55
1983	17.76	2.44	0.54	14.78
1984	13.79	2.81	0.34	10.64
1985	5.10	2.60	0.13	2.37
1986	4.70			

Notes

1. See Ford (1983), Williams (1971) and Díaz Alejandro (1970) for Argentine economic history prior to World War II.
2. Quoted by Cardoso (1987) and Ford (1983, p. 92).
3. This is the series reported regularly by Morgan Guaranty Trust, *World Financial Markets*. We are indebted to Rimmer de Vries for making available the historical series.
4. On the Perónist experience see, in particular, Di Tella (1983) and de Pablo (1982; 1984).

References

Calvo, G. (1986) "Incredible reforms." Mimeo, University of Pennsylvania.

Cardoso, E. (1987) "Latin American debt: Which way now?" *Challenge* (May).

Cavallo, D. (1984) *Volver a crecer*. Buenos Aires: Sudamericana-Planeta.

Cavallo, D., and A. Pena (1983) "Deficit fiscal, endeudamiento del gobierno y tasa de inflación: Argentina 1940–82." *Estudios*, No. 26, April–June.

Dagnino Pastore, J. M. (1983) "Progress and prospects for the adjustment in Argentina." In J. Williamson, ed., *Prospects for adjustment*. Cambridge, MA: MIT Press.

de Pablo, J. C., ed. (1980) *La economía que yo hice*. Buenos Aires: El Cronista Comercial.

de Pablo, J. C. (1981) *El processo económico*. Buenos Aires: El Cronista Comercial.

de Pablo, J. C. (1982) *Economía política del Peronismo*. Buenos Aires: El Cid.

de Pablo, J. C. (1984) *Política económica Argentina*. Buenos Aires: Ediciones Macchi.

Díaz Alejandro, C. (1964) *Exchange Devaluation in a Semi-Industrialized Country*. Cambridge, MA: MIT Press.

Díaz Alejandro, C. (1970) *Essays on the Economic History of the Argentine Republic*. New Haven, CT: Yale University Press.

di Tella, G. (1983) *Argentina under Peron 1973–76*. New York: St Martin's.

Dornbusch, R. (1985) "External debt, budget deficits and disequilibrium exchange rates."

In G. Smith and J. Cuddington, eds, *International Debt and the Developing Countries*. Washington, DC: World Bank.

Dornbusch, R., and M. Simonsen (1987) *Inflation Stabilization with Incomes Policy Support*. New York: Group of Thirty.

Feldstein, M. (1987) "Muddling through is just fine." *The Economist*, June 27.

Fernández, R. B. (1985) "The expectations management approach to stabilization in Argentina 1976–82." *World Development* 13: 871–92.

Fernández, R. B., and C. A. Rodríguez (1982) *Inflación y estabilidad*. Buenos Aires: Ediciones Macchi.

Ford, A. G. (1983) *The Gold Standard 1880–1914: Britain and Argentina*. New York: Garland, reprint.

Harberger, A. (1985) "Lessons for debtor country managers and policy makers." In G. Smith and J. Cuddington, eds, *International Debt and the Developing Countries*. Washington, DC: World Bank.

Heyman, D. (1986) *Tres ensayos sobre inflación y políticas de estabilización*. Doc. No. 18. Buenos Aires: CEPAL.

Instituto de Estudios Económicos sobre la Realidad Argentina y Latinoamericana (1986) *Estatísticas de la evolución económica de Argentina, 1913–1984*. (Published in *Estudios* 9, No. 39, July–September, Córdoba).

Mallon, R., and J. Sourrouille (1975) *Economic Policy Making in a Conflict Society*. Cambridge, MA: Harvard University Press.

McCarthy, D. (1987) "Argentina towards the year 2000." Mimeo, World Bank.

Morgan Guaranty Trust. *World Financial Markets*, various issues.

Nogues, J. (1986) "The nature of Argentina's policy reforms during 1976–81." World Bank Staff Working Paper No. 765. Washington, DC: World Bank.

Pazos, F. (1972) *Chronic Inflation in Latin America*. Westpoint, CT: Praeger Publishers.

Ramos, J. (1986) *Neoconservative economics in the Southern Cone of Latin America, 1973–83*. Baltimore, MD: Johns Hopkins University Press.

Rodríguez, C. A. (1983) "Políticas de estabilización en la economía Argentina, 1978–82." *Cuadernos de Economía* (April).

Summers, R., and A. Heston (1984) "Improved International Comparisons of Real Product and its Composition." *Review of Income and Wealth* 30: 207–62.

Watson, M. *et al.*, (1986) *International Capital Markets: Developments and prospects*. IMF Occasional Paper No. 43 (February). Washington, DC: International Monetary Fund.

Williams, J. H. (1971) *Argentine International Trade under Inconvertible Paper Money. 1880–1900*. New York: AMS Press (reprint).

World Bank (1987) *Argentina. Economic Recovery and Growth*. Report No. 6467-AR. Washington, DC.

Index